BAPTIST
FAITH AND WITNESS
BOOK 4

BAPTIST
FAITH AND WITNESS
BOOK 4

Papers of the Study and Research Division
of the Baptist World Alliance
2005-2010

With Foreword by Fausto A. Vasconcelos, Director
Mission, Evangelism & Theological Reflection
(Formerly Education and Evangelism/
Study and Research)

BAPTIST WORLD ALIANCE

Table of Contents

Foreword
Fausto A. Vasconcelos / ix

The Commission on Baptist Heritage and Identity
Karen O'Dell Bullock, Chair / 1

1.   John Smyth's Request for Mennonite Recognition and Admission: Four
        Newly Translated Letters, 1610-1612
            Kirsten T. Timmer / 5

2.   Rembrandt and the Waterlander Mennonites
            Kenneth Edmonds / 23

3.   The Slave Trade and the Unholy Triangle: A Caribbean Perspective
            Cawley Bolt/ 47

4.   History and Development of Baptists in Mexico
            Dinorah B. Méndez / 57

The Commission on Baptist Worship and Spirituality
Christopher J. Ellis, Chair / 71

5.   Truth on Fire: The Spirituality of Preaching
            David Coffey / 73

6.   Prayer and Theology
            Christopher J. Ellis / 85

7.   From the Edge: On Approaching the Task of Breaking Open the Word
            Lina Andronoviene / 97

8. Opportunities and Challenges of Contextualization in Baptist Worship in Mexico
       Joel Sierra / 107

The Commission on Christian Ethics
    Ross Clifford, Chair / 113

9. An Historical Evaluation of the Contribution of Baptists to Christian Ethics
       William M. Tillman, Jr. / 117

10. What Do We Owe the Embryo? The Ethical Limits to Embryonic Stem Cell Research
       Dennis L. Sansom / 131

11. Can a Sanctity-of-Human-Life Ethic Ground Christian Ecological Responsibility?
       David P. Gushee / 149

12. Christian Social Ethics in an Era of Globalization: Tensions and Methods
       Anna Robbins / 177

The Commission on Church Leadership
    Brian Winslade, Chair / 201

13. Defining Congregational Government in the 21st Century: The Nigerian (African) Experience
       Solomon A. Ishola / 205

14. How is Church Leadership Different in the 21st Century from the 20th Century?
       Michael J. Quicke / 221

15. Ordination: Does it Fit?
       Brian Winslade / 229

16. Ordination: A Case Study from Bulgaria
       Teodor Oprenov / 239

The Commission on Doctrine and Interchurch Cooperation
Paul Fiddes, Chair /245

17. A Baptist View of Ordained Ministry: Just a Function or a Way of Being?
Brian C. Brewer /249

18. The Multi-lateral Discussion on Baptism: Where are We Today?
Neville Callam /279

19. Continuing Conversations around Baptism and Membership
Curtis Freeman /291

20. Baptism, Membership and Communion: Scotland and Alabama
Kenneth B. E. Roxburgh /305

The Commission on Freedom and Justice
Regina Claas, Chair /343

21. Beyond Integration: The Caribbean Diasporan Church as an Agent of Reconciliation
Delroy A. Reid-Salmon /351

Appendix
Contributing Authors /365

Baptist Faith and Witness: Book Four

Foreword

Fausto A. Vasconcelos, METR Director

The Baptist World Alliance, through its Division on Mission, Evangelism & Theological Reflection (formerly Evangelism & Education and Study & Research), is very happy to place in your hands this copy of Baptist Faith and Witness Book 4.

This is the final book of the Study & Research Division since it was organized in 1975. In the new BWA quinquennium (2010-2015), the Division on Mission, Evangelism and Theological Reflection (METR), established at the General Council meeting in Ede, Netherlands, in 2009, will take up the historical legacy and contribution of the Divisions of Evangelism & Education and Study & Research.

This publication is being officially presented to the BWA General Council as it gathers for the 2011 Annual Gathering in Kuala Lumpur, capital city of the Federation of Malaysia.

In the tradition of the first three volumes in this series, Baptist Faith and Witness Book 4 represents a spiritual and intellectual effort to address some great issues before the church and world. This has been done by bringing together Baptist pastors and scholars who have invested time in reflecting on these matters.

The purpose of this book is to make available to BWA member bodies and local Baptist churches across the world reflections presented by Baptist theologians to study commissions at Annual Gatherings during the quinquennium 2005-2010.

The content of this book is as diverse as the issues researched by each study commission.

Introductory articles, written by commission chairs, open the chapter of each commission and provide excellent overviews of the papers included in it. From the research into the development of Baptist heritage and investigation of issues concerning Baptist identity to exploring Baptist distinctives and concerns in relation to worship and spirituality; from addressing ethical issues that are relevant to our Baptist life and witness in these strategic and global times to tackling matters related to ecclesiology and church leadership; from reflecting upon distinctive Baptist approaches to Christian doctrine to the focus on the experiences of real people in adverse circumstances and their perseverance among sufferings and struggles, this publication constitutes a rich resource of how Baptists have thought about and responded to these matters. You will certainly recognize these words as you read the commission chairs' introductory articles.

As you read this book, please bear in mind that it reflects the way Baptists around the world approach these topics and does not in any way, shape or form represent the official position of the BWA on the same topic. It is also worth noting that this publication respects the oral nature of the delivery of these papers during commission sessions at Annual Gatherings. It should go without saying that this book presents both academic and practical approaches on how Baptists deal with the array of topics included.

To further this objective, a list of all papers and presenters for this quinquennium is posted on the METR web page.

It is my privilege to acknowledge a number of Baptists who contributed to this publication:

All S&R study commission chairs and presenters whose papers are included here

Professors James Abernathy, W. Benjamin Boswell, Daniel Carro, Robert Cochran, Daniel Dapaah, Mark Olson, Andrey Shirin and Jeffrey G. Willetts, all of whom are members of the faculty of the John Leland Center for Theological Studies, Falls Church, VA.

BWA General Secretary Neville G. Callam; Director of the Division of Freedom & Justice Raimundo C. Barreto, Jr.; and Associate Director for Communications Eron Henry for their encouragement and assistance with this project and Lauren Weaver, who read the papers and offered many valuable suggestions.

Some chapters of this book have appeared in earlier publications. Portions of chapter 1 were first published in Baptist History & Heritage Journal, Winter 2009, Baptist History and Heritage Society, 3001 Mercer University Drive, Atlanta, GA 30341, USA.

Chapter 10 appeared in Ethics & Medicine: An International Journal of Bioethics Volume 26.3, August 2010 and is reprinted here with permission. A revised version of this paper, under a different title, was previously printed in Ethics & Medicine, Vol. 26.3, August 2010.

Chapter 11 was originally presented at the BICTE meeting in Prague, July 2008. Substantially similar versions of this paper were later published as "The Sacredness of God's Creation," Perspectives in Religious Studies 36, number 2 (Summer 2009): 187-197, and "Can a Sanctity-of-Human-Life Ethic Ground Christian Ecological Responsibility?" Notre Dame Journal of Law, Ethics & Public Policy 23, no. 2 (2009): 471-495.

Chapter 12 was previously published as "Universalism or Tribalism? Christian Social Ethics in an Era of Globalization" in Ecumenical and Eclectic, Anna Robbins, ed., Studies in Christian History and Thought, (Milton Keynes: Paternoster, 2007).

Chapter 17 was previously published in the Baptist Quarterly in two parts in Volume 43 (July and October 2009 issues).

As we Baptists around the world read this Baptist Faith and Witness Book 4, may we Hear the Spirit! and be "always prepared to give an answer to everyone who asks you to give the reasons for the hope that you have" (1 Peter 3:15).

Soli Deo Gloria!

Fausto A. Vasconcelos
METR Director
Baptist World Alliance

The Commission on Baptist Heritage and Identity

Karen O'Dell Bullock, Chair

In the years leading up to the Baptist 400th anniversary in 2009, the Commission on Baptist Heritage and Identity, 2006-2010, met in Mexico City, Mexico (2006); Accra, Ghana (2007); Prague, Czech Republic (2008); Ede, Netherlands (2009); and Honolulu, Hawai'i (2010). In each Annual Gathering, commission members explored the development of Baptist heritage in the host country, investigated critical issues regarding global Baptist identity, joined with other commissions to reflect upon matters of mutual concern, and worked in teams to accomplish its tasks.

In Mexico City, Dinorah B. Méndez, professor of Theology and History at the Mexican Baptist Theological Seminary, presented "The History and Development of Baptists in Mexico." Mexican Baptists have published Bibles, developed their own hymnology and popular education, conducted evangelistic outreach and cross-cultural missions, championed church-state separation, and promoted theological education. Members attending a joint session with the Commission on Freedom and Justice heard a report of Alvaro Castro, Mexico's Director of the Ministry of Religious Affairs, about the present state of religion and church life as well as a panel of global Baptist leaders who related their experiences concerning religious liberty in various countries.

In Accra, the commission hosted more than 100 visitors from seventeen countries. Kojo Oseih-Wusuh, recent president of the Ghana Baptist Convention, presented "The History of Baptists in Ghana," sharing the critical need for more trained pastors in this country where almost 80 percent of Ghanaian Baptists are young people. In the second session, Cawley Bolt, vice president of the Jamaica Baptist Union General Assembly, presented "Slave Trade and the Unholy Triangle." Bolt traced the origins and ancient tribal patterns of slavery and the European, African, and American mutations of those patterns that denied to slaves any rights whatsoever. Peter Morden, professor of Church History and Spirituality at Spurgeon's College, presented "British Baptists and Slavery" about the work of activists, like William Knibb of the Baptist Missionary Society, who helped to bring about the abolition of slavery in Britain. These papers engendered both painful and beneficial discussions and fostered a time of prayer, apology, forgiveness, and reconciliation at individual and corporate levels. On Thursday, BWA members traveled by bus up the coast to visit the slave fortress, where they participated in a deeply moving service that expressed sorrow for the atrocities perpetrated against human beings made in God's image.

Hosted by the Czech Republic Baptists, the BWA Annual Gathering in 2008 was held in the magnificent city of Prague. In its first session, the Commission on Baptist Heritage and Identity joined the Church Leadership and Doctrine and Interchurch Cooperation members to address the topic of ordination or the credentialing of ministers, one of the top Baptist identity issues worldwide. An historical overview of "Ordination in Baptist Life" was presented by Karen Bullock, followed by Brian C. Brewer's paper addressing the question of whether the Baptist view of ordained ministry was more functional or characteristic of "Being." On Thursday, Lydie Kucova, professor of Theology at the International Baptist Theological Seminary in Prague, presented "The Development of Baptists in the Czech Republic," as she explored three streams of Baptist life in Bohemia, Moravia, and Silesia and related the often extreme hardships resulting from immigration relocations, political tensions, and life under the communistic regime.

At the 400th celebration in Ede, members the commission hosted four sessions and a history corner. Teun van der Leer, rector of the Baptist Seminary in Barneveld, presented "The History of the Dutch Baptist Churches" and the work of Johannes Feisser, whose mid-19th century ministry most influenced Dutch Baptist life. In the second session, Ken Edmonds, a professional architect from Melbourne, Australia, presented "Rembrandt and the Waterlander Mennonites (Anabaptists)," which explored the nature of the relationship between the two and included a walking tour map of Amsterdam that traced their common historical sites.

On Thursday afternoon, BWA participants traveled to the city of Amsterdam to gather at the United Mennonite Church (*Singelkerk*) to celebrate the 400th anniversary of Baptists. The building, dating from 1608, was the church of the Flemish Mennonites until their merger with the Waterlander Mennonites in the 1660s. After the service, people scattered to tour the city and early Baptist sites. In the final session of the commission, Kirsten Timmer, Ph.D. student at B. H. Carroll Theological Institute, presented her research, "John Smyth's Request for Mennonite Recognition and Admission: Four Newly Translated Letters, 1610-1612," describing the first contact between the English Separatists (later earliest Baptists Smyth and Helwys) and the Waterlander Mennonites. While investigating correspondence, written in 17th century Latin and now in the Amsterdam archives, Timmer discovered evidence showing that the Waterlanders *did not accept* the Smyth group in 1610 as previously believed, but in 1615, after the death of Smyth in 1612. Commission members also presented papers in forums entitled "Major Moments in the Baptist Story in the Regions," and the commission's chair moderated "Baptist Peacemakers: Four Centuries of Reconciliation."

The commission's work of the period included hosting its annual programs, publishing a "Baptist Principles" leaflet, a children's story coloring book, and a historical walking tour brochure, freely distributed from its History Booth at both European Baptist Federation and BWA 400th celebrations, where it also displayed historical memorabilia and books on the history of Baptists around the globe. To Peter Morden for his work on the leaflet, Sheila Heneise and Bethany Bullock for their expertise on the coloring book, Kirsten Timmer for designing the walking tour brochure, and David Parker, the commission's webmaster, the commission extends deep gratitude.

The members of the Commission on Baptist Heritage and Identity gladly offer the following papers as examples of the fine work accomplished by the historical team who gratefully served together throughout this quinquennium.

Chapter 1

John Smyth's Request for MennoniteRecognition and Admission: Four Newly Translated Letters, 1610-1612

Kirsten T. Timmer

Introduction

Today, as we travel back in time to the early 1600s, we will look at the Amsterdam Waterlander Mennonites and the earliest Baptists from two perspectives. The first perspective allows us to recreate some of the circumstances under which the two groups came into contact. The second viewpoint helps us to see clearly while we zoom in on some of the details in the Mennonite correspondence regarding the English affair as the Mennonites referred to Smyth's request for recognition as a true church. Until recently, four pieces of important correspondence were known in Dutch only. Today, they are available in English translations as well. [1] These new translations provide evidence that supports and challenges some of Coggins' views regarding the Smyth group's application to the Waterlanders and the ensuing events.[2] For now, let us turn to the first perspective.

Earliest Baptists and Waterlander Mennonites

John Smyth (c. 1570-1612) was an ordained Anglican minister who turned Puritan. After being fired by the authorities for being a Puritan, Smyth and his wife moved to Gainsborough where John made a living as a physician and part-time pastor. He began meeting with a Separatist church and completely broke with the Church of England in 1606. [3] This Separatist church held to Calvinistic doctrine, infant baptism, and covenanted church membership. That same year, when the church became too large to go unnoticed, the leaders decided to split into two groups in order to avoid religious persecution under King James I. The Robinson-Brewster-Bradford group met in Scrooby Manor; the Smyth-Helwys group remained in Gainsborough.[4] Within the next two years both groups would flee to the Netherlands.

When the Smyth-Helwys group arrived in Amsterdam, the city stood at the eve of becoming "perhaps the most cosmopolitan city in the world, trafficking in both goods and ideas." From Amsterdam, both the worst and the best that the Renaissance offered was soon to spread throughout Northern Europe.[5] Amsterdam became the most important port as the trade and traffic by the Dutch East-Indies Company flourished. In 1612, Amsterdam's population numbered 50,000. Ten years later, the population had doubled.[6] In short, Amsterdam stood at the beginning of its Golden Age.

Amsterdam has been known for its religious tolerance. The city, however, could not practice religious tolerance during the time of the Spanish Inquisition (in Amsterdam from 1521-1578). Anabaptists were tortured, beheaded, drowned, or otherwise executed both in the capital and in other places.[7] Under these conditions, Menno Simons (1496-1561), "the most outstanding leader of the Anabaptist branch," worked and ministered.[8]

The Waterlanders formed one group of Mennonites and derived their name from an area in the province of North Holland. As early as 1534, many Anabaptists lived in this district. Around 1555, because they were more liberal and progressive, the Waterlanders separated from the main Mennonite branch. In 1615, the number of baptized Waterlanders in Amsterdam reached more than 1,000.[9] Compared to stricter Mennonites, the Waterlanders allowed more contact with the world (some of them held lower magisterial offices), marriage to non-Mennonites, and open communion. They also accepted Reformed believers into their congregation without re-baptizing them. In the Waterlander congregation, room existed for disagreement, and the elders had less authority than in other Mennonite congregations.[10] Hans de Ries, minister at Alkmaar, and Lubbert Gerritsz, minister at Amsterdam, were two of the most outstanding Waterlander leaders. Smyth and Helwys came in contact with them after arriving in Amsterdam.

When the Smyth-Helwys group fled religious persecution in England the group settled in Amsterdam, in Jan Munter's Bakehouse along the Amstel River, near Bakkerstraat and Engelse Pelgrimssteeg. The Bakehouse, which produced the hardtack biscuit for ships sailing to the East Indies, provided jobs for the Smyth-Helwys group as well as living quarters and a place for worship.[11]

The Smyth-Helwys group was not the only group of English refugees in Amsterdam. Many of these refugees gathered at the English Reformed Church at the Begijnhof. Francis Johnson, leader of the Ancient Church, and John Robinson with the Scrooby group lived in Amsterdam as well. Soon, however, Robinson and his people moved to Leiden. Some of his group later returned to England and from there set sail for the New World on the Mayflower - they were the Pilgrim Fathers.

Through the Waterlander Jan Munter, Smyth and Helwys came in contact with the Amsterdam Waterlanders. At that time, the Waterlander congregation met at the Church at the Tower.[12]

The theological discussions proved valuable. Likely in 1609, Smyth adopted believer's baptism, baptized himself and his group by effusion, and thus, reconstituted his group as a church - the first Baptist congregation.[13] In 1610, Smyth wrote his *Argumenta contra Baptismum Infantum*, still an important document for Baptist beliefs today. The year 1610 is where we change our perspective.

Four Newly Translated Letters

Correspondence regarding the English affair, as the Mennonites referred to Smyth's request for recognition and admission, commenced with Smyth's application to the Waterlanders in February 1610.[14] Helwys disagreed with Smyth's application to the Waterlanders because he did not think the principle of successionism necessary. He then sent a letter along with his confession of faith to the Waterlanders.[15] Helwys and his small group returned to England in 1611/12 to plant the first General Baptist church on English soil. The Waterlanders considered Helwys' objections; yet they desired to grant Smyth's request.

Valuing consensus, by means of letters the Waterlanders asked other Waterlander/Mennonite congregations for their opinion on the English affair. Although these newly translated letters provide insight into the contemporary Mennonite view and practice of consensus, our main concern is with details shedding light on the English affair. As stated, these new translations provide evidence supporting as well as challenging some of James Robert Coggins' views regarding the Smyth group's application to the Waterlanders and the ensuing events.[16] A discussion follows the translation of each letter. The translations retain some of the Dutch word order and punctuation to facilitate further research by non-Dutch historians.

A Letter Dated May 15, 1610

A Letter of Yeme de Ringh at Harlingen to Lubbert Gerritsz., Hans de Ries, and Reynier Wijbrandtsz., Dated May 15[?], 1610 To the Honorable Pious Man

Reinier Wybrants glassmaker

in Saint Luke on the

Singel in the Mennonite Church.

At Amsterdam

Pay the messenger[17]

Praise be to God XV[?] May 1610 in Harlingen

From the heart-beloved brothers and fellow servant in Christ Lubbert Ger:[ritsz.], Hans de Ries, Renier Wibrants. Your letter with the request to come there to you to discuss the English affair, has reached us; the others have been sent for immediately at my word. Our teachers, except Jacob Tiewes, have gathered and have sent their opinions regarding this to you, which you may want to review. It seems that they prefer to have first the articles which have been given to you by the English in order to review these same with the brothers so that afterwards there would come no trouble out of it since they are worried. So the friends can do what their minds think "and I do not think that even if we came there" that we perhaps would be united in the understanding and that might cause some trouble I am afraid; but that you send to here to the teachers the articles given to you and that I do not see as evil. For I am concerned that they do not take it (so it appears) on the aspect of baptism, [that is] why I hope so that they can be satisfied with our belief and household, that it could come indeed to a good end by letters as God

8

wills. So you think well, for I for my person had much preferred to see the case somewhat in a different manner than this, namely that they had undertaken themselves to hear and see all things/ or since they have not undertaken that they would have placed it in your hands completely. Then this as it appears has not been able to go this way/ and this so I notice from the care of the churches here. Therefore, I beg you to do so indeed and write after her desire the articles as you have given them to her and even if it were that the servant of the English co-signed/ then this would not harm my reservation, but do it as you think is good. I have co-signed this although it is not all according to my opinion/ so I cannot view it as evil, for when we do something without our congregations/ so we get certainly trouble/ for we have many hard heads to which we have to see a bit/ and it is not possible to live always in strife for our congregations grow now fairly, praise God, so that we now in two times in one month or within five weeks/ have received for baptism 40 people/ and it would not be good indeed to bring unrest among them. Further with this goes a letter which I have just received from Rippert and have opened without knowing it and have not yet read/ since I was still in bed when the letter came this with all my best taking away it happened unknowingly. Nothing further than be greeted from the heart along with all who are beloved to you.

Your Servant, Yeme de Rijnck

Yeme de Ringh wrote this letter some three months after the Smyth group applied for recognition as a true Mennonite congregation.[18] De Ringh's letter is a reply to Gerritsz's request to Mennonite congregations that were part of the Bevredigde Broederschap to attend the May 23, 1610, conference regarding the English affair.[19] De Ringh replied to Gerritsz that he had called the teachers of the Harlingen church together and discussed the issue together. Their conclusion was threefold: they should not attend the conference because they most likely could not come to a mutual understanding; they wanted to see A Short Confession of Faith, which de Ries and Gerritsz had drawn up and which the Smyth group had signed in agreement, so they could read Smyth's view on baptism; and they did not want to cause any unrest in their church by recognizing the Smyth group. Five other ministers of congregations in Friesland replied similarly.[20] In short, the Friesland teachers refused to decide upon the English affair until they had had a chance to discuss the articles of faith with their congregations and reach consensus. The teacher of the congregation at Rijnsburg, South Holland, however, expressed no concern regarding doctrinal issues in his May 18, 1610, letter.

A Letter Dated May 18, 1610
A Letter of Willem Janszoon, Teacher at Rijnsburg, to
Reynier Wybrantsz. at Amsterdam, Dated May 18, 1610
To the
Honorable and the pious reijner
Wybrant son living at Amsterdam[21]

Be greeted from the heart
After wishes of everything good from this side I let know (known?) my dear and in-God beloved brother and fellow worker in the gospel Reijner Wybrant's son that I have received your writing and have understood from it as that there have come some zealous hearts from England who there are seeking to unite with you and that you have spoken with them there multiple times about our household and outwardly are one with each other in confession as I understand and [you] write to us unworthy ones to come there on 23 May with some of our fellow servants to discuss with each other in order to speak on the most important [matter] with them and that I should bring some along who can understand and speak Latin, so I let my dear brother and fellow servant know that it is not convenient for me on that day since my word stands to come that day to another place which I cannot rearrange because of a reason, but I have moved Master Jacob and Cornelis van Beest to be there then with you all since they can understand and speak Latin and that you will have more help from them than from us since we do not understand that language; the Lord may give you altogether wisdom and understanding that it may take

place to the honor of the gospel, to the edification of many pious and to the praise and gratitude of God's holy name and to the salvation of our dearly bought souls, for this God may loan us his grace. Amen.

The main point of Janszoon's letter is the teacher's reply to Gerritsz's invitation. Janszoon's concern was to send two men who understood and spoke Latin. This concern supports the view that the English did not speak Dutch, nor did the Dutch speak English. The common language at the conference, then, was Latin. Not all Dutch and English, however, spoke Latin. Some men of either group, speaking both Latin and their native language, were to serve, therefore, as interpreters at the conference.[22] Janszoon himself was unable to attend. He was not the only minister to decline the invitation.

A Letter Dated May 21, 1610
A Letter from Dirk Pieters at Hoorn to Lubbert Gerritsz.
At Amsterdam, Dated May 21, 1610
To the honorable elas Iansen Bruijn
to be passed on
to Lubbert Gerretzen in
Amsterdam
Three SS [Stuivers = nickels]
The deliverer's pay [23]

God's grace for a friendly greeting. Amen.
Honorable Sir, from the heart loved and loved-in-God brother (father) and fellow servant in the Lord Lubbert Gerretsen. Since we have received the letter signed by you all of the 6th of this [May] and have thought about the same with attention (and have reviewed with worry) so we have discussed with our servants and with our fellow servants/ as well as have called for Aebell Hendericksen, Gijsbert Dircksen and Jacob Ariensen with them holding council, we find it for the best of our conscience (and for the Lord) not to come according to your desire// beg therefore hold it to us for the best/ it does not happen because you all are not worthy to us, not at all, even if it were ten more times as the Lord knows/

but [it happens] because of certain important causes which we think we have for that/ As many as now deal with the case therefore we were written, is our simple advice and request that you would indeed deal carefully and thoroughly and not lightly agree to a continuation because of some dangers that may arise over that!/ so that we do not hammer on the one side and break much more on the other side// for, dear brother, we see well when already a few separated nations come together how heavily it falls to keep the same in peace just as the present situation teaches us all too well// however, we know that the fruits of righteousness are sown in peace by those who keep the peace/ therefore, dearly beloved brother, let us keep that which the Lord has given us/ so that we do not lose what we have wrought but may receive full pay from the Lord/ with this may the Lord help and assist us now and in eternity. Amen. Be with this [letter] commended to the Lord and greeted from the heart with the peace of the Lord/ dated Hoom, 21 Mayanno 1610.

By me Dirrick Pieterzn, your fellow servant in the Lord

Writing on his own behalf and that of three other ministers, Dirk Pieters, a minister in Hoom, North Holland, declined Gerritsz's invitation. Pieters urged the Amsterdam Waterlanders to be careful and thorough in their decision because a continuation with the English group might prove dangerous. Writing of his concern that "we do not hammer on the one side and break much more on the other side," Pieters likely was afraid of the possible breakup of the Bevredigde Broederschap. The congregations aligned with the Broederschap at that time already had difficulty maintaining peace amongst each other. Despite this difficulty, the Amsterdam Waterlanders continued working on recognition and admittance of the Smyth group which would cause more unrest in the Broederschap.

The Amsterdam Waterlanders' letter of July 16, 1610, to the Mennonite leaders in Friesland contained a request for their answers to two issues. First, the Amsterdam Waterlanders wanted to know the Frisians' opinion of the confession of faith which the Smyth group

12

had signed. Second, they wanted to know their view of the baptism that the members of the Smyth group, in particular John Smyth, had undergone. The Amsterdam congregation, then, still desired national consensus on the English affair. Yet the congregation felt ashamed and pressured: "We are very surprised that this affair seems to have been taken at heart by you so very little, for which we are ashamed before these [English], and scarcely know what to answer that this affair is put off such a long time."[24]

Replying two days later, the Frisian ministers urged the Amsterdam Waterlanders to acquaint "all churches in Prussia and the whole of Germany, and wherever established" with the English affair, which "is a completely new and never heard of affair."[25] The ministers warn against "ruin, harm, hurt, and perdition of the churches concerning the [Waterlander] peace-making or union," desiring "peace, quietness, and silence" instead. According to them, the Waterlanders' intemperate zeal is partly the cause of the widespread discontentment over the English alliance or union with the Mennonite congregations.[26] The Friesland congregations, therefore, did not want to have anything to do with the discussion. No further correspondence between the Waterlanders and the Frisian Mennonites concerning this topic has survived. Most likely, these were indeed the Frisians' last words regarding the issue. The following winter, when the Amsterdam Waterlanders brought up again the union with the English as evidenced by a surviving manuscript, Mennonite ministers were gathered around Gerritsz's deathbed. According to Coggins, by then the Smyth group had been recognized as a true Mennonite congregation.[27] Coggins' threefold argument that the 1610 negotiations with the Smyth group formed a cause for the breakup of the Bevredigde Broederschap around 1613 is cogent.[28] His hypothesis that the May 23, 1610, conference ended negotiations and recognized the Smyth group as a true Mennonite congregation, however, is not as strong as it fails to account for two aspects as found in surviving manuscripts.

First, the Amsterdam Waterlanders' letter of July 16, 1610, requested the Friesland congregations to send their opinions on the English affair. The Waterlanders are ashamed that it is taking the Frisians such a long time, and they do not know what to answer the English regarding this putting off. If, as Coggins contends, the May 23 conference resulted in the recognition of the Smyth group as a Mennonite congregation, why would the Waterlanders have thought it necessary to obtain the

Frisian Mennonites' opinions? The Frisians' reply of July 18, 1610, is also inconclusive regarding Coggins' hypothesis, for the leaders wrote, "We, undersigned, may not conceal from you our astonishment at your ardent and impetuous writing to us, in which you demand our answer within a fortnight, or that we afterwards shall be quiet about the alliance or union with the English, in your town, having taken place or intended."[29] From the remainder of the reply, the Frisian leaders seem to have believed the union had not taken place yet, since they warn against it and urge the Amsterdam Waterlanders to deliberate most seriously. The second aspect which appears to discredit Coggins' hypothesis is found in the memorandum by Claes Claeszoon Anslo.

A Memorandum Dated January 17, 1611/2
A Memorandum Made by Claes Claeszoon Anslo at
Amsterdam on Jan. 17, 1611/2
Copy[30]

On the 17th of January when Lubbert Gerretsz was in bed very ill, he has asked all servants and also Hans de Ries/Jan Munter/Nittert Obbesz/Comelis Albertsz/and myself Claes Claesz/ (except Mathijs Lutso[?] who was absent) even Koefoot, his desire from the heart was so he said and [we] clearly expressed to him that it was also our desire that Reijner Wijbrans might be affirmed in the full service/ since he had served the congregation for a while in the Word of God! saying that he was at peace with that/ since he had been found being most faithful to the Word of God/ to know that the sacrament would also be well entrusted to him the best[?]/ to which we all answered yes/ and since, except for seven, it was determined peacefully by that whole congregation by silence, Lubbert Gerretsz then also asked Reynier Wybrans/ whether he was prepared to accept the heavy duty by God's grace/ who under the same also answered yes/ then Lubbert Gerretsz has placed [on] him the hand on the head/ wishing him many good wishes of God and also affirmed him and bound him to nothing but to the Word of God/ saying also that he had had great happiness that with all those men finally all concepts had been laid down and that one shall deal with everything only according to the Word of God, furthermore he has desired seriously that one, however, should not postpone the case of the English/ but complete firstly if it were possible since they had some reservations about the baptism of Mr. Smidt/ since he had no Scripture for it/ but now did want to accept all the other English without worry/ without baptizing again/ further he desired also from Nittert abbes/ that he would lead the voting happening for this/ and would let him be placed and do his best through God's grace/ which Nittert abbes also accepted under that same grace/ and it was also desired by Lubbert Gerretsz that Matheus[?] Iansz would do that, too, who was not present there but the servants promised to request that, too, and have all accepted Reynier Wybrans with a kiss and also have departed friendly in peace and have commended Lubbert Gerretsz with a kiss to the Lord's grace and have wished good night - and before that Lubbert Gerretsz asked Hans de Ries, since Reyner Wybrans was a young man, that he would come to his aid in everything with advice and deed/ and with him weigh all things and act as they had done together/ either orally or to write each other depending on the situation of the case/ also Lubbert Gerretsz expressed and desired/ that one in the handling of the sacraments would act in everything for the most edification of the congregation/ saying in some places at a table there around 20 people sat down/ in other places one should deal with it differently/ which might take place with the most peace/ that he had administered it at a table in De Rijp and also in other places etc.

Claes Claesz in Ansloo

This I have written on the very same day for a memorandum as soon as I came home.

Gerritsz's meeting with some Waterlander ministers resulted in affirming Wybrantsz into full service. While Mennonite consensus on local and intra-local levels takes place here in a practical way and provides important information regarding Mennonite consensus during this time, a more intriguing passage in the letter forms the second aspect for which Coggins' hypothesis fails to account:

> Saying also that he had had great happiness that with all those men finally all concepts had been laid down and that one shall deal with everything only according to the Word of God, furthermore he has desired seriously that one, however, should not postpone the case of the English/ but complete firstly if it were possible since they had some reservations about the baptism of Mr. Smidt/ since he had no Scripture for it/ but now did want to accept all the other English without worry/ without baptizing again/ further he desired also from Nittert abbes/ that he would lead the voting happening for this.

It is not clear to whom the phrase "all those men" refers. Perhaps, it is the concluding part of Wybrantsz's ordination. If so, then "all those men" could refer to the leaders present at Gerritsz's bedside. However, the phrase may introduce the next topic, namely "the case of the English." Although the meaning of the Dutch word, translated with "postpone," is difficult to determine, the context shows that the case of the English was still pending. The main reason, Gerritsz shared, was the reservation of the ministers regarding "Smyth's se-baptism" which had no biblical warrant. Gerritsz understood the reservations, yet encouraged the leaders to accept all the other English without rebaptizing them. The aspect of consensus played an important role since Gerrritsz asked Obbes to lead the vote on accepting the other English.

From this discussion, two observations are noteworthy. First, John Smyth was still alive at this time. If he had died already, then the Mennonite ministers would have had no reasons for their reservations. According to Burrage's description, Smyth was still alive indeed: "Smyth had long been of consumptive tendency, and in the summer of 1612 he grew rapidly weaker and died at the end of August in that year."[31] Second, a complete acceptance of the Smyth group as a true congregation does not seem to have taken place before January 17, 1612. If acceptance had been arrived at during the May 23, 1610, conference, then why did Gerritsz urge his fellow ministers to accept all the other English in January 1612? The available evidence, then, shows that most likely the May 23 conference did not finalize the discussion.[32] Wright, however, proposes an intermediate position which is well-argued and is partly based on Helwys' chiding of the Waterlanders:

> The Waterlanders could not admit Smyth and his friends formally, but offered them tacit recognition as a group, and close informal association, through continued accommodation at Munter's bakehouse. Helwys chided the Waterlanders .... [The group] found [itself] in ecclesial limbo, unable to go forward or back, the only means to properly church themselves blocked by the Broederschap.[33]

Conclusion

Baptist historians need more evidence to prove their hypotheses conclusively. As it stands today, the letters of July 16 and July 18, 1610, as well as the memorandum of January 17, 1612, contain phrases indicating the May 23, 1610, conference did not have the result for which the Amsterdam Waterlanders and Smyth had hoped. Close association between the two groups continued since the Smyth group lived at Jan Munter's Bakehouse.[34] Nothing else is known with regard to this group before their request of November 6, 1614, to merge with the Amsterdam Waterlanders.[35] Until then the other Mennonite congregations likely continued stalling negotiations. Finally, in January 1615, the Smyth group was "admitted in the community ... *without baptism.*"[36]

Finally, the union of the Smyth group with the Waterlanders was a fact. Yet it had come at great cost. The Waterlanders in Holland had alienated themselves from the Mennonite leaders in Friesland and Germany. Plausibly, this alienation contributed to the breakup of the Bevredigde Broederschap in 1613.

NOTES

[1.] For formerly known letters and translations, see Burrage, *Early English Dissenters,* voL2, 172-218; Smyth, *Works,* vol. 2, 681-709, 733-50; and Benjamin Evans, *The Early English Baptists,* vol. 1 (London: J. Heaton & Son, 1862),208-22. The English translations were published in article form: Kirsten T. Timmer,

"John Smyth's Request for Mennonite Recognition and Admission: Four Newly Translated Letters (1610*1612*)," *Baptist History and Heritage* 44, no. 1 (Winter 2009): 8-19.

2. James Robert Coggins, *John Smyth's Congregation: English Separatism, Mennonite Influence, and the Elect Nation,* Studies in Anabaptist and Mennonite History, ed. Cornelius J. Dyck, no. 32 (Scottdale, PA: Herald Press, 1991), 77-97

3. Walter H. Burgess, *John Smith the Se-Baptist, Thomas Helwys and the First Baptist Church in England with Fresh Light upon the Pilgrim Fathers 'Church* (London: James Clarke, 1911), 81.

4. H. Leon McBeth, *The Baptist Heritage* (Nashville: Broadman Press, 1987), 33.

5. John J. Murray, *Amsterdam in the Age of Rembrandt,* The Center of Civilization Series (Norman, OK: University of Oklahoma Press, 1967), ix.

6. *ibid.,* 7, 10. By 1662, the population had doubled again, to 200,000.

7. S. Blaupot ten Cate, *Geschiedenis der Doopsgezinden in Holland, Zeeland, Utl'echt en Gelderland van derzelven Ontstaan tot op dezen Tijd, uit Oorspronkelijke Stukken en Echte Berigten Opgemaakt* (Amsterdam: P. N. van Kampen, 1847), 4-16.

8. Timothy George, *Theology of the Reformers* (Nashville: Broadman and Holman, 1988), 255.

9. *The Mennonite Encyclopedia,* s.v. "Waterland," "Waterlanders." Some derogatory nicknames for the Waterlanders were Scheedemakers (schismatics; after elder Jacob Jans Scheedemaker) and Drekwagen (garbage wagon).

10. *ibid.,* s.v. "Waterlanders;" see also, W. J. Kiihler, *Geschiedenis der Nederlandsche Doopsgezinden in de Zestiende Eeuw,* 2nd ed. (Haarlem, the Netherlands: H. D. Tjeenk Willink en Zoon, 1961), 347f.

11. *The Mennonite Encyclopedia,* s.v. "Munter, Jan." Jan Munter (1570-1620) owned the bakery and put the building at the disposal of the Smyth-Helwys group. After Smyth's death, his group joined the Waterlanders in 1615. The members continued having their services there until 1639, the year their leader Thomas Pigott died and the English Waterlanders fully integrated into the Dutch Waterlander congregation. See Keith L. Sprunger, *Dutch Puritanism: A History of English and Scottish Churches of the Netherlands in the Sixteenth and Seventeenth Centuries,* Studies in the History of Christian Thought, ed. Heiko A. Oberman, vol. 31 (Leiden, the Netherlands: E. J. Brill, 1982), 84: "After Pygott's death, the English assembly in the bakery faded out as a separate body, the victim of acculturation and assimilation."

12. *Global Anabaptist Mennonite Encclopedia Online,* s.vS . "Toren;" http://www.gameo.orgiencyclopedia/contents/T672.htmlI/?searchterm=De Toren (accessed July 28, 2009): "Toren, a former meetinghouse at Amsterdam. About 1565 the Waterlander Mennonite church of Amsterdam obtained a warehouse

on the Singel Canal between Bergstraat and Torensluis close to the Jan-Rodenburgstoren (dungeon) ... In 1668, when the Waterlander congregation merged with the Lamists, both meetinghouses henceforth were used by what was then called the United Flemish and Waterlander church. In 1801, when the Zionist congregation of Amsterdam merged with this United church, the Zonist meetinghouse was closed, its pulpit and pipe organ transferred to the Toren church ... from then mostly called the "kleine" (small) church, while the Lamist church, the present Singel church, was called the "groote" (large) church."

[13.] Burgess, 149, thinks it was early 1609; J. Bakker, *John Smyth, de Stichter van het Baptisme* (Wageningen: H. Veenman en Zonen, 1964), 72, argues for a date in late 1608.

[14.] Champlin Burrage, *The Early English Dissenters in the Light of Recent Research (J 550-1 64 1)*, vol. 2, The Dissent en Nonconformity Series, no. 10 (Cambridge: University Press, 1912; reprint, Paris, AR: The Baptist Standard Bearer, n.d.), 177; and John Smyth, *The Works of John Smyth*, vol. 2, ed. W. T. Whitley (Cambridge: Cambridge University Press, 1915), 681. Cornelius J. Dyck, "The Middelburg Confession of Hans de Ries, 1578," *Mennonite Quarterly Review* 36, no. 2 (April 1962): 131-32 argues for an application date of early 1610 because the English used Old Style dating. The application consisted of *Nomina Anglorum* and *Corde Credimus*.

[15.] See Burrage, *Early English Dissenters*, vol. 2, 182-7, for *Synopsis Fidei* and Helwys's letter to the Waterlanders.

[16.] James Robert Coggins, *John Smyth's Congregation: English Separatism, Mennonite Influence, and the Elect Nation*, Studies in Anabaptist and Mennonite History, ed. Cornelius J. Dyck, no. 32 (Scottdale, PA: Herald Press, 1991), 77-97.

[17.] For the Dutch text, see Burrage, *Early English Dissenters*, vol. 2, 205-7.

[18.] Stephen Wright, *The Early English Baptists, 1603-1649* (Woodbridge, UK: The Boydell Press, 2006), 41.

[19.] Bevredigde Broederschap (Satisfied Brotherhood) was the name of a group of High German, Frisian, and Waterlander Mennonites who united around 1600. In 1613, most Frisians and High Germans separated from the Broederschap due to their stricter views on the ban and mixed marriages. Also, the Amsterdam Waterlanders' consideration of accepting the Smyth group as a true Mennonite congregation contributed to the breakup. See Coggins, *John Smyth's Congregation*, 81-4, and ibid. and "A Short Confession of Hans de Ries: Union and Separation in Early Seventeenth-Century Holland," *Mennonite Quarterly Review, 60,* no. 2 (April 1986): 126, 135.

[20.] Evans, *Early English Baptists*, vol. 1, 214.

[21.] For the Dutch text, see Burrage, *Early English Dissenters*, vol. 2, 207-8.

[22.] *ibid.*, 187.

[23.] For the Dutch text, see *ibid.* 208-9.

[24.] Evans, *Early English Baptists,* vol. 1, 215.

[25.] *ibid.,* 217. Coggins, "Short Confession," 137, argues that the Friesland ministers objected to the group's baptism because it contradicted Article 12 of the *Concept of Cologne* (an important document for the founding of the Bevredigde Broederschap). This article called for "proper succession in ordination," which rendered the Smyth group's baptism invalid since Smyth had baptized himself.

[26.] Evans, *Early English Baptists,* vol. 1, 217.

[27.] Coggins, *John Smyth's Congregation,* 84. Some historians arguing that the union of 1610 failed are B. R. White, *A History of the English Baptists,* vol. 1: *The English Baptists of the Seventeenth Century,* ed. B. R. White (London: The Baptist Historical Society, 1983), 26; and W. T. Whitley, *A History of British Baptists* (London: Charles Griffin & Company, Ltd, 1923), 22.

[28.] Coggins, "Short Confession," 136-38

[29.] Evans, *Early English Baptists,* vol. 1, 216.

[30.] For the Dutch text, see Burrage, *Early English Dissenters,* vol. 2, 213-15. The year is 1612 according to New Style dating.

[31.] Champlin Burrage, *The Early English Dissenters in the Light of Recent Research (] 550-1641),* vol. 1, The Dissent en Nonconformity Series, no. 9 (Cambridge: University Press, 1912; reprint, Paris, AR: The Baptist Standard Bearer, n.d.), 248. The burial books of the Nieuwe Kerk show an entry for John Smyth's burial and the fee paid. Smyth died September 1, 1612; the fee was paid the following Sunday, September 9, 1612.

[32.] Jason Lee, *The Theology of John Smyth. Puritan, Separatist, Baptist, Mennonite* (Macon, GA: Mercer University Press, 2003), 95, n269; and Burrage, *Early English Dissenters,* vol. 1,249. Likely without having a complete English translation available, both authors correctly refer to the memorandum of January 17, 1612.

[33.] Wright, *Early English Baptists,* 42-3. For Helwys' comments, see Thomas Helwys, *An Advertisement or Admonition unto the Congregations ... New Fryesers* (Amsterdam?, 1611), 39-40

[34.] Sprunger, 83; Wright, *Early English Baptists,* 42-3; and Evans, *Early English Baptists,* vol. 1,220.

[35.] Evans, *Early English Baptists,* vol. 1,220.

[36.] *ibid.,* 221

Selected Bibliography

Bakker, J. *John Smyth, de Stichter van het Baptisme.* Wageningen: H. Veenman en Zonen, 1964.

Blaupot ten Cate, S. *Geschiedenis der Doopsgezinden in Holland, Zeeland, Utrecht en Gelderland van derzelven Ontstaan tot op dezen Tijd, uit Oorspronkelijke Stukken en Echte Berigten Opgemaakt.* Amsterdam: P. N. van Kampen, 1847).

Burgess, Walter H. *John Smith the Se-Baptist, Thomas Helwys and the First Baptist Church in England with Fresh Light upon the Pilgrim Fathers' Church,* London: James Clarke, 1911.

Burrage, Champlin. *The Early English Dissenters in the Light of Recent Research (15501641).* Vol. 1. The Dissent and Nonconformity Series, vol. 9. Paris, AR: The Baptist Standard Bearer, 1912.

------. *The Early English Dissenters in the Light of Recent Research (1550-1641).* Vol. 2. The Dissent and   Nonconformity Series, vol. 10. Paris, AR: The Baptist Standard Bearer, 1912.

Coggins, James Robert. *John Smyth's Congregation: English Separatism, Mennonite Influence, and the Elect Nation.* Studies in Anabaptist and Mennonite History, ed. Cornelius J. Dyck, vol. 32. Scottdale: Herald Press, 1991.

------. "A Short Confession of Hans de Ries: Union and Separation in Early Seventeenth Century Holland." *The Mennonite Quarterly Review* 60, no. 2 (April 1986): 128-38.

Dyck, Cornelius J. "The First Waterlandian Confession of Faith." *The Mennonite Quarterly Review* 36, no. 1 (January 1962): 5-13.

------. "Hans de Ries and the Legacy of Menno." *The Mennonite Quarterly Review* 1988, no. 3 (July 62): 401-16.

------. "The Life of the Spirit in Anabaptism." *The Mennonite Quarterly Review* 47, no. 4 (October 1973): 309-26.

------. "The Middelburg Confession of Hans de Ries, 1578." *The Mennonite Quarterly Review* 36, no. 2 (April 1962): 147-54, 161.

------. "A Short Confession of Faith by Hans de Ries." *The Mennonite Quarterly Review 38,* no. 1 (January 1964): 5-19.

Evans, Benjamin. *The Early English Baptists.* Vol. 1. London: J. Heaton & Son, 1862.

------. *The Early English Baptists.* Vol. 2. London: J. Heaton & Son, 1864.

Helwys, Thomas. *An Advertisement or Admonition unto the Congregations ... New Fryesers.* Amsterdam? 1611.

Kühler, W. J. *Geschiedenis der Nederlandsche Doopsgezinden in de Zestiende Eeuw.* 2nd ed.

Haarlem, the Netherlands: H. D. Tjeenk Willink en Zoon, 1961.

Lee, Jason. *The Theology of John Smyth. Puritan, Separatist, Baptist, Mennonite.* Macon: Mercer University Press, 2003.

McBeth, H. Leon. *The Baptist Heritage.* Nashville: Broadman Press, 1987.

Murray, John J. *Amsterdam in the Age of Rembrandt.* The Center of Civilization Series. Norman, OK, University of Oklahoma Press, 1967.

Smyth, John. *The Works of John Smyth.* Vol. 2. Edited by W. T. Whitley. Cambridge: Cambridge University Press, 1915.

Sprunger, Keith L. *Dutch Puritanism: A History of English and Scottish Churches of the Netherlands in the Sixteenth and Seventeenth Centuries.* Studies in the History of Christian Thought, ed. Heiko A. Oberman, vol. 31. Leiden: E. J. Brill, 1982.

Timmer, Kirsten T. "John Smyth's Request for Mennonite Recognition and Admission: Four Newly Translated Letters, 1610-1612." *Baptist History and Heritage* 44, no. 1 (Winter 2009): 8-19.

White, B. R. *A History of the English Baptists.* Vol. 1: *The English Baptists of the Seventeenth Century.* Edited by B. R. White. London: The Baptist Historical Society, 1983.

Whitley, W. T. *A History of British Baptists.* London: Charles Griffin & Company, Ltd, 1923.

Wright, Stephen. *The Early English Baptists, 1603-1649.* Woodbridge: The Boydell Press, 2006.

Chapter 2

Rembrandt and the Waterlander Mennonites

Ken Edmonds[1]

Rembrandt was born in 1606 and died in 1669. He lived in the Dutch Golden Age and never traveled further than 60 miles from Amsterdam in his whole life. Rembrandt is acknowledged as one of the greatest artists of all time. It came to me as a surprise that Rembrandt was in some way connected to my own Baptist heritage, even if it was rather farfetched, being via the Anabaptists four hundred years ago. It seems the following questions require answers:

- Was Rembrandt associated with the Waterlander Mennonites?
- If so, what was the nature of the association?
- Who were the Waterlander Mennonites?
- Was Rembrandt a Waterlander Mennonite?
- Did the Waterlanders influence Rembrandt the artist and did Rembrandt the artist influence the Waterlanders?

Was Rembrandt associated with the Waterlander Mennonites? If so, what was the nature of the association?

Baptists are not generally noted for their interest in, or contribution to, the visual arts. It was exciting to think Rembrandt is part of our tradition. I discussed the possibility with others who knew nothing of an association between Rembrandt and the Mennonites and were doubtful if such a thing ever existed. As a result, I have undertaken some research into whether Rembrandt was associated with the Dutch Waterlander Mennonites and if so, what was the nature of this association. I would now like to trace the history of this matter.

Mid Nineteenth Century: The association is suspected but unproven

It appears to me that the secular art historians have not until recent years paid much attention to this matter if at all. However, Mennonite scholars have been working on the subject since the late 1940s. In fact prints made from Rembrandt's painting that portrays the wealthy Mennonite cloth merchant, ship owner and preacher, Cornelius Anslo, and his wife, began appearing in North American homes and church vestibules in the 1950s celebrating an unproven association between the great master and the Dutch Mennonites.

At the time, Mennonite scholars quoted a passage from the Italian Art critic, Filippo Baldinucci, who wrote in 1686 concerning Rembrandt:

> The artist professed in those days the religion of the Menists, which though false too, is yet opposed to that of Calvin, inasmuch as they do not practice the rite of baptism before the age of thirty. They do not elect educated preachers, but employ for such posts men of humble condition as long as they are esteemed by them honourable and just people, and for the rest they live following their caprice.

Baldinucci's source of information was the Danish painter Bernhard Keihl (1624-1687), who worked in Rembrandt's workshop between 1642 and 1644.

Poet Julia Kasdorf, Assistant Professor in Writing at Messiah College, PA, USA, wrote an article in 1996 titled, "The Master and the Mennonite," published in the newsletter of the Historical Committee & Archives of the Mennonite Church. In that article she wrote the following:

> This was a critical period in the great artist's career, following the death of his wife, when he painted his masterpiece, *The Night Watch*. It also coincides with his association with Anslo (that portrait was commissioned in 1641) and the Mennonite art students and patrons. From those years on, Rembrandt gradually sank into financial ruin, while turning increasingly to biblical subjects that

would earn him little income. It is especially in these later paintings that some have recognized a quality suggestive of contact with Mennonite spirituality. However, it is primarily through the preacher Anslo that Mennonites have staked their association with Rembrandt.

In 1947, Ira Landis published an article in the *Mennonite Historical Bulletin* suggesting incorrectly that Rembrandt's parents were Mennonites. In 1952, Cornelius Krahn reported in *Mennonite Life* the findings of Jakob Rosenberg and H.M. Rothermend, two art historians who were working independently on Rembrandt's relations with the Waterlander Mennonites. Rothermend in his article, "Rembrandt and the Mennonites," in the same issue claims Rembrandt had contact with Mennonites in his youth and was certainly affiliated with them after 1641. Both scholars claim the Mennonites affected Rembrandt's religious paintings especially the Anabaptist ordinances of the Lord's Supper, adult baptism and foot washing.

In 1956, a special edition of *Mennonite Life* was published to celebrate the 350th anniversary of Rembrandt's birth. The cover featured the Anslo portrait. The edition also included three articles on Rembrandt that were clearly intended to establish the connection between the master artist and the Dutch Mennonites. One of the articles by Irvin Horst was titled, "Rembrandt knew Mennonites." In this he traced Rembrandt's connections from boarding with a Mennonite family to associations with Mennonite art students, poets and patrons. Horst identifies thirteen Mennonites portrayed by Rembrandt together with a catalogue of possible Mennonite subjects.

Late Nineteenth Century: The association is proven

After the 1950s new research showed Rembrandt not only knew Mennonites but that he had close association with the Amsterdam Waterlander Mennonite community. This was as a result of his relationship with Hendrick Uylenburgh who was a prominent member of that community, and a most important art dealer who ran an artists' studio in which Rembrandt worked from 1631 to 1635, responsible for art production.

Rembrandt lived in the Uylenburgh house where he met his future wife, Saskia, who was Uylenburgh's niece. After their marriage in 1633, they continued to live in the Uylenburgh house for a period of one year. Clearly Uylenburgh provided Rembrandt with access to the Waterlander Mennonite circle which resulted in profitable portrait commissions. In 1631 and 1640 Rembrandt invested considerable sums of money into Uylenburgh's enterprise. Rembrandt purchased his own house in 1639 which was next door to Uylenburgh's. In his grand new residence he established a studio similar to that he had been part of with Uylenburgh. This residence is now the Rembrandt House Museum which has been set up to replicate what it was like in Rembrandt's time with the assistance of most detailed records made at that time.

In 1964 Jakob Roseburg, Professor of Fine Arts at Harvard, wrote in his book, *Rembrandt Life and Work,* the following:

> Comparatively little emphasis has been given, in the literature on Rembrandt, to the artist's relationship to the Mennonites. Some theologians have dismissed this problem, but too exclusively from the theological angle .... A study of the Mennonite literature, and Menno's own writings in particular, will reveal how close Rembrandt came in his Biblical representations to the spiritual attitude of this sect.

Christopher White in his 1984 book, *Rembrandt,* writes about the Master Painter:

> In his own unorthodox way he was a deeply religious man but it is doubtful whether he followed any one religion. His attitude can be most closely matched by that of the Mennonites, whose creed is based on the original and literal contents of the Bible and excludes all dogmas based on subsequent events.

Simon Schama, Professor in Art History and History at Columbia University in New York, has written extensively about the Dutch Golden Age in his 1991 book, *The Embarrassment of Riches,* and his 1999 book, *Rembrandt's Eyes.* These books explore a time of innovation in science, economics and the arts. Schama writes about the history of the Mennonites and their flight from Germany, Switzerland and the Netherlands for sanctuary in Poland. Schama writes in great detail about Hendrick van Uylenburgh who moved from Danzig to the Netherlands around 1625 with a large number of fellow Mennonites when a change in the Stadholder resulted in an era of toleration. Schama surmises Rembrandt first met Uylenburgh when he was studying with artist Pieter Lastman close to the Uylenburgh house. Uylenburgh traveled to Leiden three years later to purchase art from Rembrandt. Uylenburgh established himself as a prominent and versatile entrepreneur in the Amsterdam art market. His business was cash hungry and Rembrandt lent him one thousand guilders, a considerable sum at the time. In return, Rembrandt gained access to Uylenburgh's wide circle of contacts including the Waterlander Mennonite community together with workshop experience required by the artists' guild before Rembrandt could set up as an independent master. Schama's books record in a rather off hand manner the connections between Rembrandt and the Mennonites. In *The Embarrassment of Riches,* Schama writes:

> Rembrandt came from a family in which the father was a Calvinist and the mother a practising Catholic. At different times he himself was attracted to Remonstrants, Mennonites and to the highly unorthodox sects like the Collegiants and the Waterlanders whose emphasis on extreme scriptural simplicity appealed to a Christian for whom the Bible was an anthology of human drama.

Unfortunately Schama shows little interest in the association between Rembrandt and the Mennonites and spends one third of *Rembrandt's Eyes* writing about the great Catholic artist, Peter Paul Rubens, who he argues Rembrandt saw as a rival and attempted to outdo.

Twenty First Century: Serious research into the association and quadricentennial birthday celebrations

It seems to me that by the turn of the century, some art historians had accepted that Rembrandt had extensive contact with the Mennonites and were turning their attention to serious study of Mennonite influence on his prodigious work. Other art historians remained silent on this subject.

The National Gallery of Victoria in Melbourne mounted an exhibition in 1997 and published a lavish book titled, *Rembrandt – A Genius and His Impact*, with a number of chapters by art historians on various aspects of Rembrandt's life and work. It is disappointing and even amazing that although reference is made in *Rembrandt - A Genius and His Impact* to Rembrandt's association with Uylenburgh, no comment is made concerning the influence of Mennonites on Rembrandt's life and work.

It seems some scholars do not regard the association as important with respect to Rembrandt's work. This I find hard to understand.

The matter of whether Rembrandt had an association with the Mennonites, or whether the Mennonites had an influence upon him, is of great interest in the Mennonite world but apparently not taken very seriously in some parts of the secular fine arts establishment. In fact the December 2006 edition of the *Smithsonian* magazine featured an article celebrating "Rembrandt: The Master at 400" which acknowledges the association with Uylenburgh, but not that Uylenburgh was a Mennonite, or that the association was of any significance.

If there was any doubt about the association it was erased by the publication of *Uylenburgh and Son: Art and Commerce from Rembrandt to De Lairessee 1625-1675*. This impressive book was published in 2006 by the Rembrandt Huis Museum in Amsterdam.

With the publication of this book the Mennonite/Rembrandt association was confirmed beyond dispute by the in-depth research for this book undertaken by historians from the Rembrandt Huis Museum, Jaap van der Veen and Friso Lammerstse. The foreword to the book includes the following statement that sets the matter in context and is supported by detailed investigations of original documents.

> Launched by Uylenburgh, Rembrandt rapidly became the most eminent and best paid portrait painter in Holland ... The wealthy Amsterdam merchants who had their portraits painted by Rembrandt generally moved in the same Mennonite circles as Hendrick Uylenburgh.

This publication covers in great detail the activities of Hendrick Uylenburgh from agent for the King of Poland to art dealer in

Amsterdam. The authors document the Mennonite movement in 17th century Danzig and Amsterdam, together with its strong involvement with art and the business of art.

Rembrandt's association with the preacher, Anslo, is now no longer the prime evidence of his links with the Mennonites. By the 21st century, serious studies were being published which look not only at Rembrandt, but also at the nature of the Waterlander Mennonites and their emerging involvement in secular society.

Who were the Waterlander Mennonites?

The University of Amsterdam's 1994 publication titled, *From Martyr to Muppy,* deals with the Dutch Anabaptists as hunted heretics who finally became accepted Mennonite urban professionals or "muppies." It explores Mennonite contributions to the rich history of Dutch culture including the connection between economic advancement among the Dutch Mennonites in the 17th century and their extraordinary interest in art and literature.

In 1996 Mennonite scholars Piet Visser, Professor of Book History and Curator of the Mennonite Library, University Library of Amsterdam, and Mary Sprunger, Professor of History at Eastern Mennonite University in Virginia, wrote in their book, *Menno Simons: Places, Portraits and Progeny,* about the gradual emancipation of the Mennonites in the 17th century in Netherlands.

> They came out from the dark wings and played not only economic, but also technological, intellectual and artistic roles on the World's Centre Stage.

The Mennonite movement comprised a number of distinct groups with different views on points of doctrine and ethics. The two largest groups in Amsterdam were the Waterlanders and the Flemish Mennonites. The Waterlanders were the more liberal of the two. They held worship services in a building named "de Toren" or "by the Tower" and the Flemish worshipped in a building named "het lam" or "by the Lamb." The Rembrandt House Museum Scholars Lammertse and van der Veen write:

In the early seventeenth century the various Mennonite factions in Amsterdam formed approximately seven percent of the population.... Few though they were this religious minority comprised many affluent merchants and artisans and exercised a disproportionately strong influence on the city's economic life. Many Mennonite merchants traded in the Baltic, if only because ships sailing to that region did not need to carry arms. Interestingly enough, their religious leaders wrote little about economic matters, but evidently had no objection to their followers earning money. In business, Mennonites tended to form partnerships and deal with members of their own community, and in this respect Hendrick Uylenburgh was no exception.

Mary Sprunger, in her chapter in *From Martyr to Muppy*, notes:

The membership lists of "by the Tower," extant from 1612 to 1668 provide the comprehensive clues to the social composition of the congregation. Over the course of 56 years, 3137 persons joined either by baptism or by letter of transfer.

At any one time, there may have been about 1,000 members ... unfortunately it is not possible to say to what extent the Waterlanders mirrored Amsterdam society in general, because no figures for the city as a whole exist. Mennonites in Amsterdam were shut out of the most elite group in the city, the patrician or regency class, because of their non-participation in government. Nor were Mennonites present in the lowest social group, defined by contemporaries as the rabble ... which included vagrants, beggars and social undesirables. The majority of Waterlanders came from the middling class of small businessmen, skilled artisans and unskilled workers ... but also had many representatives among the prosperous class of non-ruling notables, rich merchants, businessmen, shop owners and intellectuals.

Also in *From Martyr to Muppy*, Sjouke Voolstra, Professor of Anabaptist/Mennonite Theology and History at the Mennonite Seminary, Amsterdam, argues:

> The slow integration of the Mennonite into Dutch society in the seventeenth century had historical, sociological, economic and religious reasons. In spite of the fact that the Mennonites in this 'Golden Age' remained a minority with limited religious freedom, nowhere else in Europe were Mennonites able to live in such relative tolerance as in the Republic of the Seven United Provinces. The Calvinist offensive against the Anabaptist competitor died down around the middle of the seventeenth century. The merchant had triumphed over the preacher. By this time the Mennonites had already became indispensable honey bees for the state made important contributions to both the economy and to culture.

In her summary, Mary Sprunger writes:

> The close social and family ties formed within a dissenting Church helped the Waterlanders elite to amass comfortable, not to say large, fortunes. Nevertheless, perhaps because of their rejection of weapons and political participation, the Mennonites were not highly represented on the uppermost rung of Amsterdam's social and economic ladder during the seventeenth century. This would change, however, by the eighteenth and nineteenth centuries as some Mennonite families continued to accumulate capital.

The largest concentration of prosperous Mennonites was in the textile industry and many of the Waterlander deacons were cloth merchants. Mennonite engineers made recognized leaders in land reclamation.

Cornelius Dyke, in the 1993 book, *An Introduction to Mennonite History*, writes:

The Union of Utrecht in 1579 provided that each person should be allowed to remain free in his religion. These actions did not mean that all oppression had stopped but the Mennonites were no longer forced to go to prison or to the stake for their faith ... Full freedom of worship, however, did not exist for them until the nineteenth century. Mennonites nevertheless soon made a place in the life of the nation... Trade with Greenland, whale and herring fishing were almost completely in Mennonite hands. They were very involved within the Baltic Sea trade, ship building, the lumber business, the food industry and were the backbone of the textile industry ... For the most part Mennonites were highly literate, partly from a desire to read the Bible and the martyrologies, but also by way of overcoming social disadvantage. In the seventeenth century a high percentage of the medical doctors in the Netherlands were Mennonites, this being one of the professions open to them. Since doctors were the best educated members of the congregations, they often served as pastors at the same time.

Dyck also provides some historical perspective as follows:

All this progress in material and cultural ways was not pure gain. A century or more after the Mennonites suffered deeply for their faith, they were tolerated and many were wealthy. Many no longer believed deeply in the things for which their fathers and mothers had died. Ease and luxury had done what persecution could not do... In the mid-seventeenth century the Dutch Mennonites had no serious threat to their life from without; leaders arose who tried to reverse the process of cooling off from within. They collected the stories of the martyrs, the writings of the heroes of faith, and wrote the history of their heritage, in order to renew succeeding generations.

Clearly they did succeed in making succeeding generations aware of where they had come from. Modern day Mennonites have an excellent knowledge of their history and a fine appreciation of their heritage.

The Amsterdam Waterlanders' place of worship located at Singel 158 in a former warehouse was called "by the Tower" due to the proximity of a Tower. It was rectangular in plan with men sitting on hard wooden pews lining three walls with women sitting in rows of chairs in the middle. All seats faced the elevated pulpit in the center of the remaining wall which had huge windows providing daylight for reading the scriptures. The focus was upon the exposition of the word visually reinforced by the prominent pulpit. The conservative Flemish Mennonites' (Lamist) place of worship was called "by the Lamb" due to the close proximity of a Brewery that used a lamb as its trademark. The building at Singel 452 is the present Church "bij het Lam" (also known as the Singelkerk) which is located off the street down a passage. An engraving published in 1743 shows the interior of the "Lamist" Mennonite Church during a baptismal service.

A regrouping of the Dutch Mennonites into two new branches, the Lamists and the Zonists, occurred between 1664 and 1668 as the result of theological disputes called "War of the Lambs." As part of this regrouping, the Waterlanders in Amsterdam merged with the Lamists and worshipped with them at Singel 452.

The Zonists derived their name from the warehouse building they purchased at Singel 118. The engraving published in 1691 shows the interior of the building of the Zonist Mennonite Church in Amsterdam. The church received its name from the image of a sun already on the gable of the building when it was acquired following a division from the more liberal Lamist Church. The building is still standing but is no longer used for worship. The image of a sun is still visible on the front facade of the building.

A copy of an engraving depicts the "de Zon" place of worship as it was in 1790, more than a century after Rembrandt's time, showing a large pipe organ, a symbol of the financial strength of the congregation and acceptance of music in worship.

A reconciliation of the various Mennonite groups took place in 1801 when the various factions joined to form the United Mennonite Church. A gable stone on the Singelkerk shows the sun, the lamb and the tower, together with a Latin phrase, "Bound in Love and Peace."[2]

In an article published in the *Mennonite Quarterly Review* of April 1999, Keith Sprunger, Professor of History, Bethel College, Kansas, writes:

> The Mennonite churches in the Netherlands began as simple secretive house churches. Hidden worship was required because of persecution, but after Dutch independence from Spain in the late sixteenth century, the Dutch republic tolerated but did not officially encourage Mennonites. Their meeting places had to be located off the street and "behind the houses." Without any tower or bells or public show such a place was called a hidden church.

Keith Sprunger also observed that the Dutch Mennonites were not so interested in the previous use of a building but more interested in the moral responsibility of having a good building no matter what it was used for in the past. This contrasted with the attitude of the Puritans who had crossed over from England. They were most concerned about the "purity" of the building and the influence of the "old idolatrous shapes."

Architectural historians have characterized Mennonite architecture along with that of other Christian dissenters, including Baptists, as "unadorned simplicity" contrasting with liturgical based traditions which prefer "elegant presence."

In fact, Reinbuild Janzen, Assistant Professor of Art History, Washburn University, Kansas, writing in the same issue of the *Mennonite Quarterly Review*, said, "The Anabaptist Mennonite attitude towards the visual arts in worship settings has historically been iconoclastic."

However in other areas of their life, especially their homes, the Mennonites celebrated the visual arts.

The Waterlanders and the Visual Arts

Stephanie Dickey, Assistant Professor of Art History at Herron School of Art, Indiana - Purdue University, Indianapolis, declares in an article in *The Christian Century*, published June 2000:

> Patronage of the arts converted by Protestants from a privilege of the Church to thriving private enterprise becomes a means of displaying personal success and civic virtue. Rembrandt participated in this consumer paradise as artist, art dealer and collector of artifacts.

Dickey also observed that the Waterlanders lived in an environment in which "artistic activities were regarded as worthy venues for the expression of faith and morality."

Piet Visser and Mary Sprunger wrote in *Menno Simmons: Places, Portraits and Progeny,*

> In the Netherlands, the moderate Waterlanders formed a vanguard among the Mennonites for decades. They adapted the quickest to the surrounding society, or were first to pay the price with their outward identity - judgement of their experience depends entirely on one's perspective. The fact is that Waterlander preachers were immortalised in portraits more often than those from other groups ... The general public associates the Dutch Golden Age primarily with an artistic output of unequalled quantity and quality. While elsewhere in Europe nobles and clergy promoted the arts and literature, in the Protestant Low Countries bourgeois patronage by the regent and merchant classes reigned supreme.... Out of an ethically driven, almost artisanal mentality, emerged writers and poets, painters and engravers, bright minds and technical geniuses ... Some placed their talents exclusively in the service of their own Mennonite circle. Most, however, worked for any potential client who was willing to furnish a commission, without regard to religious conviction.... In the century of Rembrandt, the grand master painter, a number of Mennonite artists availed themselves of the tremendous demand for paintings. In keeping with their religious- ethical principles, thoroughness stood at the forefront of Mennonite painters, and they applied themselves conscientiously to whatever their patrons, whoever they might be, desired. In Dutch Anabaptism there is no evidence of restriction regarding the second commandment, that against making images.
>
> Rembrandt was the most prominent artist whose work was purchased by notable Mennonite art collectors and who painted numerous portraits of Mennonites in Hendrick Uylenburgh's Waterlander circle. In addition there were many other significant Dutch Mennonite,

painters, engravers and calligraphers such as Lambert Jacobsz, Govert Flink, Salomon and Jacob Van Rysdael, Frans Hals, Carel Van Mander (also a poet) and in the next generation Jan Luyken. The latter enjoys an ongoing appreciation within the Mennonite world and a most important place in Mennonite history. Luyken, one time member of the Amsterdam Lamist Church was the illustrator of the famous book "Mirror of the Martyrs", written by Van Braght, first published in 1660. No book except for the Bible has been more influential in the perpetuating and nurturing the faith of the Mennonites than the "Mirror of the Martyrs".

Jan Luyken's engravings are in the characteristic style developed by Rembrandt and his studio. The *Mirror of the Martyrs* continues to be reprinted and is the prime resource in reminding Mennonites of their heritage of persecution and flight to new lands offering tolerance.

The historical setting of the Dutch "Golden Age" encouraged artistic endeavors. Painters, playwrights, and poets were given social status in view of the perceived moral impact of their activities.

Piet Visser in *From Martyr to Muppy* writes:

> Both the painter and the poet were generally considered as contributors to the moral standards of society. Seventeenth-century paintings, poems and plays were supposed to contain a Christian message, to serve the purpose of a moral, general edification besides providing other lessons, such as the domestic scene depicting a kitchen maid sitting by the open fire was usually not just a reproduction of cozy reality, but also contained some generally recognized truths about vices and virtues, good and evil. In that time merchants, bankers, ship owners and civil governors were in charge. In contrast to the Middle Ages when the Catholic Church patronized artistic skills, it was now primarily the new political and economic elite which created a demand for artistic products, for paintings and poetry; they dominated and promoted the moral values and world views of which the products reflect...

When we consider the Mennonite idea that the Christian artist was supposed to be guided and inspired by a Biblical way of life that should be expressed in deeds and not just in mere words, we can understand not only the Mennonite merchant as the Mennonite craftsman, but also the Mennonite truths and ethics.

Over many years, Mennonites have recognized that their artists face the perennial problem of the relationship between the individual and the community. Even today they continue to address the tension of being "in the world but not of the world" which characterizes the Mennonites' relationship with the dominant culture.

Modern day Mennonites continue to struggle with the use of visual arts in their worship. They tend toward simplicity but also see that the visual arts can play a role as long as they are not confused with "decoration," do not become icons, and understand a work of art as the "door to the spiritual."

Was Rembrandt a Waterlander Mennonite?

Was Rembrandt a Mennonite or Mennist as Baldinucci wrote? Consider these facts: following the death of his wife, Saskia, Rembrandt's sons' nurse, Geertge Dircx, became his mistress only to be later acrimoniously supplanted in 1649 by the younger Hendrickje Stoffels. Rembrandt did not marry Stoffels as to do so would have meant renouncing his life interest in the inheritance left to him by his wife. Stoffels was subsequently summoned to appear before an ecclesiastical court of the Calvinist Church. In 1654 Stoffels was exhorted a number of times by the court to renounce her illicit relationship with Rembrandt and do penance. Ignoring these exhortations, she continued to live with Rembrandt and in October 1654 gave birth to a daughter of Rembrandt named Cornelia. In that period Rembrandt's clientele diminished, he failed to meet his debts and was declared bankrupt in 1656, losing his grand residence and possessions. He even sold the space above his wife's grave.

Stephanie Dickey writes:

> Ultimately, this was as much a moral disaster as a financial one, since Rembrandt's Calvinist patrons

regarded material wealth as a sign of God's favour, good stewardship of one's assets an ethical necessity, and bankruptcy as a sin."

Rembrandt lived in close proximity to the Waterlanders' Place of Worship, businesses and residences.[3]

Notwithstanding Rembrandt's close personal and business associations with Mennonites, and in view of his personal behavior, it appears to me most unlikely that he would have been accepted as a member by the Waterlander Mennonites who were very serious about membership matters as shown by the "English Affair." However, because Rembrandt was not a member of the Waterlander Church, this doesn't mean he was not influenced by the Mennonites or they by him. There appears to be ample evidence of both.

As discussed previously, Mennonite scholars have been investigating the nature of Rembrandt's association with the Waterlanders since the 1940s and accepted long ago that a close association existed.

Jan Gleysteen in his 1984 *Mennonite Guide to West Europe* wrote:

> Although there is no documentation to suggest that Rembrandt was a Mennonite, he was close to and influenced by, the Waterlander Mennonites.

Did the Waterlanders influence Rembrandt the artist and did Rembrandt the artist influence the Waterlanders?

Jacob Rosenburg observed:

> Whether Rembrandt really became a member of the Mennonite Community or was only closely attached to it does not greatly matter for the understanding of his work .....But what really counts is Rembrandt's Spiritual affinity to this sect, with which he shared many basic beliefs, far more than Calvinism. Rembrandt shared with the Mennonites an indifference to all dogmatic notions and institutions, seeking, as they did, to go back to the simple truth of the Bible.[4] (NOTE 3) ...All in all, one gains the impression that the truly evangelical simplicity of the

Mennonites, their sobriety, sincerity and humility are reflected in Rembrandt's religious art.

An enormous number of books and articles have been written about Rembrandt and his work. A simplistic overview of Rembrandt's work shows he developed two specialties: firstly, portraits that made their sitters look both distinguished and vividly alive, and secondly, dramatic history paintings that explored the great and familiar Biblical themes. Many art historians note Rembrandt's work reflects a sound knowledge of the Bible and his ability to make Biblical stories both entertaining and profound. *(figs. 31, 32)*

Stephanie Dickey writes:

> ... Rembrandt was not, as far as we know, an active churchgoer himself. His spirituality reveals itself best in his art, arguably the greatest body of work ever produced by a Protestant painter.

Andrew Marshall, in his 1987 book, *The History and Techniques of the Great Masters - Rembrandt*, writes of Rembrandt's painting, "The Adoration of the Shepherds." This is one of several small scale Biblical works of the 1640s in which the figures are treated in the tradition of contemporary Dutch genre painting. It may possibly reflect the beliefs of the Mennonites, a Protestant sect that placed great importance on the Biblical injunction to "Love thy neighbour" and with which Rembrandt is known to have been closely associated. This could have had some bearing on the way Rembrandt expressed divine events in everyday, down to earth terms, easily accessible to his contemporaries, with an emphasis on individual humility and quiet devotion.

At this point I wish to return to Rembrandt's most well known commissions received from a Waterlander Mennonite. In 1641 Cornelius Anslo commissioned Rembrandt to paint a double portrait of Anslo and his wife to hang in Anslo's new house scheduled for completion in the following year. In addition Anslo requested a single portrait etching of himself seated at his desk which Schama assumed was for distribution among his flock. Anslo and his wife had become prosperous by this time and Schama notes that in the portrait:

The fur trim on the coats of both him and wife manages to advertise this substance without violating too blatantly the Mennonite aversion to conspicuous display ... None of his contemporaries come close to Rembrandt's instinctive ability to inject drama in simplicity and still manage not to compromise the integrity of the subject.

In both the Anslo painting and etching, Rembrandt addresses the claims of the eye and the ear in art works commissioned to promote the exposition of the word over visual imagery. This was further highlighted at the time by poet Joost Vanden Vondel, himself a one time deacon of the Waterlander congregation. Vondel, who ranks among the Dutch as Shakespeare does among the English, composed the following four lines:

> O Rembrandt, paint Cornelius's voice
> The visible part is the least of him:
> The invisible can only be known through the ears.
> Who Anslo wants to know must hear him.

Rembrandt did just that. He painted "the word;" he made the invisible visible.

The preacher Anslo had legendary oratorical skills expounding the word of God. To indicate the source of Anslo's message, Rembrandt places Anslo with an open Bible in front of him. Anslo's wife looks at the texts as she listens to her husband. Rembrandt brilliantly, and paradoxically, has created a picture that proclaims the Mennonite belief in the centrality of the word.

In the etching of Anslo, the preacher is alone in his study. His pen and inkwell suggest he has been interrupted while writing a sermon. Behind him a painting leans facing the wall and a nail in the wall above it hints that the painting has been taken down. In doing this Rembrandt responds to Vondel whose poem was found to be inscribed on the back of a preparatory drawing made for this etching. The artist presents in his Anslo portraits the Mennonite notion that verbal perception is more truthful than sight.

Simon Schama writes that Rembrandt, by creating a temple from a stack of books and a candle demonstrated

...astounding capacity for transforming the ordinary into the sublime. The extremely low angle of vision, the corner of the table thrust out at an angle to the picture plane ... all combined to give the impression of something like a high altar, atop which rest the sacred books. And those books, which catch the full illumination coming from the left, are not mere heaps of parchment and paper. The pages stir, rise and flutter with light and life. The books, like Ezekiel's dry bones, respire. The word lives.

Simon Schama claims that in the Anslo painting Rembrandt "had created what preachers had said was impossible: 'Protestant icons.'" He points out that the smoking candle in paintings often alluded to the brevity of earthly life and that "the juxtaposition of book and candle to suggest things immortal and worldly, the spirit and the flesh." He sees the double portrait as "more than a bundle of symbols, more than a painter trumping a poet.... a work that is both vision and diction."

Stephanie Dickey in her critique of Schama's book states

This poetic description incorporates an essential principle of both Mennonite and mainstream Protestant thought: the supremacy of word over image, a prejudice that Dutch painters in general and Rembrandt in particular countered by imbibing their portraits and historical subjects with the visual equivalent of sound. Anslo's parted lips and empathetic gesture almost make it possible, as the Dutch poet Vondel wrote, for the viewer to hear the preacher's voice.

Rembrandt paints "the visual equivalent of sound," artistic genius with absolute understanding of the subject matter. The Anslo portraits have been elevated as far as Mennonites are concerned to the equivalent of iconography.

Did the Waterlander Mennonites influence Rembrandt the artist? I suggest that they clearly did so. That is not to say the Mennonites were the only influence upon Rembrandt, but they were a most significant one. This was so notwithstanding Rembrandt had a lot of contact with other groups in cosmopolitan Amsterdam including the Jewish community, which lived in the immediate neighborhood and whose main synagogue was just down the street.

Conclusion

It appears that a close association existed for some time between Rembrandt and the Amsterdam Waterlander Mennonites that was important to both. The nature and outworking of this association is fascinating and still to be further explored as new research brings forth more information.

For me, the fact that the Waterlanders embraced Rembrandt, and other artists, illustrates how the Mennonites clearly accepted the visual arts unlike other dissenting faith traditions that rejected the visual arts. Non-conformist denominations, including us Baptists, have placed greater priority upon oral communication rather than visual communication. For good reason the excesses of pre-Reformation times were eliminated, however this has led us to a very sparse visual tradition.

We can learn from our Anabaptist cousins who also adopted oral communication but when given security, tolerance and opportunity, these people exhibited great creativity in the visual arts. The Hutterite ceramics in Moravia, the Amish quilts in North America, along with "Golden Age" Dutch Mennonite painting and engraving are wonderful examples of faith communities that valued both the oral and the visual.

Rembrandt remains influential to 21st century Christians. Reproduction prints of Rembrandt's "*The Return of the Prodigal Son*" are most popular today. This was Rembrandt's last work left on the easel at his death and was completed by a pupil. Schama writes concerning this painting:

> We can scarcely make out his features, so lightly has the artist drawn them, but we see enough to know this prodigal is for Everyman, for the child who has taken all the sins of the world on his shoulders.

This painting, which inspired the meditations of Henri Nouwn and others, has attained modern day iconic status in mainstream Protestant denominations including in Baptist circles.

Rembrandt was self-conscious, producing many self-portraits during his lifetime, hiding nothing, honestly recording the ravages of time. Some observers have suggested that in the good times he painted himself living it up in a "far" country and in the bad times, at the end of his life, he painted himself as the Prodigal son seeking forgiveness.

In Schama's words:

> So the son kneels against the loins of the father, eyes shut, arms across his chest, they melt together in a simple form, the pathetic shred of humanity returned to the boundlessly encompassing compassion of his creator.

There was no lengthy tolling of bells, chants, poems or prayers when Rembrandt was buried in a rented space under the floor of the Westkerk, on the eighth of October 1669.

NOTES

[1] The author wishes to thank Joel Aldefer and Forrest Moyer of The Mennonite Heritage Center of Eastern Pennsylvania, Harleysville, PA, who were of great assistance with the research carried out for this paper.

[2] Seventeenth century Mennonite places of worship were located on the west side of the Singel Canal as follows: (1) the Waterlander Mennonite place of worship was at "by the Tower," Singe I 158. This building no longer exists; (2) the Flemish (Lamist) Mennonite place of worship was at "by the Lamb," Singel 452; (3) following the "War of the Lambs" the liberal Waterlanders merged with the Lamists and worshipped together at Singel 452, known today as the "Singelkerk;" (4) following the "War of the Lambs" the conservative Mennonites in Amsterdam purchased a warehouse at Singel 118 called "the Sun." This building exists and is now business offices and apartments; (5) reconciliation of various Mennonite groups in 1801 resulted in the United Mennonite Church which still worships at the Singelkerk.

[3] Rembrandt had an association with the Waterlander Mennonites who in turn had an association with the English Baptists. Could Rembrandt have come into contact with the English when he lived in Amsterdam?

The English Separatists (led by Smyth and Helwys) gathered together for worship as the first Baptist church in the world in 1609 at the East India Bakehouse in Bakkerstraat. The Bakehouse was owned by Jan Munter, a wealthy ship owner and Mennonite. The English Baptists lived and worked as a faith community in the Bakehouse, which faced the Amstel River (Binnen Amstel). Helwys and approximately 10 of the group returned to England in late 1612. Smyth and 31 of the group remained and applied for membership with the Waterlander Mennonites. After long consultations amongst the Waterlander Mennonites they were accepted in 1612 and held services in the Bakehouse until 1639.

Rembrandt moved to Amsterdam in 1631, living at various addresses prior to the purchase of his grand residence on the Jodenbreestraat.

Rembrandt and Saskia were married in 1633 and lived with the Uylenburghs for 2 years after which they lived from 1635 to 1637 on the Dodenstraat (next door to the pensionary Boreel), Nieuw Dodenstraat, which ran alongside the Amstel away from the Munt Tower. In 1635 Rembrandt established his studio in a warehouse on the Bloengracht (the flower market), which was close to his residence.

Pascal Bonafoux, in his book, *Rembrandt Substance and Shadow*, reproduced a map of Amsterdam (Page 74 - 75) on which he indicated the location of Rembrandt's residence in the Dodenstraat in the immediate vicinity of the "Lamist" Mennonite place of worship (now the Singelkerk), and within a few minutes walking distance of the East India Bakehouse.

For the period 1637-1639 Rembrandt and Saskia moved to the Binnen Amstel district. Christopher White in his book, *Rembrandt*, records that the artist wrote in 1637: "I live on the Binnen Amstel. The house is called the sugar refinery". Bonafoux in his book, *Rembrandt Substance and Shadow*, records the artist writing: "I reside on Binnen Amstel, the house called the Sugar Bakery." Bonafoux shows on his map the location of Rembrandt's house in close proximity to the East India Bakehouse as shown on part of Pieter Bast's map of Amsterdam (1599) reproduced on the cover of the newly published, *Communities of Conviction Baptist Beginnings in Europe* by Ian Randall.

In contrast, Simon Schama writes in *Rembrandt's Eyes*:

"For a while at least, from 1637 to 1639, Rembrandt and Saskia were dwelling in sweetness, next door to the house called "the Sugar Bakery" on Vlooienburg Island at the east end of the city. The house faced out onto the Binnen Amstel, so they could see sails moving past their windows, the masts of moved lighters leaning in the wind, timber stacked up on the island shipyards. An unloading wharf was at their back door. Their front door led onto the busy large Houtstraat. Their neighbour was Jan van Veldesteyn, who owned and ran the 'Four Sugarbread' bakery close by."

Pascal Bonafoux locates Rembrandt's residence on the south side of the Amstel River whereas Simon Schama locates it on the north side of the river. In fact Schama records, "The site of the house, its view of the Amstellong obstructed by a row of houses built on land reclaimed from the river in 1660, is Zwanburgerstraat 41."

If Rembrandt's residence was on the south side, it was close to the East India Bakehouse. If Rembrandt's residence was on the north side, the East

India Bakehouse, being a substantial building (3 stories with 16 tall oven chimneys), would have been clearly visible across the river.

After Rembrandt moved in 1639 to the Jodenbreestraat, he would take walks outside the city into the countryside. For the next 15 years he prepared drawings and etchings of the landscape in the close vicinity of Amsterdam, which Christopher White described as "not just impersonalized landscape but of a definite locality". One of his earliest works was the etching "View of Amsterdam" (1640).

White regards this as a view of the city from the east and others have claimed it to be from the northwest. Neither of these viewpoints appears consistent with seventeenth century maps of Amsterdam.

Jacob Rosenberg in his book, *Rembrandt Life and Work*, refers to Frits Lugt's *Mit Rembrandt in Amsterdam* (published in 1920) as follows:

> Lugt has corrected the assumption that this view is taken from the banks of the Y, to the northwest of the Capital. He states that Rembrandt was at this point not very far from his own home, having left the city by the 8t. Anthoniespoort and, after a fifteen minute walk in a south easterly direction, reached the spot from which Amsterdam appears in the etching, although with directions reversed.

If the viewing point for the etching was, as Lugt asserts, south east of the city looking towards the Binnen Amstel, then the landmarks clearly visible on the etching are correctly located. From the left to right Rembrandt has drawn the Westkerk (with clocktower), the Munt Tower (with spire), large storehouses, single windmill, the Montelbaanstoren (without spire) and a row of windmills on the eastside embankment.

Mariet Westermann in her book, *Rembrandt* (2000), supports the concept:

> One of his first landscape prints, a "View of Amsterdam" combines direct observation and judicious composition to create a panorama of the city. Although the buildings are placed in order Rembrandt would have seen from a dyke near his house the print is less a typographic record than a rhythmic evocation of the city's profile against a towering sky.

Rosenburg writes that the storehouses in the etching were of "the East and West India companies." The geographic location of these storehouses appears to be in the Binnen Amstel district in close proximity to the East India Bakehouse. All this may be circumstantial and requires further research into primary sources.

However, these records show Rembrandt lived and worked in the same parts of Amsterdam where the "English" Baptists had also lived, worked and worshipped. It is understood the "English" merged into the Waterlander Community within a couple of generations. Prior to that period the foreign English group would have been obvious when living at the East India Bakehouse.

In summary it seems the separate identity of the "English" fades about the time Rembrandt moves from the Leiden to Amsterdam in 1631. However the presence of the English and their application to join the membership of the Waterlander Mennonites ("The English Affair") had a significant impact upon the Mennonites for many years which would have included Rembrandt's life in Amsterdam.

It seems to me most likely that Rembrandt would have known about the "English" by virtue of frequenting the same physical environs, but also as both were associated with the Waterlander Mennonites to a significant degree.

[4] Piet Visser and Mary Sprunger wrote in *Menno Simons: Places, Portraits and Progeny*:

> Although the Mennonites themselves would not lack for artistic talent, they did not, with one exception produce satirical prints from among their own ranks. They lectured each other - not always gently or with much tact - orally and in great quantity of polemic writings. One of the many conflicts concerned the question of the "written or unwritten word" among the Waterlanders between 1622 and 1627. This was conducted by the most prominent opponents Hans de Ries and Nittert Obbesz. The latter a preacher in Amsterdam, was accused of Socinianism, or literalism, in the jargon of the time, while de Ries and his supporters were accused of spiritualism or enthusiasm, or subordinating the importance of Scripture to the Spirit. This was graphically portrayed in an image from a pamphlet of 1627 by Nittert's supporter Jan Theunisz. He shows de Ries kneeling on an unprinted Bible.

Chapter 3

The Slave Trade and the Unholy Triangle:
A Caribbean Perspective
Cawley Bolt

The transatlantic trade in African slaves and the institution of slavery in the Western world constitute one of the major blots on the history of the so-called enlightened peoples of Europe and the United States of America. The reason given to excuse the action and the institution is that the context and mind-set of the times need to be taken into consideration when assessments are made about the involvement and participation of Europeans in the trade. But this is an untenable proposition if Europeans are going to maintain the adjectives of being enlightened and of being civilized.

Unholy is a rare biblical concept but one understands it to be the opposite of holy. It does not appear in some biblical reference books or concordances. It is in only two passages in the New Testament, both in the Pastoral Epistles viz., I Tim 1:9 and II Tim 3:2, and in both passages it appears among a list of vices. It is the Greek word transliterated "anosios" and means "ungodly" or "not having any regard for God or man (human beings)." Some synonyms are listed as "impious" and "hater of God." Relevant antonyms are "holy," "undefiled," "devout," "pious," and "consecrated." It is instructive that, in the list of vices in I Timothy 1:9-10, one of the vices stated is slave traders or men stealers or, more commonly, kidnappers. Kidnapping was one of the most important means of procuring Africans for slavery in the Americas. Luke Timothy Johnson notes that "slave traders" refer to those who sold into slavery free people who had been captured in war or had been kidnapped.[1]

The reference to the triangle is an allusion to what in historical study is called the "triangular trade." It refers to the route that was regularly traversed to bring the produce of the colonies of Europe to the benefit of the countries of Europe. The route began in Europe and went down to Africa where eventually goods from Europe were traded for the main product of African people to be slaves. From Africa the route went across the Atlantic Ocean into the Americas, where the captured were sold to be the main element in the production of the staples Europe needed for its own development. The produce of the Americas being accomplished, the ships crossed the Atlantic back to Europe from the Americas. On the map the route from beginning to end forms a triangle, hence the name "triangular trade."

The reference to the triangle as being unholy is somewhat tautologous because it is the inclusion of slavery in the facets of the route that primarily makes the trade unholy. While that is true, the immoral conduct of the Europeans in their dealings with the Africans also falls in the category of being unholy, for they defrauded the Africans by exploiting their innocence.

Slavery is the ownership of human beings by other human beings. Orlando Patterson defines slavery:

> Slavery is the permanent, violent, and personal domination of nationally alienated and generally dishonored persons. It is first, a form of personal domination. One individual is under the direct power of another or his agent. In practice, this usually entails the power of life and death over the slave. Second, the slave is always an excommunicated person. He more than she, does not belong to the legitimate social or moral community; he has no independent social existence; he exists only through and for the master; he is in other words, nationally alienated. As Aristotle observed, 'The slave is not only the slave of his master; he also belongs entirely to him and has no life or being other than so belonging.' Third, the slave is in a perpetual condition of dishonor. What is more, the master, and.... his group parasitically gain honor in degrading the slave.[2]

Patterson's definition shows the social death of the individual for the person is assigned no worth apart from being the property of another.

The Origins of the Unholy Triangle

The attempt to quantify the number of Africans transported across the Atlantic to the Americas to serve as slaves on the plantations of these locales remains a matter of disagreement and ranges from 15 million to as high as 100 million. Clearly the accurate figure will never be known and proposals will remain "guesstimates." What, however, is a consensus is the assertion that the transatlantic trade in Africans

> was the largest forced human migration in recorded history. The extent of human suffering associated with this involuntary relocation of men, women and children may never be known. But their shipment, packed and stored beneath the decks of ships like commodities, constitutes one of the greatest horrors of modern times.[3]

This forced migration began on this horrifying scale from about 1500 when sailing ship routes linked Western Africa to Western Europe and eventually included the Americas and the Caribbean, where the main resources for the building and sustaining of Europe were located.[4] The Portuguese had been transporting several thousand slaves annually to supply and supplement their profitable domestic labor. This situation changed dramatically when it became clear that the mines and plantations of the Americas needed hard working laborers. Africa became the source for the laborers needed in these mines and plantations and so the Africanization of the trade.

Slave Supplies for the Unholy Triangle

Slavery existed in Africa when the Europeans made their assay into the continent. It is, however, necessary to determine the nature of African slavery for apologists, for the European slave traders are quick to point out that Africans already were enslaving Africans when the Europeans came on the scene. There is no denying that Africans were enslaving Africans then. But it must be remembered that slavery was a universal practice and had existed in all known societies and so there is hardly any nation where its people were not at some time slaves. In Africa, as it was in some parts of medieval Europe, the economy was not slave based and so it is asserted that they should be referred to as "wageless workers" who were never mere chattels, that is that they were without rights or had no hope of being set free. Some of them were bought and sold and presented as gifts to others but their condition greatly differed from that of the African slaves who were transported to the Americas to work in the mines and the plantations.[5]

Sources for Africans as slaves resided in the social systems of the continent. African society was feudal in nature with rulers, vassals, and subjects. Before the coming of the Europeans, men and women were used in traditional forms of labor such as portage because there were no animals for that purpose. Also labor was obtained from some groups and individuals who had received punishment for a crime, war captives, and through conquests. Normally peasants were tied to the soil and differed little from the serfs and villeins of medieval Europe who provided forced labor. In reality, the vassal was free but owed services and tribute to their ruler who in turn was expected to provide protection and settle disputes. The vassals in turn provided protection to the subjects in exchange for labor and goods. The societies were of a communal and stratified nature with no one working for money but everyone virtually providing duties or services to someone else.

Despite this, there were groups of persons who had no freedom such as community outcasts, adulterers, debtors, prisoners of war, and those convicted of, and condemned for, witchcraft. But these persons had limited rights and were not chattels. They could marry according to the customs of society, own property, establish and preserve family connections, worship freely according to their religious traditions and at times became military commanders and have been known to rise to the rank of rulers.[6] It is therefore unwarranted to equate slavery in Africa with slavery in the Americas where the individual was chattel and defined as property and real estate.

Probably more disturbing is the fact that there were ex-slaves, particularly some from Brazil, who in the 19th century returned to Africa and engaged in the slave trade.[7] Explanations of various kinds have been given. One is that there was no work with the consequence that slave trading provided a way out. Another has to do with the complexity of human motivation that would include greed and the push for wealth. Still other reasons for participation in the trade may never be known for these would depend on the circumstance of those who took part. One thing that is clear is that universal human reasons operated in the Africans as in any other person. At the same time, it must be said that there were other ex-slaves who were skilled individuals and who brought their skills back to Africa and settled in the Jamestown section of Accra and contributed positively to the society.

The Middle Passage: Some Horrors of the Unholy Triangle

The transportation of Africans to the Americas included what has become known as the Middle Passage. However, the movement of persons from capture to deposit on the other side of the Atlantic has been conceptualized into six distinct stages that help to highlight the horror of the experiences of those transported. The six stages are:

- Capture and enslavement in Africa
- Journey to the coast and other departure points
- Storage and package for shipment
- Transatlantic crossing
- Sale and dispersion in the Americas
- Seasoning/adjustment in the Americas

Each stage of the process included fatalities and the deepening of the trauma of the persons captured. At times, some had to travel hundreds of miles to the place of shipment. Storage time for individuals differed from place to place on the journey to the coast. The loss of lives before the journey across the Atlantic was great. It took approximately fifty days for the crossing to be completed. It is estimated that up to thirty percent of those transported died.

Slavers debated whether loose or tight packing was more profitable: the former being based on the assumption that the more comfortable the captives, the better they will survive the crossing; while the latter took the position that a large percentage is going to be lost anyway. And so the more tightly the "cargo" is packed, greater will be the survival of sufficient numbers to make the enterprise maximally profitable.

The callousness and inhumanity of the operators are staggering. The surgeons on board ship had the responsibility to detect early warning of disease among the "cargo" and, to protect the healthy captives, jettisoned those considered ill. Women captives were kept separate from male captives and the sailors felt they had the right of sexual access to the female captives, some of whom arrived pregnant.

Some captives seized the opportunity to escape the horror and terror they were experiencing by jumping overboard.

One of the conclusions from studying the records left behind is that mortality among the males was higher than among the females. This was probably attributable to the fact that women had more spacious accommodation on board the ships; that they were not chained and, since they were sexually exploited, that the sailors may have ensured better treatment for those women so favored.

Life in the Caribbean: The "Cargo" from the Unholy Triangle

Upon arrival at the plantations the captives were made to pass through a period of adjustment that was called "seasoning." This was to make the Africans adjust to the condition of being a slave; and the process could last between one and three years, during which one quarter to one third of them died. Life on the plantations was harsh and hard. The norm was long hours of back-breaking labor to ensure maximum return on investment. Bear in mind that the African, in the eyes of the owners and managers of the plantation, was no longer a person but simply one of the dispensable factors of production.

The fertility rate of blacks on the plantation declined. It is calculated that the males suffered emasculation regarding their understanding of themselves as males. Slavery abolished any distinction between male and female insofar as the women were expected to work as hard as the males. The women were punished as hard as the men. In addition, the sexual favor of the female was desired by both black and white, and she was more often in alliance with the white than with the black. In the long run, the male was completely demoralized, for he was incapable of asserting his authority either as husband or father, his sexual difference was in no way recognized in his work situation by the all powerful out-group. The object of whatever affection he may possess was beaten, abused, and often raped before his very eyes, and with his female partner often in closer link with the source of all power in the society, it is no wonder that the male slave eventually came to lose all pretensions to masculine pride and to develop the irresponsible paternal and sexual attitudes that are found even today.[8]

Undermining the Unholy Triangle: The Slave Fights Back

Despite what has just been noted about the male slave, it must not be taken as the final outcome. It must not be thought that the captive and eventually slave submitted passively to the condition in which he was at any stage of his time as captive or slave. From the moment of capture, the individual begins to fight back out of a sense of dignity and awareness of the violation of his person. There was unrelieved resistance by the person in mind, body, and spirit.[9] This resistance was widespread, intercontinental, and multifaceted and, at times, it was considered "non-violent disengagement," although violent reaction would become part of their sense of dignity.[10]

In the Caribbean, violent resistance has been called "slave rebellion." However, the reference has been revised and is now identified by Caribbean historians as "slave war of liberation" in that the slaves were always conscious of their personhood, never accepting that they should be anyone's property. As a result, they decided to take their freedom since it would not be given willingly and freely by their oppressors.[11]

It was felt among slaves that any slave who did not seize the opportunity to run away had lost his self-respect and sense of dignity. In addition, the slaves engaged other means to defeat the system including infanticide, suicide, stealing, lying, and destruction of the implements of production whenever they could safely do so. No doubt God understood and sympathized with what under different circumstances would be considered immoral.

Sharing the Benefits of the Unholy Triangle

It is generally accepted that the labor of the slaves has contributed to the development of the states of Europe and was largely responsible for the industrialization of these nations. In this context, there has been the call for reparation to the descendants of those who experienced the brunt of slave production over the centuries of their enslavement.

Veront Satchell has outlined some objections that have been proffered against reparation. Some have considered it in terms mainly of monetary contribution, indicating that the suffering of the ancestors cannot be quantified in terms of dollars and cents. Others have argued that slavery was legal and the trade legitimate at that time; there was nothing criminal about it. Concomitantly, Satchell has pointed to cases offered for compensation to descendants of Africans, both in Africa and in the Americas. He further indicates that the Nuremberg War Crimes Tribunal has listed enslavement, deportation, and any other inhumane act committed against any civilian population as crimes against humanity. In addition, the slavery experience caused the rise of poverty, landlessness, and under-development, as well as the crushing of culture and language, the loss of identity, the inculcation of inferiority among black people, and the indoctrination of whites into a racist mind-set, all of which continue to this day to affect the prospects of equality of black people's lives in the Caribbean, the USA, Canada, and Europe. [12]

Mention must be made here of the controversy that arose in the United States of America as a result of a proposal put forward by Congressman Tony Hall of Ohio. His proposal was that the Congress "apologize to African-Americans whose ancestors suffered as slaves under the Constitution and laws of the United States until 1865."[13] That resolution caused a division of opinion, with two of every three whites objecting while two of every three blacks were in support. Then President, Bill Clinton, acknowledged that slavery had left deep scars on America, but that what should happen is that opportunities should be created for Americans to work hard in order to overcome the unacceptable legacies of the past. It should be noted that some agencies, including Anglicans, some Baptist groups, and the Roman Catholic Church, have apologized for involvement in slavery.

The Church and the Unholy Triangle

Missionaries and other ecclesiastical personalities accompanied the colonizers into the Caribbean. The Anglican Church, in the period before ideas of emancipation began to take shape, was reputed to be the white man's church. It did not cater to the spiritual needs of the slaves because the planters, who dominated and controlled the House of Assembly that paid the clergy of that church, had strong objections to this happening. The planters believed preaching Christ to the slaves would give them ideas of equality. The planters missed the fact that the slaves needed no one to tell them that they were human beings: they had not lost their sense of self.

When Protestant and non-Conformist missionaries began to arrive in the "new world," they were restricted by their sending bodies as to what they could say. These bodies stated categorically that their missionaries should not become involved in political matters, which effectively meant that they should not say or do anything concerning slavery. They were to confine their activities to the spiritual welfare of the slaves. They gave these instructions because they were aware of the sensitivity to the subject of the planters and their agents. Their missionaries were also at pains to show that Christianity, instead of being revolutionary, taught obedience and submission.

In Jamaica, Baptists are highly regarded for their involvement in the movement for the abolition of slavery. In this regard the name of the missionary William Knibb stands out. The reason seems to inhere in the Baptist insistence on the importance of the liberty of the individual. In 1788, the Reverend Robert Robinson preached a sermon at Cambridge on the subject, "Slavery Inconsistent with the Spirit of Christianity." In that sermon he insisted that "slavery in a state is a deep-rooted obstinate evil, and love of dominion is a disposition that thrives too well in the hearts of depraved men."[14]

The church in the Caribbean must engage the societies of the region in combating some of the legacies of slavery including rejection of blackness, racism, problems of identity and poverty. These issues are made more complex with the advance of globalization.

NOTES

[1] Luke Timothy Johnson, *Letters to Paul's Delegates: I Timothy, 2 Timothy, Titus,* (Valley Forge, Pa.: Trinity Press International, 1996), 113.

[2] Orlando Patterson, *Freedom in the Making of Western Culture,* Vol. 1, (New York: Basic Books, 1991), 9-10.

[3] Hilary McD. Beckles and Verene Shepherd, *Trading Souls: Europe's Transatlantic Trade in Africans, A Bicentennial Caribbean Reflection,* (Kingston, Jamaica: Ian Randle Publishers, 2007), *xxii.*

[4] Basil Davidson, *Africa in History,* (New York, N.Y.: Touchstone, 1991), 206.

[5] Davidson, *op. cit.,* 209

[6] Joseph Harris, *Africans and Their History,* (New York, N.Y.: Penguin Books, 1972), 73.

[7] Anne C. Bailey, *African Voices of the Atlantic Slave Trade: Beyond the Silence and the Shame,* (Kingston, Jamaica: Ian Randle Publishers, 2007), 87.

[8] Orlando Patterson, *Sociology of Slavery: An analysis of the origins, development and structure of Negro slave society in Jamaica*, (London: MacGibbon & Kee, 1967), 167-168.

[9] Bailey, *op. cit.*, 90.

[10] *Ibid.*

[11] See Neville Callam, "Hope: A Caribbean Perspective," *The Ecumenical Review*, Vol. 50, No. 2, April 1998, 137-142.

[12] Veront Satchell, *Reparation and Emancipation*, Emancipation Lecture Series, Bethel Baptist Church, Kingston, Jamaica, 2003, 6-8.

[13] For the resolution presented to the US Congress, see http://www.directblackaction.com/h_con_res356.htm. See also http://www.directblackaction.com/tony_hall.htm.

[14] Robert Robinson, *Slavery Inconsistent with the Spirit of Christianity: A sermon preached at Cambridge, on Sunday, Feb. 10, 1788* (Cambridge: J. Archdeacon, 1788), 18.

Chapter 4

History and Development of Baptists in Mexico

Dinorah B. Méndez

In Mexico, evangelical work did not arrive until the 19th century because the country was dominated by Spain for almost three centuries, and Roman Hispanic Catholicism with its Inquisition did not permit the entry of evangelicals. After Mexico's independence was consummated in 1821, the doors for evangelical work were opened, especially with liberal governments, which saw the necessity to diminish the influence of the Catholic Church. One way was permitting other religious groups to arrive in the country.

Antecedents and Controversial Beginnings

There were several important antecedents to the founding of evangelical work in Mexico. James Thomson, the noted Baptist colporteur of the British Bible Society, made two trips to Mexico during the years 1827-30 and again in 1842-43. He never established a permanent work, but he did experience some success in the sale of Bibles in the central and southern regions of the country.[1] Another important aspect was the war between the United States and Mexico. It appears the war awakened interest in sending missionaries to Mexico.[2] It is within this context that we discuss the first evangelical work in Mexico and its relationship with the Baptists.

Which denomination started evangelical work in this country? Who is really the founder of evangelical work in Mexico and what has that to do with the growing missionary presence in the country in the 19th century? These are controversial issues in Mexico. The question as to the founder of evangelical work in the country is not an easy one to answer. Examining the evidence is sometimes like trying to examine grains of sand - it slips through the fingers of the investigator.

Our first purpose is to define, as much as the historical information allows, who founded evangelical work in the country and what relationship that work had with a growing Baptist presence. The reason to establish this is not just for denominational pride, but to examine, as much as the evidence allows, what the truth is. Then and only then is it possible to define the relationship between the beginnings and development of Baptist work of the last century.

When one examines the history books, a problem appears that is not easily resolved. There are many authors who follow completely the book written by an independent missionary, basically a Presbyterian, Melinda Rankin, *Twenty Years with the Mexicans*.[3] This book states that she began the first work in Mexico, in the city of Monterrey. Others follow the idea that James Hickey was the true founder of not only Baptist work in Mexico, but also of the first evangelical work. The majority of the authors who adopt Rankin's claim are not Baptist. The majority of those who accept that Hickey established Baptist work in Mexico are Baptist. The first task at hand then is to examine these historical sources.

The first group of historians follows the idea that Rankin began the work, arriving at the border with Mexico in Brownsville in 1852. Thus began her work "with the Mexicans." Even Latourette, who is usually very meticulous in his investigation, notes that Rankin began the work, but that Hickey was the first "notable worker." He does note that Hickey gathered "... a group of believers."[4] Goslin mentions "episcopal work" as being an important beginning. Gonzalez follows this same thought, noting that the Episcopal Church was first. However, this work should probably be called an indigenous catholic movement rather than an evangelical one. Moreover, Latourette mentions that Rankin established evangelical work, but never mentions Hickey.[5] Wheeler, who is Presbyterian, states that Rankin was the first and that Hickey was her employee. The problem with these authors is that they follow only the Rankin book, often ignoring other works.[6]

Cosme Montemayor, former historian of the Mexican Baptist Convention, examined the documents of the American Bible Society, Hickey's employer in the years of the founding of the work. Alejandro Trevino, in his work on Mexican Baptist history, went no further than this to prove Hickey was the founder.[7] Goslin, in a book often cited in the history of missions, mentions that Hickey began the work, but that Rankin was the first "notable worker." He also stated that the work of

Hickey was a true "Baptist Movement."[8] Is it that easy to draw such a conclusion? The answer is probably not clear until all details of the event can be examined.

What do Baptist authors say? They and others are unanimous in recognizing Hickey as the founder of evangelical work in Mexico. The basis for this testimony is the statements of Thomas Westrup about the beginnings of the group in Monterrey. Few people, however, have investigated further than the writings of Westrup.

James Hickey

Who was James Hickey? It appears that he was born in Ireland in 1800. He arrived in the United States and perhaps became a Baptist soon after immigrating. According to Chastain and others, he worked in Bell Country in Central Texas, a center of Baptist work at the time.

Hickey moved to South Texas for two reasons. First, he held abolitionist beliefs. These beliefs alone would have made his work as a colporteur of the American Tract Society in Central Texas difficult. Secondly, he might already have entertained plans to come to Mexico. He arrived in Brownsville in 1860.

Evangelical work in Mexico began with James Hickey's travels to Mexico in 1860. There is an interesting mention made in *La Luz* that Hickey was in Mexico in 1853, preaching in the city of Durango. However, the same article says he was born in 1785, a very unlikely date. John Cheavens recorded the incident as told to him by a man in Durango in 1902.[9]

Hickey was an agent for the American Tract Society when he began his trips to Mexico. The Tract Society was famous for several anti-Catholic tracts they published. He began making trips selling Bibles and tracts in the states of Nuevo Leon and Tamaulipas. In October 1862 he made his first contact with a group of "foreign protestants" in the city of Monterrey. He arrived in Monterrey in November of the same year. In January or February of 1863, he was named as an agent of the American Bible Society. [10]

Where was Melinda Rankin at this time? With a careful reading of her book, it is possible to draw up a chronological description of her activities. She arrived in Texas in 1849, spending the majority of this time in Huntsville, Texas. She arrived in Brownsville in 1852.

She stayed on the northern side of the Rio Grande, starting a school for children. She began counting her twenty years of work with Mexicans from this point. She was apparently working with citizens of Mexican descent in Brownsville during this time. However, Rankin never learned Spanish and worked through interpreters.

Rankin spent much of her time returning to other states during these years. In 1853-54, she was in New Orleans and Mississippi collecting funds for her work. Finally, in 1862 she crossed the Rio Grande working in a school in Matamoros, Tamps. In March of 1863, she left Brownsville because of the Civil War. It appears she stayed out of the area until January 1864 when she returned to the city but, in the summer-fall of 1864, she left once again for New Orleans. She did not return to South Texas until May 1865. She arrived for the first time in Monterrey during the same month. She remained in the city some three months. She left again, and did not return to Monterrey until May 1866. This may account for the many different dates given for her work in Mexico.[11] With this analysis, it should be obvious that Hickey actually began the work in Monterrey in 1862.

The men who invited Hickey to go to Monterrey deserve to be mentioned. Hickey, in a letter to the Bible Society, described the men he found there: John Butler was an Englishman who had worked for the conversion of another man of English descent, Thomas Westrup. Matthew Starr was a citizen of the United States. He was a hat salesman who permitted Hickey and his wife to live in his Monterrey home. Others mentioned in letters or historical descriptions afterwards are a Mr. Jolly and Mr. Pardee. In 1863, the group of followers formed the "Sociedad Mexicana de Evangelizacion' (The Mexican Evangelization Society), to facilitate and organize the distribution of Bibles. In January 1863, they sent a letter to the Governor of Nuevo Leon asking for the use of a public school for their meetings. The permission was denied.[12] In March of the same year, Hickey began preaching in Spanish in the mornings and in English at night.

From late 1863 to early 1864, there was an event that troubled the group of "protestants" that had gathered together. In December 1863, the group "became disturbed ... by the fact that the Uranga brothers were soon to be baptized."[13] This decision on the part of Hickey and the new believers was to change the nature of the group. On January

30, 1864, Hickey baptized Westrup and the Uranga brothers. That evening, they formed "The Christian Church" in Monterrey. Hickey ordained Westrup who became the first pastor of the church.[14]

The question of what kind of group was formed, however, is not easy to answer. The historical evidence is at best questionable. The actors themselves at times left conflicting evidence. The letters from Hickey to the American Bible Society do not explain much about the work. However, all of the people involved identify Hickey as a "Baptist minister." Evidently, the majority of this information comes from the testimony of Thomas Westrup. But, the work that began in Monterrey did not carry the Baptist name. This would have been obvious since Hickey, as an agent of a non-denominational Bible Society, could not begin a "partisan" work. It appears Hickey worked more for these agencies than for a Baptist group. If he was a Baptist, his convictions about Baptist faith and practice would be clear. This is what one finds when one studies the reports of the people involved. Hickey baptized the new converts by immersion. He believed in closed communion. When Rankin arrived in Monterrey in 1865, she saw the young group as "ripe unto harvest." Patterson states that she really wanted to take the field, not just harvest it.[15] It is difficult to judge motives at this distant date, but her book shows that she did not like the nature of the work begun by Hickey and Westrup. She disliked the idea of not having a permanent building for the congregation. It is obvious that her priority concern was with the construction of a church building. She recognized that a congregation had already been formed; what they lacked was a building. Rankin did possibly "build the first church building" in Mexico, but she did not establish the work or establish the first congregation. [16]

She also did not like the idea that these new converts had already developed ideas about the ordinances, particularly baptism and the Lord's Supper. She stated that "my objective was to bring people to Christ in Mexico, and as they chose the manner of baptism, I had little to say about the matter." She also stated that "the believers under her care had abandoned the doctrine of closed communion that Hickey had instituted."[17] The evidence shows, however, that it did matter to her.[18]

In several places, Westrup clearly identified the work as Baptist in principle, if not in name. He could say, in 1893, "I became a Baptist," speaking of his own baptism. Or as he said, "We became Baptist," after reading several tracts about Baptist beliefs. This last statement was after the intervention of Rankin, possibly in 1869. Westrup was invited by the American Baptist Home Mission Society (ABHMS from Northern Baptists) to go to New York in the same year to officially become their representative in Mexico. Westrup stated that, while there, he arranged to place everything "in order," even his own ordination.[19] Upon his return to Monterrey in June 1870, the churches already established in Nuevo Leon joined the Baptist Home Mission Society. However, he admitted that he found the Baptist work diminished by the invasion of Rankin ideas. In fact, the first group in Monterrey had become a mixed one, some being baptized as believers, and others not. Westrup had to reorganize the congregation.[20]

Westrup has an important place in the beginnings of Baptist work in Mexico and for the evangelical work in general as an outstanding composer and translator of hymns. Unfortunately, owing to controversies among leaders, he later left the Baptist denomination to become a member of the Disciples of Christ.[21] He had been a Baptist for thirty-eight years but, in the last seven years of his life, he denied the Baptist faith. His contribution, though, is undeniable.

Hickey died on December 10, 1866, in Brownsville, Texas. He contracted pneumonia while on a horseback trip. He was buried in Texas, but facing Mexico. His last words to Tomas Sepulveda, his co-worker, were "Siga el trabajo" (Keep on working).[22] It is difficult to say if the work established by Hickey was completely a Baptist work or not. However, it is obvious that he did begin evangelical work and produced the first evangelical congregation. Later, this work became a Baptist one in both name and principle. Hickey began the first continuous work in Mexico, not just with foreigners in an ethnic church, but winning Mexican people for Christ and baptizing them. A New Testament congregation was formed. In fact, since 1870 that church was identified as "Baptist of close communion." A sign in the building of that church says: "First Baptist Church organized on January 30, 1864 by Rev. James Hickey."[23]

Development of the Baptist Work in Mexico

In 1881, the Southern Baptist Convention (SBC) also began work in Mexico. First of all, they started supporting John Westrup (brother of Thomas), but then, when he was murdered, they sent William D. Powell to investigate the circumstances of the murder of John Westrup. Later, in 1882, Powell and his wife were appointed as missionaries to Mexico. They worked very hard, organizing new churches and persuading nationals to dedicate themselves to mission work.

Southern Baptists entered Mexico in an era of expansion. During the government of President Porfirio Diaz (1876-1911) nearly 15,000 miles of rail lines were built, connecting the principal cities of Mexico and opening vast areas to settlements. In ten years, the Foreign Mission Board (FMB) of the SBC sent 26 additional missionaries to Mexico.

At the turn of the 20th century, Baptist work in Mexico had grown significantly. In 1901, Northern Baptists reported 43 churches and missions with a total of 721 members. Southern Baptists reported 37 churches, 21 missions, and 1,189 members. There were a number of Baptist day schools and Baptist periodicals, but denominational organization was limited to three associations. Simultaneously, in 1901, two missionaries and a pastor were convinced the time had come to form a Baptist convention of churches. Thus, on September 13, 1903, 42 messengers and some 20 Baptists without credentials from 13 churches and one association met at the First Baptist Church of Mexico City to organize a national convention (CNBM).

The period 1903-1910 was marked by territorial expansion. During this period, the Pacific Railway company built lines along the coast. The Southern Baptist missions provided workers, both Mexican nationals and missionaries, to plant churches along this rail line and one from Zacatecas, north to El Paso. Churches in all parts of Mexico took seriously their responsibility for extending the work in their respective districts.

At the time the convention was organized in 1903 there were a number of Baptist schools in Mexico, some supported by the ABHMS, and another for the Southern Baptists. Some new schools were established between 1903 and 1910. Some theological education institutions were also started in the 19th century. These included the Instituto Zaragoza, founded by Powell in Saltillo in 1889, and the Theological School founded by A. T. Watkins in 1901, which was the antecedent to the Mexican Baptist Theological Seminary. Moreover, the desire for a theological school supported by both mission boards was expressed in the convention meetings of 1903 and 1904. This desire never diminished. But the Mexican Revolution prevented the immediate realization of the establishment of a theological seminary.

However it did become a reality a few years later, when in 1917 the Mexican Baptist Seminary was started by Northern, Southern and Mexican Baptists.

Among the first publications were *La Luz Bautista*, the denominational newspaper in 1885, and *El Expositor Bautista*, a Sunday school quarterly, which remain until today. Moreover, in 1909, J. E. Davis, a missionary journalist, began a print shop in his home. Today it is known as the Spanish Publishing House.

The Mexican Revolution from 1910 until 1917 had different effects on the churches. They were weakened by political differences among their members. Broken communication and rail lines left many of them isolated. Moreover, the Revolution brought the destruction of church property in some instances and the death of many innocent persons. However, despite disruption, danger, destruction of property, loss of life and leadership, the churches advanced on two fronts: evangelism and the organization of a few churches.

After the Revolution, the Constitution of 1917 brought a new way of life to Mexico. It proclaimed separation of church and state and set out on a course which was socialistic in principle. Until 1940, the Baptists in Mexico lived in a reconstruction era under severe restrictions by the government.

From 1940 through 1959, a relaxation by the government on certain church restrictions favored evangelical expansion. During the first decade of this period both mission boards and the CNBM proceeded with caution. During the second decade there was determined advancement on the part of all.

The decade between 1960 and 1970 was one of expansion and evangelism. But by 1965 relations between the Mexico Mission (MM) of the FMB of the SBC and the CNBM, as represented by its executive secretary (who had ecumenical tendencies, complicating the relationship between the ABHMS (Northern) and the FMB-SBC (Southern)), were deteriorating. He finally left the office. That was the beginning of disagreements between the boards and the CNBM, especially of ABHMS, which terminated a relationship it had had with the CNBM since its beginning. The MM of the FMB-SBC continued to cooperate with the CNBM, but under less than ideal conditions. The convention had reason for exasperation. Within the convention there were multiple programs, each with its own leadership. The convention had its field work, some associations had field missionaries, and the MM had its field work, programs to some extent parallel, but not correlated. However, in 1971, the MM voted to integrate all its programs with the CNBM.

With this Integration program, the work was blessed. From 199 churches in 1970 the number of churches doubled twice in a 26-year period, reaching 1,116 in 1995. Moreover, in 1983 the CNBM adopted the challenge of reducing the financial support of FMBSBC (given as subsidy for the programs integrated to the CNBM) at 10 percent per year. In such a way, the CNBM received the last subsidy in 1992, becoming self-supporting. Additionally, the same year the convention voted the important goal of 2000 churches being self-supporting by the year 2000. From then, during four or five years the average of growth was the organization of one church per week. However, the rate of growth was not consistent and by the year 2000 the number of churches reached was only 1,700. The CNBM has adopted the continental evangelistic program promoted by the Union of Baptists in Latin America called "Hay Vida en Jesus" with emphasis on planting new churches. Now the goal established is to reach 10,000 churches by 2010. So, in theory the current projects of Baptist work in Mexico are optimistic. The question is how healthy, stable and strong are the churches to accomplish the goals in an integral and positive way.

Formation of Mexican Baptist Identity

Since the beginning, Baptists in Mexico have had problems defining their identity. As established before, the first church did not have the Baptist name from the beginning, even though its doctrines and practices were. This happened due to the commitments of the founders, such as Hickey and Westrup, with non-denominational agencies. Thus, that congregation had to fight for its identity against Presbyterian influence. Later, Westrup himself abandoned Baptist identity to lead the Disciples of Christ work.

Another difficulty was the conversion of one prominent missionary to the Roman Catholic Church. He was Guillermo H. Sloan, one of the first pastors of the First Baptist Church in Mexico City and founder of the Baptist periodical, *La Luz*, in 1885. This fact was initially an enormous scandal because the Catholic clergy tried to use it to bring discredit to Baptists and evangelicals in general. However, nobody followed the steps of Mr. Sloan and as time passed by, the issue was forgotten.

In addition to the natural fight against Catholicism, there was another menace to a healthy identity for Baptists in Mexico. In this case, it was not the Roman Catholic Church itself, but a movement coming from the USA called "Landmarkism" which was brought by some of the missionaries during the first stages of Baptist development. This movement was the Baptist equivalent of an ecclesiology of only one true church similar to the Catholic idea. There is evidence of these ideas in the Baptist literature and of their influence even until recent years. This could be considered as another impact of the Catholic context of Mexico on Baptist identity in the sense that they might have adopted a similar concept of the church to oppose Catholic persecution, showing that the real true church was Baptist. It would be a Catholic corruption by adoption or assimilation. Other doctrinal problems have been related to the ecumenism and charismatic movements. Some leaders tried to involve the CNBM in the ecumenical movement in the middle of the 20th century. However, Mexican Baptists have been much more conservative than Baptists in other countries in relation to ecumenism. Because of the strong emphasis on the local church inherited through the previous influence of Landmarkism, ecumenism is perceived by Baptists in Mexico as a danger to a healthy ecclesiology. Consequently, Baptist churches in Mexico have practiced closed communion and closed membership. On the other hand, to practice open communion for Baptists in Mexico would open the door to a sacramental view of the church, a position supported by Catholicism, the traditional religious opposition to Baptists. In addition, this position has been reinforced by experience. When churches have opened membership to people of other denominations, the common result is the loss of Baptist identity of those churches.

In relation to the charismatic movement, the enormous and fast growth of charismatic churches has been impressive for many Baptists in Mexico. In an effort to obtain a similar rate of growth, many churches, especially those led by pastors with poor motives, such as only obtaining quantitative results, have started to introduce characteristic traits of charismatic churches in worship style, with emphasis on the doctrine of the Holy Spirit and His gifts, ending with a change of denominational identity. The problem has been a lack of a healthy teaching about the Holy Spirit, giving priority to emotions and experiences over the biblical authority on these matters.

Other kinds of difficulties have been related to structural and administrative issues. Obviously, these problems have also a doctrinal side but this aspect is less evident, though not less important in reference to Baptist identity in Mexico. In general, the doctrinal issue under jeopardy is the sociological principle distinctive among Baptists. There are two aspects derived from this principle that are suffering distortion or deviation from Biblical teachings. In the first place, at the local church level, the problem is being expressed in hierarchical and autocratic leadership by many pastors, who in practice if not in words, deny the biblical doctrine of the priesthood of all believers. Some consequences include the elevation of some leaders over their congregations as privileged clergy claiming special illumination from God and special understanding of the Bible, in such a way that they are practicing a manipulative leadership instead of servant leadership. Many churches are giving up administrative meetings, eliminating the practice of congregational government. This same trend is being manifested in denominational structures, emphasizing interdependency among churches to the detriment of the autonomy of local churches arguing for a critical unity or more precisely, a kind of uniformity. Lately, there has been strong pressure on churches to adopt these criteria of leadership instead of the leaders seeing themselves as servants of the churches and to follow the vision that churches should establish. All of this has produced a lack of interest and cooperation in the denominational structures. In the past few years the number of churches supporting the convention has diminished year by year. Thus, in spite of the optimistic projects mentioned before, the current situation of the CNBM is critical as very few churches are committed to participate because they are not taken into consideration, and more importantly because of the sense that Baptist identity is being destroyed.

Conclusion

Even though this work is only a brief sketch of Baptist history and identity in Mexico, it gives us an idea of the great past of our denomination. Mission work has been a priority since the beginning. Thanks to this emphasis many churches have been organized in all the territory of our country. Of special concern is mission work among ethnic groups. However, it is necessary to intensify missionary efforts because there are still many Mexicans in need of the Gospel message. Another area of great impact at the beginning of the Baptist work in Mexico was in education. Many schools were supported by the first Baptists thus making a significant contribution to Mexican society. These efforts were slowly disappearing due to restrictive politics, but as new laws in Mexico are being established, this should be an important project for Baptists today or in the near future. Other contributions in the social arena are several hospitals, student homes and a university, as well as agricultural projects, especially in rural areas. However, at the present only one hospital has remained. Therefore, it is necessary to reinforce these kinds of projects, involving more effectively our professionals in faithful Christian service with impact in the surrounding society and its multiple needs.

In the field of theological education, the CNBM partially supports two seminaries. However, institutions and schools to train leaders have multiplied regional and locally. The challenge in this area is that such training meets the minimal standards of healthy doctrinal teaching, especially with Baptist identity, as well as an integral formation for future leaders in all areas such as spiritual formation, moral character, academic excellence and effective strategies in his/her specific ministry. Finally, another area of challenge at the present is related to relationships with the Mexican government. The new laws established in 1992 have given legal status to all churches in Mexico. Positive results are the possibility that churches may have properties, as well as liberty to establish educative or other social projects and to have access to mass media. However, there are also negative potential results such as violations of the principle of separation between the state and the church. The government requires that churches be registered, giving all kinds of internal information about its members, properties, and financial states. In addition, for Baptists, the way in which the government relates with churches is contrary to our principles because the government is accustomed to Catholic structures. The authorities try to manage all denominations approaching them as hierarchies, ignorant of our reality of local and autonomous churches. This approach has been a great temptation for some leaders to get inauthentic power. The challenge is to avoid assimilation, rejecting concepts and practices in the cultural system contrary to our Christian identity. Baptists in

Mexico need a more transformational approach in order to change our society with Biblical values and the Gospel message full of God's love.

NOTES

[1] Kennet Scott Latourette, *A History of the Expansion of Christianity*, vol. 5: *The Great Century: The Americas Australasia and Africa*. (Grand Rapids: Zondervan Publications, Co., 1943), 10; Justo Gonzalez, *Historia de las Misiones* (Buenos Aires, 1970), 333 ff.; Tomas S. Goslin, *Los Evangelicos en America_Latina* (Buenos Aires: La Aurora, undated), 37 ff.

[2] James Garvin Chastain, *Thirty Years in Mexico_*(EI Paso,Tx.: Baptist Publishing House, 1927), 98-99, 125.

[3] Melinda Rankin, *Veinte Arios entre los Mexicanos* (Mexico: Casa de Publicaciones "El Faro", 1958).

[4] Latourette, *History*, p. 110; Latourette does not even use a source other than Rankin. For that reason his paragraph is generally confusing.

[5] *ibid.*, 115.

[6] Gonzalez, *Historia de las Misiones*, pp. 404-05; Reginald Wheeler, *Modern Missions in Mexico*, (Philadelphia, Penn.: Westminster Press, 1925), 92.

[7] Cosme Montemayor, *Hickey El Fundador* (Mexico, 1962), 3; Alejandro Trevino, *Historia de Los Trabaios Bautistas en Mexico* (El Paso,Tx.: Casa Bautista de Publicaciones, 1939), 34-40.

[8] Goslin, *op. cit.*, 96-7.

[9] John Cheavens, "Una Entrevista 1nteresante," *La Luz Bautista*, (First series), August 21, 1902, 124.

[10] John Westrup, ed. *Principios por Tomas Westrup* (Monterrey, N.L., 1948), 4, 11,29,37,44; T.M. Westrup, "La Primera Iglesia Bautista en Monterrey," *La Luz Bautista*, (First series), December 7,1893, 194.

[11] Rankin, *Veinte Años*, 60-6 I, 87- 111; Latourette, *op. cit.*, p. 112; Gonzalez, *op. cit.*, 406.

[12] Montemayor, *Hickev el Fundador*, 20.

[13] *ibid.*, pp. 19-20; Westrup, *Principios*, 15.

[14] Westrup, *Principios*, p. 45; Westrup, "La Primera Iglesia Bautista," p. 194; Montemayor, *Hickey el Fundador*, pp. 21-22; Trevino, *Historia*, p. 26

[15] Frank W. Patterson, *A Century of Baptist Work in Mexico* (EI Paso, Tx.: Casa Bautista de Publicaciones, 1979), 29.

[16] I believe much of the problem stems from the fact that she wanted to "build the first church." In Spanish the word "templo" or building is used. In English it would probably be "church," which can mean either one.

[17] pendiente

[18] Patterson, *A Century*, 29.

[19] *ibid.,* 30.

[20] Chastain, *Thirty,* 102.

[21] Patterson, *op. cit.,* 70.

[22] Miguel McAleer, *"Hickey el Fundador."* (Mexico: Seminario Teologico Bautista Mexicano, 1995), 8.

[23] Patterson, *op. cit.,* 26-27.

The Commission on Baptist Worship and Spirituality

Christopher J. Ellis, Chair

The commission has been concerned with exploring Baptist distinctives and concerns in relation to worship and spirituality. Its meetings have also provided opportunities for a group of interested Baptists to reflect together on themes which cross denominational boundaries.

A significant theme through the quinquennium has been an exploration of the varied cultural contexts of worship and spirituality. In 2006, Joel Sierra presented the paper published in this volume as "Opportunities and Challenges in Mexican Worship." We also received a paper on the Lithuanian context from Lina Andronoviene, and engaged in an open discussion on "Inculturation, Globalization and Faithfulness: Baptist Spirituality around the World" which drew on the experience and reflections of the commission members. In 2007, in Accra, Paul Msiza spoke about "African Spirituality and Baptist Worship and Devotion" and William S. Epps addressed us on "African American Worship and Spirituality."

In Ede, in 2009, most of the papers were on the theme of preaching and ones by David Coffey and Lina Andronoviene are included in this publication. A third paper by Daniel Carro united the themes of contextualization and preaching by addressing the ethics of preaching with particular reference to Latin America: "Scandalous Preachers: The Perils of False Motives."

In addition, there were several "stand alone" papers which stimulated the commission meetings. In Accra, David Loder presented the interim fruit of his research in the paper, "Spiritual Formation for Baptist Ministry," and in Prague, in 2008, Ken Edmonds gave a richly illustrated presentation on "The Architectural Design of Baptist Places of Worship."

In 2008, the commission again had an open discussion, this time on "Prayer around the World," which celebrated the variety of different cultural contexts while reflecting on the shared heritage of prayer.

The following year, a paper reflecting on the interconnection between spirituality and theology was presented and it is published here.

Worship and spirituality encompass so many themes of identity, experience, faith and belief. Our sessions hardy scratched the surface of what we might have studied. I am grateful for the contributions of the speakers as well as the reflections and questions of the group as a whole. Each session included prayer because the focus of our reflection, as well as the context of our reflecting, must be the grace of God.

Chapter 5

Truth on Fire: The Spirituality of Preaching
David Coffey

William Sangster was a celebrated evangelical preacher in London in the early decades after the Second World War. He ministered at the Westminster Methodist Central Hall and his books of sermons and manuals on preaching were widely read by the budding preachers of that generation.

He was once a member of a selection panel for prospective Methodist ministers and a rather diffident candidate appeared before the committee and said shyly: "I don't think I am the kind of person who would ever set the River Thames on fire." It is reported that Dr. Sangster responded by saying: "My dear young brother – I'm not interested to know if you could set the River Thames on fire. What I want to know is this: If I picked you up by the scruff of the neck and dropped you into the River Thames would it sizzle?"[1]

My task is to address the spirituality of preaching and however we may describe this spirituality, and there will be variations, I assume we are agreed that the spiritual preparation of the preacher is what enables us to set truth on fire in the pulpit. Every notable book on preaching and preachers has a section that emphasizes the distinction between the craft of designing a sermon and the construction of the person delivering the sermon. In the memorable words of Bishop Quayle: "It is no trouble to preach, but a vast trouble to construct a preacher." So with this warning ringing in our ears we begin the task of addressing the spiritual construction of the preacher.

The first dimension is, preachers must be secure in their identity in Jesus Christ. All preachers must remember they have a spiritual worth before God before they begin serving God. God loves the preacher as a person even more than he loves the person who preaches. It is a fundamental principle for all vocations, not just preachers, that who we are in Christ precedes what we do in the name of Christ. In the ABCD of church life "A" stands for attendance figures; "B" is for building and maintenance; "C" is the cash flow that sustains us in ministry; and "D" stands for discipleship. The preacher is the prime practitioner in the congregation for what it means to be a life-long learner in the school of discipleship.

In a beautiful memoir that contains the notes of one of the last public addresses given by John Stott, he reflects on a lifetime of preaching and asks the question, "What is God's purpose?" He shares movingly with his audience where his mind has come to rest as he approaches the end of his pilgrimage on earth and concludes that Christlikeness is the will of God for the people of God.[2]

He suggests three biblical texts that provide the biblical basis for the call to Christlikeness. We need to look back and understand God's eternal purpose because "we were predestined to be conformed to the image of his son" (Romans 8:29).

We need to look at our lives today and understand God's historical purpose, that in this moment of time, we are gradually being transformed by the Holy Spirit into the likeness of Christ (2 Corinthians 3:18). But we can also look ahead to God's final eschatological purpose for this also reveals the goal of being like Christ. "Beloved we are God's children now, and it does not yet appear what we shall be but we know that when he appears we shall be like him for we shall see him as he is" (1 John 3:2). All three – the eternal, the historical, the eschatological, combine toward the same purpose, that Christlikeness is the will of God for the people of God.

The main task of the preacher is to conform to this purpose of God in producing Christ-like disciples in the congregation and this work, which will be agonizing, is likened to the pain of childbirth (Galatians 4:19). The painstaking work of discipleship formation begins in our own lives, because the most fruitful preaching comes from those who embody the message.

All the advice from great preachers of the past stresses the importance of personal discipleship. J. H. Jowett in his Yale lectures on preaching said: "A sermon must touch life where the touch is significant and therefore the preacher's message must first of all touch 'the preacher himself.'" John Newton, who was involved in the spiritual awakening of the 18th century, said: "We do not deal in unfelt truths but find ourselves that solid consolation in the gospel that we encourage others to expect from it." E. M. Bounds in his writings on the prayer life of the preacher reminds us that: "Preaching is not the performance of an hour. It is the outflow of a life." Arthur Skevington Wood captures the spirit of the preacher as a disciple of Jesus with the reminder: "It takes a lifetime to prepare a sermon because it takes a lifetime to prepare a Christ-like preacher."[3]

One of the foundation stones for the preacher is the life of private prayer and devotion. These are the moments when I am quiet before God for myself as a disciple. Everyone will have his or her own spiritual disciplines and through the years I have used many methods and many places for Bible reflections and prayer. In the early days of my ministry I began each day with the "The Ministers Prayer Book" edited by John Doberstein; I have used the Robert Murray McCheyne method for reading the Bible in a year; "The Celtic Prayer Book" produced by the Northumbria Community has been a mainstay at times; "Life Together" by Dietrich Bonhoeffer has been a constant resource to which I return. Currently I use a daily lectionary and read passages from the Old and New Testaments together with a Psalm for the day. Jesus reminds us that the real value of meditating on His word is not for head knowledge or sermon seeds: "You study the scriptures in depth because you think that by them you possess eternal life, these are the scriptures that testify about men and yet you refuse to come to me to have life" (John 5:39). The Bible is the soul food of the preacher.

The second dimension is, preachers must know they are called to preach and this calling needs a lifetime of sustained commitment. I can remember as a young teenager the thrill of reading manuals on preaching by the Scottish preacher James Stewart. My pastor had found them helpful when he was called to be a preacher, and when he discerned that God was stirring in me the call to Christian service he lent me his copies of "A Faith to Proclaim" and "Heralds of God." James Stewart's books were cult reading for my generation and the words on preaching stirred something in me long before I was certain God was calling me to be a preacher. I can still recall listening to preachers and itching to imitate their gifting. As an 18 year old I attended a youth conference and heard an Irish pastor called George

Cumming expound the book of Philippians in a week of Bible studies and I was thrilled at the practical application of God's word.

None of these experiences made me a preacher, but I was being prepared for the call of God that was beginning to stir in my life. I can remember receiving that deep fulfillment of sensing God was using my human words to be fruitful in the lives of other young people whenever I gave a Bible study. I can take you to a house in the beautiful Lake District of England where in an upstairs room the verse from Isaiah 42:6 captivated my mind and spirit. "I the Lord have called you in righteousness; I will take hold of your hand and keep you…"

Inwardly I was aware from that moment that "I was a called person." God had called me to be a preacher. I knew this inward testimony of a call would need the outward affirmation of the community of faith, but God had brought to life the fire of his gifting in my life and I later came to understand that I had a responsibility to constantly fan into flame this gift of God (2 Timothy 2:6).

If I have a scripture to underline the call, I also have a hymn verse from "O for a Thousand Tongues":

> My gracious master and my God
> Assist me to proclaim
> To spread through all the earth abroad
> The honours of your name.

This hymn verse was given to me as a teenager but you will appreciate the latter part of the hymn with its global reach has become very meaningful in my international ministry.

I have shared a personal story of being called to preach that is unique to me and all preachers will have their story to tell, but every preacher needs to be able confess with a vulnerable dependence on God: God called me; God called me; God called me.

It is this call of God that has held me firm in the darkest days of ministry. For when you have nothing else to cling to as a preacher, hold on to the adventure of the call. Philip Greenslade spells out with creativity the depth and purpose of "calling" by drawing out of the scriptures what the call of God can do to an obedient person. "The call of God often uproots us, raises many eyebrows and ruins many a career. It leaves fishing businesses managerless and hangs a 'situations vacant' sign in tax-office windows.....obedience is a mobile home; you can park it anywhere."[5]

The third dimension requires the preacher to persevere in the task of preaching the Word – "in season and out of season" (2 Timothy 4:2). There are hard times that will be experienced during our preaching ministry that will require a massive perseverance and an utter dependence on God. There can be no avoiding the mental pain and physical weariness of sermon preparation; when you are weary in well doing and spiritually burned out, the terrible realization of your unworthiness to handle sacred things comes like a flood and can bury, under the deep waters of spiritual depression, the joy and the mystery of the call.

I confess there are seasons as a preacher when I have hung onto the pulpit by my fingernails. There are times when I have failed to give time to preparation and have preached half-baked sermons with no time to reflect deeply on the specific application of God's Word to a particular congregation. Every preacher knows what it's like preaching as if to a brick wall and another Sunday comes when few people have said a meaningful word of appreciation for your sermon. All preachers experience the challenge on a Sunday morning that the last place they want to be is in the pulpit.

Your personal relationship with members of a congregation can have a damaging influence on your pulpit ministry and I don't recommend what one of my friends did out of sheer frustration with one of his deacons. My pastor friend had been trying to cast a vision for the church, but was held back by this one deacon who steadfastly opposed change. My friend attempted everything to win round this recalcitrant deacon with no success and in the end he decided on a course of action for the pulpit. He stood up to preach one Sunday morning and said, "I am dedicating this sermon to (here he names the deacon) who has held back the vision in the church for six months and this is where I believe he is wrong."

He proceeded to preach to the congregation though his words were aimed at this dissenting deacon. He spelt out the importance of God's vision for the church and the perils of disobedience. I am not sure if he used the analogy of forty years of wilderness wanderings for stiff necked people (!) but I understand that after the service half the congregation came to the minister and said, "Well done. You should have preached that sermon seven months ago." The other half of the congregation went across to comfort the distressed deacon who was the intended target of the sermon. I certainly don't recommend this method, but if you are tempted, at least improve on the percentage of support from the church members!

The point of the story is, however frustrating the people of God are, we must never allow our disappointments to disfigure the character of our preaching. The Pauline reference to preaching the Word "in season and out of season" lifts the call to preach above the harsh experiences of pastoral ministry. Peter Taylor Forsyth's antidote to the vicissitudes of the pastorate is to preach Christ in the pulpit. "We must preach Christ and not about Christ; we must set the actual constraining Christ before people and not coax or bully people into decision. If we put the veritable Christ before them he will rouse the faith before they know where they are."[6]

The fourth dimension is, the spirituality of preaching requires a conscientious preacher. There is an unavoidable discipline about sermon preparation and entering the world of the scriptures to unlock its meaning and what John Stott calls "painstaking meticulous conscientious work." Preachers cannot skimp on time consuming preparation and if you avoid this discipline you will suffer for this neglect of duty.

The preacher who has neglected the duty of careful sermon preparation knows the heavy feeling when Saturday morning arrives and there is nothing prepared; then comes the experience of Saturday night fever and the urgent prayer, "Please give me a word Lord;" and who has not felt the Sunday morning panic and the prayer of the desperate preacher, "Please send down the fire on these dry sticks?" And what can we say about the suffering hours of the Sunday evening guilt when the unprepared preacher, in despair, thinks, "I am a worthless human being and I want out of the ministry." We have all been there and we know this is not God's best.

There are sufficient sorrows to accompany the magnificent privilege of being a preacher without adding to your burdens with slovenly preparation. I know from some harsh personal experiences of attempting to feed the congregation on "scraps and leftovers," but thin preparation grows shallow, malnourished disciples.

Restoring the spiritual disciplines of conscientious preparation will take time and may require a radical re-ordering of the diary; but it will reap spiritual dividends. Preachers need solitude and space to shape a long term preaching plan. In the sermon "kitchen" there will be microwave messages which because of legitimate pastoral pressures will be instantly produced, but you must store up material in the kitchen deep freezer. The rich advantage of knowing months in advance your subjects and your Bible passages cannot be overestimated.

The conviction of Charles Haddon Spurgeon was that the call to preaching is always accompanied by the call to study: "He who has ceased to learn has ceased to teach. He who no longer sows in the study will no more reap in the pulpit."[7]

The fifth dimension concerns the preacher's spiritual authority in preaching. This requires the preacher to reflect regularly on his or her understanding of the mandate we have been given as preachers and an earnest seeking of the spiritual unction promised to preachers of the Word. I have for years made it a summer custom to read a book on preaching during the August vacation. By this method I am always called back to a high view of preaching that reminds me that preaching from God's Word is more than the imparting of knowledge about God and his Gospel if it is to actually lead the congregation to encounter the power of God in salvation. As Christoph Schwobel expresses boldly on his reading of Romans 10:13-17: "Since faith comes by hearing – Christian faith is impossible without preaching."[8]

Schwobel reminds us that the Bible commences in Genesis with the creation of the world by God's Word and culminates in Revelation with the never ending words of glory to God in the worship of heaven. Between these two events God constantly communicates his "Word" to human beings culminating in Jesus Christ, the Word made flesh.

In our preaching we are caught up in this eternal conversation of the Holy Trinity as the Holy Spirit empowers us to take the ancient words of God and bring the contemporary people of God into the eternal conversation.

In our sermons we use human words that God sanctifies. However, for true communication to happen "the human word which brings God's word points away from itself to God as the author and content of the divine word."[9]

This was the experience of the biblical messengers. When Ezekiel received the vision of God's glory he fell prostrate to the ground and the first words that shattered the silence were, "Son of Man, stand on your feet and I will speak to you" (Ezekiel 2:1). Paul had a similar encounter with God on the Damascus road. Struck to the ground by the blinding light from heaven, he heard the command, "Saul, Saul, why do you persecute me ... now get up and go into the city and you will be told what you must do" (Acts 9:3-6). John is another messenger who is overcome with the commission to speak and write God's words and receives the assurance: "Do not be afraid; I am the First and the Last. I am the Living One..." (Revelation 1:17-18).

This conviction that we are involved in pointing people away from ourselves to the divine source of "The Word" means the sermon is not so much an encounter between the preacher and the congregation as between the congregation and the biblical texts. Too often the response to the sermon is to enquire (often privately out of earshot of the preacher), "How did the preacher do today?", when the real question for the congregation is, "How did we do today?" How are we to respond to this Word from the Lord? What does this Word mean for me?

This does not elevate the word of the preacher to a level of infallibility. It does imply that God adopts our words: "He condescends, entering the congregation through the foolishness of our words, as we testify to Christ, expositing the scriptures, speaking the words that we must believe God provides, all the while knowing how profoundly flawed our best sermons are."[10]

This means that a high view of scripture is essential to our preaching. We believe in divine revelation – that God takes the initiative to make himself known; we believe in divine providence – that God who first spoke his words has preserved through the centuries the words of the Bible. All this leads us to affirm the divine power and authority of the Bible. Preachers enter the pulpit with the primary conviction that they are called to speak God's words and these are powerful "living and active" words (Hebrews 4:12).

When the preacher sits humbly under God's Word and seeks the anointing power of the Holy Spirit for the act of preaching, then with this spiritual mind set he or she can afford to be passionate about preaching, and, as John Stott says with unbridled enthusiasm, "Our heads begin to swim, our hearts to beat, our blood to flow and our eyes to sparkle with the sheer glory of having God's Word in our hands and on our lips."[11]

The sixth dimension is, the preacher who wants to apply the word of God must love God's people. Good sermons are never confined within the walls of scripture: "They are always bursting out of the Bible into the lives of people." But how does the preacher tackle the mountainous challenge of understanding the world today and how do we begin to grasp the cultural movements that shape the lives of our church members? If we are going to hear the questioning voices of people then we must know intimately the world of our congregation. Having soaked yourself in the Word you will need to soak yourself in the lives of your people.

I have found it instructive to go into my church when it is empty and sit in the places where the members of my congregation sit each week. I meditate there in the church and think myself into their world. What challenges are they facing at present? What is the specific situation that calls for prayer and pastoral care? How does the current series of sermons fit their circumstances of life? Where it is appropriate I visit members in their homes and go at their invitation to their workplaces. I stand in the supermarket queue and get feedback on last Sunday's sermon. I hang around the church organizations "time wasting" and listening to the scraps of sometimes trivial conversations that people exchange. Whatever method you want to employ you must take time with the people in order to assess the impact of your sermons on the world of your congregation.

Lee Strobel says when he was preaching to the Willow Creek congregation he reckoned at the beginning of the 1990s that people were more cynical listeners. They would sit with arms folded and their body language said, "I dare you to communicate something to me that matters." Now in the 21st century people are saying, "I am in my third marriage and failing; I have purchased my second BMW car and it has not brought satisfaction; I have risen to the top of my precarious profession and it does not fulfill in the way I thought it would." Strobel says people see the stability of the world unraveling and they are scared. "Therefore I preach the immanence of God and the closeness of a personal relationship with Jesus Christ."[12]

I share the practice of Haddon Robinson who imagines people around his study desk as he prepares a sermon. He pictures his mother-in-law who is a true believer; he thinks of a friend who is a cynic and can hear him saying, "O yes, sure;" he thinks of a business executive and imagines him saying, "What is the bottom line pastor?"; he has in mind a teenager who says, "This is boring." Robinson says, "I think of these people and many more and ask the preacher's question – 'What will this word mean to them?'"[13] Remember the double listening skills of the preacher: Humbly listening for God's Word and lovingly listening to God's people.

The seventh dimension is the conviction that when the sermon is over the Holy Spirit goes on working. An old and experienced preacher in one of my congregations once gave me this advice regarding sermons: "Ask of every sermon, 'Where is the fishing net?', and 'Where is the good news?'" He used the image of the fishing net to "catch the congregation" with the challenge of God's Word. Don't let them escape! The reference to the good news was to make sure the sermon was full of grace and truth and focused on the person of Christ.

Too often we imagine a sermon is complete in itself and we breathe a sigh of relief when it is delivered. Christoph Schwobel suggests:

> This betrays that the preacher does not expect the address begun by a human witness to be completed by God the Holy Spirit. The art of preaching consists in offering a sermon that is open to being completed by God. It consists in telling an unfinished story because God wants to catch us up into the adventure of living his story through us.[14]

The sermon is never over until the Holy Spirit has ceased speaking. The preacher may have finished preparing the manuscript but through the delivery and beyond the end of the sermon the Holy Spirit goes on speaking. So never be surprised when God speaks his word on service through Romans 12:1 and someone says, "I want to offer my body as a living sacrifice." As you preach your sermon you should be expecting this kind of commitment.

When God speaks his word on the need to persevere in the Christian life and you urge people, as in Hebrews 12:1-2, not to stop running until the race is over, anticipate a greater steadfastness in the life of your members. When God speaks through you his word from John 3 the need for born again conversion, you should expect people to be saved. When God speaks his word from Matthew 5:43-38 on loving the enemy, expect some testimonies of forgiveness and reconciliation will occur in the days following your sermon, because the Holy Spirit goes on speaking after the sermon is over.

If you want to see fire in the pulpit there needs to be a constant fire in the heart of the preacher, what the Bible terms "never lacking in zeal and maintaining spiritual fervor" (Romans 2:11), and this task is best accomplished when the preacher is as well prepared as the sermon.

NOTES

[1] Story recounted by John Stott in *I Believe in Preaching* (Hodder and Stoughton London, 1982) p.285

[2] John Stott, *The Last Word: Reflections on a Lifetime of Preaching* (Authentic Milton Keynes, 2008) p.19

[3] Arthur Skevington Wood, *Heralds of the Gospel* (Marshal Morgan and Scott London, 1963) p.91

[4] Donald English, *An Evangelical Theology of Preaching* (Abingdon Press Nashville, 1996) p. 140

[5] Philip Greenslade, *Leadership: Reflections on Biblical Leadership Today* (revised edition CWR Farnham, 2002) p. 45

[6] Peter Taylor Forsyth, *Positive Preaching and the Modern Mind* (Hodder and Stoughton London, 1907) p. 67

[7] Charles Haddon Spurgeon, *An All Round Ministry – A Collection of Addresses to Ministers and Students* 1900 (Banner of Truth, 1960) p.236

[8] Christoph Schwolbel's introduction to Colin Gunton, *Theology through Preaching* (T&T Clarke Edinburgh, 2001) p. 1

[9] Ibid. p. 3

[10] D. Hansen, *Preaching Cats and Dogs* (American Baptist Evangelical Journal 7:3 1999) p. 20

[11] John Stott, *The Contemporary Christian* (Inter Varsity Press 1992) chapter 13 on Expounding the Word, p. 210

[12] Lee Strobel, article on preaching in *Leadership* magazine, Fall issue, 1995, p.20

[13] Haddon Robinson, article on preaching in *Leadership* magazine, Fall issue, 1997, p. 25

[14] Christoph Schwobel, Ibid. p. 20

Chapter 6

Prayer and Theology

Christopher J. Ellis

Some years ago I began to research the development of worship amongst Baptists – not an easy task when most services do not follow a written liturgy and in which most prayers are not pre-composed or written down for future reference. With such a fluid liturgical landscape I found a way forward by identifying a number of core values for Baptist worship and used these as a framework for my description of British Baptist worship.[1] These values are, I believe, held together by an overarching belief in the Lordship of Jesus Christ. I argued that this belief in, and commitment to, his Lordship is expressed through four values: an attention to scripture, a belief in the church as a community, a commitment to the kingdom of God (often expressed through mission) and the value that I wish to highlight in this paper, namely, devotion – a spirituality of the heart expressed in extempore prayer, an openness to the Holy Spirit and a concern for personal faith.

Faith as Personal Faith

This valuing of personal devotion was expressed very well at a Baptist association meeting in Taunton, England, in 1654. A local congregation had asked the gathering of church representatives whether for a person to be admitted into church membership it was sufficient for a person to assent "only upon a bare confession of Christ being come in the flesh and assenting to the doctrine and order laid down by him?" The response was clear. To be accepted into the church a person needed to give evidence of a living faith and their life needed to display "evident tokens of conversion."[2]

This concern for a living, personal faith has remained a key aspect of Baptist evangelical identity and, in particular, the emphasis on extempore prayer has been a continuing expression of this heart worship.

Petitionary and Contemplative Prayer

Insofar as we are able to identify the content of such spontaneous prayer we may see that a large part of it was concerned with petitions – what we might call "asking" prayers or "prayers of faith." Baptist spirituality has often expressed a belief that God is concerned with the whole of life by people praying for God's involvement in the details of their lives. In wider circles of writing on spirituality, such an emphasis on petitionary prayer has sometimes been seen as somehow inferior to more contemplative approaches that have been more concerned with union with the divine than with bringing a list of requests.[3]

Many contemporary writers on spirituality will also assume that contemplation and adoration are higher levels of prayer than petitionary prayer, and I have some sympathy with that view, as I will explain in a moment. However, it is not that simple. To ask God for help in the living of your life, and in the material and other provisions that you believe you need, is in fact, an act of faith, an implicit claim that God is able and willing to answer such prayer. Indeed, Jesus invited his hearers to "ask and it will be given you,"[4] and the Lord's Prayer, which he gave in response to his disciples asking for guidance on how to pray, contains a number of petitions beginning with, "Give us this day our daily bread."[5] Richard Foster, in his book on prayer, lists a number of different ways of praying, but he begins with petition that he calls "simple" prayer, because it is what we do when we come honestly before the God whom we trust. It is often the starting point of prayer where we come in our need.[6]

Nonetheless, we don't need to argue about which type of prayer is "better" or "higher." We can, however, recognize that these ways of praying are complementary and that each needs to be prized. The Lord's Prayer, for example, begins with adoration and a focus upon God: "Our Father, who art in heaven, hallowed be thy name," before it moves to a series of requests. For a Baptist audience, I want to encourage the desire to explore contemplative prayer with its emphasis on our relationship with God and with the offering of love and adoration. On the other hand, for other audiences I might want to emphasize the role of petitionary prayer in exercising faith and in seeking a life of trusting discipleship. But for the present, I hope to encourage a "contemplate concern" for seeking the presence of God and I plan to do this in a roundabout way by briefly reviewing recent developments in the relationship between prayer and theology.

Prayer and Theology

If, in the middle of the twentieth century, you had asked a theologian from Europe or North America about the relationship between prayer and theology you might well be answered with silence and a peculiar look. As I look back to my own early theological education in the late sixties and early seventies I remember few links between these two areas of Christian activity. In so far as there was any link it would probably have been mediated by the philosophy of religion, asking such questions as, "Does God answer prayer?", or even, "In what sense can we speak of God acting in the world?" These are questions about the mechanics of prayer and religious faith, questions about the very validity of petitionary prayer in which prayer is subject to the overconfident scrutiny of a critical philosophical analysis.

Some might nod sagely at this point and blame the modernism of the skeptical sixties or the philosophical mind-sets that have come from the Enlightenment for this rather sterile state of affairs. However we can go further back than Descartes. Alexander Schmemann, the Russian Orthodox theologian and the father of modern liturgical theology, complained about how what he called "Scholasticism" had changed the relationship between reason and theology. Going back as far as the schoolmen of the high Middle Ages, theology had become, in his view, an analytical activity in which human reason dissected revelation and experience in such a way as to place reason above the God it sought to serve.[7] He is critical of critical theology, yet the very nature of theology has been seen, in the Western Tradition since Aquinas, as an exercise in human rationality seeking to understand the nature and purposes of God. Philip

Sheldrake makes a similar point when he dates a change in theological method as starting around the beginning of the twelfth century with the use of Aristotelian logic. He points out that contradictions were to be eliminated by means of carefully constructed distinctions ... "thinking" began to be understood as a mastery of facts and details rather than attention to the truth expressed in symbols. To put it more simply, reason began to triumph over imagination and the ability to define truth over experiences of the sacred.[8]

The Practice of Theology

Of course, the implications of arguing for a change in the twelfth century are that prior to this there was a closer relationship between spirituality and theology. Put another way, for over half the existence of Christianity there has been a positive relationship between the two spheres. Readers of patristic theology will recognize the truth of this claim for the theological texts tend to be imaginative rather than analytical, and pastoral rather than critical.

However, there has been a sea change in recent decades and now we can see a significant number of theologians[9] who want to make connections and engage in dialogue between the experience of prayer and the practice of theology. Rather than see this shift as a stark choice between critical or non-critical forms of theology, it is perhaps better to see this movement as a change of emphasis and a re-assessment about a variety of ways in which we might engage in theological activity. So, for example, in their book on practical theology, Paul Ballard and John Pritchard suggest four distinct modes of working in theology. There is, firstly, theology as a *descriptive* activity when it describes how Christians have believed and still do believe in, and live out, their faith. Secondly, there is theology as a *normative* activity, when, on the basis of scripture and tradition, it seeks to establish the inner meaning of Christian belief, to examine its norms and claims, and then to examine both the thought and life of the church in the light of its findings. This form of theology calls the community of faith back to its essential commitment, challenging it in word and deed. The mode is often called "doctrine" because it represents what the church teaches. Thirdly, theology can operate as a *critical* activity, living on the frontiers of faith and responding to the challenges posed by the insights of those engaged in other disciplines. It sees itself as being concerned with questions of truth, its own and other people's truth. Finally, theology can work as an *apologetic* activity, concerned to work out the implications, intellectual and practical, of the Christian faith.[10]

The advantage of such a typology is that it reminds us that theology has a variety of roles suited to different contexts. Theology undertaken within the church, whether within a congregation or an educational establishment preparing people for ministry, will not always be asking identical questions to those asked in the public arena of a secular university. Perhaps a surprising recent development is the way in which even within some secular universities, so-called "confessional theology" seems to have a place.

Mystical Theology

For the sake of convenience and brevity, we could describe these developments as the rediscovery of mystical theology in which prayer not only provides a source for theological reflection but in which prayer offers theology a different goal from the rational aspirations of the academy which, to quote Vladimir Lossky, "is always the possibility, the manner, or the means of union with God."[11] It seems to me that such an understanding of theology suggests an activity in which every pastor and every Christian disciple should be involved. Every doctrine, every spiritual discipline, every act of fellowship and every mission activity revolves around this center: how, through grace, God embraces us and draws us closer in love. For the present I want briefly to identify four currents in this stream of mystical theology, four invitations to see and do theology differently.

1. *Letting God be God*
The primary concern of those who criticize critical modes of theology is that they lack reverence for God and God's revelation and that consequently they are less, rather than more, truthful. Long before the recent theological receptiveness to prayer, Karl Barth and Paul Tillich reminded us of the "Godness" of God. Encountering God in prayer, we are led to reflect on the transcendence of God who created a universe beyond our ability to measure or understand. At the same time we have encountered the immanence of God, for we are known intimately by the God, who in grace, comes in search of us. In this paradox we enter a

place where we cannot stand with our reason *over* and above God in theological analysis, but where rather we need to be questioned and challenged *by* God. The primary response to such a God is not analysis but praise and trust.

2. *Falling into a Reverent Silence*

Those who describe the history of Christian thought speak of a way of thinking and writing that was very prominent in the early centuries and that has remained significant within the Eastern Orthodox tradition, but that has been absent from much Western thought. This is the so-called *"apophati"* tradition that offers a necessary corrective to the over confidence of many Western thinkers. It balances what the Greek church called the "cataphatic way," an approach to theology that relies upon being able to describe what God is like. The apophatic alternative encourages us to fall into a reverent silence. Of course, both are necessary. In the sixth century, a writer who is known as Denis the Areopagite proposed that knowing *and* unknowing are mutually related rather than mutually exclusive.[12] For example, the doctrine of the Trinity is a way of knowing that affirms something about God. Yet, at the same time, it is a way of unknowing because the affirmations we make about the Trinity immediately push us beyond what we can grasp. As Philip Sheldrake comments, "Paradoxically, the doctrine of the Trinity both reveals God and yet reveals God as beyond human knowing."[13] I believe we can learn both about this reverential way of doing theology and from its implications for the nature of prayer.

Rowan Williams comments that, "apophasis is 'not a branch of theology,' but an attitude that should under gird *all* theological discourse, and lead it towards the silence of contemplation and communion."[14] In the fourteenth century an unknown English mystic wrote *The Cloud of Unknowing* in which he observed:

> Now all rational creatures, angels and men alike, have in them, each one individually, one chief working power which is called a knowing power, and another chief working power called a loving power; and of these two powers, God, who is the maker of them, is always incomprehensible to the first, the knowing power. But

to the second, which is the loving power, he is entirely comprehensible ... Because [God] can certainly be loved but not thought. He can be taken and held by love but not by thought.[15]

3. Rediscovering Mystery

There is a sense in which the strands already discussed invite us to appreciate the importance of mystery. God who cannot be thought but who can be loved strikes me as a very biblical theme. Remember that, theologically speaking, a mystery is not the same as a riddle, or even the same as the modern use of the term. In a mystery novel, all is revealed at the end, as the clues culminate in making clear what throughout the novel has not been clear. In a riddle, all is obvious once the answer is disclosed. But the divine mystery remains a mystery to rational thought. As Isaac Watts put it:

> Almighty God! to thee
> Be endless honours done,
> The undivided Three,
> And the mysterious One:
> Where reason fails
> With all her powers,
> There faith prevails
> And love adores. [16]

This must affect the way theologians set about their task in exploring what Paul calls "the length and breadth and height and depth" and in their search "to know the love of Christ that surpasses knowledge" that they might "be filled with the fullness of God."[17] What other word can we use than the word "mystery," not as an admission of defeat, but as a prelude to worship? This leads me to the fourth strand of theological rediscovery.

4. Doxological Theology

Paul's great prayer for the Ephesians to enter into something of this wonderful mystery reaches a climax of praise in the following verses:

> Now to him who by the power at work within us is able
> to accomplish abundantly far more than all we can ask or

> imagine to him be glory in the church and in Christ Jesus
> to all generations forever and ever. Amen.[18]

For this should be the end of all seeking, whether theological or devotional. Words fall silent, concepts shatter and music gives way to silence as we are "lost in wonder love and praise."[19] Theology leads to worship, whether personal or corporate. A young man was once asked why he was dancing in the aisle in a worship service. He said, "Because I can't fly!" As Augustine explained, God has made us as rational and expressive beings; we have to speak out in the presence of the wonder of God, yet we can only be silent. But this silence is not the silence of failure, but the silence of awe and wonder, of adoration and love.

Speaking personally for a moment, I find it difficult to conceive of a theology that is not doxological. As I pray, I find myself exploring the nature of God and doing theology on my knees. And as I set out to do theology I find myself being drawn toward prayer. This is neither cleverness nor goodness on my part: it is sheer grace where thought and worship interweave. Such a perspective does not come from or lead to a neutrally objective theological analysis. It invites the theologian to be personally engaged with a personal God, to approach the mystery of God with an integrity and unity of heart and mind and to bring as an offering a capacity for wonder.

The Development of Prayer

If theology is challenged and transformed by the meeting with prayer, what happens to prayer? I want to suggest two approaches to prayer that we would do well to explore more than many of us do at present.

1. The Practice of Contemplation and the Readiness to Adore

As I mentioned at the beginning, it is important to balance our trusting inclination to bring requests to God with a readiness to seek the Giver beyond the gifts. This is often not easy and is ultimately a work of the Holy Spirit, but our desire to come close to God and our readiness to adore are an important offering that we bring in faith. In this we can learn from other parts of the church and from previous generations, from the spiritual classics both catholic and evangelical. We do tend to use a lot of words, both in worship and, I suspect, in personal prayer. Yet for persons who know each other well and love one another, silence is deep and rich. Yes words can help, but often as a prelude for something beyond words. This is true for lovers and it can be true for prayer.

2. Scripture Leading to Prayer

As Baptists, we have a deep respect for scripture. We read it for information, for inspiration and for revelation. We call it "the word of God" but how often do we read it as a means of coming close to God. In recent years the ancient, Benedictine practice of *lectio divina* has become increasingly used across many denominations. The words literally mean "divine reading" and are often paraphrased as "spiritual reading," but I prefer to speak of "prayerful reading." It is the reading of scripture in order for the words of scripture to bring me closer to God – and to be open to God coming close to me. While the term can be used quite flexibly, the practice of *lectio divina* traditionally has four stages: reading, when the scripture is read and re-read; meditating, when the reader reflects and chews over the words, asking what their relevance might be for them; praying, when the themes that have emerged from the meditation are recast and addressed to God; and contemplation, which is beyond prayer, where the one praying simply rests in the presence of God.

This is no mere formula. There is no guarantee offering a profound spiritual experience. Like each of the spiritual disciplines, *lectio divina* simply prepares the one praying to be open to the ministry of the Holy Spirit. Yet in the reading of scripture we have a practical example of theology leading to prayer. We also have a reminder that when things go well the words of theology, even when it's scripture, and the words of our prayers, all give way to silent adoration. Paul writes:

> For now we see in a mirror dimly, but then we shall see face to face. Now I know only in part; then I will know fully, even as I have been fully known.[20]

He continues to point out the importance of faith, hope, and love. But there will come a time when faith is no longer needed, theology will be unnecessary, for we shall see face to face. There will come a time when hope is no longer needed for the kingdom will have come and prayers of petition will be redundant. But love – always there will be love – for God is love – always love.

NOTES

[1] See C. J. Ellis, *Gathering: A Theology of Spirituality of Worship in Free Church Tradition*, SCM 2004, especially pp. 74-97.

[2] B. R. White, *Association Records of the Particular Baptists of England, Wales and Ireland to 1660. London: Baptist Historical Society*, 1971, p. 56 and Ellis, Gathering..., p. 141.

[3] Such a view was taken by the German phenomenologist Friedrich Heiler who made a distinction between "mystical prayer" and "evangelical" or "prophetic prayer". F. Heiler, *Prayer: A Study in the History and Psychology of Religion*, London: Oxford University Press, 1932, pp. 135-171.

[4] Matthew 7:7.

[5] Matthew 6:11.

[6] R. Foster, *Prayer, Finding the Heart's True Home*, London: Hodder and Stoughton, 1992, pp. 7-16.

[7] A. Schmemann, "Theology and Liturgical Tradition" in T. Fische (ed.), *Liturgy and Tradition: Theological Reflections of Alexander Schmemann*, Crestwood NY: St. Vladimir's Seminary Press, 1963/1990, pp. 12-20, p. 13.

[8] P. Sheldrake, *Spirituality and Theology: Christian Living and the Doctrine of God*, London: Darton, Longman and Todd, 1998, pp. 39f.

[9] For a brief survey of some examples, including, Lonergan, Rahner, von Balthasar, Moltmann, Rowan, Williams et al, see Sheldrake, *Spirituality and Theology*, pp. 65-72. Also see Mark A. McIntosh, *Mystical Theology: The Integrity of Spirituality and Theology*, Blackwell, 1998.

[10] Paul Ballard and John Pritchard, *Practical Theology in Action: Christian Thinking in the Service of Church and Society*, London: SPCK, 1996, pp. 10f.

[11] V. Lossky, *The Mystical Theology of the Eastern Church*, Crestwood NY: St Vladimir's Press, 1976, p. 10.

[12] Commonly known today as Pseudo-Dionysius the Areopagite.

[13] Sheldrake *Spirituality and Theology*, p. 26.

[14] R. Williams, 'Lossky, the *via negative* and the foundations of theology', originally published in 1979 but now reissued in Rowan Williams, ed. M. Higton, *Wrestling with Angels: Conversations in Modern Theology*, London SCM

Press, 2007, p. 2. Williams is discussing the contribution of Vladimir Lossky and refers to his *Mystical Theology of the Eastern Church,* pp. 231f.

[15] J. Walsh (ed.), *The Cloud of Unknowing,* New York: Paulist Press, 1981, pp. 23 & 30.

[16] "I give immortal praise," hymn 38 in *The Psalms and Hymns of Isaac Watts* accessed at *Christian Classics Ethereal Library*: www.ccel.org/ccel/watts/psalmshymns.html.

[17] Ephesians 3.18f.

[18] Ephesians 3.20f.

[19] "Love divine all loves excelling" by Charles Wesley.

[20] 1 Corinthians 13:12.

Chapter 7

From the Edge: On Approaching the Task of Breaking Open the Word

Lina Andronoviene

As many speakers have found out for themselves, *who* speaks—what is known about the speaker as well as what is his or her standing within that particular community or in the context of that particular event—is just as important as *what* is being said. For that reason, allow me to start with my own story.

I currently serve at a seminary which functions as a hub for the meeting of believers from many different countries[1], offering an experience of a variety of ways of preaching.[2] However, I come from a small Baptist community consisting of only a few churches and a rather established way of approaching the task of preaching. Although several churches would strongly rely on women carrying important aspects of ministry, the overall climate I grew up in has not been that of great enthusiasm in regard to the sisters' involvement in breaking the Word open.[3] Not that it greatly upset me or anything; the task of preaching seemed to be an arduous one—both for the messenger and for the congregation. I am sure sometimes it was my own fault of not concentrating appropriately; but then there are also the merciless statistics of how little people seem to remember from sermons.[4] It has been suggested that the *most* preachers can hope for is that the congregation will still remember *something* from their message by Thursday following the Sunday they preached.[5] Next Thursday as the goal! It is not exactly inspiring for the one who prepares to expound upon the Word; and it certainly did not seem inspiring to me.

Yet, with all my lack of enthusiasm, in the course of the last few years I found myself sharing from the Word of God here and there, then being asked to do it again, and sooner than I realized it, in spite of all of the above reservations, I was one of those dealing with that arduous task. It was, at times, identified by different names, as people were confused as to what to call a talk which could have a song or a dialogue or a reading in the middle. But I could not fool myself; I was engaged in the practice of preaching. This was not something I had ever imagined myself doing! [6]

My story, of course, resembles that of many "non-traditional" preachers who find themselves breaking the Word open after having experienced an unexpected "calling from the edge," so to speak. It is from the awareness of the implications of such a call that I offer the following reflection, hoping that it will encourage further deliberation on Baptist preaching which perhaps may be helpful not only for those coming from the "edges," but others too.

The following thoughts originated as a reflection on three continua preachers face that I had found important for my own ministry. During the time of sharing this presentation at the Commission on Baptist Worship and Spirituality meeting in Ede, Netherlands, and discussing it with those present, an idea came that these three continua may be imagined as spokes of a wheel. Such a suggestion seemed to be a helpful one[7], as it highlights the fact that these continua, and their ends, can be approached in any order. The wheel needs to keep turning, with different spokes touching ground at different times, aimed at stirring and changing the hearts of the people of God.

From Vulnerability to Strength

So here comes the first of the spokes: it has vulnerability on its one end and strength on the other. Let us start with **vulnerability**. If one does not possess some sort of external authority and is not naturally aggressive in terms of personality type, one can feel especially vulnerable when sensing skepticism or resistance from anybody in the congregation—and such resistance at times is connected with one being a woman, making her vulnerable to the comments conveyed by the listeners' faces or spoken out loud. Yet, vulnerability plays out in many other ways, too. To start with, it has to do with the business of struggling with the passage, or laboring over the message, as the natural way where the vulnerability and humanness of the preacher will become evident. Disclosing some of the process of struggling with the text in the sermon, and allowing the congregation to struggle with it too, takes away the cloak of omniscient authority, but facilitates the sermon's biblical narrative coming alive to the congregation.[8]

One of the responsibilities of a preacher is fostering a healthy space for such vulnerability. The need for it pertains to all of our worship, not the least our songs which tend to reflect a certain uneasiness about anything related to God that is not neat and nicely positive.[9] But how does one speak of God who at times seems to be hidden, God who may not be understandable, God who can be difficult? Such experiences of God, biblical, historical and contemporary, will be hard to convey by the authority of statements. Somewhere there, even in the most propositional sermons, there must be space for the person behind those statements who also doubts, questions, and struggles, reflecting both the personal and collective experiences of God's people. When life is tough, preaching can be an especially difficult act to do, because we then feel we cannot issue the words of encouragement and hope in the way it is expected of a preacher. And yet, listening to a preacher who has faced a crisis and has been left defenseless in it — be it a loss of a loved one, a betrayal, terminal illness, or something of a lesser and more permanent degree — can be a profound experience. Exposing oneself, which is what is happening when we allow ourselves to be vulnerable as preachers, is dangerous for the preacher: there is a risk of one's vulnerability being misused, or even abused.

Yet paradoxically, vulnerability in the pulpit cannot exist without the other end of the spoke — **strength**. Strength is required if the words of the Gospel are to be proclaimed. If we were only aware of our vulnerability and nothing else, the pulpit would have to be the place avoided at all costs. It would not help the people of God to move anywhere beyond doubt and questioning, drowning them in grief and anxiety, which would not be very good. One mounts the pulpit with as much strength as there is vulnerability. Thus, the pulpit is a place where one carries a responsibility which requires strength — strength to communicate, and to go on communicating. As preachers, we are always in the presence of God — both when God speaks clearly and when He is beyond our understanding. That both makes one vulnerable and *gives* one strength.

Personal yet Collective

Another spoke is naturally connected to the previous one. It has to do with being personal on its one end and representing, or engaging with, the congregation as a whole, and thus acting as a public figure on the other.

If one is to expose oneself to vulnerability, one will not be able to do it without being personal. This does not imply public examination of the skeletons in one's closet, but "being real," difficult as it may be to define this. It will not mean being exactly the same as when the preacher talks one on one with any member of the congregation. "Being real" can mean more than one thing, but it at least means that it should not be "not me."

My experience of teaching homiletics in the bible school of my own little community[10] may be a helpful illustration here. The students were asked to prepare a short sermon, and after its delivery, all of us, students and teachers included, commented on how we heard the message, what made an impact on us, what seemed to work and what did not quite work. It was an excellent exercise and a wonderful testing ground which I wish for every student of homiletics, or indeed each preacher, if they are to have any idea of how what they think they have preached might be different from what was actually heard by various members of the congregation and the general effect the sermon had on the community. Yet what also struck me was the depth of the discernment in regard to the reasons the student chose this or that particular passage, the needs of his or her congregation, and so on. We knew each other well enough to say, "I think you could have pushed further;" or to bless another preacher because we knew they did all they could; or to press another one regarding the choice of the text; or to gently observe, in a couple of cases, that "this didn't sound like you. What was your purpose of doing it this way? Might some other style or approach work better?" What I could see in those different personalities was a whole collection of gifts which played into preaching in very interesting ways. It was a glimpse into the "fullness of Christ" on which John H. Yoder has expounded — a demonstration of how each of us, as members of the body with our unique abilities, but also as preachers with our individual aptitudes, have a particular role to play.[11]

Bringing in one's own personality is an important contribution to the life of the church. However, there is also the other end of the spoke that necessarily has to be attended to: the **collective** or public dimension of preaching, which can be more challenging for some preachers than for others. As those among us who are more philosophically inclined would remind us, the concept of the "self" and the "person" is a certain construction reflecting the legacy of the modern Western society, now undergoing a serious crisis. As a response to this crisis, some have suggested "that the self is its relations; that a change in its relations would mean a change in its character; and that it dissolves with the dissolution of all its relations."[12] There is more to ourselves than what we consider as our selves. When it comes to those entrusted with the task of expounding upon the Word, the line where "I" ends and "we" (in their case, a congregation) begins, is blurred. It is for this reason that we are able to speak as a part of the corporate personality of the church, addressing those questions, doubts, struggles or joys which we "personally," in the strict sense of the word, may not have experienced. Consequently, the practice of preaching has to do with fostering the skills of becoming, for the right time of being, the congregation personalized. It can be a scary responsibility; what if it ends in travesty? To perform the public role faithfully, a lot of listening will need to take place. It requires much effort. The task of listening entails not only sensing what the individual members are communicating, verbally and otherwise, but also striving to hear the voice of the congregation as such when seeking the will of the Lord and then, in some sense, embodying it in the pulpit or its equivalent. This is one of the areas, it seems to me, where women preachers can often be of particular help. There are various exceptions and complexities, but in general, female identity tends to be described as more relational than that of the males. "Because of the continual crossing of self and other, women's writing [not only writing, but also speaking] may blur the public and private and defy completion."[13] Women might do well in paying special attention in coaching this sort of gift and offer it to the people of God.

The public role of the preacher can also be supported by certain disciplines, such as a Lectionary, preaching "the whole counsel of God" as a means of checking against preoccupation with one's own concerns and issues (and favorite texts!). Of course, if one really wants to preach about one's own issues, one will find a way to do it, with or without a Lectionary, but it does provide a good discipline. Moreover, reflecting on the same texts as many sister congregations helps the preachers to be more aware of the church worldwide, and thus to avoid parochialism and self-centeredness.

Sounds in Silence

The last spoke I would like to attend to has **sound** at one of its ends. There is something about even how our voices reverberate, quite uniquely, which calls for the multiplicity of preachers in order for the message to be heard in its fullness. Then, of course, there are the ways those sounds are organized — the whole issue of the skill and the gift of using words, which generally characterizes a preacher.

This is one of the reasons why preachers are needed: to fill the space with words; to name things and phenomena; to lead and accompany people through various stages of life. Perhaps the case of the funeral may illustrate it best. What would happen if there were no pastor to conduct the funeral service? Who would say something? As human beings, we need words on such occasions. At the very minimum, we need the sounds to mark and give meaning to our experiences; but we also yearn for the meaning behind those sounds.

There is a certain ritual that takes place on Sunday mornings when I'm due to preach: I pace from one end of the room to another, saying, in worry or sometimes panic, "I've nothing to say. I've nothing to say!" This is my preacher's nightmare — that what I will say will sound trite, that it will be hollow words, dropping on the floor just a few centimeters from the pulpit; and God's people will not hear any message upon which to ponder and act. Sound and the world of meaning that comes in that sound are nerve-racking for preachers.

Yet, there is another side to sound which is not so often noticed, and yet it is as powerful — at times even more powerful: that of the absence of sound. Silence. Unfortunately, it is this area where the fault of many a preacher lies: cramming the space with words; packing it tightly with sound; shoving it in huge heaps onto the listeners' heads so that the words dribble, light and low-cost. Yet, as those who have had any experience with such disciplines as theater would tell us, there is an enormous power in the absence of words. Silence can have an impact beyond words. This is true both symbolically and literally, and it has to do especially with the preaching coming from the edges. By *not* saying something, and instead leaving space for silence framed between what was going before and is coming after, a preacher can enter areas which otherwise are too fearsome to be trodden; that of the mysterious, the difficult, the controversial, the painful, the indescribable.

To use silence takes both some technical training—such as making conscious efforts not to rush through the script or thoughts—and also a deeper understanding of how God uses the process of the preparation to preach, therefore incorporating silence into the very process of the birth of the sermon. At the very least, it would mean refusing the rush of sermon preparation, but instead employing the breaks of silence filled with prayer.

Let us not forget how little of a sermon is actually remembered by those who hear it. Let us also keep in mind that they often remember only our illustrations, or a sub-point, or—scarily—a point we've never made! But that should not worry us. Rather we should be concerned to not interfere with the listening process of the congregation as it endeavors to remember our points, or our nice stories, or a lovely flow of our voice. For this, silence is to be our discipline, so that the people of God, individually and collectively, can hear God's word for them even through us—even *in spite of us*.[14]

Other spokes can be added to these three, no doubt. Yet these have always been with me, an "accidental" preacher, as I wrestled with an unexpected calling. It is my hope that reflecting on them, and perhaps adding some new spokes, may help those who engage in the act of breaking the Word open and those who have the equally complex task of listening, in our common life as Christ's followers.

NOTE

[1] International Baptist Theological Seminary (IBTS), www.ibts.eu. IBTS is owned by the unions belonging to the European Baptist Federation, and also draws students from other parts of the world.

[2] For a helpful overview of different tasks of preaching as they are perceived by the European Baptists, see Toivo Pilli, "Preaching, Baptist," in John H. Y. Briggs, gen. ed., *A Dictionary of European Baptist Life and Thought. Studies in Baptist History and Thought* Series, Vol. 33 (Milton Keynes: Paternoster/ International Baptist Theological Seminary, 2009), 400-401, and "Sermon" in *ibid*," 459-460.

[3] On approaches to women's involvement in ministry amongst Baptists in Europe, see Lina Andronoviene and Keith G Jones, "Women in Baptist Life," in Briggs, *Dictionary of European Baptist ...*, 529-531.

[4] As an example of a study of a Baptist context, see Dennis L. Price et al, "The Measurement of the Effect of Preaching and Preaching Plus Small Group Dialogue in one Baptist Church," in David Day et al, ed., *A Reader on Preaching: Making Connections. Explorations in Practical, Pastoral and Empirical Theology* Series (Aldershot: Ashgate, 2005), 255-265. The sober conclusion of the researchers was that "the preaching task, which (...) usually has the goal of creating changes in personal knowledge and behavior, might not do so, at least in the short term" (264).

[5] I was first introduced to this great hope of a preacher by David Brown, a tutor in Homiletics at the International Baptist Theological Seminary, Prague. Brown's textbook on preaching is *Transformational Preaching: Theory and Practice* (College Station: Virtualbookworm.com, 2003) and is also available in Russian. For an alternative view of the value of consistent and persistent preaching in a local congregation see the work by Michael J. Quicke, currently Professor of Preaching at Northern Seminary, Chicago. *360 Degree Preaching: Hearing, Speaking, and Living the Word* (Grand Rapids: Baker Academic, 2003).

[6] If one was to look for examples to follow, one would find that there are many books of sermons by men and very few of sermons of women. A contemporary collection of such sermons from the United Kingdom is found in Heather Walton and Susan Durber, eds., *Silence in Heaven: A Book of Women's Preaching* (London: SCM Press, 1994).

[7] Unfortunately, I do not remember who exactly came up with the idea of spokes, but I am grateful to all the participants of that meeting for the enthusiastic discussion they facilitated.

[8] For an example of a series of sermons preached in one church struggling with difficult issues see James Wm. McClendon, Jr., *Making Gospel Sense to a Troubled Church* (Cleveland: The Pilgrim Press, 1995).

[9] Lina Andronoviene, "As Songs Turn into Life and Life into Songs," in Keith G. Jones and Parush R. Parushev, eds., *Currents in Baptistic Theology of Worship Today* (Prague: International Baptist Theological Seminary, 2007), 138.

[10] Non-residential Bible School of the Baptist Union of Lithuania http://www.baptist.lt/index.php/en/bible-school.html

[11] *The Fullness of Christ* (Elgin: Brethren Press, 1987).

[12] Harold H Oliver, "The Relational Self," in Leroy S. Rouner, ed., *Selves, People and Persons: What Does It Mean to Be a Self?* (Notre Dame: University of Notre Dame Press, 1992), 48.

[13] Judith Kegan Gardinar, "On Female Identity," in Elizabeth Abel, ed., *Writing and Sexual Difference* (Chicago: University of Chicago Press, 1982),

195, quoted in Thomas H Troeger, "Emerging New Standards in Evaluation of Effective Preaching," in Day et al, *A Reader on Preaching*, 123.

[14] For reflection on the sermon in the context of the full act of worship see Michael H. Taylor, *Variations on a Theme* (London: Galliard, 1973) especially 83 ff.

Chapter 8

Opportunities and Challenges of Contextualization in Baptist Worship in Mexico

Joel Sierra

Three Preliminary Concerns

Of the three preliminary concerns about contextualization, one is the misinterpretation of contextualization as merely the translation of resources. The other two address the true nature of contextualization.

First, contextualization is in fashion. The market uses it to win more consumers around the globe. Even snack foods tend to be "contextualized" by huge transnational companies to ensure their economic domination over indigenous forms and products. Are we talking about the same phenomenon here? Is contextualization of Christian worship only a matter of finding a better way to preserve cultural dominance of the West over the rest of the world? After all, aren't we local partakers of a global faith? Shouldn't we represent such partaking by continuing to use liturgical resources coming from Europe and North America, though translated into the languages of our poor southern nations? Yet, haven't we all been enriched by translated materials coming from all parts of the globe, including the rich West? It all depends on the percentage of material used in worship which comes from outside, and the attitudes with which these translated resources are used.

Second, contextualization of the Gospel is not an accessory element of worship. It is absolutely essential because of theological reasons. God became a human being. The tremendous indiscernible words spoken by the Creator to fill the earth with sprouting life became understandable to humans through a human being who learned to speak a human language. Worship that is not contextualized in language and forms is an outpouring of Gnostic Christology: Somehow our own culture simply cannot be the container of the Word of God. He could not have been a true human being. Yet, we believe that Christ was not merely the product of his culture. He challenged his own and all human cultures as well. Jesus was God-sent though he did not reveal himself apart from a particular cultural context.

Third, the Gospel trespasses all human fences and borders and is able to transform every human culture when the culture of the apostolic instrument does not interfere with the message of the Good News. Contextualization begins with the responsible discernment of the nature of the Gospel, and of the culture of the missionary. It means accepting the Gospel and leaving the cultural wrapping in which it came. The first Christians had to deal with this issue in Acts 15.

The Spiritual Context of Mexico

There are three elements of the spiritual landscape in Mexico which conform a thick and stout religious identity, regardless of denominational or confessional lines. Religious groups (both Roman Catholic and Protestant) share these elements in the composition of their ethos and manifest them according to their particular dogmas. Protestant groups like to think that they are very different from their Roman Catholic counterparts, but a negative identity (i.e. an identity based on the negation of what the other is) like that of Mexican Protestantism is only a derivation of the same fundamental themes that conform a "positive" identity.

The first element is millenary devotion. Mexicans are generally a people of faith, mystery and contact with the spiritual reality. We have been taught that ancient Mexicans were able to perform great cultural feats as a result of their powerful faith. The Protestant reaction to this has been a rejection of what is labeled "superstition." Baptists like to think they are free from such ignorant religious behavior. However, when it comes to whether a woman should or should not be allowed use the pulpit, Mexican Baptists display a great amount of mystery in the value that they give to this piece of furniture. Women are not allowed to preach from the pulpit.

The second one is the experience of historic devastation. Mexican history has been one of conquest, invasion and foreign domination. This has contributed to a sense of fatalism in life. It also has contributed to the pervasive presence of the Lady of Guadalupe in the life of the people. People have experienced God as a mother in the Virgin of Guadalupe. She has offered consolation to a people who have seen their culture totally wiped out, and a sense of identity when everything has been taken from them. Perhaps Baptist rejection of the Virgin is a symptom of an unbalanced approach to God as a Mother. It is a matter of all or nothing. We only have God as a Father who has total control over life, and who tells us to shape up and behave ourselves, to stiffen our lips and keep going without displaying any kind of weakness in our sufferings.

The third element that makes up Mexican religiosity is the way in which Roman Catholicism shapes all of life and society. Even in Protestant groups, the influence of Roman Catholic ways is great. On the one hand, this is manifest in clericalism, the lack of congregational involvement. On the other hand, it is manifest in judgmental tendencies towards congregations which do not conform to the standard of the rest of the group. One church starts trying out a new model for their education programs, and then it is accused of not being Baptist, because they do not use the materials that everyone else uses.

Being Baptist in Mexico

Baptist identity in Mexico could be grouped around two governing issues, one of which is the renunciation of all kinds of superstition, with the adoption of a modern worldview, including freedom of conscience, democracy, and the worth of the individual. The other one is the strongest possible reaction against Roman Catholicism, especially in worship practices. One church removed all crosses from their pews! Lighting a candle in church can be interpreted as an act of idolatry. Most churches do not observe Advent or Lent, and there are some that won't even celebrate Christmas or Easter!

The first Baptists that came to Mexico were already working among Mexicans in the territories that had been taken from Mexico in 1848. They saw their work in Mexico as an extension of their work in the Frontier. For many years, the work in Mexico was administered by the

Home Mission Society of both Southern and American Baptists in the U.S. Being Baptist in Mexico has meant adopting the cultural identity of the ones taking over after winning the Mexican-American war. The evangelization of Mexico was part of one and the same domestic missionary project. It was carried out under the same underlying assumptions: "These people have been conquered and need to be taught how to be good citizens."

The first hymnbooks of Baptists in Mexico contained almost exclusively revivalist hymns of the Frontier translated into Spanish. The last hymnbook published by Baptists in Spanish (1978) has reduced the percentage of revivalist hymns to around 70 percent.

Contextualizing Baptist Worship in Mexico

What would this imply? What are the risks involved? Considering the fact that it is practically impossible to ignore or avoid the Catholic issue, any move seeking to contextualize worship would have to take into consideration some elements present in Roman Catholicism. However, it is generally believed that anything that comes from Catholics is evil. Some people left church when we started a series of sermons on the Apostles' Creed, arguing that it was that which they had left behind when they renounced Catholicism. Anybody trying to contextualize worship and church life in Mexico would have to face criticism and labeling. Using the image of the cross, observing Lent or Advent, praying the Lord's Prayer, these are some of the actions towards contextualization in Mexico which would prompt criticism from other Baptists.

Any initiative towards the healthy contextualization of the Gospel in Mexico has to consider appreciating the rich wealth of spirituality present both in Hispanic tradition as well as in Indian heritage. A careful study of Spanish mysticism, even a respectful assessment of Loyola's contribution to renewal, as well as an attentive weighing of the poems of Nezahualcoyotl, the Nahuatl king of Texcoco, and of the missionary methods and achievements of the friars in sixteenth century New Spain, are all part of a particular "conversion to culture," as Orlando Costas used to say. When we meet Christ, our conversion to him should lead to a series of subsequent conversions. We should be converted to our culture as well, in order to be more efficient missionaries among our people. We are bearers of a message that crosses human boundaries.

Some elements in Mexican culture that may enrich Baptist worship are:

- The system of co/parenting children, the "compadres" coming from infant baptismal practice. Parents select and honor friends to be their "partners in parenting." This creates a special bond of deep friendship which Baptists haven't been able to incorporate into their experience.
- The "tequio," or communal participation in the preparation of a wedding. "Tequio" is the concept of collaboration to make a banquet possible. From weddings, this concept may migrate to other areas of communal life. "Tequio" is commitment with the neighboring community and it is much needed as many churches are viewed as isolated bubbles of people disconnected from their world.
- "Fiesta" in worship. A sense of joyful celebration especially during the Lord's Supper and Baptism, in order to emphasize the wonder of God's grace for our life situations.
- Visual elements and the use of colors in the house of prayer. Lively colors in church can be a reminder of diversity, explosive creativity and the effect of light on all things, just as Jesus is the light of the world and fills all of existence with color.
- The use of symbols in objects and gestures. In weddings, for example, using tokens as a symbol of God's provision and the lasso as a symbol of the sacredness of matrimony.

All of these are Mexican traditions that have been expelled from Baptist practice because they were not part of the culture of the missionary. A careful evaluation must be made in our efforts to contextualize the Baptist experience in Mexico. God has been present in our lands even before the first Baptists came here. This realization is a starting point towards a serious life-long effort of contextualization. Sixty years before the arrival of the Spaniards and their conquest and their missionary enterprise, Nezahualcoyotl wrote poems dedicated to the "Giver of Life" (Ipalnemohuani). He came to startling conclusions regarding the absolute necessity of having a relationship with this Lord, the "Giver of Life." He said:

> *You write with flowers,*
> *Giver of Life,*
> *You colour with songs.*
> *Using songs, You outline those who will live on earth.*
> *Afterwards, You will destroy the eagle and the tiger.*
> *We only live in your book of paintings*
> *Here on earth.*
> *Only there, inside of heaven, You invent your word,*
> *Ipalnemohuani,*
> *Everywhere He is invoked,*
> *Everywhere He is honoured.*
> *His glory is sought after, His fame on earth*
> *He is the One who invents all things, He is the One*
> *who invents himself*
> *God, Moyocoyatzin (The One who invents himself)*
> *The house of the inventor of Himself cannot be anywhere.*
> *He who finds Him only knows this:*
> *He is invoked and only by His side is it possible to live on earth.*
> *Only as if in a field of flowers we were looking for somebody*
> *That is how we look for You.*
> *Those of us who are living here, on earth.*

May our faithful witness of the God incarnate in Jesus Christ help our people find this Giver of Life and stop groping, searching, guessing once and for all, with a faith that is both theirs locally and theirs globally.

The Commission on Christian Ethics

Ross Clifford, Chair

In the 2006-2010 quinquennium, the Commission on Christian Ethics has sought to address ethical issues that are particularly relevant to our life and witness as Baptists in these strategic, global times. The authors of the papers and the other presenters were drawn from all six continents of the world. They represented a variety of backgrounds including scholars, pastors and politicians.

The first meeting of the commission in Mexico City, Mexico, July 4-6, 2006, took time to reflect on a survey the commission had sent to all BWA conventions. The survey requested the conventions to indicate their ethical concerns and, whilst there was not a large response, it was representative and helped the commission shape its future program. Anna Robbins presented her paper on "Methodology in an Era of Globalization." This led to considerable discussion on globalization and interacting with other Christian groups who have similar concerns. A panel discussion then took place on ethical issues in the Mexican context led by Dinorah Mendez. Margarita Parra Benel spoke on ethical problems for women and Senator Maria de los Angeles Moreno Uriegas the ethical issues faced by the Mexican Parliament including corruption, the environment and justice. Other papers presented were Tom Provost, "Justice in Assessing Poverty: Dealing with Systems", William Tillman, Jr., "O That All of God's People Would be Prophets," and Larry Ashlock, "A Biblical Servant-Leader Ethic as a Method for Moral Change." Ross Clifford then presented a case study on the ethical issues facing West Papua and the Indonesian Government.

On July 3-6, 2007, the commission met in Accra, Ghana. Osuwa Ampofo, a Ghanaian Baptist pastor, presented a paper on "Corruption in Ghana." As a result of his paper the commission proposed a resolution on corruption which was passed at the BWA General Council. Other papers presented were Rod Benson, "Corrupting

Technology: An Integrity Check on the Organ Transplant Industry," Surajit Sahu, "Corruption in Medicine: Integrity – Every Christian's Responsibility," and Robert Cochran, "Baptists Creating Change." A panel discussion on corruption in Ghana concluded the commission meetings and the panel featured two Ghanaian church leaders, Fred Deegbe and George S. Mallett.

On July 22-24, 2008, the commission met in Prague, Czech Republic. The commission began with an open forum jointly hosted by the Commission on Baptist Worship and Spirituality. The topic was "Integrity Issues facing Preachers and Presenters of the Gospel" and papers were presented by Michael Quicke and Paul Msiza. The forum broke into small groups for discussion, then Ross Clifford responded from an ethics perspective and Chris Ellis from a worship perspective. The commission then addressed environmental issues and discussion was based on three papers from Bill Tillman, "Ecosystems, Niches, and Other Matters ignored by Baptists," Helle Liht, "Environmental Questions from a Theological Perspective," and David Gushee, "Can a 'Sanctity-of-Life' Ethic Ground Christian Environmentalism?" As a consequence, a resolution on climate change was passed by the BWA General Council. Other papers presented were Louise Kretzschmar, "The Transformation of Persons and the Moral Renewal of Society," Rod Benson, "Sacred Gift or Secular Commodity: Human Rights and Human Trafficking." Robert Cochran presented a paper on the commission's publishing project on case studies, principles, and changes brought in communities and societies.

The last meeting of the commission was held in Ede, Netherlands, July 27-August 1, 2009. The commission began with a discussion on stem cell research which was based on two papers, one from Dennis Sansom, "What Do We Owe to the Embryo? The Ethical Limits to Embryonic Stem Cell Research," and the other from Larry Ashlock, "The Future Ethical Implications of Stem Cell Technology." Bill Tillman presented a paper, "An Historical Evaluation of the Contribution of Baptists to Christian Ethics." Mary Poythress responded with a reflection, "Prominent Baptists – The Importance of Ethics."

There was also a joint forum with the Commission on Freedom and Justice on the issue of climate change. The presenters were Robert Parham and Rod Benson. Less Fussell interviewed three Baptist leaders whose countries have been severely affected by climate change, Ratna Rai Bahadur (Nepal), Maung Maung Yin (Myanmar) and Leor

Sarkar (Bangladesh). The final session addressed the question of same sex relationships and the Church today. This forum attracted a large number of attendees and two papers were presented, one by Ayodele Gbode, "Christian Ethical Response to Same-sex Relationships in the Church and in the Community" and the other by Scott Stearman, "On Racism and Sexism: On the 'Race Analogy' and our Ethical Responses to Sexual Minorities." Richard F. Wilson responded to the two addresses which resulted in considerable discussion.

The commission has been enriched by the high standard of the papers presented and the quality of the discussions.

Chapter 9

An Historical Evaluation of the Contribution of Baptists to Christian Ethics

William M. Tillman, Jr.

In a recent sermon in Logsdon Seminary's chapel, Rick McClatchy noted:

> Baptists at their best have been reforming, not reformed, but reforming. This reforming dynamic surely finds its heart in the typically named Baptist distinctives, particularly in the exercise of religious liberty. Twenty-first century Baptists owe a great deal of gratitude toward those Baptists of other centuries who have engaged in the struggle for the expression of individual conscience before God. Without exception where the struggle resided and engaged, matters of social justice were at stake.[1]

One of McClatchy's key qualifiers is "Baptists at their best." Indeed, those are the points to which we often direct attention. Quite possibly, though, some of us have developed a distorted, overestimated perception of Baptist contributions to cultural debate and dialogue. Certainly some Baptists have engaged a given cultural and theological context, a call which others undoubtedly sensed but to which they did not respond. These who responded must be identified as prophetic and Baptists at their best. I consider the term prophetic to be appropriate to their actions.

Though the prophet can be known for her or his foretelling abilities, other more important traits also mark prophets. Prophets are those who project tones of countercultural engagement, admonish failures in lifestyles expected by God – by individuals and by institutions –

and consistently apply the saying, "Thus saith the Lord." Prophets do not follow the logic of the power brokers of society or the egocentrists who try to pull all the best and most resources to their side of the table. Prophets are those who, according to Walter Brueggemann, identify the parts of the culture over which grief should be expended; give a call to follow the way of holiness, justice, mercy, and freedom; remind their hearers of the deep history of God who has walked among human beings for millennia; and jar the theological-ethical amnesia which can be pandemic among humanity.[2]

Have these historical Baptists left models for current Baptists not only to recognize but also to assimilate and perpetuate? How does one make such an evaluation, though, especially with regard to Christian ethics specifically since such an enterprise was not included as a theological discipline until the 20th century? Thus, some of the evaluation is a filtering with more contemporary gradients and characteristics over against centuries-old actions. In the United States we have a phrase which encapsulates the idea; that is, "comparing apples with oranges."

For me, however, I have come to the conclusion that the matter of religious liberty as defined by Baptists historically lies at the base of Christian ethics. The matter of individual conscience before God constitutes the essence of faith and life practice, of decision making, of extending the sense of Christian values and virtues beyond one's individual parameters. Religious liberty for individuals provides the basis for separation of church and state which takes values questions to the infrastructural level; thus, social Christian ethics can be filtered as well with the religious liberty qualifier.

Those early practitioners and proponents of religious liberty give reason for me to include other markers for Christian ethics, however. These are: biblical and theological soundness and balance; readiness to counter dominant cultural paradigms; inclusiveness of the marginalized and being globally minded.[4] In addition, you will recognize I have attempted to employ the following major modes of examination to arrive at Baptist Christian ethics considerations: personalities, theological themes, social issues, eras (even epochs), movements, and cultural milieus. The endeavor at hand demonstrates a blend of these approaches. As well, I have to provide this qualifier.

From the beginning, this presentation is heavily laced with opinion, which can carry speculative, conjectural dimensions, even prejudicial but hopefully not pejorative dimensions. I guarantee that some facets of Baptist life, globally and historically, have been overlooked. However, what follows is an evaluative look at the past with a view to possible ways of understanding Christian ethical responsibility through Baptist lenses today.

Baptist, Christian Ethics in Quick Retrospect

The prophetic voice has permeated the global Baptist experience for four centuries. Here are a few representative Baptist prophets whose death dates range from 1616 to 2008: Thomas Helwys, John Clarke, William Carey, John Leland, Johann Gerhard Oncken, Lottie Moon, Walter Rauschenbusch, Helen Barrett Montgomery, Nannie Helen Burroughs, Martin Luther King, Jr., Clarence Jordan, T. B. Maston, Henlee Barnette, Foy Valentine, James McClendon,[4] Muriel Lester, C. Anne Davis, Stanley Grenz, and Millard Fuller. [5] Others, still alive, are J. Deotis Roberts, Jimmy Carter, Tony Campolo, Ron Sider, James Dunn, Jimmy Allen, Glenn Stassen, and persons on the Commission on Christian Ethics of the BWA.[6]

Represented in this listing are males and females, black and white, American and European persons. These persons delivered their Baptist, ethical perspectives through being pastors, missionaries, teachers, laity, and denominational infrastructural spokespersons. I would be remiss if I did not give attention to some of those themes which do stand out as having been addressed by Baptists: human rights, women and society and the church, peacemaking, bioethics, AIDS, and environmental ethics. Cultural issues of family and sexuality, public policy, missions, economics, race issues, and a myriad of sub themes of these larger areas have been addressed by these characters mentioned and others not listed.[7]

Contemporary Baptists will note a Western-centrism is explicit in the listings. One of the disappointments I discovered in preparing this presentation is that few engagements have been made toward recognizing the Baptist Christian ethics work projected from the Majority World cultures. The Baptist World Alliance has provided some tracking possibilities with the formation of the six continental unions or regional fellowships making up the BWA. These are: Asia Pacific Baptist Federation, All Africa Baptist Fellowship, Caribbean Baptist Fellowship, European Baptist Federation, North American

Baptist Fellowship, and Union of Baptists in Latin America. Though Baptist work has been around for decades, even centuries, in parts of the world besides Europe and the United States, relatively little information has been provided for evaluation of the Baptist Christian ethics dimensions of those fellowships besides the North American Baptist Fellowship and European Baptist Fellowship. [8]

Why this lack of information? Perhaps it has been the heavy influence of the European and American Baptist groups setting the agenda and writing the histories. Perhaps in these other than Euro-American fellowships more emphasis has been given to evangelism, missions, and church planting, without the accompanying emphases on living the Christian life, individually and corporately. In the flow of missions and evangelism attempted, history does demonstrate the early generations of a group of Baptist Christians are not always able to obtain some authenticity in proclaiming the ethical import of the Gospel.

Thus, cultural and historical contextualization have impact on the extension of Baptist Christian ethics. Certainly in some portions of the world, for instance among the Africans, life circumstances are such that matters beyond survival cannot be addressed. As one has to deal with wars, all sorts of economic and political upheaval, hunger, AIDS, and resistance from other theological persuasions, little time and energy is left to do the kind of reflection that would provide those in the Western world analyses from those cultures.

To What Have We Come, Though – and Why?

Ironically, another challenge for analysis and development of Baptist Christian ethics is the reality that in the European and American cultures, Baptist ethics has entered a period of decline. There are some reasons which can be put forward.

We can review the Baptist heroes and heroines, consider their cultural contexts, and reflect on the models they developed or recognized to be evolving as ways to interface with their cultures. These types need to be put forward more often and with more vital, illustrative power. Too often, however, these characters have been related in ways to ask theological education students and lay people to consider these personalities akin to those who allegedly occupied Mount Olympus. All the stuff of humanity has been mashed out of them. Contemporary

Baptists can scarcely find empathy with those historical personalities as they are illustrated as bigger than life or their cultural context apparently is so different as to be unable to find correlation with our own. Perhaps the failure to develop correlative contextual appeal along with an apparent generational divide which dismisses historical reference points has contributed to a continuing lack of attention to the Baptist forebears and their modalities, typologies, and methodologies.

Ernst Troeltsch in his classic work, *The Social Teachings of the Christian Churches,* categorized Baptists in their early days as part of the sect genre.[9] This identification was posed over against those other frameworks we would recognize as denominational which he called "church." In the Western culture expressions of Baptists, a shift began early on for movement from sect to church. This shift apparently is something of a product of cultural adaptation and assimilation.[10] The movement toward cultural adaptation carried the Baptists from a counter culture movement to a cultural accomodationist perspective, a position which is less prophetic in nature than the former.

James McClendon maintained Baptists have lacked a deep and broad Christian ethics emphasis. His point was:

> Baptists have produced little theology and by definition little ethics. Why? The truth, I believe, is this: The baptists in all their variety and disunity failed to see in their own heritage, their own way of using Scripture, their own communal practices and patterns, *their own guiding vision,* a resource for theology unlike the prevailing scholasticism round about them.[11]

Not the least of how we have to come to where we are is the matter of the continuous stream of Baptist controversies; for controversies have marked Baptists from the beginning. We cannot forget Helwys and Smyth's split over doctrinal disagreements. Just as Christian ethics inroads might be made, a conflictual context ensued. The energy spent on the controversies inevitably drained the frameworks' ethical emphases. Something of a dilution happened as generations of successors to Helwys and Smyth followed contorted and perverted dimensions of the progenitors' emphases. So, the strand of those who would articulate religious liberty for all began to move into the minority.

Irony resides in this discussion if one uses the Southern Baptist Convention (SBC) as a case study. From this organization developed the most widespread mission enterprise known to Christian history.[12] Some individuals at this meeting are here because a SBC missionary made an impact in their culture years ago. However, all the rationale for limitations of contributions of Christian ethics I have just reviewed can be seen in the overall history of the SBC. Several years ago, as he and his wife, Heather, visited one of my classes at Southwestern Seminary, Dr. Noel Vose responded to a student's question of the impact of the controversies issuing from the SBC. Dr. Vose, replied, "When the SBC sneezes, the rest of the Baptist world catches the flu." Indeed, the controversies, for example, got transported from the United States to the utter most reaches of the mission board's appointees.

More specifically, observers of the SBC saw an interesting pattern: the rise, and then paradoxically what could be called the decline and fall of social ethics arms of the denomination, at the national and state convention levels. These agencies were a platform for addressing public issues. Because of the platform, people like Foy Valentine, Jimmy Allen, James Dunn, and Phil Strickland were able to articulate Baptist, Christian perspectives beyond their immediate contexts.[13] Nearly all those agencies are gone now because of divisions among the respective Baptist conventions. The fact that fewer professors of Christian ethics operate in Baptist schools is the result of fewer doctoral programs to produce the next generation of teachers and pastors with Christian ethics emphases.

Looking toward the Future: Some Needs for Baptist Contributions in Christian Ethics

Understanding what we have come to as Baptist, Christian ethicists can be recognized from retrospection. We can look over our shoulders, perhaps wag our heads in dismay of the points lacking, or even stick out our chests and draw ourselves to our full height for some of the high points. All that is well and good, but what about the future? I consider what we have as time and opportunity as points of stewardship, even calling from God, to be about the business of conveying Baptist, Christian Ethics for now and the future. We can project life into the future as well as we can look at where life and culture are headed; then, come back to our present and try to recognize how we can move more positively into that future. I put forward for your consideration ideas developing from both an historical review and future projections.

First, those Baptists who have operated from a majoritarian position taught us an assumption we must get past. That is, we cannot assume Baptists at large or anyone beyond catch the idea of Baptist distinctives. In the United States, for example, the priesthood of the believer emphasis must continually be articulated to combat the implicit and explicit individualism in the American culture. This individualism also works against the formation of *Koinonia* among a collection of priests, or the churches. With an ecclesially-based theology and ethics, Baptists should be able to understand systems, institutions, and networks for coalitions on common causes. Unfortunately the opposite has happened with a xenophic isolationism developing which precludes relevance and cultural engagement.

Second, we need to build off the spirit of risk explicit in the early Baptists. Smyth and Helwys moved outside their national culture and into Amsterdam. They moved from a regimentation to a level of not just tolerance but acceptance which is nearly breathtaking to behold. The Dutch were at the height of their Golden Era.[14] The freeing dynamics of the Renaissance, the Reformation, and the Enlightenment found incarnation in Amsterdam. Smyth and Helwys sought out this setting for practicing their faith. Further demonstrating the willingess to take risk was Helwys' determination not only to return to the furnace of state-established religion but to take on the king who had authorized the production of Scripture for the populace.

Third, move from being obsessed with single issue address and explanations. This propensity to "issuism" has stunted the overall process related to Baptist, Christian ethics. For instance, we must recognize the interface and interdependence of what we call issues. Any which could be raised carry facets of money, sex, and power and in different, relative proportions. Matters of personal morality have been emphasized to the detriment of recognizing the points of address needed toward respective cultural infrastructures.

Abortion and homosexuality, for example, have become hot button issues in recent decades in the United States. Typically, more heat than light has been shed upon these concerns. Reflections of cultural perspectives and strategies are found among Baptists in regard to both these matters, with extreme comments taking the limelight and most Baptists finding themselves in a kind of middle majority, quietly pondering but not knowing quite what or how to think or say or do on these matters. Interestingly those who oppose abortion so vehemently often have been those who are ready to go to war or impose capital punishment. This arrangement should cause us to think more in terms of working upon understanding and implementing what can be called a consistent ethic of life. Homosexuality typically in the United States is still met by rejection. Cultural observers note, however, that the current generation of students, for instance, is less apt to be negative; that, quite probably there will be movement toward more acceptability of homosexuals particularly in the economic realms of benefits for partners in civil unions. At the least, too, the debate upon homosexuality should have deepened our conversations and actions regarding gender, societal roles, and vocational pursuits. So, with regard to an issues approach, what can be addressed? What strategies and tactics are culturally appropriate?

Fourth, continue development toward the process of recognizing the need of Christian ethics emphases educationally, at whatever levels needed. A constant struggle over the last century or more among Baptists in the United States is how much theological education is acceptable. We have perverted the priesthood of the believer concept in such ways so as to give grounds for lots of people to detract from the pursuit of education. Much gets made of the expansion of Baptist thought among those who were in the lower economic classes.[15] The earliest Baptists demonstrated some traits of which we could have more, though. As I said in another place, "The First Baptists, it took more than half a mind to be one." These people were products of the Enlightenment, with emphasis on the power of the mind. Those early Baptists to whom we pay homage, like Helwys and Smyth, and John Clarke, who is given credit for establishing the first Baptist church in the young, American colonies, were educated persons. They found ways to extend their educated premises even to those who were uneducated. Charges of elitism will no doubt be made, but I more and more agree with the comment allegedly made by W. T. Conner, the first theology professor of Southwestern Seminary, that the Holy Spirit has affinity for a trained mind.

Fifth, my point with regard to education overlays with my suggestion with regard to Scripture. Some of our most challenging work as Christian ethicists is keeping Scripture in front of our constituencies. The "battle for the Bible" cry lay at the heart of the controversy among

Baptists in the last 25-30 years. Much of what was put forward is that some of the priesthood of believers decided they should be higher priests. Their interpretations of Scripture were the matters actually in the conflict. Unfortunately, human beings want to move to the lowest common denominator, be reductionists, and a concession occurred which nearly took the Bible out of the mainstream of Baptists. Therefore, what I am calling for is that we have actual conversations with Scripture, and not just buy into a propositional approach, which perpetuates biblical illiteracy and quick non-resolutionary answers to complex social "multi-limmas."

Sixth, renew the vision of being global Christians. Recognize that Baptists developed as essentially a Western culture phenomenon carrying those cultural paradigms. The Modern Mission Movement kept evolving, or maybe de-evolving, until the dynamic expressed could be labeled as imperialistic, however. Real questions need to be asked as to whether what has been exported at times has been more the American worldview or a biblically saturated outreach. The Majority World cultures sense these dynamics which too many Westerners have employed blindly. Where Western culture is heavily influenced by the more left brained Hellenistic world view, Majority World cultures are more intuitive in their expression of spirituality and theology. [16]

One of my conclusions in this evaluative overview is that all of us Baptists carry our own provincialisms. Western Baptists need to look up and out and find new ways to communicate with those of the other sectors of this planet. Those representing the other than Western Baptist fellowships should be bold and establish relationships further with the Western Baptists. We need each other. I call this the need to expand intra-faith dialogue. From my perspective, the BWA carries the most legitimate and far reaching global vision of any Baptist organization. We must not only celebrate that reality but continue to find avenues and venues by which the BWA can be a catalyst for further Baptist expansion but also interfaith dialogue in those cultures which are decidedly other than Christian. [17]

Seventh, find ways to demonstrate the natural interface of spiritual formation, evangelism, and ethics. These interfacings should reflect further consideration of the central place of worship, individually and corporately, for Baptists' theological and ethical development. Further, hardly any analysis at all has been done with regard to the power of music to shape theological and ethical reflection and action, though

I would maintain that in many Baptist churches in the United States more theological impact comes from the music than the sermons. Unfortunately hymnody and other Christian music/lyrics, for example, have been marked more by overly devotional, pietistic texts with little call to action toward personal and social transformation. The need has been there for decades for the theologians, and especially the ethicists, to influence the composition of lyrics and tunes.[18]

Eighth, conflict has been perennial with Baptists. Even Smyth and Helwys could not stay in agreement. Baptists could do a world of good, for themselves, and beyond with more emphasis toward conflict management. Not too many Baptists, including the ethicists, have articulated that conflict mediation lies at the core of Christian ethics. Different value packages struggle for a place. The address of these struggles may be identified as dealing with issues. The issue areas, though, are merely the arena through which conflict circulates. Developing more creative ways to deal with conflict must come along with further consideration of a theology of power. These two points of lacking: conflict management and theology of power lie at the heart of the longstanding struggle in the United States among Baptists.

Ninth, be wary of fundamentalistic approaches to living the Christian life. The marks of Fundamentalists' ethical systems are black and white analyses and responses, overly authoritarian implementations, hierarchical systems, creedal orientation, and belligerency unbefitting a Christian. I will be quick to note that Baptists need to be wary of both Left Wing and Right Wing Fundamentalism. The Right Wing version has been a constant detractor in the pursuit of Baptist, Christian ethics in the United States. Kirby Godsey, the former president of Mercer University, called such Fundamentalism "a fraudulent form of faith...barbaric and uncivilized, replacing creativity with control and manipulation...diminishing our higher calling to love mercy and to do justice, and places the progress of human creation in peril." [19] I agree with Godsey's assessment. Fundamentalism whether from the Left or the Right has a way of eviscerating real Baptist orientation.

Conclusion

Involving myself in the research, analysis, interpretation, and now presentation of this paper has pressed upon me the matter that we must pursue further research, analysis, review, interpretation, and application of Baptist Christian ethics. For me, there is certainly the interest in developing this paper into a broader, deeper treatment. I hope I have conveyed some of the dynamics involved so you have caught some of the same motivation. I do think through the auspices of this specific BWA commission that we have unique opportunities to build in the directions suggested here.

Some of my plea with this presentation is more of us Baptists need to move above being incurious about this heritage of ideas and personalities and not only recognize their distinctive contributions but also find interface with their vision and methodologies. Indeed, these Baptists have demonstrated what it means to be a Baptist in ways which we too rarely know and even more rarely see practiced. Their very lives are a calling to us to move into the future with the theology and ethics they applied.

NOTES

[1] Rick McClatchy, Logsdon School of Theology chapel sermon, "The Baptist Message: Ongoing Reform." October 3, 2008, Abilene. McClatchy is the coordinator of the Cooperative Baptist Fellowship of Texas.

[2] See especially Brueggeman's *The Prophetic Imagination* (Minneapolis: Fortress Press, 2001, rev. ed.), and *Hopeful Imagination: Prophetic Voices in Exile* (Philadelphia: Fortress Press, 1986). This paragraph is drawn from my *Baptist Prophets: Their Lives and Contributions* (Brentwood, TN: Baptist History and Heritage Society, 2006), 3.

[3] Gerald L. Keown, in "The Prophet as Encourager," *Perspectives in Religious Studies*. vol. 35, Number 2, Summer 2008, 155 notes how we can be caught by the words and actions of prophets for their " ... powerful, magnetic quality. There is something about the courageous individual who is willing to stand against power on behalf of the weak and marginalized that demands our attention." Such were the words and actions of Baptists in history – prophetic in the terms we usually understand them; but, their words and actions demonstrated, as well, an element of being prophetic not usually noticed, but which may be most important to us – their sense of encouragement. Somehow, they recognized that what they were about was bigger than themselves and required the talents and energies of others still to come after them.

[4] For the application and interpretation of these categories, see William M. Tillman, Jr. and W. Andrew Tillman, *"Martin, Maston, and Millard: 3 M Baptists,"* A breakout session at the Baptist History and Heritage Society

Annual Meeting, *"Baptist Contributions, 1609-2009,"* First Baptist Church, Huntsville, Alabama, June 5, 2009.

[5] One of McClendon's publications demonstrates the value of using a biographical approach to discovering ethical paradigms. See his *Biography as Theology* (Philadelphia, P A: Trinity Press International, 1974).

[6] These latter Baptists named are, at the time of this paper, alive and still contributing to the Baptist, ethical conversation.

[7] See a historical narrative of the Baptist story in Michael E. Williams, Sr. and Walter B. Shurden, eds. *Turning Points in Baptist History: A Festschrift in Honor of Harry Leon McBeth* (Macon, GA: Mercer University Press, 2008) which demonstrates the theological-ethical turning points of Baptists. Other, recent publications demonstrating the impact of these persons are William Brackney's *Baptists in North America: An Historical Perspective* (Malden, MA: Blackwell Publishing, 2006) and *A Capsule History of Baptist Principles* (Atlanta, Georgia: Baptist History and Heritage Society, 2009); William M. Pinson, Jr. *Baptists and Religious Liberty* (Dallas, Texas: BaptistWay Press, 2007); Pamela R. Durso and Keith E. Durso, *The Story of Baptists in the United States* (Brentwood, Tennessee: Baptists History and Heritage Society, 2006). A standard reference for decades has been Robert G. Torbet, *A History of the Baptists* (Valley Forge, PA: Judson Press, 1973) which has been ably complemented by H. Leon McBeth, *The Baptist Heritage: Four Centuries of Baptist Witness* (Nashville, Tennessee: Broadman Press, 1987). See as well, James Leo Garrett, *Baptist Theology: A Four-Century Study* (Macon, Georgia: Mercer University Press, 2009); Douglas Weaver, *In Search of the New Testament Church: The Baptist Story* (Macon, Georgia: Mercer University Press, 2008). Review the *Baptist History and Heritage Journal* for relatively short, but well researched articles on personalities, themes, and movements. Certainly anything by Bill Leonard for specifically American perspectives, for example: Bill J. Leonard, Editor, *Dictionary of Baptists in America* (Downers Grove, Illinois: InterVarsity Press, 1994). Also, see Charles W. Deweese, Editor, *Defining Baptists Convictions: Guidelines for the Twenty-First Century* (Franklin, Tennessee: Providence House Publishers, 1996).

[8] Sections in Torbet, McBeth, Garrett, and Weaver allude to other than western Baptist ethics and ethicists. Latin American Baptist ethics has received perhaps more attention than any of the BWA Fellowships. See Jorge Pixley, "Baptists and liberation theology: Mexico, Central America, and the Caribbean," *Baptist History and Heritage*, January 1, 2000; Pablo Moreno, "Baptists and liberation theology in South American," *Baptist History and Heritage*, January 1, 2000; possibly the most extensive treatment of Latin American Baptists is Justice C. Anderson, *An Evangelical Saga: Baptists and Their Precursors in Latin America* (Xulon Press, 2005). A particularly helpful direction of the BWA is the study underway gathering case studies of social change throughout the

world. See Robert D. Cochran, "Baptists Creating Social Change – Studying Contemporary Efforts Worldwide," a breakout session at the Baptist History and Heritage Society Annual Meeting, "Baptist Contributions, 1609-2009," First Baptist Church, Huntsville, Alabama, June 5, 2009.

[9] Ernst Troeltsch, *The Social Teaching of the Christian Churches*, Vol. II (New York: Harper & Brothers, 1960), 691-711.

[10] Two resources which illustrate this adaptation and assimilation process are Rufus Spain, *At Ease in Zion: A Social History of Southern Baptists. 1865-1900* (Nashville, TN: Vanderbilt University Press, 1967) and John Lee Eighmy, *Churches in Cultural Captivity: A History of the Social Attitudes of Southern Baptists* (Knoxville, TN: The University of Tennessee Press, 1987, rev. ed)

[11] James Wm. McClendon, Jr. *Ethics: Systematic Theology*. Volume 1 (Nashville, TN: Abingdon Press, 1986), 26.

[12] See William R. Estep, *Whole Gospel. Whole World: The Foreign Mission Board of the Southern Baptist Convention. 1845-1995* (Nashville, Tennessee: Broadman & Holman Publishers, 1994).

[13] William M. Tillman, Jr. and W. Andrew Tillman, "The Rise, Decline, and all of Christian Life Commission Entities and Voices," *Baptist History and Heritage* Vol. XLI, Summer/Fall 2006, No. 3:21-22. Another treatment demonstrating the evolution of Southern Baptist perspectives in America is Paul A. Basden, ed., *Has Our Theology Changed? Southern Baptist Thought Since 1845* (Nashville, Tennessee: Broadman & Holman Publishers, 1994).

[14] See a most interesting perspective regarding the Dutch culture of this era, Timothy Brook, *Vermeer's Hat: The Seventeenth Century and the Dawn of the Global World* (New York, New York: Bloomsbury Press, 2008).

[15] See Carol Crawford Holcomb, "Tinkers and Poormen: Baptists and Grassroots Religion 1609-2009," Presidential address, Baptist History and Heritage Society Meeting, First Baptist Church, Huntsville, Alabama, June 3, 2009.

[16] An oft referenced resource is Philip Jenkins' trilogy developed over the last decade regarding Christianity's place in the world. He maintains, for instance, that by 2050, only one Christian in five will be a non-Latino, white person and the center of gravity for Christianity will shift to the Southern Hemisphere. See his books: *The Next Christendom: The Coming of Global Christianity* (New York, New York: Oxford University Press, 2002); *The New Faces of Christianity: Believing the Bible in the Global South* (New York, New York: Oxford University Press, 2006); *God's Continent: Christianity, Islam, and Europe's Religious Crisis* (New York, New York: Oxford University Press, 2007). There are not many publications on pneumatology by many Baptists. Such realization should strike us paradoxically as one recognizes the Spirit figure of the Trinity is the one who seems most to do with ethics as articulated by Jesus and Paul, for example.

[17] Common ground can be found for dialogue with other religious expressions. Almost without exception, spiritual exploration finds conversation around ethics and ethical systems. The humanum or well being of humanity carries through these world religion systems. One example of this conversation is Robert P. Sellers, "What Baptist Traditions Teach Us About Loving Our Neighbors," Muslim-Baptist Dialogue, Andover-Newton, Boston, Massachusetts, January 2009. An excellent overview of the work of the BWA comes in Richard V. Pierard, General Editor; Elna Jean Young Bentley and Gerald L. Borchert, Associate Editors, *Baptists Together in Christ 1905-2005: A Hundred-year History of the Baptist World Alliance* (Falls Church, Virginia: Baptist World Alliance, 2005).

[18] Music--Worship services at The General Assembly of the Cooperative Baptist Fellowship which met July 2-3, 2009, in Houston, Texas made one of the better good faith attempts of which I have been a part in some time of addressing the global variety of worship music. Songs from Latin America and Africa were particularly noteworthy, along with what can be called traditional American spirituals. See 2009 General Assembly Guide, "*Embrace the World: Welcome to Your Neighborhood*," (Atlanta, GA: Cooperative Baptist Fellowship, 2009), 18, 23, 24-27.

[19] Dr. R. Kirby Godsey, "Re-centering the Church and Its Ministry," an address delivered at the Mercer Consultation on Preaching, St. Simons Island, Georgia, September 28, 2003.

Chapter 10

What Do We Owe The Embryo? The Ethical Limits to Embryonic Stem Cell Research

Dennis L. Sansom

Introduction

I want to show that because the embryo, whether *in vitro* or *in utero*, is a human, we owe it enough respect not to create it or interrupt its natural growth so to destroy it for its stem cells. To make this case, I will argue that the embryo is human and has a moral status.[1]

Up to 2007, the issue had been between beneficence for human wellbeing and the dignity of the embryo. We had to choose among four options:

A. The actual beneficence of using stem cells for medical therapies versus the actual moral worth of the embryo (i.e., inherent dignity);
B. the potential beneficence of using stem cells versus the actual moral worth of the embryo;
C. the actual beneficence versus the potential dignity of the embryo; and
D. the potential beneficence versus the potential dignity of the embryo.

However, we no longer have these four options. Two facts have changed the considerations. First, as of today, there has not been a successful therapeutic use of an embryonic cell from a zygote or embryo. Though US President Obama recently expanded the use of federal research money, 100's of millions of dollars have already gone into this research in the US alone.[2] Researchers have encountered two major problems – first, the body (of research mice) usually rejects the stem cells and, second, the stem cells tend to form tumors, some becoming cancerous. Thus embryonic stem cells have not proven to be actually beneficial for medical therapies, though they may in the future.

Second, new technology, called de-differentiation, programs cells to reverse the development back to the embryo-like stem cells without creating an embryo.[3] Dedifferentiation develops a stem cell as though it had come from an embryo. These cells are autologous, that is, from a person's own DNA, and possibly can bypass the rejection issue. Yet, it is not determined whether they will turn into tumors. If de-differentiated stem cells prove successful, then we can achieve beneficial therapies without destroying embryos to obtain their stem cells. The previous issue of either we are for using stem cells for human wellbeing or we should respect the dignity of the embryo is not as pressing as it was before 2007. We can respect the embryo's dignity and also promote embryo-like stem cell therapies.

Some people still believe we should pursue traditional embryonic stem cell research because of the potential therapeutic benefits. We may be able to solve the two problems in the future and establish successful therapies. If that is the case, then we are left with two of the above choices - B and D.

Someone could say we have another choice – the embryo is not human at all, and thus we should pursue beneficial therapies regardless of the damage done to the embryo. However, this choice does not recognize a clear point. Since a normal zygote has the organic capability of developing into an embryo and the embryo into a fetus and the fetus into a newborn human, we must say that the zygote is a potential person. We assume it is human because we want its human stem cells for human therapies. Hence the choice is whether the zygote or embryo is a potential human or an actual human, which would consequently be owed some level of moral respect.

I want to argue that the distinction between a potential human and actual human worthy of being treated with human dignity is not really all that clear. In fact, I will try to show that it is a distinction that really does not make an ethical difference for us, because we have a certain duty that is the same owed to a potential as to an actual human.

The Distinction between a Potential and Actual Human Being

James C. Patterson contends that because the pre-implanted embryo lacks a clear moral status, we should use its stem cells to develop therapies. "How can we let patients who are unmistakably people die to protect embryos that, even if implanted, may or may not turn out to someday become persons?"[4] He feels that it is intuitionally evident that the embryo lacks such a moral status and uses a thought experiment borrowed from George Annas to make this point. "If a fire broke out in a fertility lab and there was only time to save a visiting two-month-old baby in a bassinet or a test tube rack containing seven embryos, most people would save the baby without hesitation."[5] For Patterson, this scenario indicates that we see a clear distinction between an embryo, which is potentially human and a baby, which we know is actually human. In fact, he reasons that there is not a fundamental difference between an embryo and a human cell, because both are potentially human in that each has the necessary DNA instructions to become a human.

However, Patterson's argument is counterintuitive to what we know to be the difference between human cells and a human embryo. Consider another thought experiment. Suppose a fire breaks out in a fertility clinic, and we had the chance to save a rack of human embryos and a rack of skin cells. We should naturally save the rack of human embryos because we know there is a fundamental difference between an embryo and a typical cell. It may be possible through somatic cell nuclear transfer and cloning to engineer an embryo from a skin cell, but the skin cell on its own is not potentially a human embryo, whereas we know the embryo (whether pre-implanted or implanted) is already human and is thus a potential fetus, and a potential newborn. Thus, it is confusing to claim there is no real difference between a skin cell and an embryo.

I believe Brent Waters is closer to understanding the real choice over the moral status of the embryo when he says, "The most troubling aspect of the rhetoric employed by both camps, however, has been their misdirection over what is purportedly the principal object of their dispute, namely, that the human embryo is surely something more than a speck of cells but that it is also clearly something less than a child. It is precisely by entering this ambiguous stage of human life to deliberate on the moral status of the embryo that would transform the current exercise of political maneuvering into a public debate."[6] Waters' recognition highlights the obvious point that we do not treat an embryo in the same way we do a newborn, toddler, adolescent, teenager, young adult, middle-aged adult or senior adult. Each stage of human development has requisite duties owed it relative to the level of physical and social maturation. For instance, we allow adults to vote and drive but not toddlers, and this distinction does not violate the basic duties we owe toddlers. Also, we typically give family inheritance rights to infants and not to embryos, and we do not see this difference as a denial of the embryo's humanity. Thus, I think it is consistent with our basic intuitions to treat the embryo not as just a clump of cells but as a human that is potentially a fetus, infant, toddler, so on.

There are other ethicists who argue that though the zygote (i.e., the pre-implanted embryo) has the genetic distinctiveness of a human, we should still not call the zygote a human. D. Gareth Jones maintains, "Within a laboratory environment, blastocysts are 'potentially totipotent' rather than 'actually totipotent'. In this they stand in stark contrast to their counterparts within a woman's body .... In neither case is there an opportunity for these blastocysts to give rise to new individuals; their future life-giving role is nonexistent. There is no intention that they should do so, while their laboratory environment ensures they will not do so."[7] To Jones, the embryo *in vitro* lacks the necessary environment to become human, and hence we can extract its stem cells. If successful, we "glorify God and enhance the lives of human beings. As long as the aim of therapy is the alleviation of human illness, it has the potential to elevate God's images."[8] Jones may be right about what we potentially can do with embryonic stem cells, but he is wrong about his assessment of the status of the pre-implanted embryo.

His major premise is that the pre-implanted embryo cannot mature into a full embryo and consequently a fetus, and so on, because the environment will not provide the necessary conditions for such maturity. The point is that a pertinent environment is needed for an embryo to mature to the next stage. This point could also be applied to the implanted embryo that could not mature because of some problem in the uterine environment. If the umbilical cord does not form from the mother's uterine wall, then the embryo will not mature. If the mother cannot provide nutrients through the cord, then the embryo will die. The environment of the pre-implanted embryo in a petri dish may be enough to sustain its life but it is not enough to allow it to mature. The same could be said about the implanted embryo. Environmental changes are necessary for the embryo to mature. Thus, if we maintain that the implanted embryo is human because it is in an environment in which it can mature into the next stage if the new environment matures with it, then, by the same reasoning, we should say that the pre-implanted embryo kept alive *in vitro* is also human.

Another group of ethicists argue that since the pre-implanted embryo does not have the necessary relationship with the mother that it is not wrong to destroy it for its stem cells. Ted Peters, Karen Lebacqz, and Gaymon Bennett make this argument.[9] They maintain that much of the resistance to embryonic stem cell research rests on a fundamental mistake – substance dualism. This view maintains that God gives the soul to the body at conception and hence it should be respected as having inherent dignity and consequently should not be destroyed for its stem cells.

However, they believe this dualism lacks clear philosophical and biblical support, because it fails to acknowledge that human essence depends on a relationship with God, not on an immortal substance given at the point of ensoulment. Rather, human essence results from relationships with God and others. They then conclude, "The random fertilization and flushing of ova within a women's body does [sic] not qualify as such a relationship; nor does the appearance in a petri dish of a zygote produced either by *in vitro* fertilization (IVF) or sematic [sic] cell nuclear transfer (SCNT) qualify. What counts is the day a woman realizes that living within her body is the seed of a new life, a new life that she (and her partner) will welcome into this world, a nascent person whom the angels will ferry into everlasting life with God."[10] In this view, God forms a relationship with the embryo through the mother's acknowledgement that she is a mother. They furthermore reason that since personal identity forms only after the possible twinning of the embryo occurs and with the development of a primitive cerebral streak, it makes sense to say the soul forms around day fourteen of conception. "When this relationship between a mother and future individual child is established, to think of the possibility of personhood and the prospect of a future destiny with God makes sense."[11] They thus maintain human identity is relational, derived from the parents and God.

Peters et al. correctly maintain that human identity is not an abstract reality unrelated to people's necessary relationships to other persons and God. We are not just humans, but children of parents and parents of children and ultimately children of God. However, this view has several major problems. First, the view implies that God's relationship with the embryo depends on the mother establishing a relationship with the embryo. It is right to say that the embryo is a child only in the sense that it has a mother, but we could just as well reason that in God's omniscient, providential care, God establishes a parental relationship with the embryo before the mother acknowledges she is carrying her baby. In fact, there is biblical support for such a notion in the various passages where God gives a child to a woman.[12] Our human identity arises from the relationships that cause us to become a human, and, inferentially, we could reason that God creates our childhood before the woman recognizes or acknowledges that she bears a child.

Second, the Peters et al. view emphasizes only the external aspects of the necessary relationships and ignores the internal aspect. This distinction between external and internal is important for understanding what makes a human relationship possible. The external aspect refers to the necessary environment for maturation. The internal aspect refers to the organic reality of the embryo. It would not make any sense to maintain that whatever the woman defines as a child indeed would be a child. For instance, a tumor or clump of cells would never be called a child *in utero*. There has to be something unique about the embryo before the woman can acknowledge it as her child. What is this unique quality of the embryo that compels us to call it a human embryo? Robert P. George and Christopher Tollefsen give insights into this unique quality.[13] They contend, "from the zygote stage forward the major development of this organism is controlled and directed from within, that is, by the organism itself."[14] They base this claim on the following facts (below is a brief summary of their complicated analysis of embryology):

1. Although the sperm and egg have the DNA of a biologically whole person, they cannot grow into different forms; their nature is haploid, whereas the zygote is diploid, which enables it to grow;

2. the zygote at fertilization is genetically distinct from the parents in that its DNA and twenty-three pairs of

chromosomes are unique and that the DNA of the sperm and egg break up in the act of fertilization;

3. a unique individual arises when there is a single, unified, and self-integrated biological system; this occurs at syngamy – the lining up of the twenty-three pairs of chromosomes;

4. implantation enables the embryo to receive oxygen and nutrition from the mother, which is necessary for it to mature;

5. even though twinning is possible at the development of the primitive streak at fourteen days, nonetheless an embryo exists prior to the fourteen; thus if an identical twin emerges, it most likely evolves from an existing embryo;

6. although the embryo is dependent on its environment (whether in a petri dish or mother's uterus), it is an organic whole, a distinct human organism though immature;

7. therefore, we should not say that the zygote is a potential human being; we should say that the human zygote is a potential human embryo, a potential fetus, and a potential newborn child. [15]

I summarize George and Tollefsen's findings in embryology to show that Peters et al.'s claim is only partially correct. It is true that a developing zygote must have an appropriate environment in which to mature and that human identity entails relationships with parents and God, but we must also recognize that the embryo can mature into a fetus and so on and can be called a child by a mother because it has the organic wholeness of a human, just as does the mother.[16] Due to its self-integrated biological wholeness, or as Thomas Shannon describes it – the "biologic expression of human nature,"[17] it has an organic destiny to develop, dependent upon the appropriate environments. In fact, we could say at all levels of human maturation, we grow relative to the nutritional resources and safety of the environments, from zygote to adulthood. The external environment and internal organic wholeness are both necessary.

What Kind of Respect Is Owed Human Embryos?

Although Lebacqz calls the embryo a potential human, I believe she tacitly recognizes that the embryo should be treated as a human. In an article titled "On the Elusive Nature of Respect," she emphasizes the Latin root of _respect_ - _re-specere_ - _to_ look again, to look deeper. If we look deeper at the embryo, we should respect it for its particular stage in human development. The embryo has value as a human. To value something is to believe that it has moral worth in itself, apart from its usefulness to us.

To respect the embryo is to affirm that the value of the embryo or tissue is _not_ dependent on its usefulness to us. Respect sees a value in itself beyond usefulness.[18] She hence argues that if we destroy the embryo for its stem cells, we should not treat it cavalierly as though nothing of value is lost in the destruction. She believes if we use its stem cells to further medical science, which would benefit many more people, we would show respect to it (though we destroy it). In this light, embryonic stem cell research does not violate the embryo's worth as a potential human being. She then concludes, "They can show respect toward early embryonic tissue by engaging in careful practices of research ethics that involve weighing the necessity of using _this_ tissue, limiting the way it is to be handled and even spoken about, and honoring its potential to become a human person by choosing life over death where possible."[19]

Lebacqz rightly appeals to the respect owed the embryo, but I think her argument is inconsistent. To show this problem I use a point Robert Song makes in his article, "To Be Willing to Kill What for All One Knows is a Person Is to be Willing to Kill a Person."[20] Song raises concern about the way the Human Fertilisation and Embryology Act of 1990 in Great Britain justified stem cell therapies. It argued that although we cannot be certain that the embryo is a person, the embryo should be given the benefit of doubt that it is a person. However, since the embryo's personhood is not totally certain, if we can use its stem cell to help others whom we know are persons, it is more ethically compelling to err on the side of beneficence. It is a choice of probabilities.

Song thinks this reasoning is unconvincing. The argument should not be about probabilities, because "the force of the possibility that someone might be _killed_ is lost."[21] He feels that the standard is too high to insist that we must know for certain the embryo is a person before we stop the research. He gives two illustrations to make this point. A supervisor of a demolition team, who gives the order to destroy a building, would be culpable, if he believed the probability of children playing in it would even be low. Also, a surgical team would be culpable if they stopped trying to resuscitate a patient whom they thought was only probably dead. "Similarly, in the case of destructive research on embryos, the standard of proof required is much higher than a mere balance of probabilities: it must be shown beyond a reasonable doubt [though beyond an absolute doubt is not required] (or something like this) that the embryo is not a person."[22]

Because the embryo has much more at risk than the possible beneficial consequences of its stem cells, namely its life, we should respect it as though it were a person. We must factor the moral weight of its personhood, even if we think it is only a potential human (as do Peters and Lebacqz). This moral weight compels us to realize that to justify destroying it is the same as justifying killing a person. We then must decide that the moral status of the embryo, which is a potential fetus, newborn, etc. is more morally compelling on us than the potential therapies that might result from the stem cells.

If Lebacqz believes that we should respect the value of the embryo but also can destroy it possibly to benefit others, then according to Song's line of reasoning she is also saying it is morally permissible to kill a person to help therapeutically the life of another person. This seems inconsistent, because if we respect an embryo as a person, then we should not destroy it for the possible benefit of someone else.

Lebacqz and Peters could argue that though the embryo is potentially a human and should be respected as having value, the possible beneficial value of its stem cells for others is more morally important than the respect owed to it. In fact, they reason,

> Where it is not clear that there is a harm involved, we can - and possibly must - move forward. Opportunity waits for helping suffering people [whose dignity should be respected and] who could benefit from stem cell therapies. In the face of the uncertainty concerning the moral status of the embryo, those concerned about speeding up the arrival of medical benefits elect to pursue research in spite of their uncertainty. Doing nothing - or worse,

shutting down stem cell research – passively violates the principle of non-maleficence as it pertains to those now suffering who could eventually benefit.[23]

Peters even argues that a real moral choice does not exist between the value of the *ex vivo* blastocyst and the possible beneficial value of its stem cells, because the *ex vivo* blastocyst does not have dignity, and hence does not have value, because it does not have a relationship with a mother.[24] However, I think Peter's position is problematical.

First, since we can now obtain embryo-like stem cells without lethal research, the choice is not between the embryo's life and the possible beneficial value of its stem cells. Second, since embryology indicates that the *ex vivo* blastocyst is also a human, though in an immature stage, it should be treated as though it has potential human value. Furthermore, according to Song's principle, even if the embryo is only a potential person, we would be justifying destroying a person, and frankly that is problematical.

To clarify more why Peters' view is ethically problematical, I will examine the relationship between a duty and right. In *The Right and The Good*, David Ross points out that moral rights imply duties but that duties do not necessarily imply rights.[25] For instance, "a right in one being against another is a right to treat or be treated by that other in a certain way, and this plainly implies a duty for the other to behave in a certain way."[26] The moral right does not depend on others recognizing the right or feeling that they have a duty to honor it. Rather the right comes from the nature of that which has it. "[O]nly that which has a moral nature can have a right."[27] However, according to Ross, we have some duties that do not necessitate a moral right. Although we have a duty to treat animals humanely and to respect the environment, they do not have to make a claim of rights upon us to have these obligations. We have them because we are moral agents. However, if something has a moral nature, then we are obliged to show just and beneficent treatment toward it.

In this light, we can then reason that, first, if the zygote is at least a potential human being that should be treated with respect, and second, if we try to justify killing it, in fact we are justifying killing a human, then we should conclude that the zygote has a moral claim to which we should feel obliged to act beneficently. Obviously, destroying it, even in a non-cavalier way, to help someone else would violate the duty we have toward it. Peters may be right that our recognition of the respect of dignity owed a newborn and an adult is different than what we recognize in the *ex vivo* blastocyst, but this difference does not nullify the humanity of the blastocyst. It has a human destiny, which requires external conditions for it to mature, just as every stage of embryonic development requires. The fact that the blastocyst needs a uterine environment does not take away its claim of right upon us just as the implanted embryo's need for the development of an umbilical cord does not take away its claim of right upon us.

We are obligated to respect the value of the zygote because its humanity has a right to be respected. If we were to argue that our duty to respect the zygote creates its value – that is, it has value because we respect it – then we fail to recognize its humanity, which is a claim of right on us. Its right to be respected precedes our recognition of it, and the obligation we have toward it comes not from a possible value we may derive from it or impute to it, but from its human nature as a zygote.

To understand this level of respect, Brent Waters claims we should call the embryo a neighbor.

> I propose that we explore an alternative, or perhaps parallel question: is the human embryo my neighbor? The principle reason why this question may offer a more promising starting point for moral deliberation is, following Karl Barth, that it is much more difficult to think about neighbors in an abstract manner. We cannot contemplate a neighbor in isolation, but only in relationship to and with other neighbors... We have neighbors who are our friends and neighbors who are our enemies. Moreover, when encountering unfamiliar neighbors, we presume, or at least should presume, that we share a mutual bond by the fact that we both exist, however qualitatively different that existence might prove to be. In short, in order to learn what being human means requires that we treat our fellow human beings as neighbors, and we must always remember that this treatment is predicated on God's command that we love our neighbor, whoever they might be.[28]

The command to love our neighbors as ourselves does not create the value in the person. Rather love is the proper response to one who has the rightful claim on us as a neighbor. This notion of love of neighbor articulates well the relationship of our duty to respect the humanity of the zygote with its right to be treated as a human. If the zygote is our neighbor, then it is not just an artifact of our making, valuable to us because of its stem cells or because we deem it valuable, but is one who is owed the ethic of neighbor-love.

What to Do With "Spare" Embryos?

A question that now follows is, "Can we use lethal research on redundant embryos from *in vitro* fertilization?" "Are these embryos our neighbors as well?" My concern here is not with the morality of IVF, even though the practice of fertilizing more embryos than may be necessary for a successful pregnancy is ethically problematic. My concern is if we were to destroy a redundant embryo from IVF for its stem cell, would we violate its neighbor status, and hence violate our duty to it?

George and Tollefsen maintain that it is immoral to use the redundant embryos. They argue that "it is typically not right – because not fair – to ask someone to share the burdensome effects of an act that will exclusively benefit others. So even if the removal of vital organs from a homeless vagabond, for the sake of saving many, was not an instance of direct killing of the vagabond, still, it is manifestly unfair to demand of him the sacrifice of his organs, or his life, for people to whom he has no obligations, and from whom he will receive no benefits."[29] Such an ethical principle keeps society from demeaning the value of others, no matter their situation, because they may be beneficial to others. George and Tollefsen then apply the same ethical principle to the "spare" embryos. "[I]t would be wrongful because it is an unfair imposition of burden on an innocent human being. We conclude then that destructive research on [spare] human embryos cannot be morally justified."[30] Even if the embryo were not intentionally created to be used in lethal research (as in IVF), we would be treating it as though we had intentionally created it to destroy it for its possible benefits for others.

However, John A. Robertson takes another approach. He believes it is wrong to profit from an original immoral derivation, if it were intended in the first place, but that the principle "'no benefit from another's wrongdoing' theory of complicity seems much too broad to be a guide to moral or social practice."[31] He gives several illustrations. We would not condone or perpetuate the wrongness of murder, if we were to use the victim's organs to possibly help others once it is dead. Also, we would have an ethically difficult time with most of our land transactions today since much of it were taken from the Native Americans. He then concludes that "persons who think that induced abortion is immoral [or creating 'spare' embryos for IVF] could support the use of fetal tissue or ES cells derived from abortions as long as the derivation or later research or therapy had no reasonable prospect of bringing about abortion [or IVF], just as they could support organ donation from homicide victims without approving of the homicide that made the organs available."[32]

Both make good points. George and Tollefsen rightly emphasize that since the embryo is human, we are obligated to respect its right to life in all possible situations. Robertson is also right that the "no benefit" principle does not make sense in all cases in which derivative value may occur from originally immoral acts (e.g., his illustrations). I think we can reconcile both views by maintaining that we can take the stem cells from the embryos past the point of viability, but not the ones that can be viably implanted.[33]

Those past viability can no longer be successfully transplanted and hence do not have an organic destiny. They are kept alive but do not have the potential to mature into an implanted human embryo, fetus, newborn, etc. Just as we take the organs of the recent dead without being the cause of their death, we can take the stem cells from the embryos devoid of an organic destiny. They remain neighbors, though neighbors without a future as a human embryo, fetus, newborn child, etc.

Although I believe this solution is ethically legitimate, it is an imperfect one and people can reasonably differ with it. The problematical aspect is consent. To respect a person's right of self-determination, we require informed consent before we take viable organs once she or he dies. Obviously, the spare embryo cannot give an informed consent. However, parents give informed consent for their infants, because they are responsible for the infant's maturing until she or he has the capacity of selfdetermination. In the use of stem cells from spare embryos the comparison is with the latter, not former use of informed consent. Thus, to justify taking stem cells from non-viable embryos, we should require the parents of the embryo to give informed consent.

Conclusion

I have wanted to show that we should feel a profound obligation to respect the humanity of the embryo as our neighbor. This respect is not capricious or superficial. As adults we share with them an organic destiny as humans, and God commands us to love our neighbors, even when the neighbor is in the stage most unlike our stage and when it is in the most vulnerable stage of human development. Because of the tremendous technological advance of being able to create embryo-like stem cells, we can also pursue beneficence through stem cells therapies to our neighbors who are infants, toddlers, etc. and also acknowledge the duty we owe the humanity of the embryo. It is a great time in which we can do both.

NOTES

[1]Throughout, I use zygote, blastocyst, and embryo interchangeably for the various developments before implantation. The embryonic process starts with the zygote, when the oocyte and sperm merge to create a new genetic code, to the blastocyst which forms stem cells around day three when it has around sixteen cells, and then at day six, the embryo implants onto the uterine wall.

[2] In 2008 the National Institute of Health spent $88 million (and this number will rise in 2009 due to the government stimulus spending). California has spent approximately $300 million a year since 2004 on embryonic stem cell research and will till 2014. Massachusetts spent approximately $100 million in 2008 and will each year till 2018. These figures do not count the private money spent in embryonic stem cell research.

In November 2009, Advanced Cell Technology of Santa Monica, CA announced that the US Food and Drug Administration gave it permission to conduct a Phase I/II (that is, establishing the safety of the drug) on using embryonic stem cells to cure Stargardt, a photoreceptor degenerative disease which causes blindness. It will enroll twelve patients in three sites. The company had success using animals and is now exploring the safety of the drug on humans. It has therapeutic promise, but this will not be known till the protocol moves into Phase III and IV trials. Moreover, in December 2009, the journal Stem Cells reported that the North East England Stem Cell Institute successfully treated eight patients for Limbal Stem Cell Deficiency (a blinding disease) using the patients' own stem cells.

[3]This breakthrough occurred in separate labs – first by Shinya Yamanaka of Kyoto University (published in *Cell,* 25 August 2006) and then by James A. Thomson of University of Wisconsin (published in *Science,* 20 November 2007). "Successful reprogramming of differentiate human cells into a pluripotent state would allow creation of patient-and disease specific stem cells. We previously reported generation of induced pluripotent stem (iPS) cells capable of germ line transmission, from mouse somatic cells by transduction from four defined transcription factors. Here we demonstrate the generation of iPS cells from adult human dermal fibroblasts with the same four factors .... Furthermore, these cells could differentiate into cell types of three germ layers in vitro and in teratomas. These findings demonstrate that iPS cells can be generated from adult human fibroblasts." Takahashi et al., Induction of Pluripotent Stem Cells from Adult Human Fibroblasts by Defined Factors, *Cell* (2007), doi:10.1016/j. cell.2007.11.019.

[4]James c. Patterson, "Is the Human Embryo a Human Being?" in *God and the Embryo: Religious Voices on Stem Cells and Cloning,* edited by Brent Waters and Ronald Cole-Turner, Washington D.C.: Georgetown University Press, 2003, p. 85.

[5]Ibid., p. 82.

[6]Brent Waters, "The Appropriate Contribution of Religious Communities," in *God and the Embryo,* p. 27.

[7]G. Gareth Jones, "Why Should Cloning and Stem Cell Research Be of Interest to Theologians," in *Stem Cell Research and Cloning: Contemporary Challenges to our Humanity,* edited by Gareth Jones and Mary Byrne, *Interface: A Forum for Theology in the World,* volume 7, number 2, October 2004, pp. 88-89.

[8]Ibid., p. 79.

[9]Ted Peters, Karen Lebacqz, and Gaymon Bennett, *Sacred Cells? Why Christians Should Support Stem Cell Research,* New York: Rowman & Littlefield Publishers, Inc. 2008, pp. 214-218.

[10]Ibid., p. 216.

[11]Ibid.

[12]For example, the children given to Sarai, Hannah, Elizabeth, and Mary.

[13]Robert P. George and Christopher Tollefsen, *Embryo: A Defense of Human Life,* New York: Doubleday, 2008.

[14]Ibid., p. 54.

[15]Ibid., pp. 36-54.

[16]In this light, it is difficult to imagine the embryological reasons Philip J. Nickel could give when he claims embryos are "like human body parts or recently deceased persons"; in "Ethical Issues in Human Embryonic Stem Cell Research", in *Fundamentals of the Stem Cell Debate.* edited by Kristen Renwick Monroe, Ronald B. Miller and Jerome Tobis, Berkeley: University of California Press, 2008, p. 71.

[17]Thomas Shannon, "From the Micro to the Macro," in *The Human Embryonic Stem Cell Debate: Science. Ethics. and the Public Policy.* Edited by Suzanne Holland, Karen Lebacqz, and Laurie Zoloth, Cambridge, Massachusetts: The MIT Press, 2001, p. 178.

[18]Karen Lebacqz, "On the Elusive Nature of Respect," in *The Human Embryonic Stem Cell Debate.* p. 159. Andrew Dutney makes a similar point, "In my view the embryo *in vitro* is not a human being, but it is still morally significant and should be treated with respect" by respecting the couple, the embryo's symbolic value, and those who ethically differ; "A Christian Case for Allowing the Destruction of Embryos," *in Stem Cell Research and Cloning: Contemporary Challenges to our Humanity.* p. 99.

[19]Ibid., p. 160.

[20]Robert Song, "To Be Willing to Kill What for All One Knows is a Person Is to be Willing to Kill a Person," in *God and the Embryo,* ibid.

[21]Ibid., p. 100.

[22]Ibid., p. 101.

[23]*Sacred Cells,* p. 78. Elsewhere Peters and Gaymon Bennett argue that since human dignity, especially for the embryo, is eschatological found in God's final affirmation of humanity, we should emphasize the ethic of the Good Samaritan and show beneficence in all possible cases – "Our fundamental commitment is to beneficence" in "A Plea for Beneficence: Reframing the Embryo Debate," in *God and the Embryo,* p. 128.

[24]Ted Peters, *The Stem Cell Debate,* Minneapolis: Fortress Press, 2007, p. 108.

[25]Sir David Ross, "Rights" in *Readings in Ethical Theory,* second edition, edited by Wilfrid Sellars and John Hospers, New York: Appleton-Century-Crofts, 1970.

[26]Ibid., p. 573.

[27]Ibid., p. 575.

[28]Brent Waters, "Does the Human Embryo Have a Moral status?" in *God and the Embryo*, pp. 71-72.

[29] George and Tollefsen, *Embryo: A Defense of Human Life* pp. 200-201.

[30]Ibid., p. 201. Don Marquis makes a similar point – "Age discrimination is morally wrong. When we were very, very young, we were mere embryos. Therefore, destruction of human embryos for the purposes of scientific research is wrong," in Stem Cell Research, *in The Stem Cell Controversy:*

Debating the Issues, second edition, edited by Michael Ruse and Christopher A. Pynes, Amherst, New York: Prometheus Books, 2006, p. 196.

[31]John A. Robertson, "Ethics and Policy in Embryonic Stem Cell Research" in *The Stem Cell Controversy: Debating The Issues,* p. 135.

[32]Ibid., p. 136.

[33]It is unclear exactly when non-viability occurs. It may be possible to keep indefinitely an embryo in liquid nitrogen at -195.8 degrees centigrade. Though the record is thirteen years for a successful birth, most clinics recommend not keeping an embryo frozen past five years for fear of losing its viability, according to the Tennessee Reproductive Medicine Clinic.

Chapter 11

Can a Sanctity-of-Human-Life Ethic Ground Christian Ecological Responsibility?

David P. Gushee

Introduction: Finding a Central Christian Moral Paradigm

Every religious tradition known to humanity contains numerous ethical imperatives. These emerge from sacred sayings and texts and are elaborated through many years of theological-ethical development as an expression of the effort of faithful believers to live out the demands of the faith with integrity amidst changing historical circumstances.

One aspect of a faith's theological-ethical tradition is usually an intra-scriptural or intra-traditional argument related to the ranking, ordering, or organizing of the faith's moral norms, paradigms, and teachings. This reflects a basic need of believers for guidance in sifting through the faith's many demands for clarity as to its most important requirements. It also reflects a basic human need for order.

Both the Old Testament and the New Testament contain direct evidence of intra-Jewish and intra-Christian (and perhaps Jewish vs. Christian) argumentation along these lines. Already in the period of canon formation these kindred faith traditions reflect sometimes fierce arguments over moral first principles. These very arguments inform the Jewish and Christian traditions as these come down to us through the centuries.

One important framing of such an argument in the Hebrew Bible is found in Micah 6:6-8:

> With what shall I come before the Lord
> And bow down before the exalted God?
> Shall I come before him with burnt offerings,

With calves a year old?
Will the Lord be pleased with thousands of rams,
With ten thousand rivers of oil?
Shall I offer my firstborn for my transgression,
The fruit of my body for the sin of my soul?
He has showed you, O man, what is good.
And what does the Lord require of you?
To act justly and to love mercy
And to walk humbly with your God.[1]

In this text, the prophet sets the demands of the cultic system over against the true "good" of moral living. Despite chapter and verse *within the Torah itself* in which the details of the cultic system are prescribed, for this prophet (and most others), what really matters is a life characterized by the actual practice of the highest moral values of justice and mercy, and by a posture of humility in relation to God.

According to the New Testament (Mt. 22:34-40; Mk. 12:28-31), Jesus was asked to offer commentary on the ranking of moral obligations in Jewish Law. His famous answer has long been important for Christian ethics:

'Love the Lord your God with all your heart and with all your soul and with all your mind.' This is the first and greatest commandment. And the second is like it: 'Love your neighbor as yourself.' All the Law and the Prophets hang on these two commandments (Mt. 22:37-40).

Writing explicitly to Christian communities, many New Testament writers offer moral exhortations in which they also attempt to clarify the highest and most significant moral obligations of the faith. Often the answer is, again, love (cf. Jn 13:34-35; 1 Cor. 13). And yet a variety of other options are either proposed or implicitly suggested, as in the moral exhortation sections of Paul's various letters.

Through the centuries and even today, in Christian scholarship and in the preaching and teaching of the churches, arguments or proposals about a central organizing moral norm have continued.

Certainly love remains central in most treatments of Christian morality. But it is not difficult to find scholars, pastors, and other leaders who offer other proposals. These include justice, liberation, holiness, righteousness, discipleship, obedience, kingdom ethics, the Golden

Rule, compassion, mercy, sacrifice, reconciliation, peacemaking, forgiveness, responsibility, and others. It is hard to argue against any of these moral norms. All reflect aspects of what Dorothy Emmet aptly called "the moral prism."[2] As the brilliant light of scripture's moral demand is refracted through our various interpretive lenses some of us see certain colors as more brilliant while others notice different ones. No one could argue that the God who inspired the scriptures is uninterested in any of these particular moral norms for faithful living.

The Emergence of a Sanctity-of-Human-Life Ethic

In late 20th-century Christian ethics, especially in Catholic thought which was then eagerly borrowed by (mainly conservative) Protestants, a new central moral norm emerged: the "sanctity of human life" (or "sacredness of human life"). The impetus for the articulation of this moral norm in much of the western world in the 1970s was the full legalization of abortion and, secondarily, the reality or possibility of the legalization of "mercy killing," or assisted suicide. Even today the term is often used, either by its advocates or its foes, as applying primarily to those two issues. Those who were opposed to abortion claimed the sanctity of human life as their reason, no one doing so more profoundly than Pope John Paul II.[3] The term was then picked up and used freely by conservative Protestant social activists. Those who were in favor of abortion sometimes sought explicitly to undercut the validity of a sanctity-of-human-life ethic, no one more stridently than Australian philosopher Peter Singer.[4] After awhile, many Christians wearied of the association of "sanctity of life" with the Christian Right, culture wars, and the "pro-life movement" and dropped or rejected this particular moral vocabulary for other terminology. Even today most politically progressive Christians shy away from the term.

In my current scholarship in Christian ethics, I am attempting to reclaim the concept of the sanctity of human life while at the same time freeing it of this crippling association with the abortion fight and the culture wars. In my forthcoming book on life's sanctity, I trace a millennia-long historical trajectory for the development of this critically important moral norm. I argue that the idea that every human life has immeasurable, God-given value worthy of the highest respect is actually the culmination of the best of the Jewish, Christian, and western moral traditions—and a sifting out of elements of those same traditions that fall short of that ideal.

In this sense, it is incorrect to describe the sanctity of human life as a new moral norm. Like the main synagogue in Prague, it is "old new." It is as old as the Genesis concept of the *imago dei*, and as new as the liberation ethics of the 20th century. It is as old as the demand to love our neighbors as ourselves, and as new as 20th century theological personalism, the ethical writings of Martin Buber and Emmanuel Levinas with their focus on I-Thou relationships and the irreducible Other, the post-Holocaust writings of Elie Wiesel and Irving Greenberg on re-sanctifying human life after Auschwitz, Catholic social teaching from Vatican II to John Paul II, anti- and post-colonial writing, feminist thought, and the thinking of the leaders of America's civil rights movement. What all of these disparate sources have in common is a profound sense of the majesty and dignity of the human person (each and every person) and a profound resistance to his or her dehumanization and degradation.

Situating the sanctity of human life within these kinds of sources immediately helps to wrench it free from any fixation either on the beginning or the end of life. To the extent that Catholics and conservative Protestants reduced the sacredness of life to the struggle against abortion and assisted suicide, they weakened rather than strengthened their own cardinal moral norm as they undertook their otherwise laudable moral struggle. Both morally and strategically, the best way to argue for the sanctity of human life is to broaden rather than narrow its application. Human life is only sacred if every human life is sacred, at every moment of that life. Therefore, those who are "pro-life" must join their passion to every other movement for human dignity and resistance to dehumanization and degradation.

It is clear to me that my own career as a Christian ethicist has been moving for some time toward this project of unpacking a full-orbed sanctity of life ethic as a, or the, central Christian moral norm. Earlier work in developing a Christian ethic centered on the teachings of Jesus and the reign of God (*Kingdom Ethics*) and was followed by the elucidation of a consistent pro-life centrist evangelical ethic (*The Future of Faith in American Politics*).[5] These books have been groping toward an *ethical vision* in which God's reign culminates as human beings come to love one another with the only kind of love appropriate to the immeasurable value of the human person beloved by God, and a *political vision* in which my nation's public policies reflect and advance a commitment to the valuing of every human life as sacred, both here and abroad. Those who truly love God, I have argued, will commit themselves to love their neighbors in this exalted and profound way.

The working definition I have developed for the sanctity of human life has come to be articulated as follows:

> *The sanctity of life is the conviction that all human beings, at any and every stage of life, in any and every state of consciousness or self-awareness, of any and every race, color, ethnicity, level of intelligence, religion, language, nationality, gender, character, behavior, physical ability/ disability, sexual orientation, potential, class, social status, etc., of any and every particular quality of relationship to the viewing subject, are to be perceived as sacred, as persons of equal and immeasurable worth and of inviolable dignity. Therefore they must be treated with the reverence and respect commensurate with this elevated moral status, beginning with a commitment to the preservation, protection, and flourishing of their lives. The belief that human life is sacred flows from biblical faith. In particular, life is sacred because, according to scripture, God created humans in his image, declared them precious, ascribed to them a unique status in creation, blessed them with unique, god-like capacities, made them for eternal life, governs them under his sovereign lordship, commands in his moral law that they be treated with reverence and respect – and forever elevates their dignity by his decision to take human form in Jesus Christ and to give up that human life at the Cross.*[6]

There are many reasons to embrace this ethic as a/the central Christian moral norm. As articulated carefully (though undoubtedly not without error) here, this statement of what the sanctity of life means emphasizes as starkly as possible the *universality* of human moral obligations to other human beings. I have sought to craft language here that emphasizes the length, breadth, height, and depth of human moral obligation to other humans. No one can be excluded, for any reason. From womb to tomb, from home to far away, from friend to foe, all are covered. All must be viewed as sacred (moral *vision*) and treated with reverence and respect (moral *principle*). To each and to all I (we) owe particular moral *obligations*, focusing first on the protection and preservation of their lives and finally, in an open-ended way, to their flourishing in every aspect of what it means for them to flourish as human creatures made in the image of God.

The second half of the definition simply suggests the numerous biblical warrants for this vision of the worth of human persons and our obligations to them. It is not difficult for most Christians to understand why human beings should be viewed and treated in this way when these scriptural warrants are presented. Few Christians today would explicitly reject this vision of our moral obligations. It reflects a kind of exalted theocentric humanism that coheres well with the best of contemporary Christian thinking about persons and the world. If Christian leaders could find ways to motivate more Christians (and others) to live out this kind of ethic in relation to those they are least inclined to value, it would be a hugely significant accomplishment in the real world.

And yet, it is not at all clear that this kind of Christian ethic is sufficient for addressing the particular challenges created by the ecological degradation of the planet that we face today and into the rest of the 21st century. In fact, it can be argued that a sanctity-of-human-life ethic is *part of the problem and cannot be part of the solution*. What a paradox it would be, if the highest expression of a Christian ethic that values human life turns out to be at the same time a source of the ongoing devaluation of the rest of God's creation. Some very thoughtful Christian (and other) ethicists have concluded that this is in fact the case. My goal in this essay as a whole is to determine if this is true, if we do need to create a new kind of ethic to deal with the new kind of problems that are created in a context of ecological degradation and potential catastrophe.

Problems of a Sanctity-of-Human-Life Ethic for the Care of Creation

Without pretending to offer a complete list of the possible problems and limits of a sanctity-of-human-life ethic for ecological ethics, I suggest and will briefly elucidate the following problems.

First, the sanctity ethic as articulated here sharpens our sense of the immense value of the human person, but offers no account even of the existence, let alone the value, of other beings. We are trained to see human beings (each and every human being) as the pinnacle of creation, the height of God's creative work, and the center of God's concern when it comes to the affairs of this planet—and indeed, of the entire universe. Even the broad sanctity ethic proposed here still focuses the entirety of its attention on human beings. It is different from narrower versions only in the breadth of its concern for the whole human family and the flourishing of each person everywhere at every stage of existence. The drama of salvation history remains the question of the response of the human being to God our Maker and Redeemer; the drama of ethics remains the question of the response of the human being to other human beings.[7]

As for the existence of other sentient beings, and the creation itself, this account of life's sanctity remains silent. At least in Western Christianity we have lacked even the language to discuss that which goes beyond and yet includes both the vertical and the horizontal, the divine-human and human-human dramas. An earlier generation might have spoken of God's relationship with the angels or the heavenly court. They disappear here. And no mention is made of fish, squirrels, or dolphins, or of trees, rivers, air, and crabgrass. A sanctity approach does at least push Christians to pay attention to ethics and not just theology, to how people are treated and not just whether they believe in Jesus, but it does nothing to raise the visibility of the millions of other creatures with whom we share the created order, or the created order itself in which we and these many other creatures live and move and have our being.

Even when Christians do move in the direction of a theology of creation and the other creatures, a common theological move is quickly to sharpen the ontological distinctions between human and non-human creatures. The first step in this direction in many theologies (popular or scholarly) is to define the content of the *imago dei* through some delineation of the ways in which human beings and only human beings are made in God's image. Often this is done through the specification of certain capacities of the human that are set against the lack of capacity of other creatures. Only humans, we say, can reason, or plan, or create, or love, or invent and speak languages. Only humans have a "soul" that can relate to and love God. This is sometimes called "human exceptionalism," or criticized as human egocentrism, or speciesism, and it goes deep in Christian thought.[8]

Imagine how different our view of the world would be if our teachings about creation emphasized all that we shared in common with other creatures instead of all that makes humans different. Instead, our tradition tends to emphasize human uniqueness and superiority in fateful ways.

This move toward a capacity-based construal of the divine image is also susceptible to empirical attacks from those who propose or show that the distinctions between the reasoning, creative, emotive, linguistic, relational, or even spiritual capacities of humans over against the higher mammals, for example, have been overdrawn. We end up risking a core element of our theology of creation (and even salvation) with every new discovery about the surprisingly advanced capacities of other creatures.

This is one very good reason, by the way, for us to follow the suggestions of a number of biblical scholars that the image of God should be understood in terms of our unique *responsibilities*, not our unique *capacities*.[9] We image God as we bear God's delegated authority to care for the earth and its creatures. This emphasizes our unique power and responsibility in the earth, rather than our increasingly tenuous claim to have unique capacities. Again, it might be helpful here to be reminded of the existence in biblical thought of other entities, some even "higher" than us, such as the angels, to repopulate our theological imaginations with a planet and universe full of diverse forms of life, and to some extent to de-center humanity from our vision of the created order.

One consequence of defining the *imago dei* in this better-than, over-against paradigm is the implicit or explicit degradation of the status and value of non-human creatures relative to human beings. Other creatures are less than us because they cannot reason, emote, relate, love, create, or speak. It becomes very important in this approach to delineate the many specific ways in which other creatures are indeed inferior to us in their capacities. Not made in the image of God, not destined for eternal life with God, they occupy an ambiguous and certainly less important role in the divine economy. They are not part of the ultimate drama of salvation, nor are they part of the penultimate drama of ethics. They are barely more than "scenery" on the stage of the divine-human drama.[10] Human uniqueness and status are bought at a high price here—the deprecation of the status of each and every one of the other creatures on the planet.

Incidentally, this way of defining what it really means to be human, what it really means to be made in the image of God, has a dramatic unintended consequence—a weakening of the moral status of those human beings who lose or never have those distinctive capacities that we have identified as constituting the image of God. A child in the womb does not qualify as *imago dei* material as defined by capacities. The best we can really say is that one day, if all goes well, this developing child will have those capacities. (Sometimes this is handled by drawing disturbing distinctions between personhood and human being, or between actual and potential personhood.) A person in a persistent vegetative state lacks some or all of the capacities we have named. So does a person with grave mental illness or in the last stages of Alzheimer's. These weaknesses of a capacity-based defining of the image have been exploited ruthlessly by those who have had reason to do so, from the Nazis in their euthanasia campaign until today. How tragic, that the effort to buttress the elevation of what it means to be human has sometimes contributed to the degradation of lives that do not quite qualify by the definitions we have created.

Returning to our central concern in this essay, a review of our exalted definition of the sanctity of human life reveals huge implications for how human beings are to be treated by other human beings, but no ethical framework for human responsibility to other creatures and the creation itself. We can see that each and every human being is to be viewed with reverence and respect, and to be treated in a manner that contributes to the preservation, protection, and flourishing of their lives. This is concise, challenging, and clear. But how are we to view and to treat the monkeys, rats, dogs, or the roses, oceans, and air?

I think one could argue that in a world populated by millions of other species and billions of other non-human neighbors, it is impossible for human beings not to operate according to some kind of vision and ethic in relation to these creatures. Some of these are actually codified into law, as we were reminded here in Atlanta last year when our star quarterback, Michael Vick, went to jail for grossly mistreating and even murdering dogs. So the state does have laws related to how both animals and ecosystems must be treated. But it appears that the resources for such a legal or moral vision are not available in the Christian faith itself. Can that really be so?

Of course, in the history of Christian thought there has been at least one identifiable and consistently recurring vision for the moral relationship between human beings and the rest of creation — this is captured in the English word "dominion." The concept is rooted quite firmly in the soil of Genesis 1:26-30, in which human beings are charged with the responsibility to "rule" or "exercise dominion" over every kind of creature and apparently "over all the earth" itself (cf. Gen. 1:26). Recent attempts to modify either the translation or the moral vision associated with Christian dominion theology have tended to shift the focus to service and stewardship. If we "rule," it must be more like how Jesus taught us to rule — through humble service rather than lordly domination (cf. Mt. 20:20-28).

Somehow that point was lost on many generations of Christians, especially western Christians influenced by cultural currents unleashed in the modern era, including technical rationality, expansionist capitalism, and imperial colonialism. The creation and its creatures became "natural resources" to be exploited and employed for the good of humanity, especially dominant human groups which engineered amazing feats involving the reworking of the "raw materials" of creation for the pleasure and advancement of humanity. Every one of us is the beneficiary to some extent of these developments, but looked at with a long view we see that the "thingification" of the creation and the creatures within it has proven to be spiritually damaging and environmentally and even economically unsustainable.

Whether it can be fairly traced to Genesis 1 or to the modern western reading of Genesis 1 has been fiercely argued, but the cultural result in the western world is undisputed — a human understanding of the world that abstracts one part of creation (human beings) from the rest. "Man" sits at the pinnacle of creation, lord of all he surveys, free to use it as he sees fit. There is "humanity" and then there is "the world," or humanity and "the environment," or humanity and "nature" or humanity and "the creation." Even the more biblical language of "creation" is not often employed to join us to that creation, but instead to abstract us from it.

Throughout Christian history scattered saints have modeled a different way of relating to the creation — one thinks of St. Francis. But for the most part Christians have both elevated humanity and separated humanity from the fish of the sea and the birds of the air and the livestock that move along the ground — not to mention from the sea, the air, and the ground itself.

We have been trained not to see ourselves as creatures, as part of creation, as dependent upon the well-being of other creatures and of the air, land, and water which we all share. Therefore we have been and remain vulnerable to the overexploitation of these fellow creatures and the gradual degradation of the creation which we share with them. We acted as if what we did to other creatures would have no negative effects on us, lords of creation, and as if what we did to creation itself would similarly bounce off of us, its masters. It was not until the late 20th century that a number of developments—including severe environmental problems, the depletion of what had been treated as infinite "natural resources," the early environmental movement, the revival of nature religions, and the photos of our shared "terrestrial ball" from outer space—that *we finally came to understand that what we do to creation and to the other creatures we do to ourselves*. There is no escape, no place to hide, no pinnacle down from which we can benignly view a deteriorating creation. We depend on our particular ecosytems, and our shared planet, no less than the fish of the sea and the birds of the air and the livestock that move along the ground.

One final concern seems called for before we move to a different aspect of this paper.

Some have suggested that this human-centered view of reality, this theologically validated human egocentrism, is even at its best a vestige of a pre-scientific, pre-Darwinian, pre-ecological worldview in which the earth was the center of the universe, human beings were the center of events on earth, and God guaranteed the continued well-being of this planet made for humans. It is not difficult to recall how deeply threatened church leaders felt at the suggestion that the earth orbits the sun and not the other way around. Then it was discovered that this is but one sun and one solar system among other suns and other solar systems. It became harder and harder to believe that the only thing God cared about in the whole universe was what was going on in this "third rock from the sun."

This same pre-scientific worldview suggested that not only was the Earth the center of the universe, but human beings were the center of (what matters on) the Earth. Darwin's is the name most associated not only with the idea that human beings are but one species among many on this Earth (which we knew) but also with the more radical notion that human beings are but one late-evolving species on this Earth and share an ancestry with other creatures and even the humblest life forms that exist here.

This latter move has been too much to swallow even today for large sections of the human family, especially religious believers, and not only Christians. It challenged nearly every element of the historic Christian worldview we have been discussing in this section, from the elevation of humanity, to the distinctions between human and non-human creatures, to the abstraction of human beings from the ecosystems and the earth which we share with other creatures.

This is not a paper about Darwin or evolution, and I do not believe that Christians are dependent on a particular approach to evolution for a response to the ecological crisis. But I do think that what are often thought of as two separate "faith and science" issues—evolution and the environment—actually are best considered in conversation with one another. And I think that the discovery, through modern genetic research, of our considerable shared DNA with all living creatures on this planet confirms a central thesis I am pursuing here—that whatever else we may say about the special moral status of human beings before God, we must also say that we creatures of God and earth, of spirit and humus, are somehow fellows, somehow kin, somehow morally related to and responsible to, the other creatures of earth with whom we share so much—including being beneficiaries of God's creative love.[11]

The Development of Alternative Theological Paradigms

In a famous 1967 article called, "The Historical Roots of Our Ecologic Crisis," scientist Lynn White charged that "Christianity bears a huge burden of guilt" for the environmental problems afflicting western society and now the whole world. Probing many of the same issues discussed in the last section, White argued that the Bible desacralized nature, licensed human beings to dominate and overpopulate the earth, and created an anthropocentric view of creation.[12] The Bible has also been charged with promoting a dualistic view of reality that encouraged a contempt for this world and all things physical, and with nurturing an eschatological framework in which Christ's second coming distracts Christians from an ultimate commitment to the well-being of the one Earth on which we actually live.[13] While more recent scholarship has clearly demonstrated that ecological catastrophe is not a uniquely western or Christian problem, the effects of White's thesis linger still.[14]

Many have found such contentions attractive, leading or contributing both to the explicit rejection of the Bible and/or Jewish and Christian faith, and also to the embrace of starkly different religious and philosophical worldviews viewed as more nature-friendly. This association of environmental concern with a rejection of orthodox biblical Christianity has had the disastrous effect of discrediting the environmental movement in the eyes of millions of traditional-minded Christian believers. Only recently have many serious Christians been willing to consider environmentalism, or "creation care," in any significant way, and they often find their efforts resisted fiercely on the basis of these fears.

Meanwhile, various Christian thinkers have attempted to offer more ecologically sensitive versions of Christian faith—sometimes with elements drawn from other religions or sometimes from a rethinking of biblical or theological resources. Some of these revised Christian theologies stray so far from biblical categories of thought that they basically constitute the abandonment of a recognizable Christian faith. Other times the reforms stay more carefully within Christian theological boundaries.

A variety of worldviews and theological moves have been made to create or retrieve a more environmentally friendly stance. I will name just a few of these here.

For those who believe that biblical faith's primary sin was in desacralizing nature, robbing it of the felt sense of the divine presence, one option is to retrieve or create nature religions that redivinize nature in its individual parts or as a whole. Just as once the ancients experienced and worshiped the divine in the air, land, and sea, in the various creatures, and in the mysterious processes of nature on which all life depends, such as rain, sunshine, and harvest, even today some have returned to various forms of such beliefs.

Another possibility, especially appealing to some in view of the growing appreciation of the creation as a single intricate entity, a vast ecosystem that sustains all life (the "Gaia hypothesis"), has been a retrieval of a kind of pantheism in which God is all and all is God, or a panentheism in which God is to be identified with or experienced directly in everything that exists.[15]

A third move is toward a kind of feminist nature religion. Here the critique of biblical thought categories is further specified as a critique of the patriarchy or androcentrism which has distorted all of these thought categories, such as the dualism that diminishes the female in favor of the male, the natural in favor of the spiritual, the body in favor of the soul, and this life in favor of the next one.[16] In one version of this approach, the Earth is personified as our divine Mother, who/which must be loved as a whole and in her constituent elements—every tree, river, and frog. Some who are attracted to this approach seek to retrieve ancient matriarchal religions which, they argue, contained elements of this kind of mysticism and spirituality and were displaced centuries ago in most of the world by the violent patriarchal religions of Judaism, Christianity, and Islam.[17]

The full embrace of evolutionary approaches to life on earth has been embraced by some who then weave an eco-spirituality around evolution. One approach is to find a kind of life-force spirituality at work in the multi-billion-year process by which life has unfolded on this planet and presumably elsewhere. All life is related to all other life, all life seeks to extend itself, and in the development and infinite elaboration of life forms on this planet one has much material for religious awe and wonder, as well as the basis of an ethic of reverence and respect and even "sacredness of life" in all its forms.[18]

One influential philosophical rather than theological move has been the embrace of a kind of eco-utilitarianism by the philosopher Peter Singer. Singer offers a new kind of moral universalism in which at least some non-human creatures are valued equally to human beings and thus become the bearers of moral claims that must be respected by human beings. Unfortunately, the way Singer grounds his elevation of the moral status of the higher mammals is by establishing a consciousness-based or capacity-based evaluation of that status. This simultaneously elevates the moral status of the higher mammals that have been shown to near or equal human beings in their capacities and consciousness, but at the same time to demote human beings who lack such capacities and consciousness. This move lies at the root of Singer's horrifying proposal that infanticide and euthanasia should be permitted. For Singer, the capacities of an infant or an Alzheimer's patient fall below those of a fully functioning gorilla, and their respective rights should be treated correspondingly.[19]

Another move suggested in recent literature has been more explicitly political. It involves a rethinking of political community to include all creatures. If one thinks of modern history as involving a gradual recognition of the moral and thus political status of all human beings, and not just some categories of human beings (men, landowners, white people), then the extension of this status to non-human creatures can be seen as the next logical step. Animals join humans in the kingdom of ends, to reframe Immanuel Kant. In an extension of the categorical imperative, they must count as among those who are viewed as ends also and not merely as means to someone else's ends. This ultimately leads to a reframing of the concept of citizenship, with animals included in a kind of global earth community with rights that must be respected even if they cannot speak for themselves.[20]

I have already suggested that a number of Christian theologians have attempted to reframe Christian theology in radical ways that, in my view, essentially introduce elements of nature religions into Christian faith. While this is not the place to offer an introduction to all of these approaches, what they have in common is generally the explicit abandonment of core doctrinal elements of Christian faith and often the introduction of theological concepts and images that have little precedent in biblical or historical theology. Two examples of this are the mystical panentheism of Matthew Fox's creation spirituality, and the feminist embrace of a kind of Mother Earth theology such as Sallie McFague's suggestion that the earth should be viewed as God's body.[21]

Perhaps it is easy for evangelicals to dismiss all of the foregoing moves as dangerous or hysterical overreactions. They should instead be viewed as relevant evidence of the Earth's distress and of culture's responses to that distress—and some of our Christian brothers' and sisters' responses. Some represent the retrieval of centuries of wisdom about sustainable human living on this planet. Even those that go too far should speak to us about our own need as perhaps more carefully orthodox Christians to respond far better than we have done.

It is true that a number of evangelical/orthodox Christian theologians and ethicists have attempted to offer more modest reframings of Christian ethics to shift and improve our moral paradigms and thus improve Christian approaches to the environment.

One move is to tackle the "dominion mandate" and to redefine it with language such as stewardship, earth-keeping, or creation care.

The focus remains Genesis 1-2, and the goal is to pull Christians away from a reading of dominion as domination and toward dominion as a more humble stewardship, care, or earth-keeping. This move also nudges Christians to pay more attention to non-human creatures and the creation itself, as an aspect of proper obedience to the "dominion mandate." Cal DeWitt, working in the Reformed tradition, has been a pioneer in these efforts.[22]

I think it has become clear recently that at least for most evangelicals our theology and ethic of creation are too weak to bear this added pressure. In other words, we would have to really care about a theology and ethic of creation in the first place for this revision of that theology to get our attention. But, focused as we have been on soteriology, on God's saving relationship to the human, and the human response to the divine, it would require a deep revolution in our working theology to move us toward any kind of deep concern with a theology or ethic related to creation.

This helps explain why some recent theological work has moved closer to the core of classic Protestant theology, trying to take account of ecological concerns when thinking about the meaning of Jesus Christ, sin, salvation, and eschatology. A full-blown ecological theology will involve serious work in these areas. Some of the needed elements will be suggested in the next section.

Toward a Broadened Christian Sanctity-of-Life Ethic

Let me situate this sketch of theological resources for ecological concern by treating it as the potential contribution of a broadened Christian sanctity-of-life ethic. Perhaps if properly modified, the sanctity of life still can be the organizing framework or paradigm that we need for an era of ecological crisis. If this effort is successful, concern for God's creation can be, at least in part, anchored in a moral commitment that is already widely shared in the churches, which is a considerable advantage for those trying to affect the beliefs and behaviors of the average Christian today.

As suggested earlier, and developed more fully in my book on the sanctity of life, in biblical thought the majesty and holiness of God, together with the free decision of God, entirely grounds any ascription of sanctity to humanity. Therefore it is wrong to say that human beings and their lives are somehow intrinsically sacred, if we are not at the same time saying that what makes human lives sacred is God's action and declaration toward them. Perhaps a more precise way to say it is that in theocentric perspective all value is *derived value*, in that God the Creator is the one who authoritatively declares the value of all things that he has made. Only after we are clear about this can we then venture to say that an entity has *intrinsic value*, which means that God has already and permanently made his valuation of that entity clear. In the critically important Psalm 8, for example, it is God's name that is "majestic in all the earth" (8:1). It is God's decision to choose to "be mindful" of humanity amidst all of God's other majestic creations (8:4). It is God who made us "a little lower than the elohim" (8:5), and "crowned [us] with glory and honor" (8:5). It is God who chose to make us "ruler over the works of [his] hands" (8:6). Human life can be described as sacred insofar as the majesty, holiness, presence, love, and care of God touch it, are related to it, and are directed toward it. To honor human life and treat it with reverence is an appropriate theological, spiritual, and ethical response to God.

Insofar as ecological degradation and catastrophe hurt human beings, those creatures toward whom God's actions and declarations reveal such exalted value, then Christians are duty bound to respond with steps to ease the suffering of their human neighbors. Therefore one of the best things that concerned Christian environmentalists can do to advance their commitments is to a) remind our brothers and sisters of our obligations toward our human neighbors, whom God loves so dearly, and b) show concretely how ecological degradation is already sickening and killing those neighbors. This is not hard to do. Far from setting up environmental concern as a conflict of interests between babies and whales, we must instead show the ways in which the same problems hurt both babies and whales. This would be a huge step forward.

But then we must also find ways to demonstrate biblically that these whales themselves, as well as the other creatures, and the creation as a whole, are also in a sense sacred. They may not be sacred to the same degree (cf. Lk. 6:24) or in the same way that human beings are, especially if we tie sacredness in any strong way to the *imago dei*, and if we preserve some species uniqueness as part of that divine image. But they are indeed sacred—if we understand sacred, again, to mean sacred as a result of God's action and declaration toward them and relationship with them. When we then re-open the text of the Bible and look especially for God's relationship to other creatures and the creation, we find a God who creates other creatures and the creation (Gen. 1-2), who declares them good (Gen. 1:31), who feeds and sustains them (Ps. 104, Mt. 6:26), who takes delight in them, who makes covenant with them (Gen. 9), who protects them in his laws (Lev. 25, Dt. 6:14), who hears their groaning (Rom. 8:28), and who promises their ultimate liberation from bondage to decay (Rom. 8:29) and the renewal of all things (Mt. 19:28). We have ample biblical grounds for looking upon them and treating them with reverence and respect.

It is not too much to say that to the extent Christians have failed to acknowledge God's sacred relationship to other creatures and the creation, we have failed God, we have sinned against him and against other creatures and the creation we share with them. Repentance is called for, which includes both grief over sin and new commitment to a different way of relating. We must learn to perceive our moral obligations as God's people to those other creatures loved and valued by God. This is the starting point for a fresh look at the particular resources found in the scriptures that are relevant to ecological concern.

Once we open ourselves to seeing and sensing God's immense valuing of his creation and his creatures a whole new range of biblical resources becomes available to us. Significant work has already been done and more is needed to mine these extensive biblical resources that teach us in various ways a high valuing of the creation, its ecosystems, and its creatures. These can be of especially great value in church settings precisely because they do not rely on esoteric theological moves but can simply be read off of the biblical texts. Let me at least suggest a few places to look.

We should pay more attention to Genesis 1-2, and to developing a more robust theology of creation (and fall, in Gen. 3). We should work harder at "seeing" non-human life and the creation itself as they appear in Genesis, populating our Christian moral imagination with creatures that matter to God other than human beings. We must learn to read, and to tell, the primal biblical story differently.

We should spend much more time in Genesis 6-9, not arguing about whether the flood was literal or where the ark landed, but instead paying attention to the terrible suffering that befell the creation due to human sin—a paradigmatic pattern that continues today. The Ark itself has become something of a symbol of human-animal community— there creaturely life survived together. In one sense the entire Earth is an Ark — either we survive together or probably none of us will survive at all. The Noahide Covenant is rich with theological significance, for nowhere is divine-human-animal-creation community more clearly suggested. Most breathtakingly, God makes covenant through Noah and "every living creature that was with you" to and with all human beings and "every living creature…for all generations to come" (Gen. 9:8-12). This means that yesterday, today, and tomorrow God chooses to stand in an ongoing covenant relationship with every creature. This suggests a creaturely status before God that is not contingent on their status before or with humans. It also reminds us that when we mistreat any creature, we mistreat one who stands in covenant relation to God. And when our actions contribute to the destruction of all members of a species and therefore its total extinction, one might fairly say that we are reversing the obedient work of Noah and destroying a species-family with which God intended to remain in covenant relationship in perpetuity.

Strangely and suggestively, even animals are in a sense treated as moral agents when the text says that there will be accountability of both people and animals for the shedding of blood on the earth (Gen. 9:5). Can it be that before God even the animals have a kind of moral responsibility? Certainly it is clear in Old Testament law that human beings bear responsibility for the negligent care of their animals and any harm that comes to others as a result of such negligence (cf. Ex. 21:29-32). But in this same case law the animal is put to death for its killing of a human even if its owner is not found negligent (Ex. 21:28). Surely this provision aims at the protection of human life, but it also raises the interesting possibility of a kind of moral accountability for animals, as suggested in Genesis 9. This is important because it is precisely moral agency that is often specified as a key demarcation point between human beings and other species.

The Torah contains several provisions protecting both land and animals. This is especially clear in Deuteronomy's version of Sabbath law. Here rest is entirely democratized and universalized, extending not just to every human member of the household (including servants and aliens) but also to the household's oxen, donkeys, and other animals (Dt. 6:14). If all of these are resting, the land must rest as well, a point made explicit in the instructions for Sabbath years and the Jubilee Year (Lev. 25); in both cases, "the land is to have a Sabbath of rest, a Sabbath to the Lord…the land is to have a year of rest" (Lev.

25:2, 5). Even the holy war regulations—deeply problematic texts indeed—contain surprising provisions sparing fruit-bearing trees from being cut down during city sieges (Dt. 20:19). Note that there are good human reasons for these laws, and that in the end they protect the long-term sustainability of the land and therefore human well-being. But the texts are explicit in protecting animals and the land, apparently for their own sake as well.

The psalms are notable for their celebration of God as Creator and for their sometimes quite detailed descriptive celebrations of God's care for creation. A particular favorite of Christian environmentalists is Psalm 104, which like Psalm 8 begins with a celebration of God's majesty, splendor, and greatness. This is particularized through careful descriptions of phenomena of the heavens and the earth, the waters and the air. The psalm notes and celebrates the dependence of the creatures on the provisions God continually provides for them in creation, including the springs that the beasts drink from; the grass eaten by the cattle; the plants, bread, and wine that God provides and men and women eat and drink; the carefully described niches in which the various particular named creatures dwell; the cycles of day and night and the seasons. Our commonality with other creatures is marked as the psalm ends, for "all look to you to give them their food at the proper time" and for all creatures, "when you take away their breath, they die and return to the dust" (Ps. 104:27, 29). "May the Lord rejoice in his works," says the psalmist, and those works are all of us, all creatures, entirely dependent on God's creation, provision, and care, in a fundamental sense a democracy of creaturely gratitude and need, a fact so often forgotten by proud human image-bearers. A similarly detailed and awe-inspiring text of this sort is Job 38-41, in which God takes the questioning Job on a detailed tour of creation. These are profound, passionate, loving depictions of the details of creaturely existence and the created world. They reflect a sense of sacredness.

Constructive resources for a Christian ecologically friendly ethic extend to the wisdom sayings of both the Old Testament and the New. These regularly refer to the created order, its regularities and moral structure established from the beginning of creation (Prov. 8), and the behaviors of other creatures which in various ways teach human beings lessons for the living of our lives (Prov. 17:12, 25:13-14, 25-26, 26:1-3, 11, 17, 27:8, 28:3, 15, 30:17-19, 24-31). One text even describes the character of a righteous person as one who "cares for the needs of his animal" (Prov. 12:10), reminiscent of a similar saying by St. Francis. These observations and exhortations can broaden our sense of the way God stands in relationship to the entirety of the creation, as well as our sense of sharing a kind of moral community with other creatures whose lives are also governed by the loving and just God of the universe.

The sorrowful brokenness of the creation despite God's ongoing care becomes a theme in the prophetic writings — along with promises of the renewal of the whole creation, and the healing of the conflicts and fears that separate not just humans from each other but animals and humans. So indeed at the end, in that blessed Day of the Lord, predators will no longer kill, animals will live in community with each other, and neither children nor their parents need fear animals any longer — "they will neither harm nor destroy in all my holy mountain" (Isa. 11:9).

When "the Spirit is poured upon us from on high" (Isa. 32:15), the creation will be renewed. Deserts will become fertile ground, peace will prevail in human community, the land will be fruitful and both people and animals shall dwell in safety (cf. Isa. 32:16-20). The later prophetic writings mix warnings of a fierce coming judgment on God's enemies with promises of the glorious transformation that will then come upon both Israel and the world. First there will be a purgative judgment, then a holistic planetary renewal leading to secure, joyful existence for all creatures. How often does our treatment of biblical eschatology address these themes? Does our love and hope extend this far?

Jesus reflects this thoroughly Jewish and prophetic eschatology when he speaks in passing of the restoration (Mt. 17:11) and "the renewal of all things" (Mt 19:28). Along with Glen Stassen and others I have sought to contribute to a recovery of understanding of the centrality of the kingdom or reign of God in the ministry of Jesus, and here would only add that part of that reign was and is the renewal and healing of the broken creation and broken creatures (cf. Isa. 35/Lk. 4:16-20). Not only did Jesus heal the sick and raise the dead, he also calmed the threatening storm and pointed to the future renewal of all things — a renewal gloriously depicted in Revelation in the same words used by Isaiah. One day there shall be no more hurting or destroying, no more suffering or crying or mourning or pain (Rev. 21:1-5). Is it too much to wonder whether this end of suffering, crying, and pain extends to our non-human neighbors who also suffer and die? Can that be what Paul refers to when he speaks of the liberation of creation from its bondage to decay (Rom 8:28ff.)?

These themes take us right into the heart of our theology of salvation, which is logically interconnected with our theology of creation, sin, covenant, and eschatology. Here we are well beyond tweaking an ethic of dominion.

A thoroughgoing concern for God's creation is today contributing to a discovery or rediscovery of a planetary or cosmic rather than human-centered biblical narrative. The whole biblical story is being reframed, moving away from the divine-human drama of creation, fall, and redemption toward a planetary drama involving all God's creatures. Admittedly, staying close to the biblical text entails a special place for humanity — in creation, in sin (and in evoking a divine judgment that sweeps up all creatures into its effects), in redemption, and in the final eschatological drama. But the rest of the created order has begun to reappear in Christian theological treatments of soteriology and eschatology.[23]

In this more cosmic vision, as we have already seen, from the beginning a theology of creation is much more attentive to the full range of God's creatures. While sin is (apparently) a possibility only for human beings (and higher beings, such as the angels?), all creation and its creatures are affected. God's long march of redemption begins with Noah and a covenant made with all creatures.

As for the decisive covenant that centers in Jesus Christ, more and more attention is being paid to grand texts like John 1 and Colossians 1. Together, these texts do several profound things:

a) position the Word as the One through whom all things were made (Jn. 1:3, Col. 1:16) and as the source of "life," apparently both physical and spiritual life (Jn. 1:3), if the distinction is relevant;

b) describe the Word as "becoming flesh" (Jn. 1:14) in Jesus Christ, forever elevating the value of fleshly life through the reality of the incarnation;

c) describe Christ as the "image of the invisible God" and thus present him as the source and beginning of a renewal of human nature (Col. 1:15);

d) list a mysterious and extensive array of entities and creatures created by Christ (Col. 1:16);

e) assert that all of these were not only created by him but also for him (Col. 1:16) — he is their source, their purpose, and their destiny;

f) state that "in him all things hold together" (Col. 1:17), which suggests that Christ is somehow the sustaining and centering power of the universe in an ongoing way;

g) by being "before all things" and "the firstborn from among the dead," Christ has the supremacy in everything — he is Lord of all who exist, all that exists (Col. 1:17-18);

h) assert that God's purpose through Christ is to reconcile to himself "all things…whether things on earth or things in heaven" (Col. 1:20).

These are exalted themes, high points of biblical revelation. They offer a much bigger story than the relationship between God and humanity. Jesus Christ becomes the hinge and pivot of the entire planetary drama from beginning to end; no creature came into existence or stays in existence apart from him; and no creature is unaffected by the gospel, the good news that "God was in Christ, reconciling the world to himself" (2 Cor. 5:19; cf. Mk. 16:15).

Paul's treatment of these themes in Romans 8 seems to suggest a relationship between the salvation of humans and the rest of creation in which just as human sin brought creation's groaning, so the salvation of human beings in Christ brings creation's reclamation. That is why a (personified) creation can be depicted as "wait[ing] in eager expectation for the children of God to be revealed" (Rom. 8:19). In Adam, humans sinned and creation suffered; in Christ, redemption begins and creation rejoices. We are the God-designated servant-leaders of the rest of creation — after all, that is the meaning of Gen. 1:26-28 — but we are forever connected to that creation as well. When God sent Christ into the world, Paul seems to be saying, his central purpose was to reclaim humanity, but in so doing he acted to reclaim the entirety of the created order, which of course only needed to be reclaimed because human sin brought it low. When we see this, when we see that God was in Christ, reconciling the world to himself, every creature included, we see the ultimate evidence of God's immense valuing of a universe made sacred by his design, decision, and declaration.

This, finally, is the theological reason why it cannot be that God's ultimate intention for this planet is its destruction by fire. It is hard to overstate how much damage has been done by this particular

171

interpretation of the events of the end, and especially of 2 Peter 3. I call on our biblical scholars and theologians to work hard on this text in light of the eschatology of the rest of the scriptures. It seems clear that 2 Peter 3 is much better interpreted as a purgative judgment preliminary to the final renewal of all things. That coheres better with the rest of scriptures in which warnings of ultimate judgment at the Day of the Lord are coupled with promises of the final "renewal of all things." The "new heaven and the new earth" of 2 Peter 3 and Revelation 21 is actually a renewed heaven and renewed earth, where God's intention for this planet at the creation is at last fulfilled. It is hard to see how a God who cares so profoundly for the creatures and all creation could end the planetary drama with raw destruction rather than renewal.

Conclusion

I began this essay by describing the sanctity-of-human-life ethic as it has emerged as an "old new" theme in Christian ethics. I talked about its profound power and appeal for addressing the perennial problem of how human beings should view and treat one another under the majestic and loving sovereignty of God.

But then I asked whether it can serve as an adequate ethic for an age of ecological degradation and possible catastrophe. I named a number of very serious objections to even a strong and holistic articulation of this kind of Christian ethic, and surveyed various theological and philosophical alternatives that essentially abandon it and the biblical framework that undergirds it.

I turned to the question of whether a modified sanctity of life ethic is possible that does not sacrifice the exalted moral valuation of the human person but can stretch to include non-human creatures and the creation itself. I turned to the scriptures to see whether there were legitimate resources there for an eco-friendly sanctity-of-life ethic.

My happy discovery is that the scriptures very clearly reveal "a wideness in God's mercy," and that the Bible is full of evidence that God has revealed his profound care for non-human creatures and the creation in ways that, to our shame, Christians often miss. It is fair to say from scripture that a sanctity-of-created-life ethic can be found that includes but is not limited to the sanctity of human life. Human beings occupy a special leadership role in creation, but as scripture consistently teaches, leadership roles entail disproportionate responsibility and not unique status or special privileges. Human failures before God, neighbor, and fellow creatures damaged relationships at every level. The good news is that Christ's redeeming love is big enough to include the entire created order, which was after all, made by him, through him, and for him.

It turns out that a sanctity-of-human-life ethic can be (must be) expanded to include other creaturely neighbors. As Helen Fein wrote in relation to the sad history of indifference to the plight of the Jews during the Holocaust, what is needed is an *expansion* (not abandonment) of a "sacred universe of moral obligation."[24] Christians who turned away from Jews when the Nazis were trying to kill them believed that certain lives were sacred, but just not Jewish lives. They would lay down their lives for their own family members, but not for Jewish strangers. This may be understandable at a human level but did not reflect the teaching of Jesus. He taught that the stranger and even the enemy must be treated as falling within that sacred universe of moral obligation, and he proved it by dying for them — for us.

I do not believe that we must abandon a biblically based sanctity-of-human-life ethic in order to care adequately for God's creation. To the contrary, having recovered the majestic worth of the human person, we can also discover the extraordinary value of God's other creatures — and the foundation of both in the majesty and love of God. Indeed, we can make the argument more strongly to say that to recover the true roots of the sanctity of human life in God is also to recover the true roots of the sanctity of all created life. This is at least as much a spiritual experience as it is a theological move. Those who tremble in loving awe before the God of all creation will in turn love all of God's creatures. One might say that worship of God is the ultimate origin of a true appreciation for life's sanctity in any of its forms.

As we fall on our knees before God, may we also (re)discover the God-given connectedness of all created life. The evidence is clear all around us that as we care for God's creation well, we care for each other well, and that, sadly, the reverse is also true. Human beings are permanently and inextricably connected to other creatures and the rest of the creation. We may be the planetary servant-leaders, but our story is the story of those whom we lead, our destiny intertwined with theirs, from creation to eschaton. WE are as dependent on the rest of creation as it is on us, with the whole dependent on God-in-Christ. The astonishing discovery from scripture is that God revealed this long ago, through the Word written and the Word made flesh. We lost track of it for a long while under the impact of many factors. May we Christians recover, internalize, and be transformed by these truths without further delay, taking an appropriate role in the global effort to restore God's good yet damaged creation.

NOTES

[1] All Scripture is taken from the New International Version.

[2] Dorothy Emmet, *The Moral Prism* (London: Palgrave Macmillan, 1979).

[3] John Paul II, *The Gospel of Life* (New York: Random House, 1995).

[4] For example, Peter Singer, *Unsanctifying Human Life* (Oxford: Blackwell, 2002).

[5] Glen H. Stassen and David P. Gushee, *Kingdom Ethics* (Downers Grove, IL: Intervarsity Press, 2003); David P. Gushee, *The Future of Faith in American Politics* (Waco: Baylor University Press, 2008).

[6] David P. Gushee, *The Sanctity of Life: A Christian Exploration* (Grand Rapids: Eerdmans, forthcoming). This definition is a composite of numerous other definitions along with my own contributions. It could be described as essentially a standard account with certain intensifying elements.

[7] Richard A. Young, *Healing the Earth* (Nashville: Broadman & Holman, 1994), p. 48.

[8] On the problem of "exceptionalism," see the excellent discussion in Anna L. Peterson, *Being Human* (Berkeley: University of California Press, 2001), ch. 2.

[9] For example, Claus Westermann, *Creation*. Translated by John J. Scullion. London: SPCK, 1974.

[10] This was actually claimed by Emil Brunner, *Revelation and Reason* (Philadelphia: Westminster Press, 1946), p. 34.

[11] A theme beautifully expressed in Larry L. Rasmussen, *Earth Community, Earth Ethics* (Maryknoll, NY: Orbis Books, 1996)

[12] Lynn White, "The Historical Roots of Our Ecologic Crisis, *Science* 155 (March 10, 1967): 1203-1207.

[13] For a careful analysis and response, see Young, *Healing the Earth*.

[14] Jared Diamond, *Collapse* (New York: Penguin, 2005), an immensely important book, tells the story of numerous societies that collapsed ecologically for a variety of reasons.

[15] The concept began as a scientific hypothesis and developed in a metaphysical/religious direction. See James Lovelock, *Gaia: A New Look at Life on Earth* (New York: Oxford University Press, 2000)

[16] Anna L. Peterson, *Being Human: ethics, environment, and our place in the world* (Berkeley, CA.: UC Press, 2001), ch. 2.

[17] See, for example, Riane Eisler, *The Chalice and the Blade* (Gloucester, MA: Peter Smith, 1994)

[18] Thomas Berry, *The Dream of the Earth* (San Francisco: Sierra Club, 1988), esp. ch. 10.

[19] Peter Singer, *Practical Ethics*, 2nd ed. (Cambridge: Cambridge University Press, 1993).

[20] This can be framed philosophically, as an expansion of Kant--as in Paul Taylor, *Respect for Nature: A Theory of Environmental Ethics,* (Princeton NJ: Princeton University Press, 1986)--or Mill--as in Peter Singer, op. cit.--or theologically, as in Larry Rasmussen, *Earth Community, Earth Ethics* (Maryknoll, NY.: Orbis Books, 1996).

[21] Matthew Fox, *Original Blessing* (Santa Fe: Bear & Co., 1983); Sallie McFague, *Models of God* (Minneapolis: Augsburg Fortress, 1987).

[22] Among other sources, Calvin B. DeWitt, *Caring for Creation* (Grand Rapids: Baker, 1998).

[23] See, most recently, N.T. Wright, *Surprised by Hope* (New York: Harper One, 2008).

[24] Helen Fein, *Accounting for Genocide* (New York: Free Press, 1979), p. 33.

Chapter 12

Christian Social Ethics in an Era of Globalization: Tensions and Methods

Anna Robbins

"Globalization" may be narrowly defined in economic terms as the increasing integration of economies across national borders through trade in goods and services, the migration of labor and the investment of capital. More widely, it also involves the spread of cultural influences and ease of communication across borders. The principal cause of globalization has been the dramatic reduction in both durations and costs of international transport and communication – be it the container ship or the Internet. Since the interwar period, the average real charge for ocean freight tonnage has fallen by 70 percent, average revenue per air passenger mile by 85 percent and the cost of a 3-minute trans-atlantic telephone call by 99 percent. These technological enhancements have been accompanied by a reduction in regulatory barriers to trade, financial flows and investment.[1]

In our contemporary world, the very processes of globalization, driven as they are by economic power, depend on universal principles, and develop universalizing tendencies. Sameness permeates our world, soaking into once diverse cultures under brand names and advertising. Sociologists and others highlight the recognition of a common youth culture that is seen to be developing globally, in addition to the common economic culture that emerges from the application of principles of capitalism.[2] Telecommunications and information technology introduce us to concepts and images that are the same the world over, offering icons as the symbols around which we organize our common identity. As Max Stackhouse comments:

> The process we call globalization seems to be creating the conditions for a new super-ethos, a worldwide set of operating values and norms that will influence most, if not all, peoples, cultures, and societies. It is quite possible that most of the contexts in which humans now live, and their roots in particular sets of values and norms, will be modified by a new comprehending context that owes its allegiance to no particular society, local ethos, or political order, even if it is advanced by 'western' influences.[3]

The development of this universal "super-ethos" has not been welcomed by everyone. Indeed, many interpretations of globalization "see in it the triumph of a global capitalism that manifests the interests of the already rich, leads to the exploitation of the less rich, pollutes the environment, commodifies every resource and relationship, creates worldwide inequality, and generates a cultural homogeneity that devastates regional diversity."[4] Moreover, as

Kofi Annan pointed out, "Many see globalization less as a term describing objective reality about the creation of a new social order or civilizational possibility than as an ideology of predatory capitalism" which they experience as a kind of siege.[5]

Stackhouse has identified a backlash against the universalizing tendencies of globalization that he suggests takes three forms: "growing nationalism sometimes threatening multiethnic states; call for strong leaders, seldom democratic, who seek to mobilize these national interests against internationalism; an attempt to use globalization as a scapegoat for all the political and social ills that in fact have domestic roots."[6] Others, however, welcome the developments, suggesting that we need to learn to live well with this new reality, arguing that eventually, it will benefit all those who participate in it.[7] It should not surprise us that there is no consensus on this process.

So, on the one hand, the world is growing more and more connected, more and more homogeneous. On the other hand, the world seems to be fragmenting through the recognition of difference, plurality and the significance of context and culture. Even in the realm of Christian ethics, it is no longer true that what must be done is evident and obvious to all, even if how it ought to be done has always been somewhat more complex.[8] Moreover, we wonder now if we even are speaking the same language across diverse contexts, let alone employing the same concepts or engaging the same rationality. We are more and more the same, and yet more and more wanting to stress our difference and the truth of plurality as the only truth. So how do these opposing tendencies relate together? Do they relate at all? And what is the relevance for the way we approach ethics as Baptists in the contemporary world?

The matter of defining the problem of adjustment between the global or universal and the tribal or plural is complex. There is a primary tension between the global-universal and the tribal-plural tendency that has profound implications for ethics. At least some ethical aspects of this primary tension may be identified and explored through the following three categories:

- Moral Ontology - ways of being
- Moral Epistemology - ways of knowing
- Moral Praxis - ways of doing

Within each category, we may more clearly describe how the tendency towards global or universal culture contrasts with a simultaneous pull in the opposite direction towards tribal or plural culture. This may help us to reflect further on how the church might relate to these tensions, and hopefully, we may gain some insight for how we might approach the ethical task in a globalized world.

Ontology

Let's begin with the ontological tension, reflecting on how 'ways of being' play themselves out in response to the two tendencies. We will do this by considering how the self of the globalized-universal world differs from the self of the contrasting tribal-plural realm. It is my contention that the self of the global-universal world is formed by a frontier context, while the self of the tribal-plural realm is formed by a local, bordered context, thus producing a tension within the self that compromises moral responsibility.

In a globalizing world, human persons are identified by their consumer patterns and practices. This identification is both external and internal. It is reflected externally through the categorization of peoples and populations by economic and political researchers, who maintain databases of spending, consumption and voting patterns, or income and educational levels. For example, major supermarket chains keep track of our spending through loyalty cards, and attempt to direct marketing at us on the basis of a determined set of characteristics. People are identified according to their consumer habits. Moreover, political parties demarcate populations according to defined characteristics derived from sociological and commercial data. They are able to chart, with unsettling accuracy, how an individual will vote in an election on the basis of these external identifications. Such information drives the marketing and advertising which then goes on to continue to shape the self in the direction of these gathered indicators. In many ways, these external characteristics define the consumer self. The stability of the global economy depends on the creation of the consumer self through media and advertising; the self who will purchase and consume in an ongoing cycle of unsatisfied desire. So even while the majority of the world's population does not actively participate in consumer structures due to poverty and powerlessness, to bring them within the parameters of a consumer identity is part of the agenda of economic and political globalization.

These external factors then, go on to shape the internal self. Through branding and imaging, the consumer uses the signs of the global culture to express who they think they are. As individuals purchase and rearrange the signs of the global economy in attempts at self-expression, the process of identity creation is ongoing.[9] But in such a context, the choice is actually limited by the products that companies choose to offer, and prescribed by the forces of advertising, which subtly erodes the moral sense of the self as one who truly has freedom to choose.

In a consumer culture it is important to maintain the illusion that moral authority rests with the individual self. The individual is seen to possess authority because the individual is the one who chooses from amongst the signs and images of a global market culture. Yet, it is clear that choice is limited and prescribed, at least to some degree.[10] The consumer self, then, is discouraged from active, creative responsibility as a moral agent. Instead, the moral self is conditioned by marketing to become morally passive, interested in moral action only insofar as it may be expressed through consumer habits (as in commitment to purchase fair trade products for example) or insofar as it is an acceptable media-generated trend that expresses something positive about the moral self (as in the *Live 8* concerts, for example). Individual loyalty to global signs and symbols shifts moral authority away from local communities and even away from national institutions. Their moral influence is consequently eroded, but the consumer self as a passive self is not able to fill the moral gap.

The consumer self becomes the morally passive self through the constant manipulation of image. The image of the self is easily disconnected from the real self, and the image is constantly created and recreated through the symbols of global culture.[11] We become enchanted with our own image, and unaware of the world around us. The consumer culture depends on us becoming mesmerized with our own image, in order for it to propagate itself. From the resulting *anomie*, there is an emerging sense of normlessness that results in community and individual fragmentation. The global context needs to be addressed by a global moral sense, which fragmented communities and selves are unable to provide. We become fragmented moral selves submerged in a homogenizing collective, without the moral resources to grasp, let alone confront, the accompanying global issues. Active communities coordinate and negotiate the needs of individual members in light of the whole, but in a global culture, such responsibility is easily surrendered to the media and marketers to coordinate. The consumer self is fashioned then in opposition to foundationalism and universal values, even though consumer culture operates out of such assumptions. There is the possibility of some active participation at the local level, but it is more often expressed in fragmented form than sustained, interested involvement.

In many ways, the moral self is deferred, or is expressed in assertions of difference and contextualization. In the west, such expressions may be liquid in nature, akin to Bauman's "peg communities," which form and dissolve at tribal levels.[12] Elsewhere, they may be found in assertions of difference in the face of globalization, through attempts to preserve some valued aspects of rapidly fading cultures, or in assertions of nationalism or various fundamentalisms. They may even be asserted as badges of difference, like images left slowly fading from a screen after the power has been shut off. The most committed are left discouraged and dismayed at the lack of moral progress they are able to generate. There is a recognition that the moral self rooted in the active community is the basic "way of being" that corresponds with a sense of moral responsibility.[13] There is an acknowledgement that many such communities exist in parallel, and share borders with one another. Some are convinced that the way to counter the passive moral self of the global culture is to reinforce local activity. And yet we cannot fail to miss the fact that wherever television goes, the global economy follows. How are such local communities able to prevent and confront the passive moral self from developing an allegiance to the symbols of the consumer society? Moreover, how does the active community equip potentially fragmented moral selves to address the ethical issues of a global world? There is clearly an ontological tension that is not easily overcome.

Epistemology

If we find a tension emerging in our 'way of being' as moral selves in the contemporary world, we may discover it is exacerbated when we move on to consider matters of epistemology, or our "way of knowing."[14] Here, we see the same tension work itself out in terms of our access to, and understanding of, that which we know. Our epistemology goes on to inform the way that we respond to the world in which we find ourselves. In some respects, epistemology then, could also be thought of as a tension between basic assumptions about the nature of our worldviews.[15]

On the tribal-plural level, there may be an emphasis on local values within a culture or community. The local community is the context in which access to knowledge and understanding is formed. The culture that exists in a particular place and time conditions the way that the world is understood. One assumption is that only that which is local and contextual can be known, since it is impossible for any single person or community to perceive the whole. Moral values then, are also local and contextual, if not culturally relative. Since epistemology at the local-tribal level is considered to be culturally conditioned and endemic to a particular time, place and environment, communities who engage with each other may well encounter the other as "different."[16] Encounters may enable them to compare and contrast their values, to understand how and why they differ, while at the same time reinforcing their allegiance to be "different" from others around them. Reinforcing difference may become a means of forging a common local identity in the face of the moral passivity discussed earlier. This may be understood positively as a means of developing healthy local values in the face of globalized values. It may be understood negatively as reinforcing sectarianisms that may lead to conflict, or as becoming so ruggedly contextual that moral relativism, fragmentation and disorientation results. For some, the relativism that is implied, particularly in a world where those who are "different" are encountered at every turn, may simply lead to moral paralysis or even nihilism. If our values are simply the projected hopes and fears of our communities, what meaning is there for the ethical life in the contemporary world?

A tribal-plural understanding of moral values is reinforced by much of contemporary scholarship. One of the more pervasive influences has been that of Alasdair MacIntyre, whose understanding of cultures and ethics is very much one that reinforces the local-plural dimension.[17] Such a perspective is reinforced by several postmodern ethicists who emphasize not only the local fragmentation of ethics, but also suggest the impossibility of transcending the culturally conditioned self with regards to epistemology and ethics. The notion is that since all we can know is what we have experienced, we are unable to generalize from our local context to a wider context in any way that does not do violence to another self or community. Any attempt at dialogue becomes simply a disguised effort to impose our views on others. The best we can do is to divest ourselves of self-interest, and encounter the ethical "other." In the "other" one finds one's true self.

It seems, however, that such a localized, experience-based approach differs significantly in its epistemology from that of the universalized experience of globalization. The processes of globalization depend on an epistemology often dismissed by scholars as "modern" and passé, as they hail the end of the enlightenment project in grand, sweeping generalizations. While epistemology fragments, even within local communities, convincing them of the "myth" of progress, globalization progresses on assumptions and conditions of universality.

"Foundationalism" is the term given to an epistemology that begins with first principles of knowledge gained through reason. Once these first principles are accessed, they can be laid down like the cornerstone of an edifice, and built upon with other assumptions of reason that depend upon them. The skepticism of causality that was raised by Hume, and carried on in diverse forms by other philosophers, found particular manifestation in the nihilistic thought of Nietzsche, who seems to have been resurrected in contemporary times as a postmodern guru. His program of radical doubt wanted to push Descartes to the point even of self-doubt, such that no aspect of reasoned thought could have any confidence that it is necessarily rooted to reality. Thus, the cornerstone of reason was itself called into question, which led to the entire edifice crumbling. Some contemporary understandings of foundationalism are consequently suspicious of ethical systems that rely on universalisms of any kind.[18] Where foundationalist approaches to reason exist, it is suggested that a belief in progress, and the general ability of humanity to harness all the powers of nature to serve itself at the expense of the other is folly, if not self-deception. The lack of moral progress in history is posited as evidence that foundationalism is an illusion. Some suggest that it leads only to imperialism and violence. In response, many have emphasized instead the local-plural dynamic of contextualism that we discussed previously as a means of countering violent claims of universalist moral truth.

Much of this discussion provides a philosophical explanation of what we see happening at the grassroots and what we experience ourselves in our lives today. However, a globalizing world actually depends for its survival and growth on a foundationalist approach, with universal assumptions and applications. The assumptions of global capitalism, for example, grow out of a reasoned approach to human nature, growth, competition, desire and accumulation. As such, it depends on stability, reliability and predictability. It not only assumes a certain universality of reason and human behavior, it reinforces universal principles and universal values, whether they are values of consumerism, development, or even greed. Through the icons of advertising, for example, a global culture emerges that may appear diverse and fragmenting, but that actually promotes similarity over difference, sameness over diversity. The homogenizing influence allows its foundationalist values to replicate themselves, and a local pluralist ethic of difference is not able to counter its more destructive aspects. For if ethics are local and contextual only, what voice is there to critique prophetically, and constructively, the instruments of global capital that often leave the weak and hungry despairing in their wake? How can a voice that emphasizes the "difference" of knowledge be heard in the corridors of the power of those who believe in the "sameness" of knowledge, in a way that actually connects with the concerns of those who occupy such corridors? Moreover, how does one community that finds itself in a position of power, relative to another community, overcome contextuality in order to stand together against exploitation and injustice? The tension is a real one in the contemporary world.

Praxis

Again, we see the tension between the global-universal and the tribal-plural emphasized in the way global ethics may work out in an era of globalization. On the tribal-plural level, there is a sense of emerging independence amongst some that may lead to a complete disenfranchisement amongst others. In any case, a sense of being in control of one's own affairs may be a positive achievement in a world where many communities feel forgotten and left out of the global picture. There may be, amongst such communities, a belief that public (or social) ethics must be discussed with, and addressed to, the local or national political authorities. Political involvement, protest, and social action are all designed to encourage governments to change policies, and generally to "make the world a better place." In a community that emphasizes its difference, this may happen on a relatively local level, though it sometimes may extend to national governments. Often times, Christians lobby governments on the basis of their local knowledge, but demonstrate a distinct lack of sophistication or savvy in terms of how politics work. Or, they are so ruggedly contextual that their appeals have little more than minimal relevance to a wider population. The Berlin Group that emerged from an assembly of disgruntled ethicists in the WCC lamented the contextuality they encountered among Christians and Christian bodies that displayed a distinct naivety about global politics and economics. Their observations have become rather acute when applied to the contemporary world. Theology, while helpful, cannot replace good knowledge about the universal power of economics, nor is a contextual praxis able to address the universalizing issues of a new imperialism from a perspective that is wider than itself.

An example of how this tension works itself out in praxis may be seen in an incident from just a few years ago. An international chocolate company was called to account by a news organization that discovered it was, in essence, trading child slaves in West Africa in order to harvest its cocoa. In an interview on the evening news, the anchor questioned both a managing director of the company and a representative from UNICEF who was among those documenting the atrocity. When the UNICEF rep was asked why he hadn't raised the issue before, he suggested that, in fact, he had been doing so for quite some time. He insisted that he had been lobbying the British government for years on the matter. The company director interrupted, suggesting that he wished the UNICEF rep had approached him instead, insisting he had no knowledge of the situation until it was recently "discovered." "Did you ever tell him what you'd discovered?" the news anchor demanded. The answer was one word, "No." Leaving aside the issue of whether the director was aware of the situation or not, watching this newscast left me rather downcast. Why do organizations, including the church, direct all of their activities towards political groups and governments, while increasingly, the real power is held in the hands of a few, massive, multinational companies, whose global tentacles stretch far beyond the authority of any single political body or government? Surely there is a place for local and national political action. But how well is the church equipped to meet the challenge of discussing ethical issues with multinational corporations with a degree of wisdom, savvy and expertise? Do we even recognize the need to expand our ethical interest beyond the level of governments to address the almost universal power of economics?

If we hope for our social ethics to have any effective outcomes, we will need to address the nature of the global-universal/local-plural tension in terms of praxis. So where do we go from here? I suggest that we may approach ethics in the contemporary, globalizing world from one of three perspectives: frontiers, borders, or networks.[19] Let us consider each of these in turn.

Frontiers

Come with me, if you will, to the frontier. We saddle up our horses, and ride out, blazing a trail across the plains. Everything is a new world to be discovered ... and to be conquered. It is a great adventure. Our encounters with others are rare, and often result in confrontation, either because of misunderstanding, or because one wishes to conquer the other and impose a certain cultural and moral "sameness" upon the other. There is no pretending that we have anything significant in common with the ones we meet. Our differences are obvious and mutually acknowledged, even with a certain respect, if not fear or hatred. The values we take with us we hold dear and we wish to see them taken up by others. Our values are the truth. They are what give us our identity, and our difference. We are willing to suffer and to die – or even to kill for that difference, and we believe in a future that will see our values realized everywhere and by all.

On the positive side, the frontier conjures up the exciting images of uncharted territory; the notions of challenge and adventure. The frontier is most closely associated with images of the American "wild west," where brave individuals and families rode out into the wild blue yonder, looking to blaze a trail to a new life. They had a belief that they were moving into free land in order to stake their claim. There, they could remove any who impinged upon their freedom to live and establish life according to their own ideals. To conquer, rather than encounter, was the norm. The real goal was self-determination; a desire to forge out an authentic existence true to the individual or community vision. But the myth of the frontier, though well entrenched in western culture, both through the "wild west" metaphor, and the European notion of empire, demands critique.

Theologian Roberto Goizueta offers a helpful initial critique of the frontier myth in western culture. He refers to the romantic frontier myth, such as that epitomized in the words of Tennyson's *Ulysses*, as our foundational myth of modernity – our creation myth.[20] Though the great frontier no longer exists in reality, its image remains. He suggests we should awake to the reality of its demise, and turn our attention instead to the existence of borders, which bring people into direct encounter on an equal footing. Certainly the idea of conquering and defeating an enemy for reasons of self-determination is not a popular one in our contemporary world.

But should we dispense so readily with the image of the frontier as a metaphor for our socio-ethical engagement just because it is unpopular? Has it ceased to exist in reality? Niall Ferguson has recently elaborated a thesis that posits the role America plays in the contemporary globalizing world.[21] He defines the globalization process as America's new empire-building process. Though he suggests there are positive aspects to America's role in the international order, he admits that there are also problems, mostly owing to lack of commitment to the outposts of empire, and confidence to see the empire clearly established. It seems he is calling for a renewal of a frontier mentality in order to make globalization work for those who seem at present to endure it rather than enjoy it. Moreover, recent world events suggest that we are not far removed from a world of conflicting value systems that seem resolved only by severe clashes of ideology.[21]

At very least, there are still many people in the contemporary world who have strong ideological commitments, and who engage the world as though it were a frontier to be conquered by the moral values of an "empire." Not least, we have already demonstrated how the global-universal suggests a frontier mentality in terms of its desire to take its foundational, universal values around the world.

And yet, Goizueta seems to have a valid point in beckoning us to consider a different paradigm of public ethical engagement, particularly when we consider Fergusson's description of the weaknesses of the new imperialism. Although the world seems ever full of conflict and confrontation, and it seems reasonable to stake out our territory – even to conquer new territories – there is no doubt that we have more neighbors to contend with than ever before, and our contact with those from outside of the moral tradition where we are most comfortable has increased in a world of plurality and mobility. Rather than simply facing a global-universal frontier, perhaps we do also live in a world of regular border crossings that influence the way we engage God's world.

Borders

We stand at the border and peer across to the other side. Travelling under the identity of the passport in our hand, we move into unknown territory, excited by what we may discover. We encounter all sorts of people from different backgrounds, and they encounter us, as they travel across our border too. We share many things, and yet we are different. There is so much mobility it is hard sometimes to remember where we are, or who we are. But we travel light, so we can always check our passport, and go back home for a while. Even there, things have changed.

Perhaps the metaphor of borders is preferable to that of frontiers, as it acknowledges the value of the tribal-plural context. It acknowledges an unavoidable confrontation between cultures and values. It recognizes that Christian morality encounters other moralities in a context where they all exist, in a manner of speaking, as cultures, with their own commitments and self-defining languages. It recognizes the reality of pluralistic existence, and yet in maintaining its own identity, a Christian morality is able to make its own claims about reality, and engage the ethical task.

Doing social ethics at the borderlines implies several things. For example, it implies an initial confidence in the task, with a clear sense of identity, and potential for idea exchanges. It indicates an openness to learn from others, and not only to teach or impose a single worldview. There is a degree of mutual trust; if one does not impose morality by force, they may expect respect of their value system in return. Inevitably there is an ongoing, integral dialogue.

Doing theology at the borderlines also provides several insights through numerous mutual exchanges of cultural practice, ideas and beliefs. It provides a measure of objectivity that may highlight moral differences between individuals and groups. Yet, at the same time, it may artificially harmonize observed similarities. We seek points of contact and mutuality with others, but without commitment to them, and rejecting responsibility for them. When anything is demanded of us, it is possible to withdraw behind the borderline of encounter to more familiar territory. Our contacts may clarify allegiances through reinforced tribal identity, whilst encouraging us to find at least artificial commonalities. If it is at all true that we know and are known through our relationships, then it must also be true that our public theology is best defined through an examination of its relations with other views. A border context makes this a real possibility.

For example, Kathryn Tanner alludes to the potential of positive identity-giving functions in her discussion of Christian identity in virtue of a cultural boundary.[23] Tanner believes the critical caricature of post-liberals regarding the self-contained and self-originating character of Christian identity is at least in part an accurate reflection of reality. While post-liberals might want to acknowledge the composite nature of the Christian way, they will not acknowledge the composite nature of their identity. She writes,

> By taking two strategies, post-liberals are able to suggest that, while a Christian way may not be self-contained and self-originating, Christian identity still is; though Christian practices are mixed-up for example, with wider cultural spheres, the Christian identity of those practices

- what makes them Christian - has nothing to do with such mixing.[24]

In contrast, she wishes to argue that the boundaries are indeed essential in understanding Christian - and consequently theological and ethical - identity. Boundaries, or borders, imply differences.

> The nature ... of any boundary distinguishing Christian from non-Christian ways of life cannot be determined by looking at Christianity alone ..... Boundaries are determined, in sum, by how a Christian way of life is situated within a whole field of alternatives. The boundaries distinguishing a Christian way of life from others will shift with shifts in the practices of the other ways of life making up the field.[25]

Following Michel DeCerteau, Tanner suggests that the appropriation of cultural material is not a passive action; rather there is a "creativity of consumption. Material borrowed from elsewhere is twisted and turned, used in different ways, when set in a different context."[26] For contemporary public theology, this activity represents a clear and present danger: there is often no recognition that the material passed off as theology has but a bare semblance to it. Perhaps there is a need to recognize the dangers of consumptive behavior for public theology at the borders.

The tendency towards identity consumption in the border context suggests several problems presented by this metaphor. First, in the metaphor of public encounter as border crossings, we can behave merely as tourists, and so never really engage the differences of others. We may fail to gain any external critique from our encounters, and similarly perceive no responsibility for the other in our travels.[27]

Second, travelling without responsibility means that we may be little more than consumers generating a false image for our identity: we may have a reputation for ethical concern, or even a spoken one, but we risk a separation of image from reality if we are not willing to enter authentic transformative relationships rather than capitulate to a consumerist attitude to others.[28]

Third, frequent, almost constant, border crossings can undermine our confidence in our moral values, and can confuse our identity.

Unlike the frontier, the border metaphor may have the effect of watering down identity as it harmonizes differences, highlighting the cultural relativity of moral values. Rather than divide and conquer, we unite and cohere. Or, according to Bauman, we can become fearful, uncertain, and insecure.[29] If, as Jean Baudrillard suggests, we consume others (or at least their images) and we allow others to consume ours, do evangelicals in a border context risk losing our distinct identity, and our ethical voice altogether? If, in the uncertainty of relativism we retreat from making any public proclamation, do we end up like the student of Prague, committing ethical suicide, and with it whatever public voice we might have in society?[30]

This is not simply a vague possibility, but a real one, similar to that which some members of the evangelical church have experienced before.[31] In his exposition of Abraham Kuyper's American Public theology, John Bolt indicates the situation that resulted from the great reversal of the 1960s and 70s in America. We have something to learn from their experience, just as we have to learn from the experience of the ecumenical activists in the WCC from the same period, who faltered in their social engagement for the opposite reason. Where one group began to lose confidence in public theology, the other became ruggedly ideological. Both ended up failing the enterprise, as eventually they swapped roles; the WCC losing its confidence, and evangelicalism turning to ideology. Bolt reminds us that:

> moving through the later decades of the 20th century, American evangelicals have increasingly been marginalized from public life by a dominant liberal-secular mindset. This has not occurred without some complicity on its own part, as evangelical Christianity in its conflicts with modernism retreated into fundamentalism. Along the way, the public identity and character of America, historically seen by many as "Christian America," was fundamentally altered. The process of change, hidden for many years as the nation continued to live under the influence of Christian America's moral capital, became obvious in the countercultural upheavals of the 1960s. In the 1970s and 1980s, shocked to discover that "their" America had been taken from them, conservative American evangelicals reacted by forming political

action groups - moral majorities and Christian coalitions. Politically engaged evangelical Christians, particularly in the so-called "Christian Right," have become a significant force in American political life in the last decades of the 20th century. The boldness of evangelical activism was not always supported by clearly thought out, principled political strategy. In addition to covering too many issues to do any of them full justice, evangelical activists often failed to set political and strategic priorities in their campaigns. It soon became clear that not only were they out of practice for the political battles and culture wars they entered, they were also – by some of their leaders' own admission – theologically and philosophically ill-equipped for the task.[32]

This conclusion coheres with my own research on social ethics in the WCC – and offers us caveats for the present time.[33] The retreat into fundamentalism (at one time evangelicalism, but now in all forms, including liberalism) may have the effect of abandoning the institutions of society to secularization.[34] Once that retreat has taken place, Christians of all sorts, including evangelicals, will need to discover new methods for engagement, since the moral capital once latent in the culture cannot be expected to linger. Moreover, Christians will need to continue to find ways of addressing the terrorism that has recently been directed against the Western world, but which some of our brothers and sisters have endured for generations. Driven by contextual ideology, the public enterprise is bound to fail, a fact admitted on the evangelical side by writers Cal Thomas and Ed Dobson, and on the ecumenical side by a whole host of writers and ethical participants.[35] Despite its relevance, simply trading a metaphor of frontiers for one of borders, therefore, does not seem to offer much promise for successful public ethical engagement that takes global power seriously.

Networks

Our lives are made up of countless connections, some random, some intentional. Within the parameters of space and time, we have limitless mobility, and a seemingly liquid identity. Depending on the company we keep, we can be very different things to different people. We have close contacts around the world, and may live far away from families and traditions. In the comfort of a sparsely furnished room at home, we do our shopping, conduct our business, and engage relationships with a global community. This is truly a different context from the frontier or even the border. I am an online activist. I can engage the world at the touch of a button. But I haven't actually seen anybody today. This is the network society.

As individuals and communities, we occupy myriad communities and engage in countless, seemingly random encounters and deeper relationships. There is a sense of connectedness, but not with linearity. This is the contemporary network – not completely unrelated to its early description by Harvey Cox as the secular city with its networks of traffic, and both casual and meaningful connections.[36] More recently, the rise of the network society has been described in depth by Manuel Castells.[37] Information technology and globalization have led people into new forms of communicating and relating in the contemporary world. Regardless of whether one accepts all of Castells' observations and conclusions, there can be little doubt that "as a historical trend, dominant functions and processes in the information age are increasingly organized around networks."[38] With an increasing dominance over the social structure of globalized society, networks are dominated by flows rather than power,[39] and presence in the network, and the interaction of networks defines control. In Castells' observation, network society becomes characterized by social morphology rather than social action.[40]

But what is a network? According to Castells, it is a set of interconnected nodes, with infinite possibilities for communication. In his words, they are "open structures, able to expand without limits, integrating new nodes as long as they are able to communicate within the network, namely as long as they share the same communication codes" (for example, values or performance goals). "A network-based social structure is a highly dynamic, open system, susceptible to innovating without threatening its balance." He suggests that the appropriateness of networks to global culture will go on to shape the structure of society itself.[41]

What might a network context suggest for social ethics? It will define relationships as intentional, based around common interests and goals. Power for change will be in the hands of those who participate in the network, and control the entry of new nodes into the network. There exists the possibility to compare differences universally, rather than simply with those sharing a border, as the potential for relationship within the network is limited only by who has the capacity to participate, and identification of shared goals. Relationships may be temporary, and utilitarian, suggesting that once goals are achieved, they may dissolve with the network.[42]

We can see positive and negative potential in a network context. The potential for universality, and for providing power to the potentially marginalized voice is significant. Shared goals may forge relationships on a global level, increasing flows and the opportunity to make a social impact beyond one's immediate neighborhood. On the other hand, it may simply provide a new and complete form of marginalization to those who, for whatever reason, lack the ability to participate in a network society. The opportunity to compare differences may reinforce identity, but it may also leave it fluid, as networks appear and dissolve according to shifting goals and values. The lack of permanence in relationship means that rather than cultures consuming one another, there is potential for individuals to consume one another through relationships that are forged and dissolved according to whim or interest.[43] We may or may not like what we may become as evangelicals in a network society. But we must reckon with its challenge nonetheless, not least because of its potential to weaken moral discernment and community commitment.

In fact, I believe that the church is uniquely poised to approach ethics through a network method; to make the most of its opportunities, and to ameliorate its excesses. I further suggest that engaging a network method in a globalizing world is the only means we have of overcoming the divide that emerges from the global-universal/tribal-plural tension.

The Networked Church

In his work on apologetic method in the contemporary world, Alan Sell suggests a model of the church that connects the local and global, the plural and the universal.[44] Balancing reason, faith and experience, his work suggests that the church functions as a community of local experience, but that filters the development of faith through an understanding of reason that is not necessarily foundationalist, but that offers evidence for its belief beyond fideistic claims. Such evidence does not establish the church, however.

All reason, faith and experience must be filtered through revelation, a universal reality that stands outside of, and critiques all experience, even as it enters into our experience of the church, and breathes into us God's life. As such, the global-local tension or divide is overcome: in the church, the moral self and the active self is the self of community, in particular the community that confesses that Jesus Christ is Lord. In praxis, the church is formed by the action of confession; it further overcomes the divide between universal principles and the particularities of lived experience: Christians are those who confess what it means to follow Jesus Christ as Lord in various contexts and circumstances, and yet we also recognize in one another that we have been found by the good news of Jesus Christ beyond our local circumstances. The body that confesses is local and global, plural and universal. As we confess we express in every language that which is beyond expression; as a statement of worship, the words "Jesus Christ is Lord" stand beyond linguistic analysis as a first order statement. But this is not to say that the utterance is meaningless. To the contrary, the act of confession points to the fact of the confession - the ontological reality that Jesus Christ really is Lord, within and beyond all of our attempts to understand and explain who he is and what he has done. He is not Lord because we say that he is; he is Lord because He Is. He incarnates into all of our contexts in the person of the Holy Spirit, and yet his work is of universal relevance, for the whole of the cosmos.

The church then, perhaps uniquely in the contemporary world, is poised to be an already-established network that unites the global and the local, the universal and the plural. As a body that recognizes its calling to be morally active in the local community, it also finds itself in international expression. It is a hub of networks that potentially makes connections between the rich and the poor, the powerful and the weak, the hungry and the satisfied. And it is through the intentional development and use of networks that it may find a way of addressing the needs of local Christians while addressing prophetically those who could do a lot more to ameliorate those needs. I can't say exactly what such intentions should look like. Indeed, some broader Christian identities are already being formed as global urban communities. Evangelical and Pentecostal expressions in particular unite a global Christian community of urban poor; a reality that is slowly being recognized by evangelicals in the West, though its ethical implications remain largely unexplored by both rich and poor.[45]

The church depends on such a network for its own survival: being a network is part of the essence of the church. Particularly for Baptists, with no central authority apart from Christ, and with no denominational hierarchy, the network is a particularly important way of viewing the church. But embracing this reality in a globalized world, and directing it with ethical intention will mean fostering our international denominational links at a time when locally, denominationalism is falling on seemingly hard times; it will mean Baptists forging network links with other like-minded Christians, at least with evangelicals and Pentecostals who are emerging as a new global culture; it will mean encouraging the comfortable to get out of their comfort zones and to assume greater responsibility for brothers and sisters around the world by changing personal and local community behavior within a global consumer culture; it will mean finding ways as international networks to connect Christians and economists and politicians rather than retreat into our respective epistemological hubs (and such expertise certainly is available in the Christian world, if theologians avail themselves of it); it will mean finding more ways of connecting like-minded Christians across contexts to share ideas and stories while pushing beyond the narrative to ask the question, "What does this story mean for me, demand of my community?" It will mean finding way of connecting diverse Christians across contexts to not only encourage but to challenge one another; (the former is often much easier than the latter); it will mean reaffirming our confidence that a body that affirms its powerlessness in a world of power can actually make a difference, not for its own glory but for the glory of Christ. For Baptists, all of this may entail particular challenges and opportunities. For example, what does the principle separation of church and state mean for those of us who live in democracies, where I would suggest that we have not only the legal right but also the moral obligation to be politically involved on behalf of our brothers and sisters who do not enjoy the same freedom of worship and assembly? If we do not use our rights are we bound to lose them? How can we be publicly active communities whilst respecting the liberty of individual members of the community to dissent? How do we account for the diversity in our ethical perspectives when we all claim to be "people of the book"?

Perhaps some of us have occasionally hidden behind our Baptist principles in order to avoid some of the tough questions rather than allow them to direct and influence our ethical endeavors. If we are a priesthood of believers, do we not have the obligation to prevail upon the authorities on behalf of one another in a globalized world as part of our priestly function and to present a biblical worldview in a prophetic and perhaps even constructive manner? Equally, if we are to be willing to confront the principalities and powers, we must be willing to divest ourselves of power too. This is costly for those of us who think we have much to lose. How precious is the freedom of self-determination, expressed through the economics of a consumer society, to those of us who don't have to think too hard about whether we can afford to attend Baptist World Alliance (BWA) meetings year after year? What does it mean for me, when I'm buying my new iPod that I've just met a pastor from a country where many of his friends have been martyred in the previous few years? Our networks, if they are to mean anything, have to be of the mutually life-changing kind. They must involve more than platitudinous statements: they must have real implications for action at the grassroots.

Where might we start on this journey? Well, here in the BWA we have a ready made network; with inbuilt opportunities to meet together and hear from one another. Let us work hard to ensure that this becomes a hub of networks that not only informs and radically challenges our ethics, but that leads to effective ethical action in local contexts, and global ones. For despite its fallen condition, this is the world that Christ yet surveys and cries, "Mine!"[46]

NOTES

[1] Paul S. Mills, "Globalization and the World Economy: for richer or poorer, for better or worse?" *Cambridge Papers* 14/1 March 2005.

[2] See for example, Marcelo Vargas, "Can the Global Replace the Local?: Globalization and Contextualization" in *One World or Many? The Impact of Globalization on Mission*, Richard Tiplady, ed. (Pasadena: William Carey Library, 2003), 203-209.

[3] Max Stackhouse, "General Introduction" in *God and Globalization: Religion and the Powers of the Common Life*, Vol 1, Max L. Stackhouse and Peter J. Paris, eds. (Harrisburg, PA.: Trinity Press, 2000), 19.

[4] Ibid.

[5] Ibid., 4-5.

[6] Ibid.

[7] See for example, Peter Heslam ed., *Globalization and the Good*, (Grand Rapids, MI : William B. Eerdmans Pub. Co.), 2004; and Philippe Legrain, *Open World: The Truth about Globalization* (London : Abacus, 2002).

[8] See Douglas John Hall, "The State of the Ark: Lessons from Seoul," *Between the Flood and the Rainbow: Interpreting the Conciliar Process of Mutual Commitment (Covenant) to Justice, Peace, and the Integrity of Creation*, compiled by D. Preman Niles (Geneva: WCC, 1992), 37. Hall highlights the need for churches to be able to relate across contexts in order to meet uniquely global challenges.

[9] See D. Slater, op. cit.: Gordon Wenham in *Christ and Consumerism*, Craig Bartholemew and Thorsten Moritz, eds. (Carlisle: Paternoster, 2000), 121.

[10] Slater, cit. Wenham, 130.

[11] For an analysis of the self-replicating nature of the postmodern image as the 'hyperreal' see Jean Baudrillard, *The Consumer Society* (London: Sage, 1998). Baurdrillard is here dependent on Marshall McLuhan's work on the media.

[12] See Zygmunt Bauman, *In Search of Politics* (Oxford: Polity Press, 1999), 47-48.

[13] See Marcia Y. Riggs "Living into Tensions: Christian Ethics as Mediating Process" in *Many Voices One God*, Walter Brueggemann and George W. Stroup, eds. (Louisville: WJK, 1998), 181-192.

[14] This is not unrelated to ways of being. Certainly, how you understand ontology will influence the way you understand epistemology, and vice-versa.

[15] A discussion on worldviews is relevant here, but space prohibits it. See James Sire, *Naming the Elephant: The Concept of Worldview* (Downers Grove: IVP, 2004), and David Naugle's *Worldview: The History of A Concept* (Grand Rapids, Mich. : W.B. Eerdmans Pub., 2002) Of course such work is preceded by Kant and Dilthey amongst others.

[16] The ethical importance of the term *difference* is a popular topic within postmodern philosophy, including the work of Paul Ricoeur and Jaques Derrida.

[17] See Alasdair *MacIntyre, After Virtue: A Study in Moral Theory* (Notre Dame, Ind.: University of Notre Dame Press, 1981); cf. MacIntyre, *Whose Justice, Which Rationality?*(Notre Dame, Ind. : University of Notre Dame Press, c1988). In the latter work, MacIntyre allows for dialogue across contexts, though its potential is not really made clear. In a recent article in *Studies in Christian Ethics*, Michael Taylor highlights the contrast between MacIntyre and Ronald Preston. Much of what he says in the article is instructive for the present discussion. See Michael Taylor, *Faith in the Global Economic System: The Future of Christian Social Ethics: Essays on the World of Ronald H. Preston 1913-2001, Studies in Christian Ethics,* 17/2, 2004, 197-215.

[18] Even some secular ethicists who have no biblical reason for doing so, attempt to establish some sort of universalism for ethics. See, for example, John Rawls, *A Theory of Justice* (Cambridge, Mass. : Belknap Press, 1972).

[19] *Cf. Anna Robbins, Sharing the Feast (Milton Keynes: Authentic Media), 2005.*

[20] Roberto Giozueta, "There You Will See Him: Christianity Beyond the Frontier Myth," in *The Church as Counterculture*, eds. Michael Budde and Robert Brirnlow (Albany: SUNY, 2000), 174.

[21] Niall Ferguson, *Colossus: The Price of America's Empire* (New York and London: Penguin, 2004).

[22] See, for example, Samuel Huntington, *The Clash of Civilizations and the Remaking of World Order*, (London: Simon & Schuster, 1997).

[23] Kathryn Tanner, *Theories of Culture: A New Agenda for Theology* (Minneapolis: Augsburg Fortress, 1997).

[24] Ibid., 105

[25] Ibid., 111. While we may wish to go beyond Tanner and say that the essential *content* of Christian theology is at least in some respects self-defining, (or God-defined insofar as it relates to the revelation of the gospel), the *activity* of theology, especially public theology, is one of relationship with other insights and disciplines. Indeed, Archbishop Rowan Williams rightly suggests this recognition is essential to integrity in moral discourse, and that the activity of discourse itself presupposes such relationships. Rowan Williams, *On Christian Theology* (Oxford, Blackwell, 2000), 4-5.

[26] Tanner, 112.

[27] Zygmunt Bauman has identified the stroller, vagabond, tourist and player as alternative identities to that of the pilgrim in postmodern life. See Bauman's *Life in Fragments: Essays in Postmodern Morality* (Oxford, Blackwell,1995).

[28] This calls to mind Jean Baudrillard's four orders of simulation that results in the separation of image from reality: the image first reflects reality; then masks reality; then masks the absence of a profound reality; then has no relation to reality whatsoever (hyperreality). See Jean Baudrillard, *Simulacra and Simulation* (University of Michigan, 1994).

[29] Zygmunt Bauman, *In Search of Politics* (Oxford, UK : Polity Press, 1999), 9-57.

[30] See Jean Baudrillard, *The Consumer Society: Myths and Structures* (London: Sage, 1998).

[31] I would suggest this possibility is particularly real in the life of popular British evangelicalism at the moment, much of which brings to mind the social gospel emerging from 19th Century Liberal Protestantism. Cf. Gary Dorrien, *The Making of American Liberal Theology: Imagining Progressive Religion 1805-1900* (Louisville: WJKP, 2001).

[32] John Bolt, *A Free Church, A Holy Nation: Abraham Kuyper's American Public Theology* (Cambridge and Grand Rapids: Eerdmans, 2001), xiv.

[33] Anna Robbins, *Methods in the Madness: Methodological Diversity in Twentieth-Century Christian Social Ethics* (Carlisle: Paternoster, 2004).

[34] Secularisation is defined by Peter Berger as 'the process by which sectors of society and culture and removed from the domination of religious institutions

and symbols.' Berger, *The Sacred Canopy: Elements of a Sociological theory of Religion* (Garden City NY: Doubleday Anchor, 1967), 106.

[35] In particular, a group of ecumenical participants formed the ad hoc 'Berlin group' which convened on several occasions to explore the future of the social ethical enterprise in the WCC. They acknowledged that ideology and dogmatism are insufficient equipping for the task of public theology, and highlighted instead the crucial role of dialogue in reversing the ideological and contextual trend. In particular, they highlighted several issues of dialogue that I have adapted as elements of practical unity within a model of moral integrity. The first report of the Berlin Group was issued as *A Statement to the World Council of Church on the Future of Ecumenical Social Thought: Report of An Informal Discussion of Church Leaders, Theologians, Social Ethicists, and Laity* (Berlin, May 29-June 3, 1992). The majority of their documents and official responses are unpublished. Cf. Roger Shinn, "Friendly Dialogue" *One World* (April 1994), 13.

[36] Harvey Cox, *The Secular City: Secularization and Urbanization in Theological Perspective* (London: SCM, 1965).

[37] Manuel Castells, ed. *The Network Society: A Cross-Cultural Perspective* (Cheltenham, UK ; Northampton, MA : Edward Elgar Pub., 2004).

[38] Castells, 469

[39] Castells describes this as the dominance of the "power of flows over the flows of power." 469.

[40] Ibid.

[41] Ibid., 470.

[42] This is exemplified in Bauman's description of the 'peg-style community' as a liquid form of political action in a postmodern age. See Zygmunt Bauman, *In Search of Politics*, op. cit., 9-49, especially 47-48.

[43] The existence of liquid church models in theory, and emerging church networks in practice are examples of varied responses to these cultural trends, and provide evidence for their influence on Christian (particularly evangelical) life and thought.

[44] Alan P. F. Sell, *Confessing and Commending the Faith* (Cardiff: University of Wales Press, 2002).

[45] Andrew Davey, *Urban Christianity and Global Order* (London: SPCK, 2001), 30.

[46] Abraham Kuyper's famous phrase, 'There is not a square inch in the whole domain of our human experience over which Christ, who is Sovereign over ALL, does not cry, 'Mine!'" Cited in John Bolt, *A Free Church, a Holy Nation : Abraham Kuyper's American public theology* (Grand Rapids, Mich. : W.B. Eerdmans, 2000), xiii.

The Commission on Church Leadership

Brian Winslade, Chair

During the 2006-2010 quinquennium, the Commission on Church Leadership has met during the Annual Gathering of the BWA and enjoyed well-attended and robust discussions. Given the relatively broad definition of the commission's title, and whom it might attract whenever it meets, attempts were made to distill topics for dialogue that addressed areas of most felt need.

In 2006 the commission met in Mexico City around the general theme: "In what ways is church leadership different in the 21st century from the 20th century?" Was the dawn of the new millennium a simple "click" in our watch, or did it signal something more profound, requiring a change in how leadership is perceived and practiced? As a prior resource to our meetings, commission members were asked to read a paper, "Kingdom Leadership in the Postmodern Era," by Leonard Hjalmarson.[1]

Papers were then presented in response by Michael Quicke (UK/USA), Gilberto Gutiérrez Lucero (Mexico), Raquel Contreras (Chile), Mal Malena (Canada), Bonny Resu (India) and Bruce Powell (USA).

In 2007 the commission meetings took place in Accra, Ghana, and focused around the topic: "Defining Congregational Government in the 21st Century." This topic had surfaced as one of highest interest when future theme options were canvassed the previous year. Does historical understanding of congregational polity still fit our contemporary world and diverse cultural contexts? Prior to commission meetings members were forwarded a paper by Nigel Wright entitled: "Biblical and Theological Foundations of Congregational Polity." An attempt was made, largely unsuccessful, to establish an online dialogue in preparation for commission meetings. When the commission met, Solomon Ishola (Nigeria) and Angelo Scheepers (South Africa) reflected on how congregational polity is outworked in the African context. This was followed by a panel of short presentations around the expression of "Leadership, Power and Authority within a Baptist Polity" with contributions coming from Keith Jones (UK/Czech Republic), Craig Vernall (New Zealand), Mayrinkellison Peres Wanderley (Brazil), Teddy Oprenov (Bulgaria), and Rachael Tan (Taiwan).

Commission meetings in 2008 were held in Prague, Czech Republic, and focused on the theme: "The Place of Ordination within Baptist Ecclesiology." Prior to when the commission gathered, two preparatory papers were circulated to members, one by Brian Winslade, "Ordination – Does it Fit?", and a second (section of a chapter) by the late David Bosch, "Mission as Ministry by the Whole People of God."[2]

Given the nature of the topic, an approach was made, and accepted, to hold a joint session with two other commissions, namely the Commission on Baptist Heritage and Identity and the Commission on Doctrine and Interchurch Cooperation. An excellent (and large) joint session heard papers on "An Historical Survey of How Baptists have Ordained/Credentialed Ministers of the Gospel across the Past Four Centuries" and "Is the Baptist Concept of Ordained Ministry just a Function, or a Way of Being?" In the second session a formal debate was held around the provocative proposition: "The day of ordaining people to pastoral ministry is over!" In the third session, presentations were made by Rodney Macann (New Zealand), Ken Bellous (Canada), Jonathan Edwards (UK) and Teddy Oprenov (Bulgaria) on practical systems of credentialling pastors within their respective unions/ conventions.

The 2009 meetings of the commission were held in Ede, Netherlands, amidst the 400 year anniversary celebrations of the Baptist movement. Two particular themes were addressed. In the first session, the topic was, "Discipline and Restoration of Leaders who Fall." Presentations were made by Roy Medley (USA), Jan Kornholt (Denmark) and Bill Slack (Scotland). In the second and third sessions, the theme was around intentional development of emerging leaders. David Coffey (UK/ BWA President) presented a paper on "The Imperative of Developing Emerging Leaders" and this was followed by presentations from three members of the Emerging Leaders Network, Craig Vernal (New Zealand), Koffi Soké Kpomgbe (West Africa) and Blake Killingsworth (USA).

On two occasions during the quinquennium, members of the Emerging Leaders Network attended meetings of the Commission on Church Leadership en masse and made an excellent contribution.

While the initiative for the Emerging Leaders Network was not with the Commission on Church Leadership, it was a venture that the commission fully supported and sought to resource, where possible. We have much to be grateful for in the crop of outstanding emerging leaders God is raising up across our movement.

NOTES

[1] Leonard Hjalmarson, http://www.christianity.ca/church/leadership/2005/05.000.html

[2] David Bosch, *Transforming Mission: Paradigm Shifts in Theology of Mission*, (Maryknoll, NY: Orbis Books, 1999), 467-470.

Chapter 13

Defining Congregational Government in the 21st Century The Nigerian (African) Experience

Solomon A. Ishola

In the Beginning

Until recent years, especially from the 1990s, not much debate arose within our practice of congregational church government in the Nigerian Baptist Convention. This may have been due to the fact that the leadership pattern established by American missionaries of the Southern Baptist Convention adapted very much to the model of leadership they found in traditional African society where leadership ethos is essentially patriarchal. Looking back, one wonders the criteria used by the missionaries to ascertain what aspect of traditional African leadership values were acceptable in administering the indigenous congregations and which were not. The problem of adaptation of African leadership ethos in regard to congregational polity in the Nigerian setting was not peculiar to the Southern Baptists. It was indeed a problem faced by virtually all Western missions blazing the trail for the gospel in Africa, especially during the high tide of late 19th century Western imperialism. It may be recalled that it was in the tension between African cultural values and the Christian faith, as the latter was understood by Western missionaries at this time, that the first schisms took place in the churches of Africa and gave birth to what became known as Ethiopianism [1] in African Christianity.

In spite of the difficulties that mission churches had, the growing confidence of African Christians and their contention with the missionaries for cultural authenticity in their practice of the new found faith, definite patterns emerged in the 20th century, both in the churches initiated by Africans and those that were established by foreign missions. While the African churches intuitively appropriated African values and religious geniuses in various ways, the mission-founded churches also adapted to local realities, taking each step with trepidation, particularly in matters of ethics. Among the mission churches, it appears the Southern Baptists were the most radical in their appropriation of local realities to their pattern of church government. This is not because they practiced Congregationalism in contradistinction to the other missions whose Episcopal and Presbyterian traditions were simply taken for granted and bequeathed the new churches in Africa. For one thing, these modes of governance are very much at home with indigenous Africa and it is not surprising that the people have no problem with their hierarchical structures.

The radical nature of Southern Baptist missionaries' approach to church government in Nigeria lies in the contrast between the liberal ethos of congregational governance that characterized Southern Baptist churches in America and the near-hierarchical pattern of governance they practiced in Nigeria and subsequently bequeathed the early leadership of the Nigerian Baptist Convention. Of course, their work would have proved more difficult if they were to introduce early such liberal ethos into church government. Nevertheless, one is bound to wonder about the source of this contrast. Was it a case of intentional adaptation wherein the missionaries' understanding of African peoples and society required that they adapt Congregationalism to their context of mission? Or did the modified form of Congregationalism evolve as events unfolded? Could it also be that the missionaries were just being opportunistic by arrogating to themselves the power to make some decisions without the people's input?

If one is to go by the schismatic exchanges that took place between Western missionaries and their African converts in the late 19th and early 20th centuries, especially as led by Mojola Agbebi's Africanist affirmation, it appears the adaptation evolved within the scheme of church development. For while national churchmen like Rev. James Johnson of the Anglican Church and Mojola Agbebi of the Baptists challenged the racial pretensions of Western missionaries in the churches the missionaries founded, these men were in their essential element patriarchal. It is, therefore, not surprising that in the resolution of the conflicts between Agbebi and the American Baptist missionaries, the Nigerian churchman, as an African that he was, took for granted an African hierarchical model of leadership. Like that of his colleagues in the Anglican Church, his racial counter-response to missionaries' pretensions, for all its fieriness, did not see anything wrong with African rule of elders in community affairs. In fact, for him, it was normative and constituted an aspect of the people's genius. Hence, his quarrel with the missionaries was not occasioned by the quest for a liberal, congregational pattern of church government in the emerging Nigerian Baptist churches of the late 19th and early 20th centuries. Rather it was directed at their feelings of racial superiority toward their African converts and the consequent, perceived domination of the nationals in church matters.

It was thus by *default* that the Nigerian Baptist Convention emerged as a national entity and thrived for 76 years, that is from 1914 to 1990, as a denomination governed by what may be called modified Congregationalism. Governance modified in the sense that while most of the churches maintained their autonomy in self-governance and voluntarily contributed resources toward the national denomination, the leadership in the latter exercised authority with wide latitude. This is evident in the unquestioned, far-reaching influence and authority of some of the leaders in the affairs of some of the local congregations. Examples in this regard abound in the recommendations of pastors to local churches and in the processes of resolving local churches' internal conflicts by the general secretaries of the denomination. And the internal conflicts sometimes included those that have to do with pastor-church relationships and appointments of deacons; matters that are, in congregational polities, internal affairs of the churches and should court "external" intervention only by invitation. Although some of the local churches' crises that received intervention from denominational leaders could hardly be said to be resolved to the various parties' satisfaction, no one challenged the authority of the leaders to intervene in these crises. It was taken for granted that such intervention was normal, and the denomination has since formalized the process into its conflict-resolution mechanism.

A Critical Turning Point

However, beginning in the 1990s a new experience began to unfold in the denomination. Deep fissures became evident as annual convention sessions became combative. The turbulent nature of annual sessions was not new, but from this period the resolution of issues at stake were protracted and impugned on the credibility of the leadership. Several factors combined to generate this state of affairs. A remote factor was the inflow of a new cadre of students, from mid-1980s, into the theological training schools of the denomination in preparation for pastoral ministry. These students were university graduates, and a few of them held higher degrees prior to their enlisting for theological training. While a few university graduates had passed through the seminary in the past, this type of student began to enroll in increasing numbers from the 1980s. By the time they were taking up appointments in the churches at the end of the decade, the ground was prepared for leaders who would not take things on their face value. They questioned suspicious denominational policies and raised issues with members of their congregations on the policies and decisions of the denomination on current, sensitive issues.

While this quiet change was creeping into the profile of the denomination's ministerial personnel, critical leadership struggles began to manifest in the late 1980s in the bid to get a successor to the then outgoing general secretary of the denomination, Dr. S. T. Ola Akande, well known to many in the BWA. The process was perceived to be fraught with intrigues and led to a spontaneous mass action in which a new general secretary emerged in the person of Dr. S. Ola Fadeji, also well known to the BWA, at the annual session held in Ibadan in 1991. Although it was hardly seen at this time that the spontaneous election of a general secretary of the convention by a process of mass action was damaging to the credibility of the leadership of the denomination, the seed of suspicion was thereby sown and the decade of the 1990s would see to its nurture, flowering, and eventual fruition toward the first decade of our 21st century. What followed in that closing decade of the 20th century was a series of protests and disaffection with the way the leadership handled sensitive issues that arose within the denomination and in its institutions.

A particularly damaging crisis, in fact bordering on schism, lasted between 1995 and 1997, giving rise to the "Stand-Up for Jesus Baptist Movement" among young ministers from one of our cities.[3] The magnitude of the shock the crisis sent through the system can only be appreciated by observing the campaigns launched in its aftermath by the denomination's leadership. Churches were told to add to their media signposts, as part of their identity, that they belong to the Nigerian Baptist Convention. Several churches responded accordingly; and a few were indifferent. The tragedy of this crisis was not so much in the fact that it arose at all; it was in the fact that it did not seem to motivate the leaders to do business in ways sensitive to the aspiration of the people they led. Rather it appears the whole process of denominational leadership continued as if nothing had happened when, in reality, its credibility had been challenged and authority undermined.

Even though the leaders tried to wish away the sad onslaught of the movement, it was obvious that the system could no longer take for granted unqualified loyalty of its local congregations. This was overtly manifested in the wholesale rejection of the Executive Committee's proposals toward the restructuring of the convention at the 2000 Annual Session held at Abeokuta. Following the crisis of the "Stand-Up for Jesus Movement" and the incessant and suspect constitutional amendments with which they had been inundated all through the decade, the people had become wary of the restructuring agenda. Some of the churches being led by young ministers had become more assertive of their autonomy as voluntary members of the convention. The credo of voluntary association of churches to form cooperative organs, purely for the purposes of mission and institutional development, became the argument of some of these ministers for the existence of cooperative work at all among the churches.

Another factor that cannot be discounted in this climate of seemingly weakening ties in our denomination is the effect of global politics. Ordinarily, this will appear farfetched, but the change that came upon the international society in the dissolution of the Union of Soviet Socialist Republics (USSR) in the wake of Premier Gorbachev's vision of *Glasnost* and *Perestroika* for communist Russia had ripple effects in the global South. In Africa it excited agitation for the liberalization of national political spaces that had been dominated for decades by sit-tight rulers. The wave of national conferences that swept Francophone African countries in the 1990s well attested to this process. In Nigeria, the massive agitation of civil right groups for the validation of the annulled presidential election of 1993 and the attendant restiveness put the country in the league of nations of the South groaning for liberal democratic governance over and against the dictatorship of the military class. It was in this age of dissatisfaction with autocracy, in whatever form it might be cloaked, that the assertiveness of the autonomy of our congregations became a vexing issue to our cooperative organs.

By the closing years of the 1990s it was clear to the leadership of the Nigerian Baptist Convention that ties were weakening in the denomination. To address the issue, the subject of congregational polity came to the front burner at the annual workers' conference. A committee was also set up to look into the matter and make recommendations to the Executive Committee of the convention. Both approaches came to naught as they did not stem the tide. The pastors in the congregations were not interested in anything that would compromise the autonomy of the churches they led. Further, the churches would not trade their autonomy for anything. In the last five years, several papers have been issued from different constituencies of the denomination with regard to how Congregationalism should be practiced in the Nigerian church environment. One of these, titled, "A Critical Re-Evaluation of the Baptist Church Polity and Its Application in the Nigerian Baptist Convention," was presented by Prof. Osadolor Imasogie at the annual workers' conference of the convention held in February 1999.[4] The fact that the paper addressed the issue in the context of the denomination's procedure for resolving conflicts itself is revealing. The activities of the convention were conflict-ridden in the decade of the 1990s. The great disconnect, however, was that the establishment did not realize that each conflict it managed poorly undermined its credibility and added to the disillusionment of its member churches, hence their brazen affirmation of autonomy. Dr. Imasogie's submission attested to this disconnect when he wrote:

> [O]ur present polity as understood and practiced ….is not effective, to put it lightly. As a matter of fact it is unworkable. A polity that tacitly guarantees member bodies the option to accept or not to accept the decision of the corporate body cuts the ground off the feet of the corporate body. Any wonder then that some churches write insulting letters to the General Secretary, Boards and Committees of the Convention and get by with it when decisions taken do not favor them! The same understanding of autonomy of the local church makes churches to refuse to have pastors for years in disregard of

the directive of the constitutionally appointed Convention officers to do so.[5]

From this statement, it is clear that the churches were contesting with the convention, its authority over them, vis-à-vis the issues of discipline and leadership. What Rev. Imasogie failed to appreciate was that the anomaly he called "the option to accept or not to accept the decision of the corporate body" was not always the attitude of the churches to the denomination. While it is true that a few among the local congregations have had disagreements with the denomination at one time or another, the scale of these disagreements in the 1990s was unprecedented, especially when it is observed that the crises involved were primarily within the structures of the denomination. The development is a product of specific realities that set in at a particular time, that is, beginning from the late 1980s, in the climate of global appreciation for liberal, democratic values and, more specifically, Nigerian Baptist people's increasing disillusionment with the way the denomination's leadership carried on. And because the retired seminary teacher failed to look beyond the trend itself and see the events that led to this systematic weakening of denominational ties, he missed the mark in his recommending to the convention a modified model of the Baptist World Alliance's operational method. According to him, the denomination could avoid the discordance at the annual sessions by establishing a General Council *"as a substitute for the functions of our present Convention-in-Session."* The recommendation was completely oblivious of the dynamics at play and only confirmed that the leaders would rather marginalize the people than be accountable to them. This perception by the local churches of the unwillingness of the denomination's leadership to be accountable to them was at the root of the crisis.

Accountability to the church-in-community is a fundamental ethos of Congregationalism, including denominational cooperative organs, however it is adapted to contexts. As a voice from the establishment, the views shared by one of the elders of the Nigerian Baptists could not have done more damage to the image of the convention's leadership among its people and unwittingly confirmed their suspicion. In response to Prof. Imasogie, another pastor and critic of this recommendation wrote a 20-page critical response in 2003:

[I]n spite of the unwieldy nature of the annual sessions, the recommendation is oblivious of the grave social and financial conditions of the Convention. A denomination in which our history has repeatedly demonstrated that different segments of our polity are at one time or another suspicious of the leadership, [Prof. Imasogie] is suggesting that another statutory layer be added to the existing set-up to finally hijack it beyond the people's reach. Who are the people that will operate at this new level? Angels? Or outsiders who have never been interested in the politics of the denomination hitherto? There is no prospect that the proposed, additional layer will be effective.[6]

Recognizing Forces of Change

Having looked into the factors that led to crisis in our practice of Congregational church government, it needs to be said that the difficulties we have encountered should not be surprising. This is so when it is viewed against the background of the way modernity has impinged on Africa's traditions and ways. The new paradigm for human socialization and leadership ushered in by western colonization through education, liberal political institutions, and the egalitarian ethos implicit in it logically means that primal Africa and its institutions cannot remain sacrosanct. The rule of the elders, previously taken for granted and unchallenged, has first been demystified by the new generations that have tasted the fruit of freedom and self-determination in their tradition of socialization. The new generations would not be expected to give unqualified loyalty to the old way. And what is more? The teachings of the Scriptures, especially as they are understood in evangelical tradition, and their theme of complete freedom to self-determination under God could not but have finished up what was left undone by the new paradigm of modernity.

What this implies is that when the number of highly educated persons continued to increase in our local congregations and among our pastoral team, and the number of young people acceding to the faith continued to rise, we should not be surprised by the call for reformation in our polity as a Congregational tradition. This is to state the fact simply, but it is more complicated. The reality is that the old has refused to yield the rein of power to the new, and Africa, as Timothy Monsma wrote in the 1980s, is a crisscross of the old and the new. Sometimes their harmony defies logic; but their disharmony and, indeed, violent opposition, which has bedeviled modern African nation states, the ultimate legacy of colonialism, can be destructive.

So where do we go from here? Two things have to be settled in our mind. First, Africa is no longer pristine, and however desirous of the old way for its seeming order and balance, the pristine past is irretrievably lost. In fact we may find ourselves unnecessarily romanticizing the past as if everything was good about Africa's pristine past. Worse still, if we do not keep this fact before ourselves, we may be stepping out of tune with God in his plan for here and now. Jewish history has a lesson to instruct us in this regard. The second is that while we cannot retrieve the past in its entirety, necessity urges us to mediate the noble values of the past to the present liberal order and save it from its self-destruction. The danger of isolation, unwittingly expressed in, "we-are-sufficient and we-can-go-it-alone attitude," which attends churches like ours in the Congregational tradition calls for a non-threatening relationship between denominational leadership and these churches. This is to say that there is the need to recognize that modernity, from which the prosperity of our religious tradition of Congregationalism cannot be completely detached, has overtaken us. Yet in view of the other fact that its fruit of liberty now borders on the edge of disorder we cannot let things run on as they are unfolding unrestrainedly.

What Should We Expect? What Can We Do?

Before we address how we have attended and how we may attend to this it is proper for us to establish the signs we expect to see as evidence of a thriving denomination. In other words, how do we expect our churches to show that they are in step with us in the leadership of the denomination? And what do the churches expect from us as signs of their worthy commitment to the denomination? It is important for us to establish this as the temptation is also present with us to see our activities as denominational leaders as essentially to manage crisis in the local churches, the sole premise on which Professor Imasogie constructed his argument. It is also important for us to acknowledge that the congregations should expect results from us for our own good and in the overall interest of all.

Basically, I suppose we can say that our local congregations are cooperating with the denomination when they actively participate in the programs of the various organs of cooperation – local associations, state or regional conferences and the convention. This is to say that we expect them to send their representatives to contribute to the programs and activities of these cooperative organs. We also expect them to give faithfully toward the activities of the various organs as established by our Constitution: 21 percent, 5 percent and 20 percent of their tithes and offerings as basic contributions to the three levels of cooperation – association, conference and convention respectively. The present situation is that many of our churches do not give faithfully and so deprive the denomination of the funds we need to run our institutions and projects. Of course the third is that we expect them to abide by the decisions of the denomination in the interest of order and discipline, and ultimately for the prosperity of our denomination. And really, there ought to be no reason for them to dissent from these decisions if they have been constitutionally represented in the formation of the various bodies that constitute the decision making arms of our organs of cooperation.

It may also be said that the churches have a right to expect from us a judicious use of the funds they send to us, and this we try to show through our accounting reports at the annual sessions. They also have the right to know how we have handled sensitive issues in the denomination and how we have arrived at the various decisions we may be recommending to them. This is another issue of accountability. I must admit our denominational leadership in the 1990s was not sensitive to this and made the people believe the leaders were being bossy. In this respect, the present team has the challenge of restoring credibility to the denominational leadership. The final thing is that the churches may rightly expect us to run our institutions with integrity so that they achieve the purposes for which they were established. There has been in the past a lot of acrimonies in our institutions – colleges, seminaries, hospitals and medical centers, and the convention itself – and truly the way some matters have been handled left much to be desired.

Cooperative Identity

So far, in the Nigerian Baptist Convention, we have revisited the state of affairs between the churches and the denomination. The Executive Committee set up in 2005 a sub-committee to look into the matter with a view to addressing the issue of cooperation and identity.[8] In the document, there are some essentials that must not be mortgaged in the attempt to restructure, and these focus on the distinctive elements of Baptist organizations, mainly what Baptists believe: the Lordship of Christ; the Bible as the sole written authority for faith and practice; believer's baptism; soul competency; liberty or freedom of conscience; the priesthood of believers; salvation from sin only by faith in Jesus Christ as Lord and Savior; church membership composed of regenerate people; and religious freedom. There are three other distinctive elements built on the above biblical essentials which are, congregational polity, the autonomy of the local churches and a cooperative program where we pool our financial resources together for our collective responsibilities embedded in the Great Commission. Closely related to these are four emphases that are non-negotiable: evangelism and missions, Christian education, ministry, and social concern.

The recommendations brought forward by the committee have not achieved much. Essentially they addressed:

- Nomenclature and the nature of the annual gatherings. The committee recommended standardization of names such that they follow the same pattern among the churches. It also made attempts to re-designate the title of the office of the General Secretary as *General Overseer*. [9]
- With regard to the annual gathering it was recommended that they should be more of a time of spiritual retreat than a time of business. The recommendations, especially the first one, did not go down well with our people. The second one, while it was not contested, was also suspected to be a ploy to make the leaders unaccountable to the people. While there were arguments within the denominational structure in favor of our plans at restructuring, as expected, there have been critical responses from the pastors who represent the voice of the churches; that also is expected.

- In view of the fact that the attitude of some of our young pastors toward the denomination leaves much to be desired, we have also adopted the policy that final year students of our theological institutions, as part of their senior seminar, should attend the denomination's annual workers' conference as a way of introducing them to the activities of the convention and thereby bridge the gap between the churches where they will minister and the various cooperative organs of our denomination. At the 94th Convention session held in May 2007, the issue of cooperative program (how we pool our financial resources together – 20 percent of churches' tithes and offering for the convention, while 10-12 percent go to association and state conference) received attention. The problem of many churches that are unfaithful to our decision on the Cooperative Program has been traced to lack of enthusiasm by the church leaders, particularly pastors. Disciplinary action is being considered, such as decertifying defaulting pastors through the withdrawal of their preaching licenses and revocation of their ordination. The response so far has been encouraging in favor of strengthening the Cooperative Program.
- While our efforts have been largely administrative in that we have been making efforts to restructure the system, we need to appreciate the fact that the crisis of weakening ties among our churches with regard to the organs of cooperation, particularly the convention, is a spiritual problem. And this is no less serious than the crisis now being posed by the ideology of freedom and liberty in the modern world. It needs to be recognized that human nature, for what it is, will not relinquish freedom, and we need not expect that. In fact freedom, as a gift, is a cardinal promise of God in our faith. The issue is how to balance this freedom with community. How do our churches, while remaining autonomous, keep nurturing faithfully their ties with one other? This is the ultimate issue, and tackling it requires our understanding the four dynamics we are up against, among others.
- The first is the pitfall inherent in Congregational polity, which is the temptation of the churches to slip into isolationism.
- The second is the secularization of our polity; our tendency to see denominational machinery as a kind of civil service with

a hierarchical ladder to be ascended, as we find in Episcopal tradition.

- The pedestrian quality of pastoral training forms the third dynamic; here programs and courses do not creatively respond to contemporary challenges and needs within and outside the church.

- The fourth is the spirit of the age – the quest for boundless freedom. Ultimately, without denying the reforms necessary in our institutions to make them more efficient, the answer to these are fundamentally spiritual, requiring us to be more humble in our leadership of the denomination so that we do not give offence by the way we do things, but demonstrate the servant leadership we find in Jesus, *"who did not consider equality with God something to be grasped, but made himself nothing, taking the very nature of a servant ... and became obedient to death-even death on a cross"* (Phil. 2:6-8). As with many paradoxes inherent in our faith, following His model of leadership, both as denominational leaders and as voluntarily cooperating congregations, may be the ultimate answer to our dilemma

Conclusion

Congregationalism as a form of church government resonates with human desire for self-determination under God. Yet, on the other hand, we are also made for community as, in Christ, "the whole body, joined and held together by every supporting ligament, grows and builds itself up in love, as each part does its work" (Eph. 4:12). At bottom, therefore, our challenge is to keep the balance between the seeming opposites of autonomy and control and avoid, on our part, denominational leadership pressures that may inhibit our local congregations from being faithful to ministry in their local contexts. We also hope that our local churches and their leaders too will grow in their appreciation of the strength that comes with mutual cooperation as a denominational establishment and be faithful in their various contributions to its growth. More power to the leadership of the denomination or more intense assertion of autonomy from the local congregations will not do us or our mission any good. Power without accountability has not done the world any good. Intemperate self-assertions have, at best, led the world to wars and conflicts. A world that has seen both extremes needs respite. The question is, can we as Congregational people, model to the world the grace of living out the balance between community and autonomy. If we keep our eye on the model of the head of the church, all things will be possible.

NOTES

[1] This cultural movement was an ideological self-affirmation of African Christians, drawn from a fusion of Biblical prophecies on their conversion – "Ethiopia shall soon stretch out her hands unto God"[KJV] (cf. Psalms 68:31; 87:4)-and a contemporary event during which Ethiopia defeated the Italians in the latter's attempt to subjugate and colonize the country in the late 19th century.

[2] For further insight into the intricacies of the conflict see, E. A. Ayandele, *A Visionary of the African Church: Mojola Agbebi, 1860-1917* (Nairobi: East Africa Publishing House, 1971) and E. A. Ayandele, *Holy Johnson: Pioneer of African Nationalism, 1836-1917* (New York: Humanities Press, 1970)

[3] "Stand-Up for Jesus Baptist Group" was mainly made up of young pastors serving in Lagos, many of whom are still actively involved in the convention life today as moderators of associations, state conference and convention leaders, and whose churches are still contributing generously and faithfully to the Cooperative Program of the convention.

[4] The 22-page document was the author's presentation at the Seminar organized by the Nigerian Baptist Convention held at Camp Young, Ede, Osun State, February 2-5, 1999. Some of the papers presented at the Seminar were compiled by Baptist Institution's Forum under the title, *The Nigerian Baptist Convention in the 21st Century: Path to Greater Heights to the Glory of God* (April 1999).

[5] *A Critical Re-Evaluation of the Baptist Church Polity and its Application in the Nigerian Baptist Convention*, p. ll.

[6] Kehinde Olabimtan, "Renewing a Battered Polity; A Response to Professor Imasogie's *A Critical Re-Evaluation of the Baptist Church Polity and its Application in the Nigerian Baptist Convention*. p. 6.

[7] See Timothy Monsma, *An Urban Strategy for Africa* (Pasadena: William Carey Library, 179) p. 35.

[8] An overview of the report of the committee was presented to the 93rd Convention-in-Session (2006) for churches to consider with a view to send in their views and comments. Copies of *Restructuring and the Nigerian Baptist Convention, An Overview,* complied by S. Ademola Ishola, the current General Secretary were distributed to the messengers. A collation of the submissions

was to be presented to the 94th session with expectation for a decision at the 95th session in 2008.

[9] The attempt here is to consider the title from biblical perspective as in I Timothy 3:1 where pastors or church leaders are referred to as "overseer" or "bishop." The nomenclature "General Secretary" does not seem to elicit the perception of a spiritual leader who is the chief executive of a spiritual body by outside denomination, governments or international organizations. The designation is too secular and political in outlook. The nomenclature however remains the same as it has been deleted from the document submitted.

[10] Ordination within the Nigerian Baptist Convention is not a local church's affair. The convention has a Ministerial Board that handles the issues of pastors' ordination through the Sub-Ministerial Board in each state conference. Those pastors who qualify are presented at the annual session for ratification before they are ordained.

Chapter 14

In What Ways is Church Leadership Different in the 21ˢᵗ Century?

Michael J. Quicke

This brief paper looks in two directions. It offers paradigms and patterns of churches in transition and also identifies some key implications for the future.

Paradigms and Patterns

How best may I sum up changes in church leadership from the wide perspective of evangelical church life in North America and Western Europe? Though inevitably suffering from over-simplification, it is helpful to reflect on overviews provided by two studies about how changing culture has impacted church life, with descriptions of some consequent church models.

First, Baptist authors Jim Herrington, Mike Bonem and James H. Furr argue that "the role of the church in American culture is a key mental model that needs to be examined. The environment in which we serve has shifted dramatically."[1] They describe two paradigms for understanding the church – "Stable Institution and Context" and "Rapidly Changing Mission Field." The older paradigm operated throughout much of the 20ᵗʰ century, and characterizes the church as a stable institution set within relatively slow-changing society. Because the church largely shared the same values as surrounding culture, pastors were regarded primarily as chaplain-managers who organized church life to draw in like-minded people. Their strategy for leadership was therefore largely developed by denominations which also provided one-size-fits-all programs. Church leadership expected to be able to manage incremental changes with a minimum of disruption.

However, a second paradigm has emerged in the late 20th century, of the church set within a rapidly changing mission field. Instead of enjoying stability there is uncomfortably rapid discontinuous change. Rather than church and culture sharing the same values there is now strident divergence. Pastors can no longer remain as chaplain-managers successfully applying standardized programs designed by denominational headquarters. Managing such programs is no longer effective. Instead, pastors must become leaders working within distinctive demands of each church's missionary context. They have to become missional leaders.

These two paradigms reveal dramatic changes from when churches could assume they shared values with predominant culture, to responding to the current widening gap between gospel and culture. Today's church now lives in a mission field of rapid change with widely different contexts requiring widely different approaches. Perhaps, music in worship illustrates this contrast more than any other aspect of congregational life, as churches have moved from being stable institutions to mission fields. Instead of one primary form of music in worship - often with organ and hymn book - contemporary churches face a bewildering diversity of contemporary musical expression. Formerly, pastors supervised largely unified non-controversial music expectations, but now need to lead congregations through conflicts over preferred styles while developing fresh mission strategies.

In a second study, Aubrey Malphurs has focused some implications of this paradigm shift by describing different models of evangelical churches in North America.[2] Some of these fit more easily into the older paradigm of the stable institution and context. For example, the "Classroom Church" has a unifying value of information with the pastor viewed primarily as teacher with the people as students. It has a key emphasis "to know," with teaching sermons educating Christians in knowledge of the Bible. The "Family Reunion Church" has a unifying value of loyalty, with the pastor mainly seen as chaplain relating to people as siblings. Its key emphasis is "to belong" with tools like potluck suppers enabling people to feel secure in their identity together. Also, the "Soul-winning Church" sees the pastor as evangelist who, through altar calls, calls people to faith, adding such born-again people to the church. Each of these models was strongly evident in the old paradigm of stable church leadership.

However, in this time of dramatic discontinuous change, Malphurs identifies other church models. The "Experiential Church" has a unifying value of experience and regards the pastor as performer with the people as audience. Its key emphasis is "to feel" with an end result of empowered Christians who participate with vitality. The "Life-Development Church" has a unifying value of "character" with the pastor viewed as "coach" and with the people involved in ministry as in Ephesians 4:11-13. Here the key emphasis is "to be" with concern to develop disciples with changed lives in community. Note especially how the "Life Development Church" presents many characteristics of postmodernity because of its unifying value of "character" and its pastors as "player-coaches" leading by example. What a contrast with, for example, the "Classroom Church" with its didactic pastor, and knowledge and authority connecting within a stable hierarchical leadership pattern!

These paradigms and patterns offer insights into contemporary churches in transition. What are some key implications for the future?

Some Key Implications

- *Take culture seriously*

While oversimplifying complex issues in the relationship between culture and church, these paradigms – "stable institution" and "rapidly changing mission field" – illustrate two primary aspects of the contrast between modernity and postmodernity: the latter's increased rate of change and its divergent values. Of course, much more is at stake when considering such a major culture shift. In westernized society, postmodernity is a broad-brush term that attempts to describe the consequences of a powerful philosophical shift combined with a massive communications change to electronic literacy. Philosophers such as Derrida, Foucalt, and Rorty deconstructing knowledge as something "certain, objective and good" have instead claimed it to be uncertain, subjective and far from inherently good.[3] Obviously this threatens classic 20th century evangelicalism by the specter of relativism, rejecting the possibility of absolute truth in Christ. Consequently, some church leaders have treated postmodernity as a taboo subject, as though by rejecting it, King Canute-style, it will somehow retreat.

Of course, much in postmodernity does threaten "modern" (old paradigm) Christianity, but western churches must respond positively and learn to express the gospel as "rationality is expanded to include experience."[4] Leonard Sweet calls for a constructive response to post-modernity by advocating EPIC churches, marked by four mnemonic qualities: *experiential, participatory, image driven and connected*. Churches cannot avoid the consequences of living in culture, and being exposed to its major shifts, but their leaders must take full responsibility to critique such changes from gospel perspective and respond positively. As Leonard Hjalmarson comments: "When Church leaders fail to engage the postmodern movement, they risk becoming isolated from the culture they live in. This in turn guarantees that the church communities they build will gradually stagnate and die."[5]

- *Recognize how complicated is the relationship between church and culture*

In North America and Western Europe culture is in messy transition. Modernity and postmodernity will continue to live alongside each other for a long time. Some even argue that for all the hype about postmodernity, history will eventually show it to be no more than a large ripple on the surface of developing "modernity." Certainly, the church scene represents a mosaic of modern and post-modern characteristics. Indeed, in many churches postmodernity has made little impact – class room churches still hold considerable cache (though contemporary music has made inroads). Many black and Hispanic churches in the USA frankly find the postmodern analysis less relevant to their situations. (How interesting it will be to see the range of perspectives in the BWA commission!)

Many serious issues facing contemporary churches and their leadership cannot be simply categorized as consequences of postmodernity. It is arguable, for example, that western values like individualism, consumerism, security, personal happiness and corporate success (all nurtured by modernity) continue to dominate and damage churches by their leadership aspirations. Such values encourage leadership to see its prime responsibility as building up congregations of individuals who gain personal fulfillment.

Swallowing secular goals, such church leadership commits to help people find self-satisfaction in their personal salvation without any further ethical or kingdom consequences.

- *Keep focus on Biblical leadership*

Henry and Richard Blackaby comment on Christian leaders' obsessive immersion into popular leadership writings of today. "The trend among many Christian leaders has been for an almost indiscriminate and uncritical acceptance of secular leadership theory without measuring it against the timeless precepts of Scripture." [6] The phenomenal rise of leadership studies can so easily displace attention to Scripture. While authors such as John Kotter and Peter Senge[7] have undeniable significance in the leadership field, beware indiscriminate and uncritical acceptance.

For example, some church leaders, looking at earlier paradigms and patterns in this paper, may be tempted to devise strategies that move a congregation from one option to another by entirely secular textbook techniques. But strategies of Christian leadership owe everything to Jesus Christ, the world's greatest leader, who incorporates us into his living body, the Church, through the Holy Spirit. Our responsibility is to stay close to Scripture. Yes, to take the best of secular thinking, but submit it to Scripture and to Jesus' modeling of leadership with his first disciples, and the consequent development of relationships in the early church. Nowhere is this more important than in renewing commitment to biblical preaching that leads.[8]

- *Be missional*

Christian leadership should always be concerned with mission. George Hunsberger has usefully summarized Lesslie Newbigin's theology of culture in the model on page 226.

Figure 1 shows a triangular model of gospel-culture relationships. It was taken from George R. Hunsberger, "The Newbigin Gauntlet: Developing a Domestic Missiology for North America," *Missiology*, 19, 4, 1991 and is reprinted with permission of the American Society of Missiology.

Figure 1: A Triangular Model of Gospel-Culture Relationships

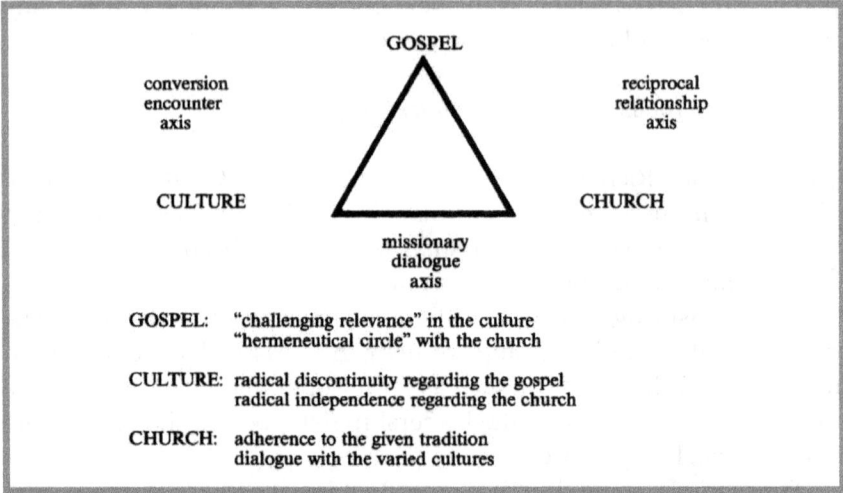

GOSPEL

conversion
encounter
axis

reciprocal
relationship
axis

CULTURE

CHURCH

missionary
dialogue
axis

GOSPEL: "challenging relevance" in the culture
"hermeneutical circle" with the church

CULTURE: radical discontinuity regarding the gospel
radical independence regarding the church

CHURCH: adherence to the given tradition
dialogue with the varied cultures

Its dynamics flow backwards and forwards within its three cornered-relationships between gospel, culture and church. Most obviously, gospel impacts culture along the *conversion encounter axis*, confronting hearers to repent from sin and believe in Jesus Christ. But the *reciprocal relationship axis* lies between the gospel and church. Assuming personal conversion, this axis represents the challenge for believers to embody the outcomes of new life in Christ, so that they grow into maturity for works of ministry (Eph. 4:11-13). Third is the *missionary dialogue axis* between church and its local culture. This axis assumes that a church community has been formed so that it can live out the gospel challenge in its own particular missionary context. Newbigin called for a relationship of true dialogue – a process of new converts (in community) being open to living out the unique implications of the gospel within the particularities of human culture. This challenge issued to God's people to live out such missionary dialogue sums up Christian leadership's primary task – enabling a people to grow together while living under God's will and seeking first his kingdom in contradistinction to society in order to witness to the world.

In New Testament times this axis was lengthy as the early missionary church modeled new ways of love and purity in their relationships and behavior that strongly contrasted with culture (e.g. 1 Peter 2:9-12). Today, the axis is lengthy again and leaders have responsibility to help the church's tri-directional dialogue, which disturbs the world by the gospel message, disturbs the church lest it accommodate too easily to the worldly culture and disturbs the particular culture in which a church lives by the witness of its common life. In other words, they must lead the missional church.

- *Be Baptist*

Classic Baptist polity has very positive contributions to make to Christian leadership during this time of cultural change. Because of our understanding of church as gathered believers, formed under Christ's headship, by the authority of his word, Baptist ecclesiology encourages communities where a "priesthood of all believers" militates against hierarchical authority. Congregational meetings that discern the mind of Christ (1 Cor. 2:16) offer a distinctive mode of decision making, and grant flexibility to be strategically missional in their contexts. Many characteristics cited in Hjalmarson's paper such as: rejection of authority in position in favor of authority in relationship, leadership by wisdom and example, communities that are missional and witnessing to reality of the gospel should be descriptive of Baptist ecclesiology. As the Commission on Church Leadership works through this quinquennium we must never lose sight of the particular strengths (and weaknesses) of our Baptist principles and practice.

NOTES

[1] Jim Herrington, Mike Bonem and James H. Furr, *Leading Congregational Change*, (San Francisco: Jossey-Bass, 2000), 116.

[2] Aubrey Malphurs, *Values-Driven Leadership: Discovering and Developing Your Core Values for Ministry*, (Grand Rapids: Baker, 1996), 54.

[3] For helpful analysis see Stanley J. Grenz, *A Primer on Post-modernity*, (Grand Rapids: Eerdmans, 1996).

[4] Leonard Sweet, *Post-modern Pilgrims. First Century Passion for the Twenty-First Century*, (Nashville: Broadman & Holman, 2000).

[5] Leonard Hjalmarson, *Kingdom Leadership in the Postmodern Era*, 2.

[6] Henry and Richard Blackaby, *Spiritual Leadership – Moving People on to God's Agenda*, (Nashville; Broadman & Holman, 2001).

[7] See John P. Kotter, *Leading Change*, (Boston: Harvard Business School Press, 1996); Peter M. Senge, *The Fifth Discipline: The Art and Practice of Learning Organizations*, (New York: Doubleday, 1990).

[8] See Michael J. Quicke, *360 Degree Leadership: Preaching to Transform Congregations*, (Grand Rapids: Baker, 2006).

Chapter 15

Ordination: Does it Fit?

Brian Winslade

In 2009 Baptists celebrated the 400th anniversary of the founding of the first Baptist church. We've come a long way in 400 years. From a small group of English dissenters fleeing their homeland to avoid persecution, Baptists today represent the largest Protestant communion in the world. An occasion such as a 400th anniversary is a time to recall our roots and to review the distinctive elements of our ecclesiology. Within the mosaic of church life around the world, what is peculiar or unique about Baptist ecclesiology? Our forebears were radical dissenters against the religious status quo, and many paid dearly for their convictions. Do we still hold to their radical views, or are we less distinctive these days?

Most Baptist conventions and unions practice a form of ordination of pastors. Meanings of words may vary but the language is fairly uniform. But does it really fit our Baptist ecclesiology, or, as the title of Albert L. Vail's provocative book from 1915 suggests, do we have *A Roman Fly in the Baptist Ointment*?

By definition, "ordination" comes from the Latin root *ordo* or *order*, meaning literally to arrange in order or rank. In its historical development the word came to mean the taking of office or orders. In Roman Catholic and Orthodox traditions ordination is considered a sacrament, by which special grace is imparted. Clearly Protestant traditions do not hold to such a high view. So what do Baptists mean when they use the term?

The purpose of this paper is not to attempt an answer to this question. That is a task for brighter minds and needs to follow the trail of robust dialogue. The purpose of this paper is merely to identify questions worthy of response. There will likely be varied responses, and the ability to live and work together within the tension of differing views is one of our strengths. Perhaps the questions that follow offer a framework for ongoing dialogue.

A doctrinal question

Does the concept of ordination conflict with our understanding of the priesthood of all believers?

The priesthood of all believers is arguably a central plank upon which Baptist ecclesiology is constructed. Popularization of the priesthood of all believers as a doctrine is generally credited to Martin Luther, although from how his later ecclesiology developed it is less clear what he actually had in mind. He certainly didn't agree with the radical Anabaptist view of elimination of a clergy class. Luther argued against the medieval distinction between "spiritual" and "temporal," with the ordained clergy being the "spiritual" and the rest being "of this world." By contrast Luther argued that every baptized Christian is a "priest" or "spiritual" in the eyes of God.

However, the term undoubtedly opens the door for a low view of clergy hierarchy. Baptists have always stressed the equal and mutual priesthood of all members of the church. Each Christian has unfettered access to God, in the Old Testament understanding of priesthood; similarly each Christian is able to represent God's grace and activity toward others. In Baptist thinking there is no theoretical or practical distinction in status between a pastor and any other member of the church. The question arises, therefore, whether the concept of separate "orders" for those appointed as pastors or ministers militates against the doctrine of the priesthood of all believers.

A theological question

To what extent does the institutional model of church, with distinctions between clergy and laity, reflect the movement Jesus began?

In a post-modern worldview we're allowed to ask questions that otherwise might be avoided. Our ecclesial "eggs" are well and truly "scrambled" after 2000 years, and it may not be possible to unscramble them. Anglican theologian, Leon Morris, dared to pose this question at the beginning of his study on formal offices of ministry in the life of the church. Was the formulation of an organized system, with officers and specified duties and rituals, something Jesus instituted, or was this foreign to Jesus original intent when he spoke of building his church (Matthew 16: 18)? While Jesus spoke of the formulation of an *ekklesia* that would reflect the values of God's kingdom come on earth, do the origins of the church as we know it today actually go back to Jesus, or do they reflect the best intent of those who succeeded Jesus' mission?[1]

Given Jesus' teaching on leadership and servant-hood as contradistinctive to models of the Gentiles, did he really envisage a community wherein only certain people had authority to perform ceremonial functions, and others were merely passive? Or was the model of church Jesus envisaged somewhat more participatory and less hierarchical?

A pneumatological question

Did Pentecost alter the paradigm for Holy Spirit empowerment for ministry?

The events of Pentecost were significant in the launch of the church, as foretold by Jesus prior to his ascension. The disciples were to wait in Jerusalem until they were imbued with power from the Holy Spirit. Pentecost marks a distinct change in the empowering work of the Holy Spirit in the lives of human beings. The Apostle Peter clea. rly interpreted the manifestation of the Holy Spirit as fulfillment of the prophecy of Joel.[2] Prior to Pentecost imbuement with Holy Spirit power was sporadic and only occurred in the lives of specially anointed individuals. At Pentecost the *modus operandi* of the Holy Spirit altered. No longer was manifestation of power for ministry limited to a select few or a particular class of people; power to serve was severally distributed and across all classes of people - men and woman, young and old, all people.

How might the Apostle Peter view the reduction of authority to minister to a select few in the church on account of their theological education and ministerial training? To what extent are models of ministry that propagate clergy separation, and elite special authority, in conflict with the effects of Pentecost? Did not Pentecost represent a death blow to the Old Testament concept of an elite priestly class, in favor of every Christian being a potential vessel through whom the Holy Spirit can minister?

A historical question

How significant do we hold the dissenting views of the earliest Baptists who argued against a clergy dominated church?

Pioneer Baptist leaders held to a low view of clergy ministry. Perhaps the first incident of Baptist conflict occurred between John Smyth and Thomas Helwys shortly after the formation of the first Baptist church. Smyth apparently doubted the efficacy of his own baptism and reached the conclusion that what he did to himself, and subsequently to others, was invalid. He came to believe his baptism should more properly have been administered by the Mennonites who had a more developed ecclesiology.[3] Helwys countered: "... *there is no succession or privilege in holy things*" and that precedence for their 1609 baptism could be drawn from John the Baptizer who "*being unbaptized preached the baptism of repentance.*" [4] The conflict was so serious Smyth was eventually excommunicated from the fledgling church he had helped form.[5] In Helwys' mind there was no special authority for the ordinance vested in the person administering it. This was a defiant challenge to the view that holy ordinances or sacraments could only be performed by ordained clergy, as representative of apostolic succession. Helwys went further in his 1611 Declaration:

> The Church ... though they be but two or three, have Christ given them, with all the means of their salvation (Matthew 18:20; Romans 8.32; 1 Corinthians 3:22) are the body of Christ (1 Corinthians 12:27) and a whole church (1 Corinthians 14:23) and therefore may, and ought, when they come together, to pray, prophesy, break bread, and administer in all the holy ordinances, although as yet they have no Officers, or that their Officers should be in Prison, sick, or by any other means hindered from the Church (1 Peter 4:10; 2:5). [6]

Church officers or ministers were not unimportant in Helwys' view, but if they were absent for some reason the church was still competent to function. A 1948 statement by the Baptist Union of Great Britain makes a similar point:

Any member of the church may be authorized by it, on occasion, to exercise the functions of the ministry, in accordance with the principle of the priesthood of all believers, to preach the word, to administer baptism, to preside at the Lord's Table, to visit, and comfort or rebuke members of the fellowship.[7]

How does this view of common priesthood of every church member fit with the concept of special rights and privileges of ordained ministry?

An ecclesiological question

To what extent does ordained ministry conflict with the Apostle Paul's teaching about spiritual gifts?

If the Apostle Paul were to visit our churches would he recognize them? In his letters to churches in Rome, Corinth and Ephesus, Paul developed the analogy of a multi-faceted human body in describing the operational function of the church. All parts of the body are essential and have a part to play in the correct functioning of the body. No one part is to be regarded as more important than others. There is mutual honor and respect for different parts of the body. Paul was at pains to point out that all parts are not equal in function, but all are necessary.

Clearly Paul was not suggesting a church that was leaderless or that every member has the same capacity for ministry. Offices such as pastor or teacher or prophet or elder are not unnecessary. Quite the reverse; they are all the more necessary in order to facilitate high level participation by church members in the varied ministerial functions of the church. How, therefore, does a model of church life that limits certain ecclesial functions to a select few with special "orders" compare with Paul's ecclesiology? Does the concept of "special vocation" or "separate orders" for a clergy class tend toward high passivity on the part of congregation members, who merely assemble to watch the professionals perform?

A nomenclature question

Have we confused ordination with credentialing of ministers and the establishing of best-practice standards?

Is the Baptist use of the term "ordination" consistent with its etymology and theology, or have we confused it with something else? In Catholic theology, ordination is a sacrament of the church. The *ordinand* is male (only), trained, formed, tested and at the end of a defined process formally separated as a member of special "orders" within the church. The conferring of ordination is said to mystically alter the very essence of the person from then on. The status is a life-long vocation (unless he resigns or is defrocked).

Could it be that Baptists have borrowed ordination as a term for the credentialing of pastors who have achieved a certain standard of competence or education? Having been recognized for their ability or sense of spiritual gifting they are commended as competent ministers of the Gospel within their denominational grouping.

Raising the standards for pastoral leadership is a worthy ideal. Nothing but good comes from raising high the bar of ministerial competence. The question remains, however, whether the language of ordination truly fits what we do. Could it be that Baptists are misusing a theological term without cognizance of its meaning or implication? Is this why some Baptist denominations use terminology like accreditation or registration rather than ordination?

Another implication of nomenclature is the title "Reverend" to distinguish ordained persons from those who are not. At what point is a pastor able to employ such a distinguishing title? Is it from the point at which they are formally ordained by their denomination, or at the point of commissioning within their local church? The use of the title is so widespread within the Baptist communion, as it is in other denominations, that it may not easily be discontinued, but it does beg the question as to its meaning. Is the title "Reverend" appropriate or defendable within Baptist ecclesiology, or more importantly within the model of church taught by the New Testament?

A vocational question

Is ordination a life calling or is it delimited to function?

In a Catholic world view the concept of ordination is life-long. Priestly ordination is a vocation, not merely a career. Origins of this view have merit when properly understood, but it raises questions for Baptists as to whether such a theological position sits well.

For hundreds of years Baptist pastors have testified to a sense of divine calling to "the Ministry." This calling has been followed with deep reverence for the mission of the church, and often at considerable personal cost. This paper does not question the sanctity or validity of such a "calling." However, it does question whether a "call" to pastoral ministry is always or necessarily a lifetime commitment. Could it be that serving as a pastor is for an episode in a person's life, rather than an irrevocable lifetime commitment? In a Catholic worldview: once a priest; always a priest. There is no such thing as retirement. The priest may no longer actively serve in a parish, but the right or authority to do so is not related to specific appointment or function. Is this how Baptists view the function of pastoral ministry?

Thinking theologically, is there not a range of vocational "callings" across the body of Christ? Is the "calling" to be a pastor of any greater significance to a "calling" to be a doctor or a teacher or a nurse or a policeman or a mother? Would the Apostle Paul contend that all "callings" are of equal validity?

We live in an age where people have multiple careers within the space of a lifetime. In some cases they completely retrain for a new career. This is true of most pastors who held a former career before their sense of "call" to pastoral ministry. Having received training and equipping for pastoral ministry do we believe the act of ordination sets a pastor apart from then on (i.e. for the rest of his/her life) in an irrevocable state? If a pastor chooses to discontinue in pastoral ministry (for whatever reason) have they broken a life-long commitment, thereafter deemed to have failed? Or could it be that we can celebrate the episode of their ministry and recognize its closure with honor, rather than veiled shame?

Some former Baptist pastors prefer to retain their ordination title as "Reverend" even though they no longer exercise a pastoral function. What does such practice imply? Does it reduce ordination to something of a qualification – perhaps similar to a degree? Or would we be better to delimit the use of such titles and credentials to those who are actually in ministry appointments, and only for as long as they do so?

A local church question

Is ordination a local church function or a denominational ordinance?

To what extent is the Baptist movement a loose collection of autonomous local churches, and to what extent are we a regional/territorial/ideological denomination? A range of views exists and this paper does not suggest one answer. Some have argued that principles of denominationalism do not easily fit a Baptist ecclesiology. Others contend for principles of association and covenantal relationships that enable local churches to do certain things "better together" than can be achieved on their own. However, it behooves Baptist conventions and unions to think through where the place of ordination or credentialing best fits. If the answer is at the wider denominational level this would imply a set of common or core competencies that are measurable and acceptable, so as to allow a recognized pastor to move ministry location within the movement. Others argue that Baptist ecclesiology focuses more squarely upon the local church as the arbiter of ministerial competence and recognition, and that the right of the local church to call whomever it wills to be its pastor is sacrosanct.

A missiological question

Does the model of ordination and distinction between clergy and laity tend toward a passive missiology?

Given the primary purpose of the Christian church is the continuation of the mission of Jesus,[8] missional ecclesiology must ask questions about models of church organization that best achieve the desired result. Are models of church that perpetuate priestly elitism (i.e. whether formally or implicitly or even unintentionally) most efficient missiologically?

The language and practice of ordination tends toward recognition of only certain people in the rhythms of church life who are competent to perform certain tasks. The sacraments cannot be celebrated unless an ordained minister is present to officiate. But the same can also be said of churches that claim a low (or lower) view of clergy. A model of church ministry that recognizes a pastor as the principal servant of the church in dispensing biblical teaching, counseling, administration and pastoral care is equally questionable.

This paper does not call into question the validity of local church pastoral ministry. This is not a veiled call for Bretheranism. The New Testament offers examples of local church servants employed, supported and honored for such work. But what is to be the focus of those appointed to such positions? The language of ordination tends to set people apart from the rest, and to afford status in the church that is crucial or central to its function. It allows for a much higher form of passive involvement in church life than the New Testament prescribes. Ordained clergy are supposedly more learned and competent in handling the scriptures and dispensing wisdom and in caring for the infirm. Yet how does this compare with the concept of "body ministry" that the Apostle Paul wrote so clearly about? Moreover, when Paul wrote to the Ephesian church (4:11-12) he implied the purpose of those gifted as apostles, prophets, evangelists, pastors and teachers was less on delivery of professional service, and more upon equipping fellow members of the church in the delivery of such ministry.

A postmodern question

To what extent are institutional models of church being deconstructed by the generations that follow?

Philosophers differ on their definitions of postmodernity, when it started or when it will end. Some have already begun to describe the term as *passé*. Suffice it to say that in the 21st century many former institutions and foundations of thinking or values have begun to crumble. Language and wisdom from the modern age is deconstructed and truth has been transformed into relative ideology – you have yours and I have mine, and all are valid.

The shape and function of the church does not escape the ravages of post-modern critique. Some might even say it deserves more particular focus than other institutions in society. The point is, everything is now being questioned, and asked to give fresh reason for being. Historical church practices like ordination are no exception. Younger members of the church are less likely to blindly accept tradition as valid reason for keeping practices going. Inherent respect for honorific roles and offices are less assumed than they once were. Churches built around systems of hierarchy may not fare as well in the years ahead than those that are more hierarchically flat or inclusive. That means the Baptists have a great opportunity within a postmodern world. Theoretically at least, we recognize the priesthood of all believers and do not defer to overlords as the soul arbiters of revelation and biblical exegesis. We say that every Christian is competent to hear the will of God or to at least participate in the process of its discernment.

All this raises questions as to where the language and practice of ordination fits in contemporary and future Baptist ecclesiology. Have we unwittingly imbibed models from other denominations, from whom we once dissented? Given the context in which we live, is it time for us to think radically again about the nature of the church and its ministry, and what best connects with a generation who hold deep suspicion concerning traditions from the past?

NOTES

[1] Leon Morris, *Ministers of God* (London: Inter-Varsity Fellowship, 1964), 12.

[2] Acts 2:16-21; Joel 2:28-32

[3] Marjorie Warkentin, *Ordination. A biblical-historical view,* (Grand Rapids: Eerdmans, 1982), 79.

[4] Laurie Guy, *Baptist Church - MB726* (Lecture Notes), (Carey Baptist College, NZ, 2005), Week Three, 6.

[5] Robert G. Torbet, *A History of the Baptists,* (Philadelphia, PA: Judson Press, 1959), 65.

[6] William L. Lumpkin, *Baptist Confessions of Faith,* (Valley Forge, PA: Judson Press, 1969), 120.

[7] A. Gilmore, *The Pattern of the Church - A Baptist View,* (London: Lutterworth Press, 1963), 47.

[8] Matthew 28:19-20; Mark 16:15; Luke 24:46-47; John 20:21, Acts 1:8

Chapter 16

Ordination: A Case Study from Bulgaria

Teodor Oprenov

The first ever Bulgarian Baptist Church traces the roots of its development to 1867 when Stephan Kurdov, a tradesman who had heard the evangelical message in Istanbul through Congregationalists from Armenia, formed a Congregational community in the town of Kazanluk. In 1875 M. Herbold, a BFBS colporteur and a Baptist, visited the congregation and convinced the majority of the members about believer's baptism. This baptism was conditional upon the participant's faith and the presence of an ordained pastor to perform it. That is how on August 10, 1880, Grigor Drumnikov wrote to the BFBS in Russe, on behalf of twenty-two Kazanluk believers, asking for a pastor and particularly for someone to baptize them. This letter was translated and published in an article, "The Macedonian Cry Re-Echoed from Macedonia Itself." Although the group in Kazanluk did not know it when they made their appeal in 1880, help was already on its way. Ivan G. Kargel, who had served the German Baptist congregation in St. Petersburg, decided to move to Bulgaria. On September 7, 1880, Kargel immersed five people from the Kazanluk group in the river – Toshka Pateva, Marijka Belcheva, Nikola Patev, Grigor Drumnikov and Petko Kurkelanov. There were at least five more people who wanted to be baptized, but after very strict testing and questioning, Kargel refused to baptize the others.

The Bulgarian Context for Ordination

The context in which the theology of ordination has developed within the Bulgarian Baptist churches features several key elements that have strongly influenced the present- day idea of ordination in

Bulgarian Baptist ecclesiology. The word "ordination," in the Bulgarian language, does not convey the meaning of "induction" or "order." The word literally means "laying-hands-upon" as in separation for service, appointing someone, or delegating responsibility. It does not naturally have the tendency toward empowerment, but rather, the opposite.

The Context of the Baptist Pioneers

The first Baptists in Bulgaria were ex-Mennonite, German-speaking Russians, who regarded ordination as:

- separation and appointment of some people to serve as officers and recognized leaders of the church community, to distinguish them from the laymen primarily in responsibility for the ministry;
- conferring responsibility and office to fulfill the ministry among certain individuals. Laying on of hands was the biblical foundation of separation for the ministry;
- appropriate only for men in pastoral and diaconal responsibility;
- effective only within the context of the local church. Missionaries were travelling pastors who were ordained for the pastorate and were later sent out on mission;
- constituting a life-time ministry, and not a task oriented service for a limited time;
- performed only by other already ordained people, representing a higher level of authority;
- installation to an office which is directly under the supervision of a national leader.

The theological convictions were based on a traditionally "only men" of a "certain age" and with "certain characteristics."[1] These convictions were understood to be derived from biblical principles found in passages including 1 Timothy 3; Ephesians 4 and Titus 1.

The separation for the believers in terms of ministry was reinforced through the years of persecution and Communist rule. To accept baptism meant to be viewed as an outcast to the society, and to undertake the responsibility for leadership – pastoral or diaconal, meant to be targeted for arrests, imprisonment or exile and deprived of the right to a job. In those years (1945 – 1989), when the leadership was always voluntary, lack of secular employment meant total lack of ability to survive financially. So ordination during that period in

Bulgaria had the essence of readiness for martyrdom and being ready to be counted for Christ. [2]

The Context of 1,000 Years of Orthodox Tradition

Because Baptists have been under constant attack from the Orthodox Church in Bulgaria, Baptist ecclesiology has been influenced by Orthodox tradition as we attempted to minimize the level of negative interaction with the Orthodox principles in terms of leadership. Following the pattern of the Orthodox Church, any Christian church may exist only through a higher national body, union or national church. Those churches are registered by the Department for Religious Confessions to the Council of Ministers in the Republic of Bulgaria, and through the high court of the country. A church cannot exist as an independent congregation, but always as a part of a wider ecclesial body. At the present time, denominations can be easily established and currently, there are 97 Christian denominations in Bulgaria, 17 of which are Baptist.

Under Bulgarian law, the person responsible for the church is the priest. In the case of the Baptist church, the pastor is deemed responsible. Pastors carry out their responsibility through election to office by the local congregation, (obtaining legal approval and registration), and being ordained in that office (spiritual approval by the denomination leaders). In 95 percent of the cases, the pastor is the official administrative, legal and spiritual representative of the church before the people and the law. Interestingly enough, the success or failure of a church is often attributed to the pastor and leaders, rather than the whole community of people in a given church.

Furthermore, in the Orthodox rite, at the moment of ordination, which is considered a sacrament, special power is given to the priest. Bulgarian Baptists do not accept that claim. Even though they often regard the pastor as having equal, or even lower standing, by virtue of his service to others, the pastor is looked upon as having higher authority enabling him to have the final word on many questions related to witness and ministry.

Following the tradition of the first founders, but conveniently complying with the Orthodox model, Bulgarian Baptists ordain only men as pastors, preachers and deacons. The forceful Orthodox claim concerning apostolic succession by the laying on of hands and the accusation of Protestants as not being in the same line of succession – although totally rejected by Bulgarian Baptists – have given way to a "direct line" of ordination and the following sacraments – baptism, the Lord's supper, and marriage.

Only men, and only men ordained in the "right" way, are allowed to baptize, perform weddings, lead the Lord's Supper, and ordain their peers. Ordination of deacons and preachers can be done by the local pastor, but ordination for pastoral ministry can only be done in agreement with the national church body (the union) and with the presence and participation of at least one officially elected union leader.

In the period, 1920-1930, leaders of the Baptist union refused to ordain some key preachers as pastors, based on the view that the existence of a church was properly attested by the existence of a building in which the church met. The community could not enjoy the leadership of an ordained minister if it did not have a building. Although this rule was never committed to writing, it was the guideline that prevailed unofficially for some time.

As in the case of the Orthodox priest, the Baptist pastor could expect to be ordained only once during his lifetime, and the ordained could lose that status only for ministerial misconduct, moral failure, etc. The office of an ordained person never expires, although the ordained person might, for some reason, be no longer engaged in active service in a local church.

Among Bulgarian Baptists, women have never been ordained for ministry. Prayers have been offered for them before they are allowed to carry out certain ministries, such as leadership, preaching, teaching, or diaconal ministry, but they serve without official appointment or a title. Most of our churches will have real difficulty allowing a woman to preach and very few Christians would ever take part in the Lord's Supper served by a woman, even if that person is a national women's ministry leader. The churches have been influenced by the Orthodox Church which does not ordain women to the priesthood.

In recent years, owing to the number of women who have been trained in theological institutions, some women have been allowed to serve with the title, "Bible Worker." In the constitution of the Baptist union, which was amended in November 2007, all Christians are said to be completely equal in the eyes of God. Both the priesthood of all believers and the right for everyone to read and interpret the word of

God are affirmed (1 Peter 2:5, 9; Rev. 1:6). However, this is what the constitution says about the Bible Worker:

> This is an office function that is given to believers, who hold the qualification and the abilities necessary for the pastoral ministry, but are not ordained for such. The Bible worker, just like the pastor, can preach the word of God, can be responsible for services, and can perform all church duties with the exception of weddings, baptism, the Lord's Supper and ordination.

Challenges

Contemporary Bulgarian Baptist ecclesiology needs to come to terms with a number of challenges.

To begin with, our theology of ordination is based on the tradition of the founders of Baptist work in Bulgaria; it has been shaped to an extent by the circumstances of life in an Orthodox environment, and it has a strong male-oriented tendency. It is not derived directly from an independent study of the Scriptures; it follows an inherited tradition.

Sometimes, we can clearly see a problem between the theological conviction of the priesthood of all believers and the power of the office given by ordination. The Communists used to have a joke: *we are all equal, but some are more equal than others.*

Ordination, and the refusal of ordination in some cases, has a limiting effect on the ministry and the acceptance of such for certain Christians, such as young people and especially women.

When the Baptist union created the term, "Bible Worker," it was seeking to overcome some of the difficulties attached to the denial of ordination to women. It seems, however, that such a term actually avoids the issue instead of dealing with it.

The "title for life" approach, over against the ordination for a specific ministry for a specific period of time, has created pressure for people whose abilities do not match the necessities of the new times. They have felt inclined to stay "in office" instead of allowing more gifted people to step forward into ministry. The celebrated slogan, "Pastors and deacons never retire," reflects the desire to recognize the sacrificial ministry some people fulfill. However, it is helping to keep people in ministry, and on pulpits, literally until their passing away, sometimes long after their natural God-given abilities have left them. It limits and discourages younger leaders from getting involved in ministry.

We need to come to a balanced biblical view of the gifts that God gives to both men and women in the Church today. The Church may wish to acknowledge these gifts and allow their use in ministry, recognizing them by appropriate forms of ordination.

Ordination as such should remain the practice of the Church, but it should be stripped of the unnecessary shield of nominal spirituality, exclusivity and counter-humbling power. It should be there to announce the commitment to serve and not to delegate additional power to rule; it should be recognition of leadership, but not elevation to office of a dictator.

NOTES

[1]Married, over 30 years of age, never divorced, and with a certain number of years within the church. Approximately five years for deacons and more for pastors and preachers.

[2] During the communist regime, from 1970-1989, official ordination was only possible with the permission of the Committee for Religious Affairs of the Communist State. This was the communist arm established to control activities of the church with a view to destroying the church. Thus, many leaders who in effect were pastors were condemning ordination as cooperation with the communists. The story of Sofia Baptist Church clearly shows that in practice. So, I remember years in which to state that you have been ordained for anything, was to be considered unfaithful in some way, and in cooperation with the State. It was indeed very confusing.

The Commission on Doctrine and Interchurch Cooperation
Paul Fiddes, Chair

Gathered in the heady atmosphere of the centenary celebrations of the Baptist World Alliance in the Congress at Birmingham, UK, in July 2005, the members of the commission who were present met to consider their priorities for the next quinquennium, opening the second century of BWA global partnership. Three general concerns emerged from those preliminary meetings, which the commission has worked to implement since then. First, the members gathered were anxious that the fruits of the conversations with the Anglican Communion held during the previous five years, and just published under the title *Conversations around the World 2000-2005*, should not be lost. Reception of the report needed to be encouraged, and its conclusions should be reflected upon.

Second, the members of the commission were anxious that a proposed second series of conversations with the Roman Catholic Church should be agreed by the constituent bodies of the BWA during the next year, and then that the commission should be kept in close contact with their progress, making as much input to the discussion as would be possible.

Third, among the distinctive Baptist approaches to Christian doctrine that the commission should concern itself with, there was a particular concern to highlight the doctrine of the Church, and the key aspect of the meaning of "membership." A fourth major emphasis had not yet appeared on the horizon, though it came to occupy a huge amount of time and effort during this period – namely a response to the letter from Islamic scholars to world Christian communions called, *A Common Word Between Us and You* (October 2007).

The annual meeting in Mexico City, July 2006, gave an opportunity to start on all of the issues identified, though the first took up the most attention and – perhaps regrettably – turned out to be the only occasion for explicit reflection on it in the four meetings available. Sections were chosen from the report on the Anglican-Baptist Conversations, one on the nature of oversight or *episkope* in the Church, and the other on baptism and church membership. Papers offering responses to these sections were given by commission members from many parts of the world. The particular sections from the Anglican-Baptist report were also chosen to facilitate discussion on the third theme highlighted the year before - that of the nature of the church and its membership.

Our second main concern, relations with the Roman Catholic Church, was covered by reflections on the fruits of previous conversations, and by a successful recommendation to the BWA Council for a new round in this quinquennium. The aim was to build on the earlier series of conversations in 1985-89, taking our discussions beyond the initial "getting-to-know-you" exercise into a real attempt at sharing a life of discipleship and developing a common witness. The partners envisaged that they could move towards the fulfillment of these aims by focusing on the overall theme: "The Word of God in the Life of the Church: Scripture, Tradition and Koinonia."

The policy of close involvement between the Commission and the Conversations has been continued during the last four years. Of the thirteen Baptist participants or consultants, eight have been members of the commission. In Accra in 2007, papers given by Baptist participants on the theme of the Bible and the Word of God were reviewed, and each year since then some of the key Baptist papers written for the conversations have been presented and discussed at the commission meetings. In Accra the earlier concern for Baptist ecclesiology was also not forgotten, as papers were given on Baptist ecclesiology "beyond the local church" and on progress with ideas of baptism on the world ecumenical scene.

At the next meeting of the commission in Prague, July 2008, papers were given on the sacraments as visible Word of God, the theme of the Baptist-Roman Catholic Conversations in December 2007. Continuing our study of Baptist ecclesiology, papers were offered on church membership among Baptists in Sweden, Scotland and Alabama. The commission had further been invited to join with two other commissions in a united session on the meaning of ordained ministry. But it was in Prague that the commission also began the task that it had not anticipated at the beginning of the quinquennium - a huge responsibility shared with the Commission on Freedom and Justice at the invitation of the General Secretary. That is, the two commissions were asked to prepare a response from the Baptist World Alliance to a document, signed originally by 138 world-ranking Muslim scholars and leaders (later augmented to 299), addressed to the leaders of the major Christian communions.

Called *A Common Word Between Us and You*, the Muslim document proposed - in the most friendly and irenic way - that all future conversations between Christians and Muslims should be based on two principles - the Oneness of God and the command of Jesus to love God and neighbor. An open forum was held in the Prague gathering in which reactions and advice were sought from all those present. Following the Prague meeting, the chairpersons of the two commissions drafted an extensive response which was then sent for comment to the president and general secretary of the BWA, and to the presidents and general secretaries of the six regional fellowships of the BWA for their comments. In the light of comments received, a final draft was sent in December 2008 to the Royal Aal-Bayt Institute for Islamic Thought in Jordan from which the original letter had emerged. The BWA response, while highly appreciative of the initiative, gently affirmed that Baptists could not separate the two great love commands from a vision of a triune God of love; this response was received warmly by the Islamic scholars there, who published it along with a few other responses they selected from the many received.

When the commission met in Ede, July 2009, papers were given which reflected on positive conversations with Islamic scholars in Jordan, and on Baptist-Islamic conversations in the USA. The continuing theme of the Baptist-Roman Catholic conversations was not, however, neglected, since two Baptist papers were presented which originated in a session on the Virgin Mary in December 2008. Concerns for ecclesiology were connected with issues of liberation among Baptists, one paper being about the Sam Sharpe rebellion of 1832 in Jamaica, when a Baptist slave and deacon organized a sit-down strike against the inhuman institution of slavery.

These are the ways in which the commission has aimed to carry through the goals it set itself in 2005, with the notable and unexpected addition of the beginning of a Baptist-Islamic dialogue, and the papers that follow are a sample of this program.

Chapter 17

A Baptist View of Ordained Ministry:
Just a Function, or a Way of Being?

Brian C. Brewer

The rite of ordination, that "act of setting a person apart for ministerial office,"[1] has long been assimilated into the Baptist tradition as a customary practice. It is often thought by its churches to have biblical precedent and to serve as a means by which a congregation might affirm in an official way, both spiritually and ceremonially, the ordinand's divine calling to the gospel ministry. Additionally, the act of setting an individual apart, often through the use of laying on of hands, usually has demonstrated a congregation's recognition of the candidate's gifts, character, and often, proper training for a ministerial vocation.

However, upon closer examination, assumptions regarding the practice can be questioned and a lucid theology of ordination might become more problematic. One aspect of this uncertainty is the question of whether or to what extent the rite of ordination actually has a biblical foundation. Secondly, one might question how Baptists have represented the calling of those ordained both from "above," as from God, and also from "below," as from the church, its denominational leadership, and even the local congregation needful of the ordinand's gifts and ministry of the Gospel.[2] Both questions are significant for developing a third, which shall be the underlying question of this study: to what extent is ordained ministry simply an official installation of a person to fulfill an ecclesial or liturgical function for the church (e.g., preaching, administering the ordinances, pastoral care, leadership, etc.) and to what extent is the life of ordination an ontological reality (i.e., a special and particular way of being unparalleled in the life of a layperson)?

Biblical Background and Assumptions

Baptists and other Christians have turned as far back as the Old Testament to find practical precedent for the rite of ordination. Isaac blessed Jacob instead of Esau through the laying on of hands in Genesis 27, thus setting the younger son apart with authority and inheritance. Jacob, in turn, would bless the sons of Joseph by laying his hands on the boys (Gen. 48:8-22). Subsequently, blessings were passed down from one generation to another, but these blessings were to have binding implications upon the recipient. When Samuel anointed Saul and later David (I Sam. 9 and 16, respectively), it was to grant them God's leadership of the chosen people.[3]

Likewise, Christians look to the Jewish precedent of ordination for rabbis and add to that background the New Testament passages which describe a kind of formal induction into an office (Titus 1:5; Hebrews 5:1; 8:3). Lastly, many Christians understand the practice of laying on of hands as indicative of a biblical and solemn event for all those involved (Acts 6:6; 13:3; I Timothy 4:14; 5:22; 2 Timothy 1:6). Yet Biblical scholars, Baptists among them, have argued that there is very little actually said in Scripture regarding this rite, and that "ecclesial biases, the influence of post-canonical developments, and an unhistorical reading of rabbinic literature ... have been allowed to skew the reading of the NT texts when looking for guidance on the topic of ordination."[4] Consequently, one must look to the historical development of ordination among Christian churches to have a better understanding of its current position among Baptists today.

Reformation Heritage

Over the centuries, a number of challenges to the Catholic notion of ordination as a sacrament have emerged. Scholars have traced the development of a more egalitarian priesthood dating as early as the Waldensian movement in the 12th century and continued through the Lollard and Hussite movements in the 14th and 15th centuries as evidence of pre-Reformation attempts at a shared notion of a universal priesthood for all Christians.[5] However, much of the Baptist understanding for ordination originates more directly from the development of early Protestant thought, most specifically from Martin Luther. In eschewing the hierarchical priesthood in the Catholic Church, Luther instead theologically rent asunder the Temple curtain for all by arguing for the priesthood of every Christian. Each Christian's ordination, Luther posited, was enacted through baptism. Thus, in the then new Protestant thought, all Christians bore most of the responsibilities for and the privileges of ordained ministry.[6] Luther would cite I Peter 2:9 as a biblical basis for the egalitarian priesthood, which declares: "But you are a chosen race, a royal priesthood, a holy nation, God's own people, in order that you may proclaim the mighty acts of him who called you out of darkness into his marvelous light" (NRSV).

Ironically, it is on the action of proclamation (i.e., preaching) that Luther finally separated clergy from laity. While all Christians share the same authority in regard to the Word and sacraments, for the sake of good order only a person who has received the consent of the congregation or been called by the majority thereof should actually administer them. The public tasks of preaching, baptism and communion seem to be the only demarcated privileges and/or responsibilities of an ordained priest in contrast to the laity. Consequently, Luther redefined the long-held Catholic view of ordination as no longer a sacrament in which the ordinand's character is "indelibly impressed"[7] by the rite, thus affecting an ontological change in the person, to merely being a rite through which one is set apart for his clerical duties. Argues Luther, "The sacrament of ordination, if it has any validity at all, is only the right through which someone is called to the ministry of the church, since the priesthood is simply the ministry of the word; the word, I say; not the law, but the gospel."[8] Such an ecclesial ceremony is only carried out after the vocation has been discerned both by the individual and by the congregation who examined the ordinand. Thus for Luther, ordination is merely a pragmatic matter, a process through which some are identified as gifted for ministerial tasks and tapped by the congregation for its public duties in worship. Yet, one should not miss Luther's primary point: all Christians are priests, and the ontological hierarchy that had once separated priest and layperson is now abolished. All Christians are qualified to participate in the mission and ministry of the Church with the gifts each is given. But for the purpose of good order, the priestly acts of preaching and administering the sacraments are reserved for the chosen and ordained few to represent the whole of all Christians. Thereafter, ordination is one among the five Catholic sacraments that loses its sacramental status within Protestantism, baptism and the Eucharist remaining as the only two for most Protestant churches and Christians.

One significant implication for Luther's radical redefinition of ordination is the shifting of the locus of power within the two sacraments which continued to be practiced by the German Church.[9] In the case of baptism and the Eucharist, the authority of the rite did not emanate from its administrator. This notion was in contradistinction to the Roman Catholic Church which had generally accepted the teaching called sacerdotalism, an idea in which a priest, by virtue of his ordination, is granted the ability not only to administer the sacraments but also to dispense grace through them. Thus, for the late medieval period,, a person not properly ordained by the Church (i.e., not in direct line with apostolic succession) who nevertheless attempted to administer the sacraments would render them impotent and invalid.

For Luther, however, the rite of ordination does not provide a sacramental potency to the ordinances. Arguing in the case of baptism, for instance, Luther notes that

> we can clearly see the difference in baptism between man who administers the sacrament and God who is its author. For man baptizes, and yet does not baptize. He baptizes in that he performs the work of immersing the person to be baptized; he does not baptize, because in so doing he acts not on his own authority but in God's stead. ... Ascribe both to God alone, and look upon the person administering it as simply the vicarious instrument of God, by which the Lord sitting in heaven thrusts you under the water with his own hands, and promises you forgiveness of your sins, speaking to you upon earth with a human voice by the mouth of his minister.[10]

Instead, the minister is a designated person "placed in the church for the preaching of the Word and the administration of the sacraments."[11] Ordination is nothing more than the designation of those who are to serve these purposes.

It is worth noting at this juncture that the Catholic Church responded to Luther's charges and reforms through the Council of Trent. Held in three periods which spanned from 1545 to 1563, Trent regarded the new Protestant teachings as "innovations" and reaffirmed not only the hierarchical priesthood of seven orders (bishops, priests and deacons being the most essential) but also the notion that ordination was sacramental, a rite which conferred a special status on the individual. David Steinmetz observed:

> Unlike Luther, Trent taught that priesthood is not merely a vocation like any other and priests are not laity on special assignment. Ordination effects an ontological change in the one ordained. No layperson, however gifted and pious, can confect a valid eucharist, but any priest, however limited and unworthy, can.[12]

The sacramental nature of ordination for Catholicism imprints the soul of the priest, granting him not only authority but also power to dispense grace to the laity.

Thus, the cleavage between the Catholic and Lutheran positions was particularly pronounced on the issue of ordination. For the Catholic Church, ordination was a sacrament which indelibly changed the priest so he might spiritually change the faithful laypersons in his charge. For Protestantism, ordination was a rite serving utilitarian purposes, vetting out those within the Church who were called by God to preach the Word. Luther would conclude then that the ordination for the priesthood was for an exclusively functional purpose. He argued:

> The duty of a priest is to preach, and if he does not preach he is as much a priest as a picture of a man is a man. Does ordaining such babbling priests make one a bishop? Or blessing churches and bells? Or confirming children? Certainly not. Any deacon or layman could do as much. It is the ministry of the Word that makes the priest and the bishop.[13]

Likewise, John Calvin, who would follow Luther's German Reformation with the Reformation in Geneva, saw the purpose of the pastoral office as being primarily for the purpose of preaching the

Word. However, Calvin's argument also includes some sense of an ontological means to carry out the practical ends: *"Through the ministers to whom [God] has entrusted this office and has conferred the grace to carry it out,* he dispenses and distributes his gifts to the church."[14] Indeed, utilizing Isaiah 52:7 ("Beautiful are the feet and blessed the coming of those who announce peace"), Calvin argues for a certain "prestige" of those who are called and appointed to the preaching office. While each pastor is bound to his own congregation, he can, on occasion, be useful to other churches in times of emergency or when outside advice might be needful. But the tenor of Calvin's writings certainly elevates pastors not only for what they do but also for who they are: dispensers of God's revelation. Likening the ordained pastor to the apostolic ministry and authority of Peter and Paul, Calvin argued for the uniqueness of the apostle then and today by virtue of the fact that Christ entrusts to him God's teaching to humanity. God entrusts his message to the modern-day apostle or pastor just as God entrusted his Word to Paul, Calvin wrote,

> that very Paul whom he had determined to catch up into the third heaven and make worthy to receive a wonderful revelation of things unspeakable [II Corinthians 12:2-4]. Who, then, would dare despise that ministry or dispense with it as something superfluous, whose use God willed to attest with such proofs?[15]

Calvin then argued that while significant for the church, ordination is not a sacramental ceremony because it is "not ordinary or common with all believers."[16] Additionally priests are not given special powers to convey the Holy Spirit into others, nor are they capable of instituting a sacrifice through the Mass, thus "there is no reason why the papist priests should be proud." [17]

With this balanced argument for both honor for but humility in the pastoral office, Calvin also then echoed Luther's theme of a universal priesthood of believers. The Church is still called upon to institute a sacrifice, though not through a Eucharistic transubstantiation. Instead, as Christ is all Christians' Pontiff, every Christian offers to God a sacrifice of praise: "From this office of sacrificing, all Christians are called to a royal priesthood" [I Peter 2:9]. Through the Altar who is also Christ [Heb. 13:10], the Christian can acknowledge that Jesus "has made us a kingdom and priests unto the Father" [Rev. 1:6][18]

A final group from the Reformation period one should evaluate in order to understand the background of Baptist thinking on ordination practices is the Anabaptists. Frank Littell calls early Anabaptism "one of the first patterns of lay organization in Christian history."[19] So strongly did these Radical Reformers hold to Luther's concept of the priesthood of all believers, it is thought that ordination was not a part of the first Anabaptist congregations. Indeed, Conrad Grebel was probably never ordained, and early Anabaptists even eschewed the notion of a professional class of clergy, especially those who received salaries from the state church system.[20]

At the same time, 16th century Anabaptist theology was somewhat nebulous, particularly regarding the concept of ordination. Menno Simons and other second generation Anabaptists in northern Holland enjoyed a greater sense of distinction between clergy and laity and depended upon "a small circle of elders" to carry out baptisms and do other ministerial tasks.[21] Likewise, Hutterite Peter Riedeman would write in 1542 that

> It is not for all and sundry to take upon themselves such an office, namely that of teaching and baptizing; as James declares, saying, "Dear brothers, let not each strive to be a teacher, for we all sin much, and shall then receive all the greater condemnation." For which reasons none must take upon himself or accept such power, unless he be chosen properly and rightly by God in his church and community.... [Just as] "Christ glorified not himself to be made an high priest," thus his ministers likewise must not press themselves forward and come to the fore, but wait until God draws them out and chooses them. [22]

On the other hand, Mennonites in the southern region of Holland and what is today Belgium continued to maintain authority within the congregation as a whole. Baptisms were performed by the unordained, and the ban, the discipline of excommunicating unfaithful members, was carried out not by any particular group of presbyters but by the entire congregation. Only later, by the 17th century, did these congregations begin to imitate their northern counterparts and attach a greater significance to ordination.[23]

Thus, while early Anabaptists apparently make no mention of ordination practices, probably by virtue of their great emphasis on the universal priesthood of all Christians, later Anabaptists varied in practice, while seeming to elevate the pastorate to a position not only of responsibility but also of distinction, power and honor. Regardless, in all three Reformation traditions, Lutheran, Reformed, and Anabaptist, a greater emphasis on lay participation is underscored as all believers began to take on roles which heretofore in the Catholic tradition had been reserved exclusively for the cleric. Robert G. Torbet argues that during the Reformation, the Protestant movement sought less to "unfrock the clergy as it ordained the laity."[24]

Across the English Channel, the Church of England attempted to reform some of the abuses of the Catholic notion of sacramental ordination while still maintaining the ecclesial structure and hierarchy. Frustrated at retard in reformatory progress, Puritans called for further modifications in both the theology and the practice of ordination. Most prominent among these, Puritan Separatists followed Calvin's thinking by rejecting the episcopal hierarchy and transferred the authority for ordination to the congregation itself.[25] More radical forms of Christianity, especially the Quakers, argued for the idea that the Spirit worked without human means thus making ordination unnecessary. More conservative Christians held that the Holy Spirit worked through the human rite of ordination and did not work immediately, as had been the case in the apostolic era. Subsequently, through pressure from more conservative influences, parliament voted through a series of bills in 1644, 1645 and 1646 which required ordination for preaching and outlawed lay preaching. While conservatives argued primarily on the basis of good order and education as a check for public preaching, the British government codified the notion that God worked through the human means of ordination.[26]

Early Baptist Thought and Subsequent Development in England and America

It would be difficult to diminish accurately the influences Martin Luther, John Calvin, and the Anabaptists played in informing early Baptist thought on the subject of ordination. It is quite plausible that the rapids of variation of Baptist thinking on this topic come as outflows from these three major originating Reformation streams, the former two sifted by British Separatism and the latter by the Dutch Mennonites.

The first Baptist congregation emerged from the Separatist church led by John Smyth and Thomas Helwys which had fled to Holland to avoid persecution in Britain. Both Smyth and Helwys originally believed that the entire congregation should lay hands on the ordained, for, as Helwys observed in 1609, "If elders must ordain elders, then from whence did your eldership come?"[27] And Smyth would write in the same year, "The body of the church has in it all ministerial power immediately from Christ."[28] Smyth's use of the word "power" here is unclear and left to interpretation. In his own *Short Confession of Faith* of 1609, Smyth used this word several times, arguing "that the church of Christ has power delegated to themselves of announcing the Word, administering the sacraments, appointing ministers, disclaiming them," etc. and "that the ministers of the church are, not only bishops ('Episcopos'), to whom the power is given of dispensing both the Word and the sacraments, but also deacons," etc.[29] Thus, both Baptist leaders initially eschewed the practice of the Mennonite congregation they encountered in Amsterdam which had opted to grant presbyterian authority for vetting and ordaining. Instead, Smyth and Helwys both seemed to view the clergy as emerging from the laity, and were probably tapped merely to serve ministerial functions. However, Smyth's use of the word "power" might be construed to suggest a kind of sacramental authority for those who are ordained.

It is worth noting that Smyth would finally separate from Helwys on this issue and several others, as was his tendency in his ever-changing theology, and he joined the Mennonite thinking not only by investing the elders only in ordination, but also by coming to terms with the Dutch Mennonites in most other matters of faith as he and a group from the exiled English Separatist church eventually joined the Mennonite congregation in Amsterdam.[30]

Helwys, for his part, maintained an exclusively pragmatic and non-sacramental understanding of ordination. He would again reemphasize the theme in his *English Declaration at Amsterdam* in 1611 that "officers are to be chosen ... by election and approbation of [the] ... church whereof they are members with fasting, prayer, and laying on of hands." In this document, touted as "the first English Baptist

Confession of Faith,"[31] Helwys argued for a two-tiered system of church officers, namely, elders "who by their office do especially feed the flock concerning their soules," and Deacons, "Men, and Women who by their office relieve the necessities off the poore and impotent brethren concerning their bodies"[32] (Acts 6: 1-4). Understanding the important and distinct functions of these ordinations, Helwys also noted that "officers are to be chosen when there are persons qualified according to the rules of Christ," citing several scripture passages which describe the requisite disposition of the ordained.[33] Thus, ordination seemed to exist to serve a purpose, but it also required persons of high integrity and Christian character. Limiting ordination only to the calling church, a church officer could not transfer his or her ordination to another congregation. Thus, for Helwys, ordination originated from those selected from the church's laity. They are selected by the local church for the purpose of serving the local church. But to serve at the pleasure of the congregation, the officer must already fulfill the scriptural mandates requisite of the position. A few months after writing the *Declaration*, Helwys and a remnant of followers returned to England to establish the first Baptist church on English soil.

Thomas Helwys' functional understanding of ordination undoubtedly held sway among the first generation of Baptists and their congregations.[34] However, by the writing of *The Second London Confession* in 1677, British Baptists seemed to undergo a marked shift in their ordination practice which might suggest a parallel alteration in their theology. This confession limited the investment of ordination to the "eldership" of the congregation. And in the following year, *The Orthodox Creed*[35] broke the ordained offices into three groups, namely, "Bishops, or Messengers [36]; and Elders, or Pastors; and Deacons, or Overseers of the poor." Also notable, the creed states that only those who were "fitted and gifted by the holy ghost" for the office of bishop would be "chosen thereunto by the common suffrage of the church, [but] solemnly set apart by fasting and prayer, with imposition of hands, by the bishops of the same function." Likewise, elders (pastors) were chosen by the congregation and "ordained by the bishop or messenger God hath placed in the church he hath charge of."[37]

That the ordained were elected by the congregation points to the early Baptist understanding of congregational polity through its theology of a priesthood of all Christians. That the actual investment of the offices were left to the bishops seems to distinguish different classes of priesthood among laity and clergy and, interestingly enough, be a nod toward the Catholic doctrine of apostolic succession, thus implying a kind of sacramental quality to the later 17th century Baptist ordinations. To this point one might observe that several 17th century Baptist documents seem to indicate that an ordained elder is ordained again to the office of bishop. While this observation might be argued to underscore ordination's functionality, it is noted that before one is selected by the congregation God makes one a minister. This point might antithetically convey, then, an ontological quality that is either conveyed or at least confirmed at ordination.[38]

Over the next three centuries, most Baptists would tend towards either Helwys' functionality of the ordained office or towards a more ontological approach of the Orthodox Creed, perhaps suggesting a mild sacramentalism in ordination. It is worth noting, however, that some Baptists rejected the notion of ordination altogether. Notably, Baptist Edmund Chillendon, undoubtedly influenced by the Puritan anticlericalism of his age,[39] authored a book in 1647 titled, *Preaching Without Ordination,* in which he argued that one need only be called and given the opportunity to carry out the gospel ministry and that a formal laying on of hands by an official or a church was superfluous. Two centuries later, Charles Spurgeon would also reject the rite of ordination for any church office, and he was popularly believed to have described the service as "laying idle hands on empty heads." Thus, either in an attempt to underscore the power of the priesthood of all believers or simply to avoid the theological complexities of ordination as a function and a way of being, a small minority of Baptists chose to disregard the rite altogether,[40] though scholars have noted that Spurgeon's views of eschewing all ordinations was rather influential in Britain in his day.[41]

However, Baptists initially may have been slow regularly to ordain their ministers less out of anticlericalism or fear of falling into Catholic sacertodalism and more for pragmatic reasons. In the 17th century, Baptists were viewed in England as nonconformists, and in light of the Conventicle Act of 1664, Particular Baptists in particular were reluctant to practice ordination because their official leaders would then be subject to heavier penalties.[42] However, this hesitancy to carry out the rite should not be conflated to be representative of Baptist theology but merely as necessary pragmatics, for by the time the Act of Toleration was passed in 1689 more than one hundred "Baptized

Churches" were said to have met in London where they declared it "evil" for their congregations to not practice "that sacred Ordinance of Ordination."[43] Likewise, in that same period, the Philadelphia Baptist Association (1707) also condemned those who did not exercise "laying on of hands for any purpose." And a half-century later, the Sandy Creek Association (Liberty, North Carolina, 1758) even argued for full-fledged Baptist sacerdotalism, holding that the ordinances of the church would be invalid without the proper ordination of its administrator.[44]

Perhaps the greatest Particular Baptist theologian in the eighteenth century was John Gill (1697-1771). Gill argued that a minister receives two callings, one inward and one outward. Through the inward calling, the person receives the gifts for carrying out his ministry by the work of the Holy Spirit. Through the outward calling, the church endorses the candidate to exercise his gifts, confirms the reception of the divine handsel, and sends the minister forth "in the name of Christ, to preach the gospel, where he may be directed in providence to do it."[45] What is notable in Gill's theology is that while he rejected the actual practice of laying on of hands,[46] he not only endorsed the general practice of ordination but also saw it as carrying a universal implication (i.e., an endorsement for ministry beyond the local congregation). Thus, through the confirmatory mediation of the local congregation, the minister is liberated to practice freely his inward calling. And, through the authority of ordination, the congregation, in Gill's mind, was empowered with a great deal of responsibility in its choice of a candidate in such an endorsement.

On the other hand, Andrew Fuller (1754-1815), who was instrumental in creating the Baptist Missionary Society, saw ordination merely as a "brotherly concurrence" and completely rejected the notion that through ordination a minister becomes "a successor to the apostles" or is somehow imparted the authority to preach the Word or administer the ordinances. While he encouraged the assistance of outside preachers to participate in a congregation's ordination of its minister, he also sought to avoid the idea that such an ordination might convey "my having to impart to another minister some power or authority." Fuller then saw ordination to be a prudent but not an essential practice.[47]

What Gill and Fuller demonstrated in their time then is the ebb and flow of Baptist thought on ordination. While both men accepted the practice as important, they diverged on whether ordination somehow authorized the minister for his responsibilities. This tension was not only evident by varying practices among British Baptists but also among their contemporaries in America, Hugh Wamble noting that "among early Baptists ordination was a function of the church, assisted by ministers, with ordination [also] being viewed as installation into a specific office."[48] However, it is unclear whether Baptists during this time viewed ordained ministry simply for the purpose of tapping an individual to discharge the pastoral responsibilities or whether it might also have been intended to convey a "way of being" for the person exemplified by the office and its requisite characteristics, thus living up to its Southampton billing as a "sacred Ordinance."

The 19th century manifested an even greater cleavage in the Baptist understanding of ordained ministry. For many decades it was not uncommon for one to find the practice of multiple clergymen participating in the ordination services of their fellow ministers. While many Baptists remained somewhat sectarian, the tradition also reflected a growing sense of ecumenism, especially in relation to other Dissenting Protestants. One reflection of this was the use not only of other Baptist ministers during the ordination of fellow clergy but also the participation of ministers from other denominations. Indeed, in at least the case of Rev. J. Statham, formerly a missionary to Bengal, some 30 ministers of various denominations were present for his ordination. J. H. Y. Briggs notes that this practice represented not only a more ecumenical outlook for Baptists in general, but it also "clearly indicated that ordination was not to a separate Baptist ministry but to the Christian ministry."[49] But whether they be Baptists or otherwise, the presence and apparent desire for other clergy to officiate an ordination, lay hands on the candidate and "give the

SMARDEN
PARTICULAR BAPTIST
CHAPEL.

ORDINATION
OF
MR. R. W. MANN,
WILL TAKE PLACE (D.V.)
ON TUESDAY, THE 8TH OF JULY, 1862,
ON WHICH OCCASION

MR. WYARD,
OF LONDON
Will state the nature of a Gospel Church, and the usual questions, receive the Confession of Faith,
AND
MR. FOREMAN
Will give the right hand of Fellowship to Pastor and People,
AFTER WHICH ABOVE WILL BE OFFERED, AND
Mr. FOREMAN will give the Charge to the Elected Pastor.
IN THE EVENING,
Mr. WYARD will read the Scriptures and offer Prayer,
AND
Mr. FOREMAN will preach to the Church and Congregation.

Service to commence in the Afternoon at Two, and in the Evening at a quarter-past Six o'Clock.
Tea will be provided at Six-pence each.

right hand of fellowship" to the newly ordained reflected a sense of apostolic or ministerial authority intrinsic to the office. The bill[50] at the left, announcing the ordination of Robert W. Mann, is indicative of this practice.

Wyard and Foreman, listed in the bill, were said to be "leading men in the denomination."[51] This kind of pomp and ceremony, combined with the participation of other clergy, with the "right hand of fellowship" or hands laid upon the candidate by denomination officials, might again seem to be influenced by a kind of moderate sacerdotalism. At the very least, it conveyed a new understanding of ordination being a setting apart not only for the task at hand but also, as Gill had argued a century before, for the work of the universal Church. Indeed, J.M. Stifler, pastor of the First Baptist Church of New Haven, Connecticut, in 1880, would argue even further. Citing I Thessalonians 5:12 ("We beseech you, brethren, to know them which labor among you, and are over you in the Lord, and admonish you; and to esteem them very highly in love for their work's sake"), Stifler would posit:

> This exhortation to know God's ministers is useful for all time, the present especially. The churches should recognize the men among them whom God has qualified to be overseers. Their divine credentials are in their hearts... But whence came these men with holy aspirations for this as yet but half acknowledged office? They were in the church, participating in all its privileges, its work, its trials, and yet they were something more than the standard church member. They promised something more .... The elders had a secret preappointment of the Lord. The Scriptures give abundant answer to the question of their source .... When [Christ] ascended on high he gave gifts to men. These gifts were (and are) special, qualifying them for, and warranting them to seek, the office of bishop. It was a gift not of nature, but of grace. [52]

Thus, for Stifler, ordination was a formal setting apart of those who had already distinguished themselves by their character and giftedness, and God conveyed his gifts to them even before the congregation had set them apart, through his grace. Four years later, Edward T. Hiscox would write:

The pastor is to be loved, honored and obeyed, in the Lord. He is placed over the Church by both the Head of the body, and by the free and voluntary act of the body itself. Though he professes no magisterial authority, and has no power, either spiritual or temporal, to enforce mandates or inflict penalties, yet the very position he occupies as teacher and leader supposes authority vested in him .... As a preacher of the gospel his authority is of another and a higher kind, in that he is an ambassador from the king, and speaks with an authority more than human.[53]

For Hiscox, whose New Directory significantly influenced Baptists in America, the pastor, while freely chosen by the congregation, is granted extraordinary authority not by his own character or personality but by the authoritative God who the congregation perceives speaks through him. Ordination, it would follow, was the voluntary act of recognizing the minister as God's mouthpiece and would expect the compliance of the congregation to follow him who was ordained. Such an act would suggest that an ordination service was far more than a perfunctory ceremony to serve a pragmatic purpose. It encompasses the church's recognition of a person's giftedness by God and its willingness to listen, follow and obey that person's voice as refracting the very voice of God.

At the same time, the course of the 19th century, ironically, saw the diminution of the rite of ordination among many Baptist churches in Britain and the United States. In part, out of the influence of Spurgeon and other leading anti-ordination figures, Baptist churches began to practice ordination less regularly. But a pervading anti-Catholic sentiment also directed Baptists to oppose any rite which might smack of ritualism. [54] Lastly, Baptists began to interpret the word "ordain" as "to appoint" and that a subsequent service to follow a pastor's selection by a congregation would be unnecessary.[55] Thus, while some 19th century theologians and church officials welcomed ordination as a significant service demarcating the pastor as authoritative, in other Baptist circles, the practice was on the wane and seen as inessential, unbiblical and even a "Catholic" practice. One humorous anecdote to exemplify the 19th century cleavage regarding understanding and appreciation of ordination was that of John Howard Hinton and Joseph Angus. Upon Hinton's officiating Angus' ordination service in

1838, Hinton published his ordination sermon in the *Baptist Magazine*, stating that such an act was needful, for ordination "has of late been all but abandoned, as by common consent, to an almost hopeless obscurity," and that it was "ready to vanish away." And yet, Angus the ordinand would reply in the publication, "I cannot but wish that the solemn assumptions of a modern ordination service were exchanged for the 'affectionate greetings of a public recognition.'"[56] Indeed, the "solemn assumptions of a modern ordination" were surely undergoing enervation among Baptists.

Finally, while the practice of ordination did continue among Baptists worldwide in the 20th century, an understanding as to what the rite conferred upon the ordinand was diverse. Writing about Southern Baptists in the United States during this period, Thomas Halbrooks observed one unity: " ... Baptists were almost unanimous in their opinions of what [ordination] did not confer. They repeatedly asserted that it did not confer any grace, spiritual gifts, abilities, power, priestly authority, special rights or privileges, mysterious virtues, or magic 'fluid.' For Baptists, ordination was by no means a sacerdotal action."[57] However, 20th century Baptists did commonly see ordination as conferring the authority to perform certain acts on behalf of the church and the state, such as marriage. And Baptists who argued on the basis of church order saw ordination as the qualifying mark for administering the ordinances, while other Baptists saw no clergy-laity distinction in these matters.[58] Nevertheless, Baptists generally recovered the use of ordination in many parts of the world, understanding the ceremony to be important but differing on its implications.

Baptist Practice Today

It undoubtedly comes as little surprise that the practices of ordination among Baptists are as varied today as their capricious past. What this brief history of the predecessors of the Baptists and of Baptists themselves has shown is that there has been a great deal of differences and even confusion among Baptists regarding this rite. Baptist historian Robert A. Baker rightly observed: "At least one statement may be made about the Baptist view of ordination without any possibility of successful contradiction: Baptists anywhere in the world have never totally agreed on the question of ordination."[59] And central to the thesis of this paper, Baptists have not agreed over the centuries whether the ordained are set apart simply to carry out ecclesial and liturgical functions on behalf of the church or whether their ministry is also, in some sense, a way of being.

Most Baptists in the United States still practice some form of ordination upon their leaders, especially pastors and deacons. However, such practice often is accompanied by little theological reflection upon the spiritual significance of the rite. Thus, while it is safe to say that the majority of Baptists in America have leaned towards a non-sacramental and even a merely pragmatic understanding of ordination as a kind of installation for service, it is the contention of this paper that the majority might learn from the historic minority view(s) on this issue as well, indeed each learning from the other, for a more balanced appropriation of what ordination is theologically to intend.

On the one hand, Canadian theologian Stanley Grenz argued for a functional view of ordination, stating:

> Ordained officers, then, are leaders who have been designated by the people themselves, and not a small hierarchy perpetuating themselves and their power. Baptist ecclesiology stresses the leadership function of the ordained person. Such a one is called chiefly to lead the people of God in service (Ephesians 4:1-13) and not to be the mediator of God's grace or Christ's will. Therefore, rather than being set in a position over the people, the ordained person stands with them as together they seek to be obedient to the Lord of the church. [60]

Clearly what Grenz outlines above is a position which staunchly upholds the priesthood of all believers; thus he wished to diminish any actual distinctions between clergy and laity. His argument markedly separates itself from any kind of hierarchical position resembling Catholicism. And such a point is well taken and has become a part of the fabric of both Protestant and Baptist congregational life, at least in theory. Martin Luther, from whom Baptists received this understanding of a common priesthood, demonstrated that one might hold that all Christians have access to God and are to carry out their share of Christian ministry, while he still upheld the need for specific leadership and human guidance of other Christians within the congregation. Luther did not intend to convey the idea of a priesthood for *each* Christian but rather to stress the priesthood of *all* believers collectively. Christians, as Augustine explained, "all are priests because they are members of the one Priest [Christ Jesus]."[61] Thus, Baptists can affirm with other Protestants the priesthood of all believers on the one hand and the specialty of ordination as the selection of its leaders in preaching and administering the ordinances on the other, without contradiction. While every Christian has a vocation in life, responding to the call of God in what he or she does, this is not intended to convey a radical individualism in the faith. John Howard Yoder observed how this kind of thinking developed:

> Now the priesthood of all believers can foster individualism. The high priest has access to God. Every priest is authorized to do his sacrificial, sacramental duties to have access to God. If we are all priests then we all have access to God and we do not need each other. This notion has developed in recent Protestant thought but was certainly not involved in the biblical phrasing from which it took off. Priesthood is, in biblical thought, collective .... Israel and the church are to have - as peoples - a priestly function, rather than being a group of individuals each with his or her own priestly status. The function of a priest is not to have access to God. That is the presupposition of his function, an aspect of his work. The function of a priest is to mediate for others. So to be priests is to be bridges between others and God, not to be persons of privilege who can get along on their own.

However, over the course of time, especially in the last two centuries, Protestant Christians in general and Baptist Christians specifically have begun to exaggerate the notion of the priesthood of all Christians beyond the intended corrective of Martin Luther and the Reformation. John Steely observed that "the denial of any sacramental efficacy for the ceremony or of the bestowal of special sacerdotal powers is quite typical of Baptist [conviction today]. The denial expresses resistance, partly conscious, partly unconscious, to the prevailing concept of priesthood and ordination in the dominant established churches among which Baptists had their beginning."[63] In other words, Baptists may have over-compensated their theology of ordination out of an anti-high church sentiment. Yet, ironically, the one who gave Baptists their priesthood of every Christian conviction, namely Martin Luther, also might bequeath to them the antidote to their nearly Quaker-like anti-clericalism that many Baptist churches exemplify today.

In arguing for the priesthood of all believers and against the notion that ordination is one of the seven holy sacraments of the church, there instead being two, Luther described ordination as "an ecclesiastical ceremony, like many others which have been introduced by the Church Fathers ... [as] rites employed solely to prepare men for certain duties."[64] Thus, ordination should be practiced as a significant church ceremony, but not one on which an indelible character is somehow impressed upon the ordinand during the service.

Starting with Luther, Protestant Christians have emphasized the priesthood of all believers. As Luther argued, "Christ is a priest, therefore Christians are priests; ... that we are his brethren is true only because of the new birth. Wherefore we are priests, as he is a Priest, sons as he is Son, kings as he is King."[65] It follows then, in Luther's Protestant argument, that priests are born (through the new birth) and not made. By virtue of their baptisms, all Christians are given priestly authority "to teach, to preach and proclaim the Word of God, to baptize, to consecrate or administer the Eucharist, to bind and loose sins, to pray for others, to sacrifice, and to judge all doctrine and spirits."[66] As a common right of all Christians, no one Christian can arise by his own authority and assume alone that which belongs to the entire church. Instead, Luther argued, each congregation should choose "faithful men" who are "able to teach," and to entrust to them the responsibility of carrying out these priestly functions on behalf of all.[67] While any Christian, Luther argued, can preach, baptize, and pray, and all should at times, especially in emergencies, the selected minister(s) should normally carry out these rights and perform these functions publicly so that everything might be done in order [I Corinthians 14:40]. Those chosen for this specific function should be called "ministers, deacons, stewards, [or] presbyters," and not "priests," for, again, all Christians are priests. [68]

And yet, this same founder of the Protestant movement argued a kind of specialty of those who were to be set apart for these priestly acts on behalf of the church: "Proceed in the name of the Lord to elect one or more whom you desire, and who appear to be worthy and able. Then let those who are leaders among you lay hands upon them, and certify and commend them to the people and the church or community. In this way let them become your bishops, ministers or pastors. Amen. The qualifications of those to be elected are fully described by Paul, in Titus 1 [:6ff], and I Timothy 3 [:2ff]."[69] Thus, while seeming to argue at first that ordained ministry was merely a function carried out by one or some on behalf of the many, Luther subsequently implied that those chosen must exemplify a kind of life which is worthy of the function they carry out.

In our own time, in order to counter-balance both the individualistic trends and also the anti-clerical trajectory among modern Baptists, a number of Baptists[70] have begun to argue for the recovery of a more sacramental position regarding ordination, positing that something of the nature of the ministry is lost when it is reduced to serving a functional purpose only. Echoing Luther's sentiments, for instance, John Colwell argues that the call to Christian ministry is "inherently ecclesial; Jesus does not by-pass his Church; he mediates his call through his Church."[71] It is through this means that a person's call to vocational ministry is tested and confirmed. The Church acts on behalf of Christ to declare and confirm this calling.

However, the unfortunate state of the universal church is a divided one. Thus, no one group might adequately and appropriately represent the Church catholic fully. The authority to grant ordination is bequeathed today to a denomination or even to a local church. However, theologically, that same ordination is to God's Church, for as Colwell argues, "ordination can never be sectarian. That which does not acknowledge the Church catholic, and itself as part of the Church catholic, has no authority to ordain." Colwell then concludes:

> I am arguing, therefore, that ordination is not merely an outward and supplementary expression of an inward call: it is rather the definitive uttering and effecting of that call and its consequent authority and responsibility. It is an action of the Holy Spirit in and through an action on behalf of the Church and the name of Christ. It is a mediation of grace (understood as an action of the Spirit). It is sacramental. [72]

For many Baptists today, such a claim might at first seem "un-Baptist." However, what Colwell intends is not an *ex opere operato* function in ordination, whereby the Holy Spirit is made captive to human manipulation (i.e., the laying on of hands as the means to convey God's grace). Instead, he argues: "In the act of ordination, therefore, we humbly and prayerfully appropriate the promise that God will speak through, act through, and mediate his presence through the one being ordained. But God is not restricted by this promise or this act. He remains free to speak and act through others."[73]

Thus, as this essay has attempted to outline, Baptists have historically held the notions of ordained ministry as function and as way of being in tension. While ministers must carry out a function in accordance with their calling, Baptists have also used the terminology of "separation" or "setting apart" for this purpose. These ideas seem to convey at least some sort of ontological reality for ordained ministry. Colwell articulates the fine line Baptists and all Protestant Christians should walk within this tension: " ... Others may minister the Word, but those ordained have been separated to this ministry of the Word. Similarly others may celebrate the sacraments, but again those ordained have been separated to this celebration." [74]

Both Function and Being

It is the conclusion of this paper, upon reviewing the historical evidence and compelling theological reflection of other Baptists and Protestants, that ordination, out of necessity, carries qualities both functional and ontological. Baptists ordain their ministers to the "Gospel ministry," which is typically understood as the function of proclaiming the gospel of Christ. Additionally, Baptists join most other Protestants as seeing the pastor as the normative representative on behalf of the congregation to administer the ordinances, and as the most gifted and qualified for pastoral care and to lead the congregation in theological reflection. This understanding is pragmatic; it serves an ecclesial purpose. However, this leadership is not granted to certain individuals willy-nilly or in a vacuum. Traditionally, Baptists have sought out the personal, ethical and spiritual qualities in their ordained leadership, both in their pastors and in the deacons, in accordance with their understanding of Scripture. Ordination exams, councils and sometimes denominational committees seek to ascertain the qualities and lifestyle of a candidate for ordination, especially regarding the pastorate. And upon ordination, these characteristics (often taken from the list in I

Timothy: "temperate, sensible, respectable, hospitable, an apt teacher, not a drunkard, not violent but gentle, not quarrelsome, not a lover of money," etc.) are expected to correspond to the proclaiming function with which the ordained are charged. In other words, ministers' lives should as much reflect the gospel as their words in the pulpit. And Baptist ministers, for good or for ill, have been held accountable not only for their theology and pastoral gifts but also for their personal conduct. Indeed, most Baptists would agree with the notion that pastors are to be held to a higher ethical and lifestyle standard than the rest of the congregation. Additionally, Baptist Christians historically have understood their pastors as "worthy of double honor" (I Timothy 5:17) in that they are granted with some form of leadership and some sense of authority within the congregation, even as that leadership and authority can vary from church to church. Arguably, then, ordained ministry for Baptists is as much a way of being as it is a job description. Baptist historian Robert A. Baker concludes that "Baptist scholars have never agreed whether ordination is simply functional (by which a person is set apart to a particular ministry) or whether it includes some official status (by which the person is given an office with new authority for ministry). Probably the correct answer is 'both/and' rather than 'either/or.'"[75] Additionally, ordained ministry is given a legal status within the statues of many countries Baptists inhabit. Thus, ordination often gives a person legal authority to officiate wedding ceremonies for couples and perform other services on behalf of the government. Such a practice exemplifies a public understanding regarding the authority of ordination, even among secular magistrates.

Most Baptists tend to shy away from "sacramental" terminology as it regards ordination[76] but still, at least unwittingly, grant it an ontological status. Ordained ministry embodies as much a life "set apart" as a duty to be carried out. Learning from the Apostle Paul, however, such a way of being actually initiates in the life of ministers before they are ordained and thus gives reason for their official "setting apart." Paradoxically, pastors and deacons are "set apart" not to be removed from the rest of the church as a separate class but to be the normative leaders for the church by word and deed. David Garland even suggests that "it would not be inappropriate to imagine the ministers …as player-coaches who prepare and support the starting line-up, the saints." [77] As players, they are among the priestly class that encompasses all Christians. As coaches, they are set apart and expected to be a significant example of Christian ministry to be imitated by all.

Ordination for Baptists then is more often an ecclesial recognition of the character and gifts already inherent in the individual, but one now formally recognized and endorsed by the church for her leadership and advancement. Baptists may debate the semantics of whether one has to have the character to be an ordained pastor or whether one is a pastor because he or she has the character. But students of this tradition would have difficulty divorcing the function of one who is ordained from his way of being. Baker, who was one such student, then concludes: "Thus, although Baptists hold a non-sacramental view of ordination, most of them have felt that the ordination service, so briefly described in the New Testament, should set apart a person to function in Christian ministry and, in addition, should confer on him new powers (ecclesiastical, not spiritual) by virtue of his office. In that sense, Baptist ordination historically has been a formal dedication of the spiritual gifts of a person called by God for service and a notification to the Christian community that the person was qualified to administer the ordinances and carry on the duties for which he was set apart."[78] Thus, it is a calling to carry out a function and to subsist in that calling both. In the "Declaration and Blessing" for ordination services in *Gathering for Worship* (Baptist Union of Great Britain), the suggested prayer strikes this balance:

> *In the name of the Father, the Son and the Holy Spirit,*
> *we declare you, A, to be ordained ...*
> *in the church of Jesus Christ*
> *and commissioned for ministry*
> *within the Baptist Union of Great Britain.*
> *Seek the kingdom of God,*
> *be faithful and true in your ministry*
> *so that your* whole life *may bear witness*
> *to the crucified and risen Christ.* [79]

It is essential for Baptists to revive a view of ordained ministry which understands its authority as emanating surely not from its office and certainly not from its ecclesial functions only, as significant as those are, but also from the character of humility, Christlike service, and faithful witness of the gospel of those who are called by the risen Lord

271

and his Church. Writing of Paul's authority as an apostle, Anthony C. Thiselton notes: "Paul sees his apostleship not as an instrument of power but as a call to become a transparent agency through whom the crucified and raised Christ becomes portrayed through lifestyle, thought, and utterance."[80] So must be the case for ordained "apostles" or ministers today.

NOTES

[1]Millard J. Erickson, *A Concise Dictionary of Christian Theology* (Grand Rapids: Baker Book House, 1986), 120.

[2]Methodist Bishop William H. Willimon argues both the notion of ordination as coming from "above" and from "below" is essential for understanding true, biblical, and balanced notion of ordination. See his *Pastor: The Theology and Practice of Ordained Ministry* (Nashville: Abingdon Press, 2002), 37- 40.

[3]Alton H. McEachern, *Set Apart for Service* (Nashville: Broadman Press, 1980), 12-13.

[4]David E. Garland, "The Absence of an Ordained Ministry in the Churches of Paul," from *Baptist and Ordination: Studies Conducted by Baylor University and the Baptist General Convention of Texas,* William H. Brackney, ed. (Macon, GA: The National Association of Baptist Professors of Religion, 2003), 25.

[5]Richard L Greaves is one scholar who has outlined these attempts as predating the 16th century. See his study, "The Ordination Controversy and the Spirit of Reform in Puritan England," *Journal of Ecclesiastical History* XXI, no. 3 (July 1970), 225

[6]Luther would write: "If [the Catholic Church] were forced to grant that all of us that have been baptized are equally priests, as indeed we are, and that only the ministry was committed to them, yet with our common consent, they would then know that they have no right to rule over us except insofar as we freely concede it." Martin Luther, "The Babylonian Captivity of the Church," in *Luther's Works* [hereafter *LW*], vol. 36. Abdel Ross Wentz, ed. (Philadelphia: Muhlenberg Press, 1959), 112.

[7]Luther here is arguing against the Catholic notion of *character indelibilis,* which conveys that an indelible mark is received through ordination upon the new priest as a divine gift. This marking of the soul creates a kind of alteration in those ordained to the priesthood to distinguish them from others. Thus, Catholic authorities would argue "once a priest, always a priest." *Character indelibilis* received its official status through the bull *Exultate Deo* in 1439. See fn. 201, *LW* vol. 36, lll. However, in the *Canons on the Sacraments in General,* a document written in 1547 by the Council of Trent, the Catholic Church argued

that baptism, confirmation and ordination, all three, imprinted on the soul a certain character, "a spiritual and indelible mark," in such a way that all three sacraments could not be repeated for any one person. See H.J. Schroder, trans., *Canons and Decrees of the Council of Trent* (Rockford, Ill.: Tan Books, 1978), 29-46.

[8]*LW*, Vol 36, 116.

[9]Luther writes: "For Christ established the sacrament on himself and not on the person of the minister. It rests on the Word. Accordingly, when there is a confession of the Word, no matter what kind of knave the minister may be, this detracts not at all from the sacrament," *L W*, vol. 54, 101.

[10]*LW*, Vol. 36, 62-3. For further study in this topic, see Hans-Wilhelm Kelling, "Martin Luther: The First Forty Years In Remembrance of the 500th Anniversary of His Birth," *Brigham Young University Studies*, vol. 23 (Spring 1983), 31-146.

[11]*LW*, Vol. 54, 100.

[12]David C. Steinmetz, "The Council of Trent," in *The Cambridge Companion to Reformation Theology*. David Bagchi and David C. Steinmetz, eds. (New York: Cambridge University Press, 2004), 242-3.

[13]*LW, V*ol. 36,115.

[14] John Calvin, *Institutes of the Christian Religion*, IV, III, 2. John T. McNeill, ed. Ford Lewis Battles, transl. (Philadelphia: Westminster Press, 1960), 1055 [italics mine].

[15]Ibid., 1056.

[16] Ibid., IV, XIX, 28, 1476.

[17]Ibid.

[18]Ibid., IV, XVIII, 17, 1444-5.

[19]Frank Littell, *The Anabaptist View of the Church* (Boston: Starr King Press, 1958), 94.

[20]One example of this rejection of professional clergy can be seen in Conrad Grebel's September 5, 1524, letter to Thomas Müntzer inquiring whether the latter "still accepted a salary," here cited in C. Penrose St. Amant, "Sources of Baptist Views on Ordination," *Baptist History and Heritage*, vol. 23, no. 3 (July 1988), 8.

[21] See C. Penrose St. Amant, 8-9.

[22] From Peter Riedeman, "The Manner of Baptizing," in *Account* (1542), 79-81, here cited in *Anabaptism in Outline*, Walter Klaassen, ed. (Scottdale, PA: Herald Press, 1981), 129-30.

[23]St. Amant, 9.

[24] Robert G. Torbet, *The Baptist Ministry Then and Now* (Philadelphia: Judson Press, 1953), 9.

[25]E. Glenn Hinson, "Ordination in Christian History," *Review and Expositor*, vol. 78, no. 4 (Fall 1981),492.

[26]Richard Greaves notes that Baptists and other Independents held a position between that of the conservatives and the radicals, arguing that ordination should not be condemned, neither should it be made requisite for preaching, 228.

[27]Thomas Helwys, quoted by W.T. Whitley, *The Works of John Smyth*, vol. 1, cix.

[28]John Smyth, quoted by Whitley, vol. 2, cxii.

[29]John Smyth, *Short Confession of Faith* (1609), articles 13 & 16, here cited in John A. Broadus, *Baptist Confessions, Covenants, and Catechisms*, Timothy and Denise George, eds. (Nashville: Broadman & Holman Publishers, 1996),33.

[30]In the *Short Confession* of 1610, Smyth, in a document signed by all those who would join the Mennonite church from the original Separatist congregation, would write: "For although every believer is a member of the body of Christ, yet is not every one therefore a teacher, elder, or deacon, but only such as are orderly appointed to such offices. Therefore, also, the administration of the said offices or duties partaineth only to those who are ordained thereto, and not to every particular common person. The vocation or election of the said officers is performed by the church, with fasting, and prayer to God; for God knoweth the heart; he is amongst the faithful who are gathered together in his name; and by his Holy Spirit doth so govern the minds and hearts of his people, that he by them bringeth to light and propoundeth whom he knoweth to be profitable to his church. And although the election and vocation to the said offices is performed by the aforesaid means, yet, nevertheless, the investing into the said service is accomplished by the elders of the church through the laying on of hands." See articles 24, 25, & 26 in *Short Confession* of 1610, here cited from *Baptist Confessions of Faith*, William L. Lumpkin, ed. (Philadelphia: Judson Press, 1959), 109.

[31]William L. Lumpkin makes this argument. See his *Baptist Confessions of Faith* (Philadelphia: Judson Press, 1959), 115.

[32]Thomas Helwys, "A Declaration of Faith of English People Remaining at Amsterdam in Holland," in Lumpkin, *Baptist Confessions of Faith*, 121-2.

[33]Ibid., 122.

[34]The First London Confession (1644) seems to corroborate this initial consistency. Section XXXVI of the confession states: "That being thus joyned, every Church has power given them from Christ for their better well-being, to choose to themselves meet persons into the office of Pastors, Teachers, Elders, Deacons, being qualified according to the Word, as those which Christ has appointed in his Testament, for the feeding, governing, serving and building up of his Church, and that none other have power to impose them, either these or any other," here cited in H. Leon McBeth, *A Sourcebook for Baptist Heritage* (Nashville: Broadman, 1990), 50. Here one might observe that it is

the congregation that does the ordaining and that the rite is exclusively for a functional and not an ontological purpose.

[35]In order to show theological unity with other Protestants, especially Presbyterians and Congregationalists, during a period of religious turmoil in England, the General Baptists wrote this confession in 1679. Taking its origin from the same source as the Particular Baptist's Second London Confession, the Orthodox Creed was patterned after the Westminster Confession. See W. Madison Grace, II, "Transcriber's Preface to An Orthodox Creed: An Unabridged Seventeenth Century General Baptist Confession," *Southwestern Journal of Theology*, vol. 48, no. 2 (Spr 2006), 125f.

[36]Citing Thomas Grantham's *The Successors of the Apostles* (1647), G. Hugh Wamble explains that by the mid-17th century, General Baptists had accepted the office of bishop or messenger...and as "the most prominent [of] ministers" and "it appears, major guardians of ordination. Viewed as 'successors to the apostles,' they constituted a 'travelling ministry' for spreading the gospel, planting churches, confirming churches in the faith, setting 'in order such Churches as want officers,' and aiding 'faithful Pastours or churches against usurpers' and purveyors of false doctrine." See Wamble, "Baptist Ordination Practices to 1845," *Baptist History and Heritage*, vol. 23, no. 3 (July 1988), 17.

[37]Edward Bean Underhill, ed., *Confessions of Faith and Other Public Documents illustrative of the History of the Baptist Churches in England in the 17th Century* (London: Haddon, Brothers, & Co., 1854),150. See also C. Penrose St. Amant's observations of these texts from his "Sources of Baptist Views on Ordination," 9. St. Amant argues that the shift in ordination practice at this juncture is indicative of Mennonite influence "probably through John Smyth" on these later Baptists.

[38]Wamble, 17.

[39]See James Fulton MacLear, "The Making of the Lay Tradition," in *The Journal of Religion*, vol. 33, No.2 (Apr. 1953), 113-136.

[40]St. Amant, 9-10.

[41]J. H. Y. Briggs noted that Spurgeon's rejection of ordination for himself was deliberate and that "his example was nationally very influential." See Brigg's *English Baptists of the Nineteenth Century, A History of the English Baptists*, vol. 3 (London: Baptist Historical Society, 1994), 88.

[42]Wamble, 17.

[43]Originally cited from "Ordination at Southampton, 1691, in *Transactions*, vol. 2:66, 1910-11; here cited in Wamble, 18.

[44]Robert A. Baker, "Ordination: The Baptist Heritage," *The Baptist Standard* (February 14, 1979), 14.

[45]Originally cited from John Gill, *A Body of Practical Divinity*, bk. 2, ch. 3, "Of the Officers of a Church, Particularly Pastors," The Baptist Faith Series,

no. 2 (Paris, Arkansas: The Baptist Standard Bearer, Inc., 2000); here cited in Wamble, 18.

⁴⁶Wamble notes that Gill translated Acts 14:23 as "stretching of hands" and not an imposing of hands, and he viewed the Apostle's work of laying on of hands as empowering in their day because they were extraordinary, but in the post-apostolic era such practice would be "empty" for Christian authorities because they are ordinary persons and thus have "no gifts to convey" to one another. See Wamble, 18-19. Nevertheless, the act of ordination for Gill carried with it the authority and approval of the church for the Church universal.

⁴⁷Briggs, 37.

⁴⁸Wamble, 23.

⁴⁹Briggs, 86.

⁵⁰This bill, originally printed by a relative of one of the deacons of the Smarden Baptist Chapel is here reprinted in Norman L. Hopkins, *The Baptists of Smarden and the Weald of Kent, 1640-2000* (Kent: Mickle Print Ltd., n.d.), 87.

⁵¹Hopkins, 87.

⁵²J.M. Stifler, "The Gospel Ministry," in *Baptist Doctrines*, Charles A. Jenkens, ed. (St. Louis: Chancy R. Barnes, 1880), 250.

⁵³ Edward T. Hiscox, *The New Directory for Baptist Churches* (Philadelphia: Judson Press, 1894), 100-101. J.B. Jeter seems to agree with Hiscox's notion of the origin of authority for the pastor, as he wrote in 1902, "The preacher is the mightiest human force in the world. He is the forerunner of civilization. He is the most effective reformer known to men. His power lies in his message. The word of God, which is quick and powerful, he lays on the hearts of the people." See Jeremiah B. Jeter, *Baptist Principles Reset* (Dallas: Standard Publishing Co., 1902), 252.

⁵⁴For instance, P.H. Mell writes: "There is no invisible gift imparted by the imposition of hand [in ordination]; nor does the ceremony bring the subject into a line of succession from apostles, or make him a link in a ministerial chain from primitive times." Originally cited from his "Corrective Church Discipline," *Baptist Champion* (February 23, 1860),1; here cited in John E. Steely, "Ministerial Certification in Southern Baptist History: Ordination," *Baptist History and Heritage*, vol. 15, no. 1 (Jan 1980), 26.

⁵⁵Briggs, 87.

⁵⁶Originally published in the *Baptist Magazine* (1838), 100 and 147,8 respectively; here cited from Briggs, 87-8.

⁵⁷G. Thomas Halbrooks, "The Meaning and Significance of Ordination Among Southern Baptists, 1845-1945," *Baptist History and Heritage*, vol. 23, no. 3 (July 1988), 28.

⁵⁸Ibid.

⁵⁹Robert A. Baker, "Ordination: The Baptist Heritage," in *The Baptist Standard* (February 14, 1979), 14.

[60]Stanley J. Grenz, *The Baptist Congregation* (Vancouver: Regent College Publishing, 1985), 68- 9.

[61]St. Augustine, *City of God*, XX.10.

[62] John Howard Yoder, *Preface to Theology: Christology and Method* (Brazos Press, 2002), 283-4.

[63]Steely, 26-7.

[64]Luther, "Pagan Servitude of the Church," here cited in *Martin Luther: Selections from His Writings*, John Dillenberger, ed. (New York: Anchor Books, 1962), 342.

[65]*LW*, "Concerning the Ministry," vol. 40, 20.

[66]Ibid., 36.

[67] Ibid.

[68] Ibid., 34-5.

[69] Ibid., 40.

[70]For examples, see John E. Colwell, "The Sacramental Nature of Ordination: An Attempt to Reengage a Catholic Understanding and Practice," *Baptist Sacramentalism*, Anthony R. Cross and Phillip E. Thompson, eds. (Milton Keyes, Great Britain: Paternoster Press, 2003), 228-246; Stephen R. Holmes, "Toward a Baptist Theology of Ordained Ministry," *Baptist Sacramentalism*, 247-262; and Paul S. Fiddes, *Participating in God: A Pastoral Doctrine of the Trinity* (London: Darton Longman and Todd, 2000). Fiddes would argue in this latter work: "The vocation to Christian ministry is a call to a way of being, not just the exercise of skills or the carrying out of a set of functions," 294.

[71]Colwell, 240.

[72]Ibid., 241.

[73]Ibid., 242.

[74]Ibid., 244-5.

[75]Baker, 14.

[76]Indeed, Herschel Hobbs wrote, as part of the entry for "Ordination: Ministers" in the *Encyclopedia of Southern Baptists*, the following: "Baptists do not hold to the ecclesiastical tradition which leads some to consider ordination the channel through which the ordained receives special ministerial grace or powers not afforded to others." However, he does concede that it is a "setting apart" for service. See vol. n (Nashville: Broadman, 1958), 1057.

[77]Garland, 29.

[78]Baker, 14.

[79]Christopher J. Ellis and Myra Blyth, eds. *Gathering for Worship: Patterns and Prayers for the Community of Disciples* (Norwich: Canterbury Press, 2005), 130 [emphasis mine].

[80]Anthony C. Thiselton, *The First Epistle to the Corinthians* (Grand Rapids: Eerdmans/Carlisle: Paternoster, 2000), 45.

Chapter 18

The Multi-lateral Discussion on Baptism: Where are we Today?

Neville Callam

With the publication of *Baptism, Eucharist and Ministry* (*BEM*)[1] twenty-five years ago, many churches manifested a remarkable degree of convergence around their understanding of the meaning of baptism. Whatever may have been their reservations regarding the text, some Baptist groups expressed a measure of appreciation for the section of *BEM* dealing with baptism. These groups include the Burma Baptist Convention; the Union of Evangelical Free Churches (Baptists) in the German Democratic Republic; the American Baptist Churches, USA; the Covenanted Baptist Churches in Wales; and the Baptist unions of Sweden, Scotland, Denmark and Great Britain and Ireland.[2]

Burmese Baptists responded "with a spirit of thanksgiving" to *BEM*, which they described as marking a "historic ecumenical milestone."[3] They declared that the understanding of the meaning and practice of baptism reflected in *BEM* suggested that "mutual recognition of baptism [had] become a possibility."[4] Meanwhile, the Baptist Union of Great Britain and Ireland welcomed *BEM* as "a notable milestone in the search for sufficient theological consensus to make possible mutual recognition among separated churches."[5]

The Baptist Union of Sweden agreed that *BEM* reflected "a common understanding of baptism in many respects, especially regarding the meaning and importance of baptism."[6] Meanwhile, the Baptist Union of Scotland said that *BEM* "brought sharply into focus the real issues in the search for unity, and [would] provide fresh impetus and relevance to dialogue on these issues."[7] For their part, the Baptist Union of Denmark remarked that *BEM* was "an enriching and, on several points, correcting perspective" for their own Christian tradition.[8]

While affirming that some of its member churches already embraced the view that infant baptism followed by a later personal confession of faith was "a sufficient basis for church membership,"[9] American Baptist Churches, USA said that study of *BEM* might "be an occasion of growth and reformation" for them as Baptists.[10] On the other hand, Baptists in the German Democratic Republic were rather more critical of *BEM*, regarding it as "relativizing" the "holy scripture as the norm of faith, life and teaching" and bestowing upon its themes "a weight of their own which does not properly belong to them."[11]

Baptists, like other churches evaluating *BEM*, raised questions about the ecclesiological presumptions informing the baptism section of *BEM*. They also pointed to the need for further discussion on the question of sacrament and sacramentality in relation to baptism. They affirmed the conventional understanding of the relation of baptism and faith as comprehended in the perspective of "believers' baptism," and raised questions on what this implies for the understanding of infant and believers' baptism being two different forms of baptism that are on the same level. They also called for greater clarity in the use of the term "baptism" as signifying both an initial step in the overall process of Christian initiation and as a term used to cover the entire initiation process.[12]

The Journey Since *BEM*

Since the publication in 1990 of the report on the process and responses to *BEM*,[13] work has continued on several fronts to advance the cause of visible unity among the churches based on a common understanding of the faith.

One route has gone through the minefield of ecclesiology, producing a first report entitled *The Nature and Purpose of the Church*[14] and a second report, building on the first, entitled *The Nature and Mission of the Church*.[15] Responses are awaited from churches and their agencies and institutions in order to facilitate the ongoing process in the direction of a convergence text dealing with basic ecclesiological perspectives.

A second route has traversed the zone of a common form for the affirmation of the apostolic faith. It produced the text, *Confessing the One Faith*.[16] A third route has climbed the hills surrounding the area of hermeneutics. It involved a systematic effort to probe how the churches use signs, symbols and texts in the process of articulating the faith. This journey produced *A Treasure in Earthen Vessels*.[17] Yet another route has featured the relation of ecclesiology and the renewal of the human community. This journey has produced *Church and World*,[18] and also *Koinonia and Justice, Peace and Creation: Costly Unity* (1993), *Costly Commitment* (1995), *Costly Obedience* (1996).[19] See also *Ecclesiology and Ethics*.[20] Still another route has meandered through the pathways of the church's corporate worship life and has produced, in its wake, *So We Believe, So We Pray*,[21] as well as *Becoming a Christian*.[22]

It is especially from the last route mentioned above that another study text on baptism will spring. Of course, those who embarked on this particular journey were not unmindful of the other journeys being simultaneously pursued. Indeed, many of them participated in some of those other journeys, though they did not go on every trip.

Several Baptist thinkers have participated in the process leading to the upcoming publication, which attempts to serve the churches' concern for greater convergence around the question of baptism, but grounds the discussion in the context of the church's worship life instead of on systematic theological principles alone. Such Baptists include Paul Fiddes, Timothy George, Christopher Ellis, Paul Sheppy, Burchell Taylor and this author.

Developments on the Way

The conduct of effective multi-lateral dialogue on issues related to the faith, life and witness of the church best happens in a context in which participants are aware of significant developments affecting relations between two or more Christian World Communions. In this regard, the draft study document on baptism points to a number of developments.

It refers to formal agreements that result in mutual recognition of church congregations. One example is the 2003 affirmation, "Baptismal Practice in an Ecumenical Context" by the Commission on Christian Unity in the US state of Massachusetts. [23]

Another example is the formal convergence on baptism reached in 2000 by a Theological Commission of the Roman Catholic in Poland and the Polish Ecumenical Council.[24] In addition, on April 29, 2007, eleven churches in Germany, including Orthodox, Roman Catholic, Anglican and Protestant churches, signed a text reflecting mutual recognition of baptism.[25]

Churches continue to affirm "the ... existence of common baptism [as] a decisive factor of unity beyond [their] divisions."[26] Furthermore, significant multilateral, ecumenical texts at the world level have confirmed and extended these results, urging the churches to put mutual recognition into practice wherever possible.[27]

There is a growing consensus among some Christian traditions concerning the fundamental unity in the so-called "sacraments of Christian initiation" (baptism, chrismation/confirmation, eucharist). In some traditions, these have been separated and performed at different points in the life of the believer, often with each action acquiring a distinct and self-contained meaning. When the unity of these actions is acknowledged, differences in understanding and practice may no longer appear divisive. As a result, some churches have begun to take practical steps to give expression to their mutual recognition of baptism. These include the recovery of a common process of instructing new believers in the faith prior to their baptism. Some are also utilizing a common baptismal certificate recognized by different churches. These are considerably important developments.

The Upcoming Study Document on Baptism

The text in Ephesians, stating that: "There is one body and one Spirit, just as you were called to the one hope of your calling, one Lord, one faith, one baptism, one God and Father of all, who is above all and through all and in all" (Eph. 4:4-6. NRSV) lies at the heart of the baptism text that is being prepared. This text,[28] which should be published in the coming months, has three aims in view, namely: "to clarify the meaning of the mutual recognition of baptism; to call upon the churches to put the consequences of mutual recognition fully into practice; and to clarify issues which may still prevent such mutual recognition." The text is divided into six sections:

Section One deals with the meaning of the notion of recognition, principally, but not only, with respect to baptism. According to the text, mutual recognition of baptism may reflect "a condition of full sharing in faith and life among the churches, marked by eucharistic communion, and including common discernment and decision-making, service and mission." Mutual recognition may exist where there are "significant limitations in sharing, particularly at the eucharistic table – raising questions for some about the meaning of recognition, if not of baptism itself." Mutual recognition may be said to exist "but without further shared life and mission." Where mutual recognition is lacking, "some churches [or congregations within church traditions] require the baptism of all persons seeking membership, even if they have already been baptised in another church."

The text identifies three dimensions of mutual recognition, namely: churches recognizing one another as churches, that is, as authentic expressions of the one Church of Jesus Christ; churches recognizing the baptism of a person from one church who seeks entrance into another church; and persons recognizing one another individually as Christians.

Explaining that mutual recognition indicates that "one party *acknowledges* an already existing quality, identity or status which it has discerned in another," the text grounds the mutual recognition of baptism in "an acknowledgement of apostolicity in the other. Apostolicity indicates coherence and continuity with the faith, life, witness and ministry of the apostolic community, chosen and sent by Christ." This recognition of baptism involves three movements:

- First, "discerning the apostolicity of the rite itself. The elements of the rite – proclamation, profession of faith, thanksgiving, the use of water and the triune name – function as signs of the common faith which Christians through the ages share. In particular, the use of water and the triune name of God as "Father, Son, and Holy Spirit [which is] at the heart of the baptismal rite" is said to initiate the believer "into the wealth of meanings of the biblical teaching on baptism."

- Second, "discerning apostolicity in the larger pattern of Christian initiation [which may include] formation in faith, baptism in water (and in some cases chrismation and/or the laying on of hands), leading to eucharistic communion."

- Third, "discerning apostolicity in the ongoing life and witness of the church which baptises and forms the new Christian."

Section Two discusses "Baptism: Symbol and Pattern of the New Life in Christ." It unfolds the rich tableau of images related to baptism in the Bible and it explores both "the biblical language and the liturgical history of baptism," stressing the common dimensions of most churches' baptismal liturgies and the relation of the event of baptism itself to the continuing, life-long process of growth into Christ.

"The baptismal waters are both death-dealing to sin and life-giving" the text explains, adding that, through baptism, "each Christian is entrusted with the mission of the Church to bring the good news to the world. Christians intercede for the life of the world, exercise ministries of discipleship and mission, and work for justice and peace."

This section should be of great interest to Baptists, especially in the way it posits the relation of baptism as sacrament and ordinance. Pointing to the fact that these terms are often regarded as opposing terms, the text seeks to show, through historical reflection, "that they are not necessarily incompatible."

According to the text:

Most traditions, whether they use the term 'sacrament' or 'ordinance,' affirm that these events are both *instrumental* (in that God uses them to bring about a new reality), and *expressive* (of an already-existing reality). Some traditions emphasize the instrumental dimension, recognizing baptism as an action in which God transforms the life of the candidate as he or she is brought into the Christian community. Others emphasize the expressive dimension. They see in baptism a God-given and eloquent demonstration, within the Christian community, of the gospel and its saving power for the person who, being already a believer through his or her encounter and continuing relationship with Christ, is then baptized.

Section Three explores the relation of baptism and the church. It explains how baptism serves as entry into the church; it explores the relation between baptism and the eucharist and it raises issues about the relation of baptism and church membership.

Section Four, which discusses baptism and faith, deals with "the relationship between God's gracious initiative and the faith, both of the individual being baptised and of the community in which the baptism takes place." This section also addresses aspects of the context and content of Christian formation.

Section Five probes possible further steps for the journey towards mutual recognition. It "suggests steps which may be necessary on the way to fuller mutual recognition of baptism." These include questions that are related to each of the previous sections of the text. Churches are invited to reflect on "the developments in their own traditions and in their relation with other churches, since the publication of *BEM*" and also to determine what steps they can take toward the recognition of other churches' baptism.

In Section Six, the *One Baptism* text reminds the churches of "the wider goal of the ecumenical quest: full visible unity as realised in eucharistic fellowship."

The text states:

> Baptism looks beyond itself. ... As the basis of our common identity in the one body of Christ, it yearns to be completed through the full eucharistic fellowship of all the members of Christ's body. We should be one at the one Table of our one Lord.

The *One Baptism* text invites the churches "to renewed efforts towards full ecclesial communion, in order that the unity which is theirs in Christ through the waters of baptism may find its fulfilment at His one table."

Concluding Word

At the heart of the text on *One Baptism* is the location of the act of baptism within the process of initiation and of lifelong growth into Christ. According to the *One Baptism* study document: "The unique event of baptism reflects and recapitulates the catechumenate, and the processes of nurture and growth guided by the Holy Spirit, that lead to and follow it." Christian history has seen the development of diverse patterns of Christian nurture marked by three discernible elements "which encompass the believer's full incorporation into Christ: (1) formation in faith, (2) baptism and Christian initiation ... and (3) participation in the life of the Christian community, fostering life-long growth into Christ."

If the churches are able to discern this common pattern in each other, is it not possible for them to at least affirm each others baptismal intentions? And if the whole process is taken together, is it not possible for churches to affirm each other's baptism as an authentic expression of the one baptism into Christ?

Various editions of the *One Baptism* text have been produced, but to date, the Faith and Order Commission has not been able agree on the final form of the text to be sent to the churches. One main reason for this may be that the text raises a fundamental question that some churches may not be ready to answer. If a church says that it recognizes the baptism of persons not baptized in that particular church, does it not logically ascribe a measure of authenticity to the ecclesial character of the church in which the baptism takes place? If this is so, cannot progress be made in terms of all baptized persons sharing at the Lord's Table?

Put another way, if the baptism of a person is acknowledged to be truly an authentic expression of the one baptism into Christ, does this not mean that, while the locus of a baptism is a specific believing community, the one baptized enters into one universal ecclesial community? Should not churches claiming to share mutual recognition of baptism make a tacit recognition of the authenticity of the churches in which baptisms take place? It is precisely at this point that there is hesitation. True mutual recognition of baptism has serious ecclesiological implications for the churches and some church leaders are hesitant to call upon the churches to respond to this important question.

No useful purpose is served if churches simply act as if the upcoming publication does not exist. We need to engage in discussion on the issues the *One Baptism* text raises with a fervent desire to discern how, and in what direction, the Holy Spirit is leading God's church to discover its unity. Where the Spirit leads, we ought to follow, humbly and joyfully.

NOTES

[1] *Baptism, Eucharist and Ministry.* Faith and Order Paper No. 111 (Geneva: WCC, 1982).

[2] Baptist responses appear in Volumes I, III and IV of the published reports entitled, *Churches respond to BEM: Official Responses to the "Baptism, Eucharist and Ministry" text,* vols. I – VI. Max Thurian, ed., Faith and Order Paper Nos. 129, 132, 135, 137, 143, 144, (Geneva: WCC, 1986-1988). The published Baptist responses are available as follows: Baptist Union of Great Britain and Ireland (Vol. 1,70-77); All-Union Council of Evangelical Christians-Baptists in the USSR (Volume 3, 227-229); Baptist Union of Scotland (Volume 3, 230-245); Baptist Union of Denmark (Volume 3, 246-253); Covenanted Baptist Churches in Wales (Volume 3, 254-256); American Baptist Churches in the USA (Volume 3, 257-263); Burma Baptist Convention, (Volume 4, 184-190); Union of Evangelical Free Churches in the GDR (Baptists), (Volume 4, 191-199); and the Baptist Union of Sweden, (Volume 4, 200-213).

[3] *Churches respond,* Volume 4, 185.

[4] *Ibid.,* 187.

[5] *Churches respond,* Volume I, 70.

[6] *Churches respond,* Volume IV, 200.

[7] *Churches respond,* Volume III, 231.

[8] *Ibid.,* 247.

[9] *Churches respond,* Volume III, 259.

[10] *Ibid.,* 258.

[11] *Churches respond,* Volume 4, 190.

[12] See, for example, the response of the Baptist Union of Great Britain and Ireland.

[13] *Baptism, Eucharist & Ministry 1982-1990: Report on the Process and Responses.* Faith and Order Paper No. 149 (Geneva: WCC Publications, 1990).

[14] Faith and Order Paper No. 181 (Geneva: WCC Publications, 1998).

[15] *The Nature and Mission of the Church: A Stage on the Way to a Common Statement, Faith and Order* Paper No. 198 (Geneva: WCC, 2005).

[16] *Confessing the One Faith: An Ecumenical Explication of the Apostolic Faith as it is Confessed in the Nicene-Constantinopolitan Creed (381).* Faith and Order Paper No. 153 (Geneva: WCC Publications, 1991). Readers may wish to explore some papers related to the main project that have been published in *One, Holy, Catholic and Apostolic: Ecumenical Reflections on the Church.* Tamara Grdzelidze, ed., Faith and Order Paper No. 197 (Geneva: WCC Publications, 2005).

[17] *A Treasure in Earthen Vessels: An Instrument for an Ecumenical Reflection on Hermeneutics.* Faith and Order Paper No. 182 (Geneva: WCC, 1998).

[18] *Church and World: The Unity of the Church and the Renewal of Human Community*. Faith and Order Paper No. 151 (Geneva: WCC Publications, 1992).

[19] *Costly Unity, Costly Commitment* and *Costly Obedience* have been published together in *Ecclesiology and Ethics: Ecumenical Ethical Engagement, Moral Formation and the Nature of the Church*. Thomas Best and Martin Robra, eds., (Geneva: WCC Publications, 1997).

[20] *Ecclesiology and Ethics: Christian Perspectives on Theological Anthropology*. Faith and Order Paper No. 199 (Geneva: WCC Publications, 2005).

[21] *So We Believe, So We Pray: Towards Koinonia in Worship*. Faith and Order Paper No. 171 (Geneva: WCC Publications, 1995).

[22] Thomas Best and Dagmar Heller, eds., *Becoming a Christian: The Ecumenical Implications of our Common Baptism*. Faith and Order Paper No. 184 (Geneva: WCC Publications, 1999).

[23] Following *BEM*, the statement on baptism describes baptism as "a gift of God, and is administered in the name of the Father, the Son and the Holy Spirit." It urges the liberal use of water explaining that "the significance of water and the symbolism of immersion in baptism is central" to one's understanding of Christian servanthood and discipleship. The Agreement affirms baptism at any age, explaining that baptism "is a corporate event in the life of an individual. Both the church community and the individual's baptismal party commit themselves to support and sustain the newly baptized. It makes no sense to baptize if such conditions are not likely to be honoured" the Statement declares.

[24] See, for example, the address delivered in Warsaw by Pope Benedict during his pastoral visit to the country in 2006. This is available at: https://w2.vatican.va/content/benedict-_xvi/en/speeches/_2006/may/_documents/hf_ben-xvi_spe_20060525_incontro-ecumenico.html.

[25] Readers may also examine the discussion on baptism between the European Baptist Fellowship (EBF) and the Community of Protestant Churches in Europe (CPCE). Discussions on baptism between the partners have produced a deepened communion between them at various levels – though not yet full church fellowship. Their Statement on Baptism, agreed in 2004, asserts that baptism "unites the baptized with the baptizing community and with all Christians, so that they exist as one church of Jesus Christ." The "bond of unity among Christians" which baptism creates, is "stronger and more supportive than all the divisions within the body of Christians. For this reason, the churches recognize every baptism that has been carried out in accordance with the gospel and they rejoice over every person who is baptized." They resolve the question of the relation of faith and baptism by affirming the emergence of faith "from the proclamation of the Gospel ... enabled by the Holy Spirit." Faith is affirmed as "trust in the God who meets persons as godless human beings." There is a clear call for the affirmation of "faith as a gracious gift of God and also an act of the individual

believer." The Statement locates the actual baptism in a process of initiation and describes baptism as "the sign and central event of initiation or the beginning of the Christian life." "Initiation," the text says, "is not complete unless baptism is accompanied by repentance and initial Christian nurture, until the point is reached where a person can make his or her own grateful response of 'yes' to God, is commissioned for service in the world, and shares in the Lord's Supper for the first time." Significantly, the Statement adds: "Through this whole process of initiation, whose focus is baptism, the Christian disciple comes to belong irrevocably to Jesus Christ and to the freedom of the children of God achieved through the death and resurrection of Christ." See "The Beginning of the Christian Life and the Nature of the Church: Results of the Dialogue between the CPCE and the EBF" in *Dialogue between the Community of Protestant Churches in Europe (CPCE) and the European Baptist Federation (EBF) on the Doctrine and Practice of Baptism.* Edited by Wilhelm Hüffmeier and Tony Peck, (Frankfurt am Main: Verlag Otto Lembeck, 2005), 9–29.

[26] Some Baptists insist, however, that the biblical reference to "one baptism" is not identical to the notion of "a common baptism." See, for example, Faith and Unity Executive Committee of the Baptist Union of Great Britain and the Council on Christian Unity of the Church of England, *Pushing at the Boundaries of Unity: Anglicans and Baptists in Conversation* (London: Church House Publishing, 2005), 31-41.

[27] See *The Nature and Mission of the Church*, §§74-77; "*Called to be the One Church*", the Porto Alegre [WCC Assembly] ecclesiology text, World Council of Churches, 2006, §§ 8-9 and § 14(c); and "*Ecclesiological and Ecumenical Implications of a Common Baptism: A JWG Study*", in *Eighth Report: Joint Working Group between the Roman Catholic Church and the World Council of Churches,* (Geneva-Rome: WCC Publications, 2005), 45-72.

[28] This text will be published in the Minutes of the meeting of the Faith & Order Standing Commission, which took place in Crans Montana, Switzerland in June 2007.

Chapter 19

Continuing Conversations Around Baptism and Membership
Curtis Freeman

This past spring I invited Paul Fiddes to come to North Carolina for the purpose of continuing the Anglican-Baptist conversations that he so ably led and more elegantly described in the report *Conversations Around the World*.[1] Our goal was simply to struggle together to discern what it might mean for a denominationally divided Church to understand and display our Lord's prayer "that they may all be one... that the world may believe" (Jn 17:21). We sounded out the document in two sessions: one with church leaders (mostly Episcopal and Baptist) and another among the faculty and students at Duke Divinity School. Participants were provided with copies of the report (which ought to at least temporarily boost sales and hopefully encourage the Anglican Communion Office to keep it in print). Official responses were invited from Samuel Wells, an Anglican priest and dean of the university chapel, Geoffrey Wainwright, a Methodist theologian and ecumenist, as well as from Paul Fiddes, a Baptist theologian and head of the BWA delegation.

The respondents indicated that this report succeeds in some important respects — one of which is in its approach of doing ecumenism from the ground up. Too often church leaders craft carefully worded statements that facilitate ongoing dialogue with their ecumenical conversation partners who are already in the room. *Conversations Around the World* reflects the care that was taken to listen to local practices from Anglican and Baptist communities literally around the world and then to engage practitioners in conversations structured around eight themes: continuity, confessing the faith, mission and ministry, baptism and initiation, membership, Eucharist or Lord's Supper, pastoral oversight, and mutual recognition. Roughly half of the book consists of an exposition of these eight themes, but there are two very helpful chapters that follow: one containing questions and challenges for extending the conversations and another that presents stories from various participants. If our extended conversations are representative (and I believe that they probably are) then perhaps one of the ways we can further these important conversations is to develop a strategy for this book to be read, studied, and discussed among our member churches, unions, and schools. In so doing this report could become a tool for bringing our theological reflection back to local communities that will enrich their faith and practice rather than becoming yet another ecumenical report to be archived in libraries for historical reference.

Among all the comments from the Duke conversations, one in particular stands out. Geoffrey Wainwright began his remarks with this titillating challenge: "I have always respected the emphasis that Baptists place on discipleship and baptism, but I would be even more attracted to the theology of the Baptists if they really practiced what they preached about baptism." Now as anyone here knows, it is a dangerous thing to presume to speak universally about Baptist faith and practice—even (and perhaps especially) baptismal faith and practice. But the more I thought about it, I realized that he had a point. We maintain that believer baptism is not merely the practice most clearly warranted by Scripture or simply a useful means of identifying the visible saints or even the most dramatic enactment of our Lord's burial and resurrection. We preach that when properly practiced the baptism of believers ensures the church will consist of true disciples, but in fact we do not practice what we preach. Our baptismal theology does not hold water.

From the beginnings of the Baptist movement, our forebears rightly protested against an indiscriminant and undisciplined baptismal practice that created a nominal Christianity and identified the established church with the nation state. Edward Barber, who arguably became the first Christian in England to embrace believer baptism by immersion, began his tract, *A Small Treatise of Baptism or Dipping* (1641):

> Thus it is cleare, that the Lord Christ commanded his
> Apostles; and servants of the Gospel, first of all to teach,
> and thereby to gather Disciples: And afterward to dip

those that were taught and instructed in the mysteries of the Gospell, upon the manifestation of their faith: which practice ought to continue to the end of the world, Matth. 28.20. Eph. 4.5. Heb. 13.8.[2]

From this mandate Barber concluded that "they onely are to be dipped that are made Disciples by teaching, Matth. 28.19. Infants cannot be made Disciples by teaching, therefore Infants are not to be dipt."[3] Although there is much more to say about Barber, his small treatise, and its influence on the retrieval of believer baptism by immersion, it is clear that for the early English Baptists, instituting believer baptism as an ecclesial practice was deemed to be a necessary and essential reform which they believed would ensure that the church consisted only of disciples that were committed to following the precepts of the gospel. Something like this is what Wainwright had in mind when he announced that he would be more interested in the theology of the Baptists if we really practiced what we preached about baptism.

Though the years Baptists have followed Barber in contending for credobaptism and against pedobaptism, arguing that the gospel mandates a baptismal practice which results in disciple making. More frequently questions have begun arising from within communions that historically have observed infant baptism. In 1937 the Swiss theologian Emil Brunner warned of a neo-paganism that resulted from a deficient baptismal practice. He asked: "What does the fact of having been baptized mean for a large number of contemporary people who do not know and do not even care to know whether they have been baptized?"[4] Brunner, along with his Swiss colleague Karl Barth, openly wondered whether it was possible to reform a baptismal practice that produced the sort of Christendom which became identified with National Socialism. The church, they argued, could no longer afford to abide baptism as an undisciplined induction into nominal Christianity. Baptism must be a practice that makes Christian disciples who follow Jesus as Lord or it should be suspended.

Wanting to get a little more help from our Free Church heritage, I turned to one of my favorite Baptist theologians, Will B. Dunn. In case you are not familiar with this iconic figure of Baptists in the Southern United States, Dunn is the pastor of Bypass Baptist Church in the comic strip *Kudzu* by Doug Marlette of Hillsborough, North Carolina.

Preacher Will recently received a letter from someone inquiring about his baptismal theology. It read:

> Dear Preacher,
>> Do you worry about scum in the baptismal font?
> Wondering

In the next frame, Preacher Will sits thoughtfully, as he carefully formulates his theological reflection. In the final frame he types out his response which says:

> Dear Wondering,
>> No. I'll baptize anybody.
> Preacher

There is a sense in which it is a good thing to open the doors of the church to all comers, but when openness becomes an indiscriminate and undisciplined initiatory rite we should not be surprised when it affects the spiritual PH in the baptismal pool. Those of us in the believer church tradition may be tempted to write off the problem of defective baptism as a unique trouble for churches that practice infant baptism, but as Wainwright reminded us, *our* churches do not do an effective job of making disciples of those whom we baptize. Unfortunately it is true that we do not often enough practice what we preach.

The story is told about a certain man who would get religion at the annual church revival meeting, and then backslide till the next revival came around. After several trips down to the river for the baptismal service, the preacher put him under the water, raised him up, and said: "Brother, you've been dunked so many times, the fish down here know you by your first name." Bill Leonard likes to say that there are people in Oklahoma who have been rebaptized so many times their skin is permanently wrinkled. Where I come from, repeat believer baptism— sometimes serial believer rebaptism—is more common than we care to admit, straining any attempt to hold (even in our own practice) to the biblical standard of "one Lord, one faith, one baptism" (Eph 4:5). But baptism as rededication is not the only sign that our theology and practice of baptism is in crisis. Consider a few more indicators.

For several decades, immersion of children under the age of eight has accounted for more than 10 percent of the reported baptisms in the largest Baptist denomination in the USA, and the baptism of children even four and five years old (a.k.a. "toddler baptism") is not uncommon.[5] These facts blur the line between believer and infant baptisms and strain the mystical "age of accountability" to the limit. I would further suggest that the current push by this same Baptist body to reverse the five year statistical decline in baptisms with the goal of baptizing a million people in 2006 (a mere increase of 170 percent) may make it easier for people to get into the water (although early reports indicate there will be even fewer baptisms than last year).[6] But such campaigns are not a solution. They are part of the problem. Baptism is about making disciples (Mt 28:19).

Yet another sign that our baptismal theology is in crisis is the disconnect in many churches between admission to the Lord's Table and church membership. In earlier generations of Baptists, the Lord's Supper and baptism were tightly linked. Congregations, associations, conventions, and unions frequently debated the theology of open and close communion. Twenty-five years ago it was unusual for a congregation in the Southern United States to practice open communion, that is, to admit to the Table non-believer baptized Christians and in some cases believer baptized Christians who were not members of the communing congregation. But outside of congregations whose history has been shaped by Landmark theology, today it is extremely rare to find a Baptist church in the Southern United States that still practices close communion. Yet churches that practice open communion and closed membership have rarely given thoughtful reflection to the tension and perhaps incoherence that exists between their baptismal theology and their communion practice.

Our Baptist colleagues in New South Wales report that some of their churches have responded to the need for evangelism and church growth by decoupling baptism from church membership, but here we must ask what we are then to make of such biblical declarations as "we were all baptized by one Spirit into one body" (1 Cor 12:13). Surely the apostle Paul here understands a link between baptism and membership that we dare not put asunder. George Beasley-Murray may have been right when he once said that Baptists have a baptismal theology in search of a practice to sustain it.[7] However, if what I am suggesting is anywhere near correct then Baptists no longer have a coherent theology that could be sustained by any practice. Can we recover a baptismal faith and practice that holds water? There do not seem to be any easy answers, but perhaps part of the solution is to begin talking together about these matters, and our commission's report is a good place to start.

One of the more promising features of *Conversations Around the World* is the suggestion that we understand baptism, not as an episodic event, but as a process or journey. The report states:

> This journey will include, as well as baptism, the working of the grace of God that prepares the human heart, early nurture within the community, the responsible "yes" of faith by the individual, a sharing for the first time with other Christians in the Lord's Supper, and the commissioning of the disciple for service.[8]

If divergent baptismal practices are construed as part of the journey of discipleship could Baptist Christians imagine what it might mean to realize the fulfillment of our Lord's prayer for the unity of all believers? Does an understanding of baptism as a process in discipleship help us to envision how we might bear truthful witness that with differently ordered Christian communions we serve the same Lord, share the one faith, and practice a common baptism? If we can even begin to conceive of how to embody this hope, it is worth the energy to continue these conversations.

Of course, when you look very deeply into the Baptist faith and practice of baptism, you will discover that it is not merely a matter of right faith and orderly practice. It is about the nature of the church. John Smyth, the first Baptist understood that baptism was an ecclesiological claim, and in the preface to his book, *The Character of the Beast*, written in 1609, he declared:

> We profess therefor that al those Churches that baptise infants are of the same false constitution: & al those Chu. that baptize the new creature, those that are made Disciples by teaching, men confessing their faith & their sinnes, are of one true constitution: & therefor the Chu. of the Seperation being of the same constitution with England & Rome, is a most unnatural daughter to her mother England, & her grandmother Rome.[9]

It is probably better that we not begin here in our future conversations with the Catholics and our continuing discussions with the Anglicans. Yet what is important to note is that Smyth understood that without an apostolic baptism the church cannot be the church. Common covenant was not a firm foundation. Only the work of God's own Spirit through the practice of baptism administered upon the confession of faith could establish the church.

For early English Baptists, baptism constituted the *esse*, not merely the *bene esse* of the church. In *A Treatise Concerning the Lawfull Subject of Baptism*, which became one of the classic statements of baptismal faith and practice for early English Baptists, John Spilsbury wrote: "The ordinance of baptism instituted by Christ is so essential to the constitution of the church under the New Testament that none can be true in her constitution without it." Spilsbury put the ecclesiality of baptism succinctly: "So where there is not a true constituted Church, there is no true constituted Church ordinance: and where there is a true Church ordinance in its constitution, there is at least presupposed a true Church also."[10]

The Baptist churches of the Old South in North America had a lovely image for describing entrance into church membership. They would announce that a door of the church was open. Anyone who came forward was asked to give a verbal confession of "their experience of grace." When everyone was satisfied, "the right hand of fellowship" was extended to the new members. In those days the door of church membership was open to those baptized as believers only by immersion only and into churches of like faith and order only. For all others the church door remained closed. Unlike our forebears we accept our fellow Christians as co-laborers in the extension of kingdom work and we recognize the ecclesiality of their churches. Yet as the Pauline formula "one Lord, one faith, one baptism" suggests, the three are linked. To deny that we practice a common baptism with other communions implies that we do not share a common faith or serve the same Lord. We may want to have it both ways, but neither our own theological heritage nor the integrity of our conversation partners will let us off so easily. Can we accept the validity of divergent baptismal practices and open the door to church membership without watering down our theology of baptism? As I have attempted to display, our baptismal theology is already watered down. So how might we go about revisioning our theology and practice of baptism?

The first step is to ensure a strong and intentional connection between faith and baptism. Here the sections of the report on grace and faith in baptism provide helpful treatments that are written to inform and enrich such extended conversations (3.41 and 4.4-5). As George Beasley-Murray succinctly put it in his classic work, *Baptism in the New Testament*, "Baptism is the baptism of faith and grace, so that in it faith receives what grace gives."[11] Our Baptist forebears were rightly concerned that personal faith and baptism be tightly linked. This was their major conviction and the basis of their apprehension about infant baptism. They argued that the proper order, indeed the only order explicitly warranted by Scripture, is profession of faith followed by baptism. What I am contending (and what our report suggests) is that the conviction of regenerate membership can be realized without insisting on that order as long as the link between faith and baptism is strong and intentional. Infant baptism aimed toward conversion of the baptized and believer baptism observing baptism of the converted can both share the common goal of regenerate church membership. Again Beasley-Murray offered some very helpful advice: "If a concordat between Baptists and Churches administering infant baptism with discipline is conceivable, their protest where it is *undisciplined* should be understood and their conviction respected, even if believed to be mistaken." But, he continued, "A more positive step in rehabilitating Biblical baptism would be an increase in the number of baptisms of believers of responsible age in the ordinary services of the Churches."[12] It is then both conceivable and coherent that Baptist churches might only practice believer/disciple baptism but receive non-immersed infant baptized believers/disciples into membership. In such cases infant baptism is a necessary but not a sufficient condition for membership. Baptism in whatever mode must be connected to and accompanied by discipleship.

The second step to recovering a theology of baptism that holds water is to rediscover the connection between Spirit and water baptism (contra John Bunyan and Karl Barth). Our baptismal theology has become watered down in part because we have all but lost a sense that anything might be stirring in the water besides our own feet. Our forebears rightly resisted ascribing any "magical" or "regenerative" power to the water that works *ex opere operato*. Yet in the New Testament, baptism in water and Spirit can hardly be separated. I grew up among Campbellite cousins who endlessly debated the unclear grammar of "unto forgiveness" mentioned in Acts 2:38. I held firm to what I had been taught was "the Baptist view" that the forgiveness of sin was a condition, not a consequence, of baptism. What entirely escaped my notice was that the injunction to "repent and be baptized" was followed by the grammatically clear promise that baptism was followed by "the gift of the Holy Spirit." Reading the Scriptures guided by Beasley-Murray's *Baptism in the New Testament* enabled me to see more clearly this link between baptism of water and Spirit (e.g., Acts 19:6; 1 Cor 12:13; Titus 3:5). The journey to rediscovering the work of the Holy Spirit in baptism may be further strengthened by recovering the forgotten Baptist practice of the laying on of hands at baptism, reclaiming Trinitarian doctrinal theology, and even drawing upon the positive influences of the charismatic renewal. Clearly there are strong pneumatological grounds for revisioning the theology and practice of baptism. Unfortunately this appears to be one lacuna in the baptism section of the report.

If *Conversations Around the World* (particularly sections 4.49-51) were to be more widely studied what might be the outcome for churches reconsidering their membership policy? The first might be the continued insistence on *closed membership* that accepts only those baptized as believers by immersion. The major difficulty with this view is that it denies the working of the Holy Spirit though infant baptism and consequently does not regard communities that observe this practice to be Christian churches. Such an extreme sectarian view is difficult and painful to maintain in light of contemporary ecumenical conversation.

A second possibility might be an attempt to recognize the validity of non-Baptist churches without compromising the theology of believer baptism by moving to a practice of *semi-closed membership* which regards believer baptism as a completion or renewal of infant baptism. This view is more ecumenically sensitive, but it is still received by infant-baptizing communions in the same way as closed membership: Infant baptism is not a churchly act, and their assemblies are not Christian churches.

A third alternative is *associate membership* which accepts infant baptized believers into membership but restricts the offices that they might hold and the matters on which they may vote. Associate membership is a compromise position for churches who think that open membership is too drastic, yet it leaves unresolved the deeper questions of the validity of infant baptism and the ecclesial status of those who perform it.

A fourth possibility is *semi-open membership* which receives those that have been baptized as believers (and by immersion) in churches of different faith and order. This view makes the major step of acknowledging the ecclesial status of non-Baptist congregations, but it hangs up on the question of mode about which the New Testament is all but silent and would have kept from membership John Smyth, the first English Baptist, and Roger Williams, the first American Baptist, both of whom were baptized by effusion (pouring).

A fifth option is *open membership* in which a Baptist congregation practices baptism of believers only by immersion only but allows baptized believers into full membership regardless of the mode or age of their baptism. It is important to note that open membership considers infant baptism to be tacitly incomplete until a candidate gives evidence of a personal confession of faith. Churches may wish to observe a rite of remembrance of baptism during the service for receiving Christians from non-Baptist traditions.

A recent policy statement by the Southern Baptist International Mission Board made the claim that "Baptists have emphatically and categorically denied infant baptism and have insisted on baptizing anyone who truly comes to a saving faith in Christ at some point subsequent to a prior baptism. As a true follower of Christ, one must receive baptism in its proper order—after salvation."[13] While there is strong support for the position of these guidelines as a majority view, it overstates the case by not recognizing other dissident voices within our ecclesial tradition. Among the earliest English Baptists, the Spilsbury-Kiffin churches maintained closed membership while congregations that identified with the Jessey-Bunyan theology held to open membership. Bunyan famously declared against John Kiffin his unwillingness to allow baptism to become a bar to full communion, declaiming that "the Church of Christ hath not warrant to keep out of the communion the Christian that is discovered to be a visible saint of the word, the Christian that walketh according to his own light with God."[14]

In a widely disseminated document on baptism, Reformed theologian and pastor John Piper, with support from the elders of the Bethlehem Baptist Church in Minneapolis, Minnesota (a member congregation in the Baptist General Conference), recommended changing the church constitution to permit open membership.[15] Although the pastor, staff, and elders of the church continue to support open membership, the constitution change was withdrawn. Such a case indicates not only that open membership remains a live option for Baptists in North America but that it does not always follow predictable theological lines. One of the helpful features of *Conversations Around the World* is the inclusion of statistical data (though incomplete) on Baptist church membership policies worldwide. While open membership is rare among Southern Baptists (around 1%) and National Baptists, almost one third of American Baptists (30%) have open membership.[16]

Over the last two years I have consulted with several dozen congregations in North Carolina who are considering opening their church membership policy. One of the ways I have helped them to think through the issues is to examine our local North Carolina history in addition to the broader heritage which parallels much of what I have said above. Here are a few highlights. A query at the 1778 meeting of the Kehukee Association of Regular Baptists by the church in the Isle of Wright wondered about what to "do with a minister who labors to make them believe, that difference in judgment about water baptism, ought to be no bar to communion." The answer: "Such a practice is disorderly, and [the minister] ought to be dealt with as an offender."[17] Clearly the association holds the line on closed membership, but it suggests that some Baptist minister in North Carolina was reading Bunyan. A query at the 1839 Sandy Creek Association asked whether it was "consistent with the spirit of the gospel, and according to the Scriptures, for any regular Baptist church to receive into her fellowship any member or members of another denomination, who have been baptized by immersion without baptizing them again." The answer of "no" was unanimous. The delegates went on to declare: "We cannot admit the validity of their baptisms without admitting that they are true and scriptural gospel churches, if we do this we *unchurch ourselves*."[18]

Whereas the first two centuries of Baptist life in North Carolina nearly unanimously followed a practice of closed membership, things began to change in the 20th century. In 1973 the North Carolina Baptist State Convention appointed a committee to investigate congregations with an open membership policy. The convention charged the committee to "plead with the churches differing . . . and ask that they choose the course and follow the practice followed by the other 99% of North Carolina Baptists in insisting on believer's baptism by immersion in water as a prerequisite to church membership."[19] It was discovered that there were eleven "differing" churches. It has been three decades since eleven "differing" churches in North Carolina reported to the state convention on their policy of open church membership. Since then many more have followed their example. Others are now in the process of discerning how they can open up their membership policy without watering it down. It is a hopeful sign that Baptists are beginning to understand themselves, not as a sect, but as the church united with all Christians by "one Lord, one faith, one baptism" (Eph. 4:5). It isn't a new idea. It's the oldest truth.

NOTES

[1] *Conversations Around the World 2000-2005: The Report of the International Conversations between The Anglican Communion and The Baptist World Alliance*, ed. Paul S. Fiddes and Bruce Matthews (London: The Anglican Communion Office, 2005).

[2] Edward Barber, *A Small Treatise of Baptisme or Dipping Wherein Is Cleerly shewed that the Lord Christ Ordained Dipping for those only that professe Repetance and Faith* (London, 1641), 2; in The Collection of Early English Books, Microfilm. For more about Barber and his role in the recovery of believer baptism by immersion see Stephen Wright, "Edward Barber (c. 1595-1663) and His Friends (Part 1)," *Baptist Quarterly* 41.6 (April 2006): 354-70; and Wright, *The Early English Baptists, 1603-1649* (Woodbridge, Suffolk: Boydell Press, 2006), 95-99.

[3] Barber, *A Small Treatise of Baptisme*, 4.

[4] Emil Brunner, *The Divine Human Encounter* (Philadelphia: Westminster Press, 1943), 181.

[5] Thorwald Lorenzen observed that in 1976 Baptist congregations connected with the Southern Baptist Convention baptized 35,562 children under eight years of age, in "Baptists and Ecumenicity with Special Reference to Baptism," *Review and Expositor* 72 (Winter 1980): 42, note 2. In 1989 out of a total of 351,107 recorded baptisms, SBC congregations baptized 45,224 children eight years of age or younger, *Quarterly Review* 50 (July-September 1990): 21.

[6] Trennis Henderson, "2005 Southern Baptist Statistics: Baptisms Down, Membership Up," *Associated Baptist Press* (25 April 2006).

[7] George Beasley-Murray, article on baptism in *Foundations*.

[8] *Conversations Around the World*, 3.42, 45.

[9] John Smyth, *The Character of the Beast or The False Constitution of the Church*, The epistle to the reader, in *The Works of John Smyth*, ed. W. T. Whitley (Cambridge: The University Press, 1915), 2:565.

[10] John Spilsbury, *A Treatise Concerning The Lawfull Subject of Baptism* (London: Henry Hills, 1652), 52.

[11] George Beasley-Murray, *Baptism in the New Testament* (Grand Rapids: William B. Eerdmans, 1973), 151.

[12] Ibid. 389.

[13] International Mission Board of the Southern Baptist Convention, "Guideline on Baptism," 6 March 2006.

[14] John Bunyan, *Differences in Judgement about Water-Baptism no Bar to Communion*, in *The Works of John Bunyan*, 3 vols., ed. George Offor (London: Blackie and Son, 1862), 2:616-47.

[15] John Piper, "Should We Require Agreement of All Members On the Doctrine and Practice of Baptism?" (29 March 2002).

[16] *Conversations Around the World 2000-2005*, 4.49-50.

[17] Joseph Biggs, *A Concise History of the Kehukee Baptist Association* (Tarborough, North Carolina: George Howard, 1834), 46.

[18] George W. Purefoy, *A History of the Sandy Creek Baptist Association* (New York: Sheldon & Co. Publishers, 1859, 179. Italics in original.

[19] G. McLeod Bryan, cited in the foreward of *Documents Concerning Baptism and Church Membership: A Controversy Among North Carolina Baptists, Perspectives in Religious Studies*, Special Studies Series No. 1 (Macon: Association of Baptist Professors of Religion, 1977), v.

Chapter 20

Baptism, Membership and Communion: Scotland and Alabama

Kenneth B. E. Roxburgh[1]

In this paper, I intend to contrast and compare Baptist identity in Scotland and Alabama to demonstrate the way in which the religious history and cultural setting of two different contexts have shaped the expression of what it means to be a Baptist. In particular, I will examine the way in which Baptists in Scotland and Alabama have understood the relationship between baptism and church membership, as well as their understanding of communion.

Scotland[2]

There has been a Baptist presence in Scotland since the 1650s during the Cromwellian era. This presence had disappeared by the end of the 17th century and re-emerged in Keiss in Caithness when Sir William Sinclair, influenced by Baptists in England, established a congregation in the area.

In the 18th century, Baptists made up a very small number of the church-going population of Scotland. It is unlikely that around 1766 there were more than 100 Baptists in Keiss and Edinburgh. By 1800, there were two Baptists groups operating in Scotland: the "English" Baptists with 42 members and up to 100 hearers and the Scotch Baptists with around 400 members and approximately 1,000[3] hearers. Scotch Baptists affirmed the plurality of elders and deacons in contrast to the sole pastor and diaconal model of the "English" Baptists. They also believed that pastors/elders should be present when the Lord's Supper was celebrated.

Scotch Baptists started in Edinburgh in 1765, and were influenced by John Glas[4] and the Old Scotch Independents. The earliest leaders, Robert Carmichael and Archibald McLean, were former Presbyterians and, after reading John Glas on the connection between church and state, they became Glasites. McLean becoming a member of the Glasite congregation in Glasgow in 1761. By 1764, he had adopted baptistic convictions and, in 1768, became an elder of a Baptist congregation in Edinburgh. The Glasites believed that there was a clear blueprint for church life in the New Testament. Weekly communion, unanimity of decision-making, and plurality of lay eldership were major features of their congregations. They held to a definition of faith as a bare belief in, or assent to, the facts of the gospel without including the element of trust (Sandemanianism).[5] Although never stronger than a thousand in numbers, the Glasites influenced many early Scotch Baptist leaders. Alexander McLean and his followers formed churches in various parts of Scotland and in almost every area where there was a Glasite church, a Scotch Baptist congregation also developed. McLean held that baptism was an indispensable prerequisite to church fellowship because "Christ had commanded it, because the apostles ... did not admit any to church fellowship until they had been baptized ... and by disregarding the authority of Christ in one ordinance, he thought he would be showing his disregard to it in all."[6] Carmichael and McLean left the Glasites in 1763 and were baptized along with five others to form the first congregation in Edinburgh. Under the leadership of McLean this became the first of ten societies set up during the 18th century in Scotland and England.[7] Independent in theory, the churches were, in practice, closely dependent on each other. Their early insistence on an elder being present to celebrate the Lord's Supper led to two major divisions within the movement in 1810 and 1834.

The wider context from which Baptists emerged in Scotland was that of Presbyterianism which, during the 18th century, had experienced several schisms over the issue of patronage.[8] When the Scotch Baptists first emerged in Edinburgh in the 1760s, the only church which encouraged the practice of allowing non-members to partake in communion was the Presbytery of Relief.[9] Within the structure of Scottish piety, the communion season was a highlight, not only for those who took the elements, but also for the hundreds, and sometimes thousands, of hearers who often attended several sacramental festivals during the summer months.[10] Thomas Gillespie, founder of the Relief

Church in 1761, remained convinced throughout his ministry that the Lord's Supper was open to "all His disciples, whether they apprehend themselves prepared or not ... all for whom the Body was broken and Blood was shed are bound to come."[11] Gillespie believed that all who were part of the "Universal Visible Church, who make credible profession of Faith and Obedience in him and to him ... may be admitted to partake of the seals of the covenant."[12] To those who professed faith and manifested a life of integrity, an invitation was offered to partake of the elements whether or not they were Presbyterian. This attitude was unique within the Scottish context.

The Haldanes

James Haldane and his older brother, Robert, members of the Established Church of Scotland, became itinerant evangelists in 1797, having an interest and involvement in evangelism in Britain and overseas. In 1798, Robert Haldane sold a large part of his Airthrey estate near Stirling to finance the work of home evangelism and began to open preaching centers where evangelicals of different denominations preached to the poor. By 1798, both brothers had become Congregationalist Independents and James was ordained pastor of the Edinburgh church in February 1799. In 1803, they adopted some Glasite views. The church began to "break bread every Lord's Day" and to practice mutual exhortation, church discipline and to have a plurality of elders.[13] The Haldane connection grew rapidly. By 1805 there were 25 congregations in existence and, by 1808, the number had grown to 85.[14] Those who attended the services were encouraged to return to the Established Church to receive the Lord's Supper. Their Edinburgh building was eventually located in 1801 to the head of Leith Walk, with seating for over 3,000 people.[15]

Both brothers became Baptists in 1808. Although "a considerable number" left the church at this time and formed an "Independent church," James and Robert never made baptism an issue which barred people from communion or membership.[16] They spoke of it as a matter of Christian forbearance and believed "it highly important to be understood by all the disciples of Christ."[17] Writing in 1811, James Haldane said that:

> the moment anything but the knowledge of Christ is
> made a term of communion, or that any acknowledged

disciple of Jesus is refused access to a church, that church is Anti-Christian ... Though all the members of the first churches were baptized, there is no example of baptism being made a term of communion; it had no connection with entering a church.[18]

In 1818, Haldane admitted that only on one occasion had the church "been put to the test by such an application being made, and we saw it our duty to receive the person, although unbaptized."[19] He argued that the person was not baptized because of "being ashamed to confess Christ, but from not understanding his will on the subject." And, on the basis that the "church of Christ is a school for training up disciples," they had been more than willing to "receive" one who was "weak in the faith."[20] It seems that Haldane, like Robert Hall in England, had become involved with Christians from various denominations working alongside them in the furtherance of the kingdom of God, and he could "acknowledge" such people "as disciples of Christ" when meeting them in these circumstances and not "in the church."[21] This did not mean that he would not try to help him understand the meaning and purpose of baptism, but it did mean that he would never coerce anyone into being baptized because "no ordinance can profit them, unless they observe it from conviction."[22]

Samuel Jones

Haldane's view did not go unchallenged. Samuel Jones, an elder of a Scotch Baptist congregation in London, wrote to oppose his views on forbearance.[23] Jones refers back to the disputes surrounding John Bunyan, who had argued "on the ground" of "the non-importance of baptism as to the evidence of a person's Christianity."[24] Yet to Jones, proper church order, which included believer's baptism, was as important as "the publication of the gospel."[25] He believed that the rule of forbearance which is found in Romans 14 "is not applicable to all believers" because the circumstances in Rome, which dealt with the dispute of Jews and Gentiles over food regulations related to a very specific circumstance which could not be applied to the issue of believer's baptism.[26] Haldane responded to Jones' attack in *Remarks on Mr. Jones' Review of Observances on Forbearance* in 1812 which he began by admitting that his views were very "different from the practice of most of the churches in this country" and that he had expected them to be "warmly opposed."[27] Haldane showed that complete obedience to all of Christ's commands is impossible and thus cannot be the "essential character of a disciple"[28] and thus baptism should not become such a test of spirituality.

Later Developments

When in 1869, Jonathan Watson, a minister in Edinburgh, became the first president of the Baptist Union of Scotland, his address was entitled, "Ecclesiastical Liberty, Equality and Fraternity." Watson also wrote on "Christian Communion versus Sectarian Communion"[29] in 1875. He confessed that all Christians are "fallible expounders of the Word of God" and both Baptist and Paedo-Baptists have been "honestly led to a different....scriptural view of the matter [of baptism]."[30] Because "both are equally the disciples of Christ," it would be wrong to "exclude or to keep back any whom he has received" into the fellowship of the local church.[31]

The English Baptists 1796-1852

The English Baptists, at the beginning of the 19th century, were a small and weak minority within the ranks of Scottish Baptists. Yet within three decades, it was the "English"-style churches that had grown and become more numerous. Two of their most influential pastors were George Barclay of Kilwinning and Christopher Anderson of Edinburgh. The differences between the English and Scotch model were with regard to the manner of observing the Lord's Supper, the status of the ministry, style of preaching, nature of faith, and the autonomy of the local church.

One of the major controversies in England, in which John Bunyan was involved, was that of the relationship between baptism and communion. John Bunyan's *Differences in Judgement about Water Baptism, no Bar to Communion*, published in 1673, contended that "Christ, not Baptism, is the way into the Sheep-fold"[32] because entry into the life of the church came on the basis of faith and the demonstration of holiness, rather than acceptance of any particular ordinance. Bunyan believed in the New Testament model of believer's baptism by immersion, but he disagreed with many contemporaries such as Thomas Paul,[33] William

Kiffin[34] and John Denne[35] who all asserted the necessity of believer's baptism for church membership and communion.[36] Bunyan felt that his opponents overvalued the ordinance and denied "that baptism was ever ordained of God to be a wall of division between the holy and the holy."[37] He was convinced that debates over such secondary issues "tended to divide the church and divert it from the work of evangelism."[38]

Controversy broke out afresh among English Baptists in the early part of the 19th century. Although "the majority of Baptist churches practiced closed communion"[39] in 1815, Robert Hall, minister of Harvey Lane, Leicester, published a work, *On Terms of Communion,* in which he advocated an open table. Hall had associated with Christians of other denominations in the work of the Bible Society, the London Missionary Society, and the British and Foreign School Society and could not justify any attitude which closed the communion table to those who were obviously Christians. Joseph Kinghorn, minister of St. Mary's Baptist Church in Norwich, responded to Hall in 1816 by writing, *Baptism, a Term of Communion at the Lord's Supper.* Kinghorn argued that correctness of church order was of vital importance, otherwise the existence of Baptist churches as a separate identity was unjustified. The controversy generated inevitable divisions and hostilities. However, by the end of the century, open communion churches outnumbered the closed, and two out of every three of the leading Particular Baptist churches were open membership.[40] The impact of such "English Baptist" thinking on Scottish Baptists, however, was small.

Baptist churches in Scotland which have adopted an "open membership" policy are in a minority. They include some of the historically significant congregations such as Hillhead and Adelaide Place in Glasgow, Crown Terrace in Aberdeen, Coats Memorial in Paisley and Morningside Baptist Church in Edinburgh.

20th Century Developments

The Inter-Church Relations Committee of the Baptist Union of Scotland debated the issue of open and closed membership in October 1965 when "opinion on closed membership was seriously divided."[41] In November 1966, the subject was "vigorously discussed" within the Church Extension Committee of the Baptist Union of Scotland, and "overwhelming support was reiterated for a policy of closed membership."[42] An amendment "that we recommend that open membership be considered by new churches" was carried by an overwhelming majority.[43] The decision was strongly defended by Andrew MacRae, the newly appointed secretary of the union.[44] Indeed the evidence suggests that down through the years, although several churches have moved from a closed to an open position,[45] several others have changed in the opposite direction.[46]

In 1967, Andrew MacRae presented a document on *Christian Baptism* which was adopted as the policy of the union. MacRae addressed the issue of "Baptism and Church Membership" and argued for a policy of "closed membership" for five reasons:

- No church admits to membership without some form of baptism, except the Quakers and the Salvation Army; if we admit to membership without baptism, we deny its necessity as an act of obedience to Christ.
- If baptism is rightly demanded for church membership, and we reject the validity of infant baptism, we have no option but to maintain "closed" membership.
- If we do not recognize infant baptism, we MUST enquire as to the baptismal status of every candidate, and refuse to baptize any who were baptized as children.
- The Biblical practice - and this rather than the preceding factors must govern our conduct - was for all believers to be baptized following their profession of faith, and received into fellowship in the church. To observe open membership is to depart from that practice, which we declare to be our ultimate authority.
- If we are to maintain our Baptist witness, with its stress on personal commitment to Christ, and obedience to His will in baptism, we must restrict the control of church life to those who have themselves been obedient to the call of Christ to baptism. It should be remembered that the call to baptism was part of the apostolic message. Men were called to repent, believe, be baptized and they would receive the Holy Spirit. Anything which plays down these elements is to be avoided, and open membership carries such dangers.[47]

More recently, churches which have moved from a closed to an open position have done so on pragmatic grounds. In an increasingly mobile society, churches find that members of other denominations become active adherents but are denied admission to membership unless they are baptized as believers by immersion. In March 1987, St. Andrews Baptist Church, which had been a "closed membership" church since its foundation, made the basis of its membership "profession of faith in Jesus Christ as Saviour and Lord."[48] The initial consequence of this decision was a growth in membership from 108 in 1987 to 131 in 1989. In Cupar, a church which had moved from an open to a closed membership position, took over a Church of Scotland building in 1973. They once again changed their basis of membership to an "open" position and received new members from the Church of Scotland congregation, and grew from 61 members to 104 and a year later to 128.[49]

Coats Memorial Baptist Church in Paisley, founded in 1785, was originally a Scotch Baptist congregation. During the ministry of Robert M. Armstrong (1965-1978), the congregation adopted the policy of admitting to membership all who were already baptized members of other Christian denominations, whether they had been baptized as infants or believers. During the ministry of Kerr Spiers (1986-1991) the church decided to admit members on the basis of profession of faith.[50]

The Theology of Baptism

Scottish Baptists have always defined themselves over against the theology of baptism as espoused by Presbyterianism, especially that of the national church, the Church of Scotland.[51] The 1950s and 1960s witnessed an extensive investigation by the Church of Scotland into the subject of baptism and in 1953, a commission was set up under the convenorship of T. F. Torrance.[52] The commission published a series of reports in the Church of Scotland General Assembly papers from 1956 to 1963, including an assessment of Baptist teaching in 1959.[53] An overture, which was sent down to the Presbyteries that the report become "an authoritative interpretation of the Biblical and Reformed doctrine of baptism" was frustrated.[54] The majority of Presbyteries accepted it as a valid statement of biblical and reformed doctrine and commended it for consideration, and the assembly published a brief *Doctrine of Baptism* in 1964. The assembly required that, for the baptism of a child to take place, one parent should be a member of the church or a permanent adherent. The rather diffident response to the report within the church was considered by many to be due to "the theologically questionable notion that baptism refers primarily to 'the one, all inclusive, vicarious baptism of Christ for all men.'"[55] For Torrance, "Baptism is grounded objectively in the saving work of Christ, which is also the work of the divine Trinity. Baptism is an act of God in his Church, and the faith confessed is Christ's obedient faithfulness in his saving ministry and mission."[56]

Baptist ministers within the Edinburgh and Lothian Baptist Fraternal (ELBA) entered into an extended discussion on the subject which began in April 1956 and continued for ten consecutive meetings of the fraternal, coming to a conclusion in September 1957. The fraternal obviously felt that their position as Baptists was coming under threat in the context of Presbyterian Scotland. The initial discussion centered on the report on New Testament doctrine which appeared in the General Assembly of 1955.[57] The fraternal took the opportunity of meeting with Professor Torrance and felt that the main issue which divided Baptists from the Church of Scotland was "the definition and description of the nature of the Church" and that the "idea of the 'gathered church' was the solution."[58] The fraternal remained convinced throughout their discussions that "the Report had not challenged our position seriously, and could be countered very effectively, by sound Biblical exegesis."[59] William Whyte, Minister of Portobello, led the discussion on seven occasions, engaging in a detailed analysis of the report, which he referred to in his presidential address in October 1960, concluding that "infant baptism is a gross denial of all evangelistic activity ... it is a denial of the Gospel of the Grace of God. We believe that infant baptism has no place whatsoever in the New Testament."[60] This debate was widespread within the denomination and, between May 1960 and January 1961, seven articles on the subject of baptism appeared in the Scottish Baptist magazine.[61]

One of the most significant contributions to this discussion was that of R. E. O. White. White was minister of Rutherglen Baptist Church in Glasgow from 1950 to 1954. From 1951, he also acted as New Testament tutor in the Baptist Theological College of Scotland.[62] White contributed a brief response to the Church of Scotland Report in 1956.[63] In 1960 White published *A Biblical Doctrine of Initiation*, which was a detailed biblical and theological investigation of the subject of baptism, one which saw baptism as a sacrament, closely related to membership of the Christian church. White argued that "baptism was a rite of spiritual enduement, eschatologically effective, conferring remission ... in the assurance that God as well as man was at work in each administration."[64] He contended that while this sacramental understanding should not be confused with "magico-ritualist notions of infused grace," Baptists needed to reject the view that baptism was "an idle form or traditional symbol performed without spiritual profit."[65] White maintained that "believer's baptism loses much of its scriptural significance ... when baptism and church membership are treated as two questions, and baptism into the church, into the body of Christ, is allowed to disappear from baptismal theology and practice."[66] White argued that Baptist churches ought to welcome the newly baptized person immediately into the membership of the local congregation, rather than waiting until the next celebration of the Lord's Supper, even though, within the Scottish Baptist setting, this regularly took place each Sunday. When the ELBA fraternal met in October 1960, a debate took place on White's book which led to a "vigorous discussion which made it clear that to some, a simpler and less elaborate view of baptism was more congenial,"[67] an indication that within the fraternal there were signs of contrasting churchmanship, both high and low.

When the Council of the Baptist Union of Scotland published a "brief statement" on the Baptist position on baptism in 1967, it argued for Baptism being recognized as a sacrament.[68] The booklet defined baptism as a

> Biblical sacrament ... of Divine grace, a sign of the death and resurrection of Christ, with which the believer is consciously identified. It is the recognition and seal of the work of the Holy Spirit and the incorporation of the baptized into the fellowship and witness of the Church.[69]

This language was modified somewhat in 1987 when the Doctrine and Inter-Church Relations Committee responded to the WCC *Baptism, Eucharist and Ministry* document. While they affirmed the "rich theology of baptism expounded in the report," they felt that it contained "too sacramentarian an understanding of baptism" which was too "institutional, impersonal, magical and lacking in evangelical thrust." They did however welcome the link between baptism and church membership and confessed that there had been a "tendency for many Baptists to divorce these and thus to rob baptism of part of its corporate significance."[70]

Scottish Baptists have generally held that the mode by which baptism is administered must be by total immersion in water, and many churches do not allow believers who have been baptized by the mode of effusion or sprinkling to become full members. It seems clear, however, that the recognition of believer's baptism by another mode than that of immersion will become increasingly important as society becomes more secular and many who enter into the life of the wider church will do so by believer's baptism within the Church of Scotland. Indeed, the Church of Scotland now administers more believers' baptisms than Scottish Baptists.[71] As believer's baptism becomes more and more the norm in the wider church, Scottish Baptists must address the question of whether they will insist on a re-baptism of believers by immersion. Scottish Baptists who continue to insist that the mode of baptism must be by immersion are implying that the quantity of water is the decisive factor rather than the experience of faith and spirituality.

Even within those Scottish Baptist churches which have adopted an open membership policy, there are variations of practice. For some churches it means the acceptance of members on the basis of personal faith and experience without the requirement of any form of baptism. This raises the question of whether we are devaluing, as well as de-emphasizing, the place of baptism and following the tradition of Quakers and the Salvation Army rather than other historic churches. This policy would appear to be a radical departure from the New Testament and later church tradition by eliminating any form of water baptism as required for membership in a Christian church.

For others, open membership means permitting the transfer of baptized and confirmed members of other Christian denominations of the Reformed faith without the requirement of baptism by immersion. This addresses the question of whether Baptists can accept forms of baptism other than by immersion, and thereby affirm that person's previous Christian faith and experience. Some congregations would also insist that no one who has been raised within the life of the congregation will be able to join the church without being baptized as a believer. The issue of open membership challenges Scottish Baptists to adopt a greater flexibility in their traditional views on the relationship of believer's baptism by immersion to church membership. Open membership is not a betrayal of the heritage. There has been a diversity of belief and practice in Baptist churches in Scotland, at different times and places, since the 19th century.

Influence of Christian Brethren on Scottish Baptists[72]

The Christian Brethren movement in Scotland grew out of Protestant Evangelicalism in the 19th century. It emerged initially in Dublin in the 1820s, and by 1848 had divided into two groups: those known as the "Exclusive Brethren" who followed John Nelson Darby and the "Open Brethren." Both groups grew in Scotland and were particularly strong in areas where Baptists developed in the 19th and 20th centuries, in Glasgow, Ayrshire, Lanarkshire and Fife. Movement of membership between the Baptists and Brethren occurred in both directions, although, in the latter part of 20th century, the transfer of members has largely been from Brethren Assemblies to Baptist congregations.[73] Both groups share a common commitment to baptism by immersion and frequent communion. Indeed, one of the chief characteristics of Brethren Assemblies is the centrality of the "Breaking of Bread" within the main "morning meeting," which Dickson describes as its "most distinctive service."[74] The presence of former "Brethren" members within Baptist churches will continue to ensure the importance of a weekly celebration of the Lord's Supper.

This emphasis on a frequent celebration of communion was reaffirmed in 1987, when the Doctrine and Inter-Church Relations Committee spoke of its "central position in worship" among Scottish Baptists and noted that in many churches it is "held weekly, on a Sunday morning and in others fortnightly or monthly .... In several churches the Eucharist has been taken into the whole service, and in others a quarterly or monthly celebration is 'integrated.'" This would seem, they suggested, "to be a move back to an authentic Baptist tradition." [75]

Scottish Baptists in the 21st Century

The population of Scotland is currently just over five million. Since the 1960s, the membership of all denominations in Scotland has fallen. The membership of Baptist churches has fallen from 20,139 in 1959 to 13,417 in 2007. One feature of Scottish Baptist churches, however, is that they have always had more people attending worship than their membership (normally referred to as adherents), although the number of those attending churches is declining. Baptist churches were the only denomination in Scotland to show a slight growth of attendance in 2002.

Churchgoers in Baptist Churches 1984-2002[76]

1984	*% change*	1994	*% change*	2002
29,240	-16	24,530	+1	24,830

Overall, however, the picture of church attendance in Scotland indicates continuing decline. This is especially true among children. Of the 142,000 children aged 0-9 who attended church in 1984, only 76,000 (now aged 10-19) were attending in 1994, and by 2002 (aged 20-29), only 37,000 were attending church.[77] Baptists, along with all other churches in Scotland, face the challenge of living in a society which is becoming increasingly secular, where less children are being baptized in the Church of Scotland, and yet a country where about 11 percent of the population still attends church, a figure that is still higher than in many other European countries.

Baptism and Membership

The number of baptisms has fluctuated during this same period, averaging 444 per year during the 1960s; 557 per year during the 1970s; 607 per year during the 1980s; 413 per year during the 1990s and 397 between 2000 and 2007. One unusual feature, in recent years, has been the number of people who are baptized in Scottish Baptist churches who do not become members. In 2000, only 68 percent of believers who were baptized became members and this dropped to 61 percent in 2007.[78] This may be due to some young teenagers delaying membership until they are older or some people who are already members of other churches being baptized by immersion but keeping their membership in Paedobaptist congregations. It probably also reflects a lack of theological understanding of baptism as an initiation into the church.

Alabama Baptists [79]

Although there is a significant difference between Scotland and Alabama, both in terms of geography, religious heritage and culture, the population of Scotland and Alabama are similar in size and both contexts experienced the presence of the Baptist "witness" within the early 19th century. By the middle of the 19th century Marion, Alabama, was the center of Southern Baptist Home Mission, along with Howard College and Judson College.

The first Baptist congregation in Alabama was constituted in October 1808, the first of many small congregations which emerged in the frontier.[80] These congregations defined themselves, both individually and also within Baptist associations, [81] in various statements of principles or abstracts of faith, to clarify their understanding of their faith. The majority of these congregations were Calvinistic in their theology. The Flint River Association, formed in 1814, declared their faith in "the doctrine of election; and that God chose his people in Christ before the foundation of the world."[82] In 1818, the Salem-Troy association amplified its statement on election to include "detrimental and particular election."[83] A minority view was expressed by the United Baptist Churches of Jesus Christ in 1843, when they stated their belief in "the doctrine of free salvation and a general atonement."[84]

Ecclesiologically, these Baptists were united in their adherence to viewing baptism and the Lord's Supper as ordinances, only to be administered by ordained ministers, and that only baptized believers should be admitted to communion. When First Baptist Huntsville was constituted in 1809,[85] it spoke of "water baptism by immersion and the Lord's Supper" as being "ordinances of the gospel" and that "none but regularly baptized members have a right to commune at the Lord's Table."[86] The Flint River Association, of which Huntsville became a member, maintained that "no ministers have a right to the administration of the ordinances, only such as are regularly baptized, called and come under the imposition of hands by the presbytery."[87] The Baptists of Cullman Country developed this language to speak of baptism as "the immersion of the believers, in water ... to show forth in a solemn and beautiful emblem our faith in a crucified and risen Saviour, with its purifying power; and that it is a prerequisite to the relatives of a church relation and to the Lord's Supper, in which the members of the church, by the use of bread and wine, are to commemorate together the dying love of Christ."[88]

The most consistent aspect of their polity was their commitment to baptism, which should be by complete immersion, and the Lord's Supper as ordinances, which could only be administered by properly ordained ministers. Ordination was "by the imposition of hands by a presbytery of ministers gathered to evaluate the applicant's character, mental qualifications, and doctrinal soundness."[89] So, in 1849, *Alabama Baptist*, the state Baptist newspaper, asked "whether in our whole connection, a church can be named, in which a member would not be promptly excluded, who would venture to administer baptism or the Lord's Supper, in the absence of regularly ordination as a Minister."[90] Communion services were normally celebrated on a quarterly or semiannual basis, in part due to the bi-vocational nature of ministry and the fact that many congregations met on a monthly basis for public worship.

Influences on Baptist Development in the South

Alexander Campbell and the Church of Christ

Alexander Campbell (1788-1866) was one of the founders of the Disciples of Christ or Churches of Christ. Campbell was raised within the Scottish secession movement in Ireland and immigrated to America in 1808. The journey was interrupted by a shipwreck off the coast of Scotland and Campbell spent a year in Glasgow studying at the University of Glasgow. During this year in Glasgow he met Greville Ewing, a Scottish Congregational minister, who persuaded him of the merits of Independent church order and the weekly celebration of the Lord's Supper, and came into contact with Robert and James Haldane.[91] His father had been disciplined by the Secession Church in Pennsylvania for admitting non-members to the celebration of the Lord's Supper, and in August 1809, 21 people formed the Christian Association of Washington as an agency for the restoration of the unity of the church on the basis of the New Testament. On May 4, 1811, the association constituted itself a church, which practiced Congregational church government along with the weekly celebration of the Lord's Supper. Alexander Campbell was ordained to the ministry in 1812 at Brush Run. During that year, Campbell became convinced of the biblical basis of believer's baptism and he, his wife, father and mother were all baptized by a Baptist minister, with the majority of the congregation joining them. Three years later, the congregation joined the Redstone Baptist Association. This connection with Baptists lasted until 1830,[92] when his theological position on "baptismal regeneration" and other theological issues[93] led to a separation from Baptist connections. His association with Barton Stone led them both to be convinced that a "restoration of the ancient order of things" was possible, which would unite all Christians on the basis of the New Testament. Campbell was influenced by the writings of William Jones, a Scotch Baptist from England. Jones published, *History of the Christian Church*, which argued that the history and presence of "Baptist" churches could be traced back to the time of Christ. His book went through several American editions by the middle of the 19th century.[94] Campbell's continued impact on Baptist churches led many congregations to join his connection.[95]

Landmark Baptists

One of the most significant debates among Baptists in the south during the 19th century was Landmarkism, which began in Tennessee and Kentucky when J. R. Graves repudiated the authenticity of non-Baptist churches, ministers and ordinances. Graves joined the congregation of First Baptist, Nashville, in 1845, whose minister R. B. C. Howell was a prominent member of the emerging Southern Baptist Convention and an ardent opponent of Alexander Campbell and Paedo-Baptism. Graves argued that there was no need to seek to "restore" churches to their primitive state, because authentic Baptist churches had always existed from the time of Christ.

Graves became minister of Second Baptist Church in Nashville, which had become depleted in numbers due to a split over Alexander Campbell's views. In 1846, Howell appointed Graves as associate editor of the *Tennessee Baptist*, a newspaper which Howell had started in 1835. Graves embarked on a campaign to attack alien immersion, any form of believer's baptism which was not by immersion or administered by a properly ordained "Baptist" minister. Hall maintains that his message was "heard by all Baptists, accepted by many, rejected by few."[96] Landmarkism is a Baptist "high-church" position with regard to ecclesiology, ordination and ordinances. It claims that only Baptist churches are true churches and all others are merely "religious societies." It argues that baptism by immersion is not adequate - it must be performed by a recognized Baptist minister - and that taking the Lord's Supper is contingent on being properly baptized. It can only be celebrated in a Baptist church. Consequently, co-operation with other "societies" or their "ministers," must not take place. Graves' views were adopted by many Baptists in the south. The circulation of the *Tennessee Baptist* grew from about 1,000 readers in 1846 to over 13,000 readers in 1859. K. B. C. Howell noted some years later that the Baptist state papers of Arkansas, Mississippi, Texas, North Carolina, Alabama and "some other papers [were] mere echoes of *The Tennessee Baptist*."[97]

Not all Baptists in the South, however, fully adopted Graves' interpretation of Baptist identity. J. L. Dagg, professor of theology and president of Mercer University, published, *A Manual of Church Order*, in which he argued against the exclusive view of the local church. Dagg was one of the leading theological thinkers of his time and he maintained that "the church universal includes all the local churches ... the members of the universal church as individual Christians ... [furthermore] there may be many saints on earth, as the Ethiopian Eunuch, who belong to the family of the saints, and have not been received into any local church."[98] Prior to the Landmark controversy, W. B. Johnson, elected first president of the SBC, said,

> whoever is authorized to preach is authorized to baptize - the latter being a minor work. I therefore receive those who are recognized as preachers by Episcopalians, Presbyterians, Methodists and all orthodox bodies of believers, as preachers of the gospel and I receive them as baptizers, and when the ordinance is administered by any of them, to one who professed faith in the Lord Jesus, I accept it as valid.[99]

In Alabama, it appears that the majority of Baptists accepted the argument on "alien baptism," which they had adopted prior to Graves' views being made known in 1846. As early as 1820, the Cahawba Association issued a "circular letter" in which it argued against an open communion policy of eating at the Lord's Table "with our brethren of other denominations."[100] They maintained that "baptism is (in order) the first Gospel ordinance, and that no person ought to be admitted to the Lord's Supper without first submitting to that ordinance."[101] The reason why they rejected any invitation to sit at the Lord's Table with Paedo-Baptists was the fact that they rejected their form of baptism "as being no part of gospel baptism."[102] Twelve years later, the association's circular letter returned to the theme of "Terms of Communion" and stated that "regeneration, baptism and a conversation such as becometh the Gospel of Christ" were "indispensible terms of communion."[103] In 1843, the association once again stressed their adherence to "close or restricted communion" and that "immersion, only, is baptism, and that believers are its proper subjects."[104] Yet, it was not only the mode of baptism which was important, so in November 1843 the *Alabama Baptist* stated their "opposition to receiving persons immersed by Pedobaptists, into the fellowship of Baptist Churches:

> ... if we can, conscientiously allow Pedobaptists to immerse for us, why not allow them to administer the Lord's Supper...and why not go still further, and invite all such to commune. This ... would be giving up ground which has been occupied by the Baptist denomination from the days of John the Baptist.[105]

In 1879, J. L. West argued that an applicant for membership in a Baptist church who had been immersed by a Methodist minister "must be baptized; not baptized *again*, for he must admit that the ordinance has not yet been properly administered upon him." [106]

In 1844, R. B. C. Howell of Nashville published an article in the *Alabama Baptist* in which he spoke of the number of Baptist churches "adopting the 'open' system were once very few; but have much increased during the last 20 or 30 years" a fact that he put down to the influence of Robert Hall's views in England.[107] In 1849, an editorial in the *Alabama Baptist* spoke of churches in London which either welcomed unbaptized believers to the Lord's Table or even into full membership.[108] In 1882, J. J. D. Renfroe maintained that "Baptists in the United States were never more fixed in strict communion than they are today. We have for the last century always had some men who ... blurted forth open communion sentiments" but indicated that "if such men remained quiet, our people have tolerated them."[109]

In the 1880s, however, Graves added one further feature to his Landmark doctrine which received opposition in Alabama from J. J. D. Renfroe, pastor of the Baptist church in Talladega.[110] Renfroe argued that although "the members of one Baptist church cannot *claim it as a right* to commune with another Baptist church" they would be able to "accept it as a courtesy."[111] Graves developed his Landmark theology to reject "intercommunion among Baptists."[112] Renfroe believed that this development was inconsistent with common practice among Baptists in Alabama.

The lasting influence of Landmarkism throughout the 19th century can be seen in the resignation of William H. Whitsitt as President of Southern Seminary in 1899.[114] Whitsitt joined the faculty of Southern Seminary in 1872 following study at Union University, the University of Virginia, Southern Seminary and the University of Berlin, Germany. Whitsitt had been raised in Tennessee, and J. R. Graves was a personal friend of his family and "was often a guest in their home." Graves had preached Whitsitt's ordination sermon. Yet, Whitsitt gradually moved away from his Landmark roots to publish, in 1893, an article on "Baptists" in *Johnson's Universal Cyclopedia* in which he argued that the practice of immersion began in 17th century England and that Roger William's church in Rhode Island did not initially immerse.[115] In 1895, the seminary trustees elected Whitsitt as their third president. In a context in which Landmark Baptists expressed their concern over Whitsitt's views, he published, *A Question in Baptist History*, in which he developed his earlier argument on the origins of baptism by immersion, dating it no earlier than 1641. The reaction to Whitsitt's views and the threat of the withdrawal of financial support for the seminary led Whitsitt to resign as president. [116]

Whitsitt was succeeded by E. J. Mullins in 1899, despite the fact that during the controversy, Mullins had defended Whitsitt in a series of articles in the *Religious Herald*, the Baptist newspaper in Virginia, describing Landmarkism as "a Roman Catholic party among the Baptists."[117] In 1908, Mullins published a series of lectures which he had delivered in various locations during the previous few years. The book was called, *Axioms of Religion*, a book which "did more to shape Baptist identity and self-understanding in the 20th century than any other source."[118] Mullins argued that although "baptism is not declared formally to be a condition of church-membership, but only as a duty universally binding upon penitent believers," he claimed that "without fail believers who became members were baptized."[119] On this basis he maintained that any concept of "open membership" which did not require baptism would "abolish the church itself." He also rejected the notion that baptism by sprinkling could be accepted as a valid alternative to immersion, as it "destroys the meaning of the ordinance from the Baptist point of view." Mullins also expressed his concern that some Baptists were suggesting that baptism and the

Lord's Supper were no longer to be considered to be ordinances but sacraments.[120] His arguments, however, contained no note whatsoever of an appeal to Landmark principles, and they have remained influential among Southern Baptists.

Methodists

The two bodies which became the largest Protestant denominations in America were Methodists and Baptists, and both "capitalized on the power of the revivals" of the 19th century, making "full use of frontier evangelism." This vibrant experience of growth, nurtured by "many points of similarity in the evangelical spirit and teachings of Methodists and Baptists," also provoked "intense competition" between them.[121] Baptists differed from Methodists primarily on the issue of infant baptism, which the Baptists believed to have no scriptural basis. In 1818, the number of Methodists in Alabama was around 1,600.[122] By 1839, both denominations had around 25,000 members. [123]

John Wesley never questioned the correctness of infant baptism. He believed that when converts are baptized the sacrament "functions as an assurance of salvation."[124] As the Methodist movement grew in America in the latter half of the 18th century, Methodists "were expected to receive the sacraments from local Anglican priests." But as the movement grew and moved into new areas during the expansion of the country in the 19th century, local preachers wanted the authority to administer the sacraments of baptism and the Lord's Supper, [125] an issue that was settled in 1784 when Wesley made provision for ordained ministers in America. As Methodists and Baptists began to engage in controversy over baptism, Methodist preachers were willing to immerse people who requested that particular mode, and in 1779 the Methodist Conference allowed for baptism by "sprinkling or plunging." In 1884 the church provided a choice of immersion, sprinkling, or pouring for infants or adults.[126]

During the latter part of the 18th century, Methodists were divided over the question of rebaptism, when those who had been baptized in infancy now questioned the authenticity of their experience. The annual conferences in 1779, 1784 and 1786 went back and forth between disallowing, allowing and then ignoring the issue, eventually describing rebaptism as "utterly wrong."[127] As Methodists experienced a period of spiritual awakening, in the early part of the 19th century, large camp meetings nurtured a revivalist atmosphere in which baptism and the Lord's Supper were administered to large numbers. During the 19th century, Felton argued that the rebaptism of Methodists who had previously been sprinkled as babies "continued to be practiced" although "scholarly opinion was unequivocally opposed to it."[128] Felton contends that "requests for 'rebaptism' will dwindle when the theological significance of the sacrament is clearly taught and when meaningful occasions for ritualizing subsequent spiritual experiences are effectively offered."[129] However, as late as the Annual Conference which met in Denver in 1996, the United Methodist Conference published and debated a report on *By Water and Spirit* which had been discussed over the previous four years by the church. During the debate, an amendment to the report asked that the conference delete the statement that "the sacrament of baptism may not be repeated" and to insert these words: "The practice of rebaptism does not conform with God's action in baptism and is not consistent with Wesleyan tradition and the historic teaching of the church. Therefore, the pastor should counsel any persons seeking rebaptism to participate in a rite of re-affirmation of baptismal vows."[130] When the conference voted, a minority viewpoint that rebaptism should never be allowed to take place was defeated 599 to 348.

Rebaptism in Baptist Churches

The question of allowing someone who had been baptized in a Baptist church to be "rebaptized" was raised in 1889. J. C. Wright spoke of several circumstances when such requests might be received. He speaks of "one who comes, who has been regularly baptized by a Baptist minister ... but finds that he was not regenerated at the time of his baptism." Wright argued that "he should not be re-baptized" because, prior to his baptism, he had made a "credible profession of faith."[131] In 1880 in an editorial article, E. T. Winkler suggested that if everyone who, during a "season of spiritual exaltation" concluded that they had "never believed before" and asked to be rebaptized then the "sacredness of the ordinance would be affected...it is best to decide once for all that one baptism upon a confession of Christ suffices."[132]

The rebaptism of believers within Baptist churches in the South is, in part, exacerbated by the practice of baptizing very young children, as young as four or five.[133] In each Baptist History and Theology class that I have taught over the past six years, I have always had one or two students who have been rebaptized, sometimes within the same congregation in which their original baptism took place, occasionally by the same pastor. Bill Leonard suggests that "the proportion of annual baptisms ... reflect[s] second or third 'conversions,' not first time converts."

The question of the appropriate age at which we baptize children continues to receive a variety of responses. In 1980, Bill Hull presented a paper on "The Child in the Church," in which he argued that Baptists needed to develop a theology of the child that recognizes the Old Testament insight of nurture within the community and the New Testament insight of the necessity of conversion, along with the findings of developmental psychology. He suggested that baptism and church membership would come in the middle of childhood, approximately ages nine through twelve.[135] In 1983, Glenn Stassen suggested that although every effort should be made for churches to "welcome children" and enable them to be a vital part of the life of the church, "baptism should be for believers who can experience its fuller meaning."[136] A brief survey of Baptist pastors in Alabama who are connected to CBF churches revealed a willingness to baptize children from the age of 8, although there was a preference for children to be at least 10 years old.[137] One pastor commented that he was "very cautious about baptizing children under nine years of age."[138]

One pastor in Birmingham, Alabama, offers a creative way in which people of all ages may have an opportunity to reaffirm their faith and commitment to Christ within the context of a baptismal service. She writes:

> I offer (about every two to three years) an invitation to the entire congregation to re-visit the waters of baptism. It is usually during a Sunday morning service where I have done a baptism. I scoop up the water in a pitcher and pass it down through the choir to a designated person at the Lord's Supper table. Each person who holds the pitcher says loudly, like a pronouncement, "The waters of baptism!" The person at the communion table, pours the water into a pitcher, says a prayer and then anyone who would like to re-visit the waters comes forward. They are told that they may do with the water whatever they need.

We have towels available as well...in fact, that is often my
"job." I stand there to dry hands, faces, etc. They often
want me to take the water and make the sign of the cross
on their foreheads. I have watched individuals splash
water on their faces, and some to stand and just "soak"
their hands in the water. I had one woman who came
up with tears running down her cheeks to say, "I don't
remember the day I was baptized." So we sprinkled her.
It is different every time we do it, but it seems to meet
a need. I will admit that I am always surprised by who
comes forward. [139]

As long as Baptists in the South continue to emphasize baptism as
an act of obedience, rather than the action of God in incorporating the
believer into the body of Christ, relating that event to the anointing
of the Holy Spirit, the stress will continue to fall upon human activity
rather than the assurance of God's grace through the ministry of the
Holy Spirit. In this context, it is inevitable that believers will desire
fresh opportunities to be baptized rather than focusing on the once for
all activity of God in the baptismal waters.

Baptism and Membership

In Scotland, applications for membership in Baptist churches
normally require two members of the congregation to "interview" the
candidate and report their conversations to a church meeting prior to
accepting them as members.[140] In the vast majority of Baptist churches
in the South, applicants for membership are received at the front of the
church at the conclusion of the service and are immediately presented
to, and approved by, the congregation. Although most of these people
will have already spoken to the pastor of the church of their intention
to join the church, it appears that several churches are receiving
members who were not necessarily baptized as believers. But as one
pastor commented, if they have had "a genuine conversion experience
and their baptism is valid to them, I receive them by statement, asking
only that they accept that immersion is the only form of baptism we
practice."[141] One other pastor in Alabama made the comment, "We
do not require re-baptism for those baptized in other traditions,
including those that practice infant baptism. Though not in writing,

our practice is to interview potential members from other traditions about their baptism and other Christian experiences. If their baptism is a meaningful part of their experience, either through a confirmation process or some other reflective exercise, then it is meaningful to us."[142]

This attitude is criticized by a recent book from a conference held at Southwestern Baptist Theological Seminary in 2006.[143] John S. Hammett cites the view of Mark Dever that "if a church receives into its membership someone who refused to obey ... a clear command of Christ [baptism], it would have no choice but to discipline such a person."[144]

Baptismal Trends among Southern Baptists

Baptism figures within Southern Baptist Churches have fallen for three successive years (2005-2008). This is in line with the experience of other mainline denominations within the United States. In 2007, baptisms in Southern Baptist Churches decreased by five percent to 345,941, compared to 364,826 in 2006. Indeed, over the past 50 years, the ratio of annual baptisms per church member, a key indicator of church growth, has dropped sharply. Southern Baptists baptized one person for every 19 members in 1950. In 2007 it was one baptism for every 47. Southern Baptists reached their peak number of baptisms in 1972, when 445,725 were baptized. The denomination, which lost over 40,000 members last year, also indicates that close to two thirds of members of churches do not attend on a regular basis.[145] In 2005, out of a total of 16,270,315 members in 43,699 churches, only an average of 6,052,321, or 37.2 percent attended Sunday morning worship.[146] In Alabama, from 2000-2007, the membership of over 3,000 churches associated with the state convention grew from 1,105,615 to 1,131,747 (2.16 percent). The number of baptisms fell from 25,939 in 2000 to 22,114 in 2007, and averaged 23,392 per year from 2000-2007.

The idea of baptism in Southern Baptist churches generally lacks any sacramental understanding. In a review of R. E. O. White's book, *Christian Initiation,* published in 1962, Bill Hull suggested that it "should prove both sobering and challenging to read one who can move from a spirited attack on pedobaptism to an equally vigorous assault on the 'mere symbol' emphasis so prevalent in our ranks, defending instead a 'dynamic sacramentalism' as the richer New Testament witness."[147] Indeed, many churches and pastors seem to be more concerned for the significance of baptismal numbers as a mark of church growth than as a means of grace and spiritual nourishment for those who are baptized.[148]

Lord's Supper: Meaning and Practice

Whereas in Scotland, an appreciation of the Lord's Supper as a "means of grace" and a "sacrament" is not uncommon, the majority of Baptists in Alabama would prefer to use the term "ordinance" and adhere to a Zwinglian understanding of the Lord's Supper as a memorial. In Alabama, during the 19th century, the lack of ordained ministry and the infrequency of regular weekly services, which tended to focus on evangelizing the lost, led to a quarterly or even a semiannual observance of communion. This, along with an antipathy of anything which suggested ritualism or Catholicism, inevitably led to an undermining of its importance and theological significance in the spiritual pilgrimage of the congregation. Only occasionally do you discover some influence of the theology of John Calvin in someone like J. L. Dagg who, in 1857, wrote that "The Lord's Supper was designed to be a memorial of Christ, a representation that the communicant receives spiritual nourishment from him, and a token of fellowship among the communicants." There is more than a suggestion that the Lord's Supper is a "means of grace" to those who come in faith, love and hope. [149]

In the 20th century, W. T. Conner noted that Baptists tend to see the Lord's Supper as symbols which "contain or convey [the Lord's] spiritual presence ... they only ... picture it so that it may be the mind and thus strengthen faith."[150] Fisher Humphreys, however, suggests that Baptists "agree that Christ is present in the Lord's Supper, and we who participate in the Lord's Supper by faith are in communion with Christ who is there present for us .... At the table of the Lord we are spiritually fed."[151]

Conclusion

Issues surrounding baptism, communion and attitudes towards membership in Scotland and Alabama have been shaped by a variety of theological, historical and cultural experiences over last 200 years. Baptists in Scotland have always been a minority within the life of the wider church in Scotland. They continue to demonstrate their commitment to their heritage in a context in which the membership of the life of the church is diminishing in a society where people may continue to believe but do not belong.[152] Baptists in Alabama continue to be dominant, increasingly so with the decline of Methodism within the state. In many ways, Baptists in Alabama represent the dominant culture, whereas in Scotland they are a minority. However, it appears that, even within the "Bible Belt," changes are taking place in terms of commitment to formal membership within the life of the church, with less people joining churches through profession of faith and more church growth taking place as a result of transfer from one congregation to another. [153]

Although the number of those being baptized in Alabama is falling slightly, those who are baptized consistently join the life of the local church, whereas in Scotland almost 40 percent of those who are baptized do not commit themselves to the life of a local congregation. Without that formal membership, however, they are not able to be active in the church services where the members are seeking to discern the mind of Christ.

An understanding of baptism and the Lord's Supper as being a sacramental "means of grace" is very rare within the life of Baptist churches in Alabama. As we have seen, Scottish Baptists have formally adopted statements regarding baptism which describe the event as a sacrament. Although the majority of congregations in Scotland would speak of communion in Zwinglian terms, there has always been a strong element of viewing the Lord's Supper as a means by which the grace of God is encountered in a special way, and this has led Scottish Baptists to celebrate the service more regularly than in Alabama. One of the most popular communion hymns in Scotland is that of Horatius Bonar: [154]

> *Here, O my Lord, I see thee face to face;*
> *here would I touch and handle things unseen;*
> *here grasp with firmer hand eternal grace,*
> *and all my weariness upon thee lean.*
>
> *This is the hour of banquet and of song;*
> *this is the heavenly table spread for me;*
> *here let me feast, and feasting, still prolong*
> *the hallowed hour of fellowship with thee.*

Here would I feed upon the Bread of God,
here drink with thee the royal Wine of heaven;
here would I lay aside each earthly load,
here taste afresh the calm of sin forgiven.

I have no help but thine; nor do I need
another arm save thine to lean upon;
it is enough, my Lord, enough indeed;
my strength is in thy might, thy might alone.

Mine is the sin, but thine the righteousness:
mine is the guilt, but thine the cleansing
here is my robe, my refuge, and my peace;
thy Blood, thy righteousness, O Lord my God!

Feast after feast thus comes and passes by;
yet, passing, points to the glad feast above,
giving sweet foretaste of the festal joy,
the Lamb's great bridal feast of bliss and love.

Baptists in Scotland and Alabama will continue to be formed by a changing landscape, both theological and cultural, in which both churches are seeking to minister the grace of God. Both groups of Baptists, whether large or small, claim to be committed to an authentic pattern of Baptist identity. It remains to be seen whether Baptists in Scotland and Alabama, in an increasingly post-denominational context, are able to pass on that sense of identity to the next generation of members.

NOTES

[1] I have served as a Baptist minister in Scotland in three churches (Galashiels, Fraserburgh and Livingston, Ladywell from 1978-1994), Principal of Scottish Baptist College (1994-2002) and Chair, Religion Department, Samford University, Birmingham, Alabama (2003-present).

[2] For a fuller study, see Brian Talbot, *The Search for a Common Identity: The Origins of the Baptist Union of Scotland 1800-1870*, (Paternoster, 2003).

[3]See Derek B. Murray, The Scotch Baptist Tradition in Great Britain in *Baptist Quarterly* 33, (1989-1990), 186-198. I was minister of the Galashiels Baptist Church from 1978-1984. The church began as a Scotch Baptist Church in the 18th century.

[4]John Glas (1695-1773) was a minister of the Church of Scotland near Dundee, who adopted an Independent position in relation to churchmanship, and in 1725 gathered a group of 74 people to share communion and exercise church discipline. As a result, Glas was deposed from the ministry of the Church of Scotland in 1730. He set up an independent congregation in Dundee, where he practiced weekly communion and lay leadership. Through his influence several similar congregations were established in Perth, Edinburgh, Paisley and Galashiels. See Derek B. Murray, "The Influence of John Glas" in *Records of the Scottish Church History Society* 22 (1984), 45-56.

[5]John Glas's son-in-law, Robert Sandeman (1718-1771) became the chief publicist of the movement and he visited Boston, Massachusetts in 1764 where a few Glasite congregations were established. Sandeman stayed in Danbury, Connecticut, where he died in 1771. His commitment to the British cause in the days prior to the American Revolution meant that his views were never widely adopted. See John Howard Smith, *They Suffer only for Righteousness Sake: The Glasite-Sandemanian movement in the British-American Atlantic World 1720-1790*, PhD, University of Albany, 2003.

[6] Robert Dawson Mitchell, *Archibald McLean, 1735-1812: Baptist Pioneer in Scotland*, (Edinburgh PhD, 1950), 226. A copy of the thesis is lodged in the Scottish Baptist College Library.

[7]Scotch Baptists formed congregations in the North of England, Nottingham and London. McLean's writings influenced J. R. Jones who founded several Scotch Baptist congregations in North Wales.

[8]In 1733 the Original Secession Church was formed and then in 1761 the Presbytery of Relief was established. See Kenneth B. E. Roxburgh, *Thomas Gillespie and the Origins of the Presbytery of Relief* (Lang, 1999).

[9]See Kenneth B. E. Roxburgh, *Thomas Gillespie and the Origins of the Relief Church in Eighteenth Century Scotland*, (Edinburgh PhD, 1997).

[10]See Leigh Schmidt, *Holy Fairs*, (Princeton University Press, 1989); George B. Burnet, *The Holy Communion in the Reformed Church of Scotland 1560-1960*, (Edinburgh, Oliver and Boyd, 1960); Gwen Kennedy Neville, *Kinship and Pilgrimage: Rituals of Reunion in American Protestant Culture*, (Oxford, 1987) 35-39.

[11]Thomas Gillespie, *New College Sermons Ms*, Vol. 3, f 40v.

[12] Thomas Gillespie, *Dunfermline Sermons for 1747 Ms*, f 106v.

[13]*Letter from Church, Leith Walk, Edinburgh to Church in New York*, dated 31 July 1818. In Waugh Papers, Bundle 3, deposited in the Archives of the Baptist Union of Scotland.

[14]John MacInnes, *The Evangelical Movement in the Highlands*, (Aberdeen University Press, 1951), 128.

[15]Kenneth J. Stewart, *Restoring the Reformation: British Evangelicalism and the 'Reveil' at Geneva 1816-1849*, (Edinburgh PhD, 1991), 62. The average attendance for a Sunday evening service was about 3,600. See D. E. Wallace, *The Life and Work of James Alexander Haldane*, (Edinburgh PhD, 1955), 251.

[16]*Letter from Church*. Wallace suggests that three groups left the Leith Walk church at this time. "A small portion joined Mr. McLean's Church in Niddrie Street. Another group united with Mr. Aikman's Church, in College Street and a number withdrew and met for several years in a building known as the Bernard's Rooms." Wallace, *Haldane*, p 264. The congregation at Leith Walk was "reduced to one third of its former strength." Stewart, *Restoring the Reformation*, 136.

[17]Wallace comments that "in a short time nearly all' who remained in the Leith Walk congregation 'were baptized by immersion." *Haldane*, 269-270. Other churches within the Haldane connection split evenly between those who became Baptist and those who chose to become Congregationalist or Independent. However, it "was not uncommon for a minister who adopted Baptist views to remain the pastor of a congregation who choose to become Congregationalist on the principle of forbearance on both sides." See 272.

[18]Demetrius "On Forbearance" *The Scripture Magazine*, Vol. II, (Edinburgh, 1811), 176-7. Samuel Jones knew that Haldane had written this article under the pseudonym of Demetrius. See Samuel Jones, *A Review of Mr. J. A. Haldane's Later Publication Entitled "Observances on Forbearanc"*, (London, 1812) 52. Haldane also wrote *Observances on Forbearance* (Edinburgh, 1811). Haldane had addressed the issue as a small part of his work on *A View of Social Worship* (Edinburgh, 1805).

[19] *Letter from Church*.

[20] *Letter from Church*.

[21] Haldane, *Observances on Forbearance*, 18.

[22] Haldane, *Observances on Forbearance*, 38.

[23] See Samuel Jones, *A Review*.

[24] Samuel Jones, *A Review*, 8.

[25] Samuel Jones, *A Review*, 21.

[26] Samuel Jones, *A Review*, 44.

[27]James Haldane, *Remarks on Mr. Jones' Review of Observances on Forbearance*, (Edinburgh, 1812), 3.

[28]James Haldane, *Remarks on Mr. Jones' Review*, 39.

[29]Jonathan Watson, *Christian Communion versus Sectarian Communion*, (Edinburgh, 1875).

[30] Jonathan Watson, *Christian Communion*, 4.

[31] Jonathan Watson, *Christian Communion*, 4-5.

[32]John Bunyan's *Differences in Judgement about Water Baptism, no Bar to Communion*, (London, 1673), 5.

[33]Thomas Paul, *Some Serious Reflections on that Part of Mr. Bunion's Confession of Faith Touching ... Communion with Unbaptised Persons*, (London, 1673).

[34]William Kiffin, *A Sober Discourse of Right to Church-Communion*, (London, 1681).

[35]John Denne, *Truth outweighing Error; being an Answer to a Treatise of J. Bunyan's entitled, a Confession of his Faith*, (London, 1673). Denne was a General Baptist minister.

[36] See Richard L. Greaves, *John Bunyan*, (Michigan, 1969), 129.

[37]John Bunyan, *The Whole Works of John Bunyan*, (ed. George Offor, London, 1875), Vol. 2.648.

[38]Harry L. Poe, "John Bunyan's Controversy with the Baptists" in *Baptist History and Heritage*, Vol. XXIII, No.2, (April, 1988), 32.

[39]Michael Walker, *Baptists at the Table*, (Baptist Historical Society, 1992), 34.

[40] J. H. Y. Briggs, *The English Baptists of the Nineteenth Century*, (The Baptist Historical Society, 1994), 137.

[41] *Minutes of the Baptist Union of Scotland, February 1986-March 1968*, 1523.

[42] Scottish Baptist Year Book for 1968, 177.

[43]*Minutes of the Baptist Union of Scotland, February 1965 to March 1968*, 1756. Minutes for Church Extension Committee of 22 November 1966.

[44]See Andrew MacRae, *Christian Baptism*, (Baptist Union of Scotland, 1967), 14-15. MacRae became secretary and superintendent of the Baptist Union of Scotland in 1966. In a personal communication MacRae speaks of how he "argued fairly strongly, and unapologetically, for closed membership in our Baptist churches, but for openness to the validity of believer's baptism wrongly administered by effusion, or so administered by physical necessity."

[45] These include Coats Memorial, Paisley; Central Paisley; St Andrews; White's Causeway, Kirkcaldy.

[46]These include Ward Road, Dundee where Andrew MacRae was minister from January 1961 to November 1966. Cupar and Morningside were both open membership churches, then became closed and are now open again.

[47] MacRae, *Baptism*, 14-15.

[48]Ian G. Docherty, *A History of St Andrews Baptist Church 1841-1991*, (Privately Published, 1991), 83.

[49]See S. D. Henry, "Baptist Church Growth in Fife from 1750 to the Present" in *The Baptist Quarterly*, Vol. XXXII, No.7, (July, 1988), p 339. Under the ministry of Graeme M. Clark from 1986-1992 in Whyte's Causeway, Kirkcaldy, the congregation became an open membership church and ironically several adherents who could have become members by profession of faith decided to be baptized! I am grateful to Graeme Clark for this information. [50]I am grateful to Robert Armstrong for this information.

[51]The current Church of Scotland is composed of various Presbyterian denominations which reunited during the 19th and early 20th century to be the present Church of Scotland.

[52]The group originally consisted of 25 professors of divinity, ministers and elders of the church, although the core "came from whose who were connected in some way or other with the Scottish Church Society, the Church Service Society and the Scottish Church Theology Society." These groups represented theologians influenced by Karl Barth, although not in the area of baptism and high churchmen. See Bryan D. Spinks, "Freely by His Grace: Baptismal Doctrine and the Reform of the Baptismal Liturgy in the Church of Scotland, 1953-1994" in *Rule of Prayer, Rule of Faith*, edited by Nathan Mitchell, John F. Baldovin, (Liturgical Press, 1996), 218-242. T. F. Torrance was chiefly responsible for the final documents. The post-war saw a number of books on baptism. See K. Barth, *The Teaching of the Church regarding Baptism* (London, 1948); W. F. Flemington, *The New Testament Doctrine of Baptism*, (London, 1948); Oscar Cullman, *Baptism in the New Testament*, (London, 1950); Joachim Jeremias, *Infant Baptism in the First Four Centuries*, (London, 1962).

[53]*Report to the General Assembly of the Church of Scotland in 1959*, (Edinburgh, 1959), 629-662. See also Bryan D. Spinks, *Reformation and Modem Rituals and Theologies of Baptism: From Luther to Contemporary Practices*, (Ashgate, 2006), 147-151; George Hunsinger, "The Dimensions of Depth: Thomas F. Torrance on the Sacraments of Baptism and the Lord's Supper," *Scottish Journal of Theology*, 54 (2001), 155-176.

[54]See *Reports to the General Assembly of the Church of Scotland*, 1962, pp. 709-723; 1963, 773-783.

[55] D. F. Wright, "Baptism" in *Scottish Dictionary of Church History and Theology*, (Edinburgh, 1993), 58. Wright describes Torrance's view as "sophisticated elusiveness." For a fuller exposition of his viewpoint see T. F. Torrance, "The One Baptism Common to Christ and His Church" in *Theology in Reconciliation: Essays towards Evangelical and Catholic Unity in East and West*, (Eerdmans, 1975), 82-105 where he states that "when the Church baptizes in his name, it is actually Christ himself who is savingly at work, pouring out his Spirit upon us and drawing us within the power of his vicarious life, death and resurrection .... uniting us to Christ, so that his atoning reconciliation bears fruit in us, and lifting us up to share in the very life and love of God, in the communion of the Father, the Son and the Holy Spirit." *ibid.*, 83, 103.

[56]Spink, *Reformation and Modern Rituals*, 151.

[57]*Report to the General Assembly of the Church of Scotland in 1955*, (Edinburgh, 1955), 609-662. This was followed by a report on the Fathers in 1956 (605-646).

[58]*Minutes of the Edinburgh and Lothian Baptist Fraternal*, Vol. 2.50-51.

[59]*Minutes*, Vol. 2.53.

[60]*Scottish Baptist Year Book for 1961*, 9-10.

[61]The articles were written by A. B. Miller (two), Peter Barbour, A. W. Argyle, H. Cook, R. E. O. White and Jim Taylor.

[62]In 1966 he became full-time tutor in New Testament and then principal in 1968.

[63]R. E. O. White, "Theology and Logic" in *Baptist Quarterly*, Vol. 16, No. 8, (October, 1956), 356-364.

[64]R. E. O. White, *The Biblical Doctrine of Initiation*, (London, 1960), 305.

[65]White, *Initiation*, 308-309.

[66]*ibid.* 315.

[67]*Minutes*, Vol. 2.132

[68]This was written by Andrew D. MacRae, then General Secretary of the Baptist Union of Scotland.

[69]A. D. MacRae, *Christian Baptism*, (Glasgow, 1967), 16.

[70]See "Baptist Union of Scotland" in *Churches Respond to BEM: Official responses to the Baptism, Eucharist and Ministry text*, Vol. III, edited by Max Thurian, (Geneva, 1977), 234, 236.

[71]See Article by David F. Wright on "Baptism" in *Dictionary of Scottish Church History and Theology*, (ed. Nigel M. de S. Cameron, Edinburgh, 1993), 58.

[72]See Neil T. R. Dickson, *Brethren in Scotland 1838-2000* (Paternoster, 2002). Dickson estimates that the membership of Brethren Assemblies in Scotland in 1933 was 30,000 and in 1960 that of 25,000. In 1990 he suggested there were about 12,500 Open Brethren assembly members. See Neil Dickson, "Brethren and Baptists in Scotland" in *Baptist Quarterly*, 33, (October 1990), 378.

[73]Dickson, "Brethren and Baptists," 380. I was a former member of the Open Brethren, and had a number of former members from Open Brethren Assemblies in each of the three Baptist churches (Galashiels, Fraserburgh and Livingston [Ladywell]) where I was the minister.

[74]Dickson, *Brethren*, p. 6.

[75]*Churches Respond to BEM*, 243.

[76]See Peter Brierley, *Turning the Tide: Report of the 2002 Scottish Church Census*, (Christian Research, 2003), 16.

[77]Brierley, *Turning the Tide*, 27-28.

[78]I am grateful to Brian Talbot, minister of Broughty Ferry Baptist Church for sending me these numbers from the Scottish Baptist Year Books for 2001 and 2007. The average number of those baptized who became members between 2000 and 2007 was 65 percent.

[79]I am particularly indebted to Wayne Flynt, *Alabama Baptists: Southern Baptists in the Heart of Dixie*, (University of Alabama Press, 1998). I have concentrated on Southern Baptist churches (included CBF congregations) and not examined the views of African American Baptists, Primitive Baptists, Independent Baptist Churches or Free Will Baptists.

[80]Flynt speaks of the "blossoming of evangelical religion on the Alabama frontier," which he describes as being as being as prolific as corn and cotton. Flynt, *Alabama Baptists*, p. 4. The state of Alabama was constituted in 1819.

[81]By 1823, the 120 congregations which had been established belonged to seven geographic associations. By 1839 there were "30 associations with 500 churches, 300 ministers, and 25,000 members." Flynt, *Alabama Baptists*, 7, 11.

[82] Larry Hale, *Flint River Baptist Association Minutes and Historical Articles 1814-2004*, (N.P. 2005), 8. The Cahawba Association, formed in 1818, adopted an identical Abstract of Principles.

[83]Harold D. Wicks, *Salem-Troy Baptist Association: Past and Present*, (Troy, 1990), 22. The Country Line Baptist Church, in Chambers Country, Alabama, founded in 1835 expressed their understanding of election in terms of "Westminster Calvinism" as "the everlasting love of God to his people and the eternal election of a definite number of the human race to grace and glory and that there was a Covenant of Grace or redemption made between the Father and the Son before the world began in which their salvation is secure and that they in particular are redeemed." See Glenda Brack, *County Line Baptist Church*, (N.P. 2005), 1.

[84]They adopted the name of North River United Baptist Association. In their 5th article they stated, "We believe that Jesus Christ, the son of God, did make atonement for all men in general, but the benefits of the atonement specially are only received by the true believer."

[85]The church was originally known as West Fork of Flint, and in July 1809 it changed its name to Enon Baptist Church. At the time of its formation, Madison County had 2,223 white inhabitants and 322 slaves. See Milfred B. Bobo and C. R. Johnson, *First Baptist Church of Huntsville, Alabama*, (Huntsville, 1985).

[86]Bobo, *First Baptist*, 2.

[87]Hale, *Flint River*, 8.

[88]N. A. and Celia H. Nunnelley, *Baptists of Cullman Country 1883-1983*, (N.P. 1983), 10.

[89]Hosea Holcombe, *History of the Rise and Progress of Baptists in Alabama*, (Philadelphia, 1840), 311-322.

[90]See "Communications" in *Alabama Baptist*, 16 May, 1849, 3.

[91]In 1889 William H. Whitsitt argued that Campbell was influenced by Sandemanianism. See William H. Whitsitt, *Origin of the Disciples of Christ (Campbellites): A contribution to the centennial anniversary of the birth of Alexander Campbell*, (New York, 1888). John Howard Smith comments that 'Scottish Glasites and English Sandemanians influenced, both directly and indirectly, such sects as .... the Campbellites. See Smith, *They Suffer*, 136, fn. 105.

[92]For a fuller discussion of Campbell's relationship with Baptists see Austin Bennett Amonette, "Alexander Campbell and Baptist Identity: Contribution

and Challenges" in *Baptist Identities*, edited by Ian M. Randall, Toivo Pilli and Anthony R. Cross, (Paternoster, 2006), 125-137.

[93]Chad D. Hall suggests that "the Baptist-Campbellite conflict centered on several issues. Although both groups held the Bible to be the final source of authority, they differed in their interpretations of Scripture. For one thing, the Campbellites disfavored the Baptist's confessions and missionary alliances, both of which they thought were unwarranted by Scripture. In addition, the Campbellites sought Christian unity based on two factors: the common confession that 'Jesus is Lord,' and baptism by immersion. Baptists believed that the simple common confession left too much room for theological radicalism and could never produce real unity. Finally, Baptists believed Campbellites held too low a view of the Holy Spirit's work in regeneration. In their mind, the Campbellite emphasis on the Spirit working only through the Word meant that Campbellite Christians had never really experienced conversion, since there had been no experience of the Holy Spirit." See "When Orphans become Heirs: J. R. Graves and the Landmark Baptists" in *Baptist History and Heritage*, 37 No. I Winter 2002, 126.

[94]Editions appeared in 1824, 1826, 1831, 1832, 1837 and 1845. I am grateful to Andrew Smith, for his paper, "William Jones and the Common Roots of Landmarkist and Restorationist Ecclesiology," at conference for National Association of Baptist Professors of Religion, Nashville, May 2008.

[95]See Bill J. Leonard, *Baptists in America*, (Columbia University Press, 2005), 146. The Church of Christ website indicates that "the most recent dependable estimate lists more than 15,000 individual churches of Christ." And estimates "the total membership of the churches of Christ is now 2,000,000 .... Membership of the church is heaviest in the southern states of the United States, particularly Tennessee and Texas, though congregations exist in each of the fifty states and in more than eighty foreign countries .... The churches of Christ now have five times as many members as were reported in the U.S. Religious Census of 1936." See http://church-of-christ.org/who. html# numbers accessed on 26 May, 2008.

[96]Hall, 'J. R. Graves', 117.

[97]K B. C. Howell, 'A Memorial of the First Baptist Church, Nashville, Tennessee, from 1820 to 1863,' 219.

[98]J. L. Dagg, *Manual of Church Order*, (Charleston, 1858), 121.

[99]Cited in Western Baptist Review 4/1 (September 1848), 31-32.

[100]See *Minutes of the Cahawba Baptist Association, October 1820*, 9.

[101]*Minutes of Cahawba*, 10.

[102]*ibid*. 11.

[103]*Minutes of the Fifteenth Anniversary of the Cahaba Association*, 1832, 10.

[104]*Circular Letter of the 26th Anniversary of the Cahawba Association, 1843*, 2-3. By 1843 the association had 24 churches, 12 ordained ministers and 2,743

members. During the preceding year it had received 875 new members by baptism.

[105] See Spectator, "Immersion by Pedo-Baptists - not Baptism" in Alabama Baptist, November 30, 1844, 1.

[106]J. L. West (owner of the Alabama Baptist) "Qeery (sic) on Baptism," in Alabama Baptist, 28 August, 1879, 2. In 1886, S. Henderson admitted that it had been "the general custom, with some rare exceptions, to baptize all persons who seek membership in them, even if they have been immersed by Pedo-Baptists." His argument was based on the premise that the administrator of the ordinance must himself have been "regularly baptized, and authorized by a church that has kept the ordinances as they were delivered to them." S. Henderson, "Pedo-Baptist Immersions," in Alabama Baptist, 14 October, 1886, 2.

[107]In 1855 the newspaper published several articles refuting Robert Hall's views. See "Robert Hall on Communion" in Alabama Baptist, 30 August, 6 September, 13 September and 20 September, 1855. In 1874 the newspaper once again attacked Hall's view stating that "the loose principles of Robert Hall, in reference to communion, are fatal to their [Baptist church's] prosperity." "Strict Communion" in Alabama Baptist, 14 April, 1874, 2.

[108]See "Free Communion" in Alabama Baptist, 29 August, 1849, 2.

[109]He speaks of being able to "name a dozen or so who were tainted with loose communion." See J. J. D. Renfroe, Vindication of the Communion of Baptist Churches: A Review of the Present Views of Rev. J. R. Graves, (Selma, 1882), 16.

[110] J. M. Pendleton said that this viewpoint "results from church independence." See Renfroe, "Introduction" to Vindication, 6. Renfroe made it clear that since January 1852, when he had subscribed to the Tennessee that he "stood by Dr. Graves with ardent affection and confidence," 9.

[111] See Renfroe, "New Landmarkism" in Alabama Baptist, 29 January, 1880, 2. In 1880, Renfroe was president of the Alabama State Mission Board and one of the editors of the Alabama Baptist.

[112] Renfroe, Vindication, 14.

[113] He speaks of Graves' view as a "complete absurdity." Renfroe, Vindication, 23.

[114]For a recent analysis of Whitsitt see William E. Hull, "William Heth Whitsitt: Martyrdom of a Moderate" in Marc A. Jolley and John D. Pierce (eds.), Distinctively Baptist: Essays in Baptist History, (Mercer, 2005), 237-278.

[115]William H. Whitsitt, "Baptists" in John's Universal Cyclopedia, 8 vols., ed. Charles Kendall Adams et.al. (New York, 1893-1897) I: 489-93.

[116]In 1897, the Alabama State Convention devoted two sessions, afternoon and evening on 17 December to discuss the Whitsitt controversy. They eventually decided to recommend that the matter be left to the seminary trustees to decide, rather than call for Whitsitt's resignation. The vote was 89

votes to 62. See "Alabama Baptist Dispute" in *New York Times*, 18 December, 1897.

[117]21 May, 16 July, 8 October 1896; 14 April, 1898. Malcolm Yarnell suggests that Mullins' articles against Landmarkism went unnoticed. See M. Yarnell, "E. J. Mullins" in *Biographical Dictionary of Evangelicals*, (I.V.P.2003), 458-460.

[118]William E. Hull, "Mullins and Mohler: A Study in Strategy" in *Perspectives in Religious Studies*, 31 no 3, (Fall 2004), 311.

[119] E. Y. Mullins, *The Axioms of Religion*, (Philadelphia, 1908), 238. When Herschel Hobbs re-issued a revised and much shortened version of *Axioms* in 1978 the sections of open communion were omitted.

[120]He is referring to E. F. Snell (West Newton, Mass.) "Shall We Go Forward?" An address to American Baptists. Mullins, *Axioms*, 244, 247.

[121]Robert T. Handy, *A History of the Churches in the United States and Canada*, Oxford, 1976), 167-8. Bill Leonard comments that "in 1776 Baptists and Methodists were small sectarian movements in colonial American life. By the 1840s they had become the two largest denominations in the country." Leonard, *Baptists in America*, 24.

[122]See Marion Elias Lazenby, *History of Methodism in Alabama and West Florida*, (Birmingham, 1960). These figures increased over the following years.

[123]In 1832, there were 10,996 Methodists. 1839- 24,106; 1845 - 40,632 and in 1861 there were 69,589 members.

[124]See Gayle Carlton Felton, *This Gift of Water: The Practice and Theology of Baptism among Methodists in America*, (Abingdon, 1992), 47.

[125]Felton, *This Gift*, 49, 51.

[126] *ibid.*, 52.

[127]*ibid.*, 54.

[128]Felton cites the General Conference on 1848 which stated that "rebaptism, whether of those baptized in infancy or in adult age, is utterly inconsistent with the nature and design of baptism as set forth in the New Testament." Felton, *This Gift*, 117.

[129]Felton, *This Gift*, 177.

[130]See minutes of 1996 Methodist Conference debate on baptism at: https://email.samford.edu/   exchweb/binJredir.asp?URL=http://www.historicalsocietyunitedmethodistchurch.org/GC96/vbtim22a.html   accessed on 24 April, 2008.

[131]J. C. Wright, "Re-Baptism - Alien Immersion," in *Alabama Baptist*, June 13, 1889, 1.

[132]See E. T. W. "Queeries," in *Alabama Baptist*, 5 February, 1880, 2.

[133]Leonard comments on the practice of Primitive and Old Regular Baptists who tend to delay baptism until later in life, the average being between twenty and thirty years of age. Leonard, *Baptists in America*, 148.

[134]Bill J. Leonard, "Getting Saved in America: Conversion Event in a Pluralistic Culture" in *Review and Expositor*, 82 (1985), 124.

135 Cyril E. Bryant and Ruby J. Burke, eds., *Celebrating Christ's Presence Through the Spirit* (Nashville, 1981), 161-169.

[136]Glen H. Stassen, "Preparing Candidates for Baptism" in *Review and Expositor*, 80:2 (Spring 1983), 258-9.

[137]E-mails from pastors in three Baptist churches in Alabama.

[138]Art Murphy, children's pastor at First Baptist Church, Orlando, Florida, says, "We have found that most children who make that decision [of baptism] under the age of seven tend to need to make another decision later." Referring to rebaptisms. See Art Murphy, "Leading a Child to Christ," *SBC Life*, (June-July 1998), 9.

[139]E-mail communication from Sarah Shelton, pastor, Church of the Covenant, Birmingham, AL.

[140]*Churches Respond to BEM*, 242.

[141]Comment by a pastor in Birmingham, AL.

[142]Comment by J. E. via e-mail on 21 April, 2008. One other factor to consider is the faith journey of children, young people and adults who suffer from a variety of special needs and learning disabilities. See Bill Leonard's moving story in "At the River" in Walter B. Shurden, *Proclaiming the Baptist Vision: Baptism and the Lord's Supper*, (Smyth & Helwys, 1999), 19-20. See also Faith Bowers (ed.) *Mental Handicap and the Church*, (London Baptist Association, 1985) and Faith Bowers, *Treat with Special Honour*, (Baptist Union of Great Britain, 1997).

[143]*Restoring Integrity in Baptist Churches*, Thomas White, Jason G. Duesing and Malcolm B. Yarnell III (eds.), (Kregel, 2008).

[144]John S. Hammett, "Regenerate Church Membership" in *Restoring Integrity*, 28.

[145]The resident membership in Alabama was 70 percent of the total membership from 2000-2007.

[146]John S, Hammett, "Regenerate Church Membership" in *Restoring Integrity*, 27, fn. 23. Penny L. Marler and Kirk C. Hadaway suggest that the normal church attendance in the USA is less than 22 percent. See "How Many Americans Attend Church each Week? An Alternative Approach to Measurement" in *Journal for the Scientific Study of Religion*, Sep. 2005, Vol. 44 Issue 3, 307-322.

[147]William E. Hull, "Review of R. E. O. White, The Biblical Doctrine of Initiation," *Review & Expositor*, 59 no 3 July 1962, 402-403. Fisher Humphreys told me in a personal conversation that White's book was discussed within classes at New Orleans Seminary in the 1960s. For a recent book on this subject from a British and North American perspectives see Anthony R. Cross and

Philip E. Thompson (eds.), *Baptist Sacramentalism: Studies in Baptist History and Thought, Volume 5*, (Paternoster, 2003).

[148] The church in Gardendale, AL, was first in baptisms in the Alabama Baptist State Convention (a total of 3,100+ Baptist churches) in 1995, 1997, 1998, 1999, 2000, 2002, and 2004; (2nd in 1996, 2001 and 2003). See http://www.bellevue.org/templates/cusbellevue 11 03/details.asp?id= 1360&PID=26562 accessed on 6 June, 2008.

[149] J. L. Dagg, *Manual of Theology*, (Harrisonburg, 1982), 209-211.

[150] W. T. Conner, *Christian Doctrine*, (Nashville, 1937), 287.

[151] Fisher Humphreys, "A Baptist Theology of the Lord's Supper" in *Proclaiming the Baptist Vision: Baptism and the Lord's Supper*, 126.

[152] See Grace Davie, *Religion in Britain since 1945: Believing without Belonging*, (Oxford, 1994).

[153] See Reginald W. Bibby and Merlin B. Brinkerhoff, "Circulation of the Saints Revisited: A Longitudinal Look at Conservative Church Growth" in *Journal for the Scientific Study of Religion*, Sep. 83, Vol. 22 Issue 3, 253-262. The recent Pew Forum on Religion in Public Life indicated that "more than one-quarter of American adults (28 percent) have left the faith in which they were raised in favor of another religion - or no religion at all. If change in affiliation from one type of Protestantism to another is included, 44 percent of adults have either switched religious affiliation, moved from being unaffiliated with any religion to being affiliated with a particular faith, or dropped any connection to a specific religious tradition altogether. .. Among Americans ages 18 to 29, one-in-four said he or she is not affiliated with any religion." See http://www.npr.org/templates /storv/storv.php?storyId=] 9354039 accessed on 19 June 2008. For full report see http://religions.pewforum.org/

[154] Bonar was minister of the Church of Scotland and then, following the Disruption of 1843, the Free Church of Scotland in the 19th century.

The Commission on Freedom and Justice

Regina Claas, Chair

From its inception, the Commission on Freedom and Justice has carried out its work under the BWA Division of Study and Research. However, this commission has been working in quite a different way from all the other study commissions. The focus of the work has not been on study and research as such, but on the experiences of real people in adverse circumstances, their suffering and perseverance, their oppression, persecution and struggles, their existential needs and hopes. Naturally, the commission has over the years dealt with very sensitive issues. This is the main reason why only one paper from the past quinquennium appears in this volume.

True to the mandate of the BWA to provide "a voice for the voiceless" and to hear the testimonies, acknowledge the plight and stand alongside the suffering, the commission has heard, year after year, the stories of those who cannot publicly speak for themselves, has cried and prayed with them and initiated appropriate action through the channels of the BWA. Those whose voices have been made heard need to be protected or else more suffering may be waiting for them. But while the commission chose to keep the names and details of the witnesses and their stories confidential, at the same time, the power of a worldwide Baptist family became evident in a very tangible way. We give honor to God who, through the Holy Spirit, united believers in fervent prayer for those who suffer, who strengthened those in need and changed circumstances to their benefit, and who opened channels of intervention to pursue religious freedom, freedom of conscience and social justice through the public voice of the BWA and through its ministries.

The strength of the worldwide Baptist family called BWA is connectedness, with the resulting opportunities to share resources both spiritual as well as human, financial and material. When a need arises in one part of the world, there may be an answer available in another part of the world, gladly shared because of the love that unites us in Christ. The Commission on Freedom and Justice has in this way been much more than a study center. It has been more of a communication platform where pressing needs can be expressed in confidence and made available to the community of believers for response. Much more of this networking is needed, and the commission has often felt frustrated and helpless in the face of great need, because the BWA has not always been able to provide appropriate structures and resources to always take appropriate action.

The Commission on Freedom and Justice therefore celebrates that a new BWA ministry, that of Freedom and Justice, has been established. This new ministry will have more influence in the future to deal with the many issues of human rights, religious freedom, and ethnic conflict, which so far have been combined in the Commission on Freedom and Justice. The new ministry will have four commissions with emphasis on Religious Freedom, Peace, Social & Environmental Justice, and Human Rights Advocacy, with increased opportunity to address crucial issues among the community of Baptist believers in these areas.

During the past quinquennium, the commission tried to address the three focus areas of human rights violations, religious freedom, and ethnic conflict, while giving ample space at each BWA Gathering for the sharing of individual stories and to hear about the most urgent needs from around the world. Starting with the BWA Congress 2005 in Birmingham, UK, the commission compiled a list of themes and issues to be addressed, including the right to convert from one religion to another, discrimination and violence against women and the feminization of the HIV crisis, a call to end raging wars in Iraq, Sudan, Democratic Republic of Congo, etc., alternative ways of addressing terrorism and the fight against poverty, corruption, exploitation of resources, and protection of the environment.

In 2006 in Mexico City, Mexico, emphasis was placed on hearing the voice of the voiceless, human rights violations on the ground of ethnicity, exploitation and religious persecution. The commission learned about the problems of religious intolerance against the evangelical Christians in the Southern Mexican State of Chiapas, and particularly the Baptist churches there. During a BWA Human Rights visit, led by Denton Lotz in March 1999, the difficulties of these churches had been brought to the attention of the Baptist family, and so far no real improvement had been registered. The commission was made aware of a very complex situation where political issues and the dominating factor of poverty and a need for education were over-layered by religious controversy.

Testimonies were heard from representatives of the Myanmar Baptist Convention and supported by John F. Keith of Canada, about the difficulties of Baptists exercising their Christian faith publicly. Incidents of the violation of human rights and the restriction of religious freedom, freedom of conscience and freedom of speech were discussed. The BWA was urged to pass a resolution of concern and protest regarding the house arrest of Nobel price recipient and opposition leader, Aung San Suu Kyi.

The situation in Vietnam was also addressed through the report of a BWA Human Rights visit in May 2006, led by then BWA President, David Coffey. The Japan Baptist Convention raised great interest with their Peace Declaration in regard to World War II. Rev. Michio Hamano introduced this declaration called "The Baptist Potential for Peace, not War."

Other issues of deliberation were the internationally-owned Micah Challenge, introduced from an Asian-Pacific viewpoint by Les Fussell (Australia) and Victor Rembeth (Indonesia). The Micah Challenge is a global coalition of Christians holding governments to account for their promise to halve extreme poverty by 2015. The BWA has supported the Micah Challenge in establishing a global movement to encourage deeper Christian commitment to the poor and to speak out to leaders to act with justice.

The issue of human trafficking and HIV/AIDS has been long on the agenda of the commission. In Mexico, Sally Smith of UNAIDS and Lauran Bethall, USA, gave a moving presentation on how crucial national and global networking of all public institutions and civic organizations will be for the future. The worldwide Baptist community was called to become actively involved in the fight against the spread of HIV/AIDS and in particular the dehumanizing exploitation and endangering of women in human trafficking.

It was a great privilege to receive Gustavo Parajon, Nicaragua, the first recipient of the BWA Annual Human Rights Award, in the commission (of which he was a long-standing member) to share reflections on his personal struggle for freedom and justice.

With great enthusiasm, the new Director for Study and Research, Fausto Vasconcelos of Brazil, was greeted as well by the commission in 2006.

In 2007, in Accra, Ghana, the commission studied the experiences and impact of the "Truth and Reconciliation Commissions: The Fight against Racism and Ethnic Conflict." Moving testimonies were given from Liberia by Olu Q. Menjay, from South Africa by Terry Rae and Paul Msiza, from the Democratic Republic of Congo, from Chile by Raquel Contreras, and from Rwanda by Japanese missionary, Kasuyuki Sasaki. One person after another from the floor added their testimonies from personal experiences. It became obvious that *Truth and Reconciliation* had been an important, and often very helpful, instrument in coming to grips with the terrible atrocities experienced in many nations. However, much more healing needs to take place. There was also evidence that Baptists and other Evangelicals sometimes had the tendency to suppress the pain and anger and cover it up with shallow acts of reconciliation, without rigorously facing the truth. Many of the persons giving their testimony shared concern that their home church or home union/convention would not address the destructive issues appropriately. Emotions ran high in the session and it was a great relief to speak about these burdens of the heart and bring them before the Lord in prayer for each other and for the suffering nations. The Commission discussed the idea of "Healing and Reconciliation Teams" to be established by the BWA, to assist each other within our international Baptist family in the process of healing.

We had the privilege to receive Joao and Nora Matwawana, the second recipients of the BWA Annual Human Rights Award. Joao Matwawana was born in Angola and has lived through enough wars to know the limitations of what they accomplish. He and his family fled twice, as refugees, to the Democratic Republic of Congo (DRC). Angola's war of independence began precisely where they were studying in 1961, leading to their first refugee experience. The second flight was triggered by the approach of Cuban troops to his home area in 1975. Matwawana became deeply involved in peace and reconciliation mediation especially in Angola, DRC and Rwanda.

In 2008, in Prague, Czech Republic, emphasis was placed on the issue of refugees, migration and lost people in Europe and elsewhere. The commission learned from Anna Maffei about the boat people arriving in Italy from the North African coast. Teodor Oprenov spoke on the plight of the ethnic group of the Sinti and Roma in Bulgaria. The oppressive situation of the Chin refugees in Malaysia was brought to the attention of the commission. Elijah Brown, USA, brought an update on the situation in Sudan with the encouraging news that the different Baptist groups in Sudan had met and started to network in a positive way.

Each testimony and each background story was received not just as fact but prayerfully and empathetically as a call to share the burden. Hence, intercessory prayer always became a vital part of the meetings of the commission.

Migration, and the resulting personal, social and political challenges, is not a new thing of our time. Delroy A. Reid-Salmon, the pastor of Grace Baptist Chapel, a "Caribbean Diaspora Church," in New York City, spoke about the Caribbean Diaspora Church in the Black Atlantic Tradition. Reid-Salmon's insight into the interdependence of releasing and receiving migrants and refugees brought a broadening perspective to the discussions.

In addition, the commission engaged in discussion about Israel and the West Bank. The European Baptist Federation brought a report of its EBF Human Rights Visit in February 2008 (by Tony Peck, Anna Maffei, Toma Magda and Regina Claas). Rosemary Kidd (UK) added her own experiences from a recent visit.

The commission received Dennis Dillip Datta, Bangladesh, in 2008 as the third recipient of the Annual BWA Human Rights Award, which in 2007 was renamed the Denton and Janice Lotz Human Rights Award. Datta presented a paper on "Trafficking of Women and Children in Bangladesh."

In addition to meetings of the Commission on Freedom and Justice, a forum was held on the BWA Response to the Muslim Scholars' Letter entitled, *A Common Word*. The relationship between Christians and Muslims worldwide is seen as one of the most pressing challenges of our time. The discussion centered around theological differences and channels of communication, practical experiences of peaceful relations of people of different faith living in one community, and preventing oppression in a majority/minority situation. In the discussion, it became evident that the worldwide Baptist family enjoys a great advantage and privilege of uniting sisters and brothers from around the world, from many cultures, traditions, languages, races and ethnicities, with a great variety of social and material resources, combining a vast spread of spiritual and life experiences. The richness of this body cannot be over-estimated. Yet, it has to be counted as a Spirit-led achievement that out of the multitude of responses to the Muslim Scholars' Letter a common Baptist response could be formulated.

With great joy the commission received the announcement that finally the BWA's administrative structure was being adjusted to accommodate a separate Freedom and Justice ministry. This had long been the hope of the commission in this and in previous quinquennia, but lack of resources so far had prevented the BWA from taking this courageous step. With this decision, the BWA remained true to our original commitment to invest in freedom and justice according to the mission of Jesus Christ.

The announcement of an International Baptist Peace Conference in Rome, Italy, from February 16-21, 2009, organized by a large number of peace activists within the Baptist family, was met with approval by the commission.

The last meeting of the Commission on Freedom and Justice in its current form took place in 2009 in Ede, Netherlands. With the theme, "Defending Religious Freedom," the commission deliberated on the issue of advocacy. Under the leadership of Christer Daelander, Denmark, the commission reflected on safeguarding religious freedom by developing a plan for action in case of violation of human rights and religious freedom in the context of the Baptist community worldwide.

Lynn Buzzard, a Baptist pastor, professor of law, and member of the commission, spoke on "Religious Freedom and the Law – Forms and Threats against Religious Freedom."

However, the testimonies of those in urgent need were not to be neglected. Anita Snell gave much appreciated insight into the situation of Christians in mainland China today. Mindful of the need to protect the safety of individuals, she nevertheless spoke frankly of the persecution many Christians in China are experiencing. In light of the complexity of the situation and the difficulty to obtain reliable information about the house church movement, the commission was well aware of the danger to jump to conclusions.

The Chinese Christian Three-Self Patriotic Movement (TSPM) is led by a National Committee in Shanghai. "Three-self" stands for self-governing, self-supporting, and self-propagating, and is an idea found among Chinese Christians before 1949. Most Chinese Christians, including those in the house churches, support the three-self principle, but the house churches have sharply criticized the TSPM as a government and Party-controlled church. The TSPM was the only Protestant organization before the China Christian Council (CCC) was formed in 1980. Now the CCC and local Christian Councils have taken over much of the responsibility for church affairs, while the TSPM has become more an ideological counterpart to the authorities.

One of the long-standing areas of concern for the commission is the situation in Myanmar and with Burmese refugees in Asia and other parts of the world. The commission therefore focused on initiatives by various BWA member bodies among Burmese refugees and called for a Round Table to ensure better networking and more effective problem solving. Such a Round Table has been established. However, the plight of the Burmese refugees and those Christians remaining in the country has by no means come to an end.

Further areas of concern were the situation of Baptists and ethnic groups in West Papua, the outbreak of religiously and ethnically-motivated violent clashes in Nigeria, and alarming reports from Azerbaijan and Uzbekistan about newly-developed pressure on religious minorities in this Euro- and Central Asian region.

During this quinquennium, the issue of environmental justice became more and more acute and gained importance in the awareness of the Baptist community. Consequently, the commission held a joint session with the BWA Commission on Christian Ethics on Global Warming during its last meeting of the quinquennium. The session was led by Robert Parham, USA, and Rod Benson, Australia. It could only serve as a mind-opener for a global issue that needs much further study in the near future.

It was a great joy for the commission to meet Leena Lavanya Kumari of Andhra Pradesh, India, the fourth recipient of the Denton and Janice Lotz Annual Human Rights Award. She shared her life story and touched the commission with her deep and sacrificial commitment to elevate the poorest of the poor.

Finally, the announcement by BWA General Secretary Neville Callam of the calling of Raimundo Barreto, the first BWA Director of the Division of Freedom and Justice, was met with great enthusiasm. This is a sign that the BWA will continue to "give a voice to the voiceless" and to stand alongside those who are persecuted for their faith, race or ethnicity, violated and humiliated in their human rights, oppressed and exploited as human beings with their God-given dignity, and endangered by the evil forces of violence, hatred and destruction. This will assist the BWA to remain true to the BWA mission of "Networking the Baptist family to impact the world for Christ."

In our meetings of the commission during the quinquennium, many stories were told, many tears shed, many fervent prayers offered, and much action taken – publicly or quietly, as it seemed appropriate and faithful to the need and circumstances. Those who have had the privilege to look behind the scenes know of amazing love, selfless sacrifice and faith-induced risk-taking. One day, they will hear the Lord's appraisal: "Well done, you faithful servant!"

Chapter 21

Beyond Integration: The Caribbean Diasporan Church as an Agent of Reconciliation
Delroy A. Reid-Salmon

Introduction

This essay is part of an exploratory attempt to construct a theology of the Caribbean Diasporan church.[1] It seeks to investigate how Caribbean Diasporan Christians practice their faith as followers of Jesus Christ in a new land.[2] I advance the notion that a Caribbean Diasporan theology of the church does not begin with the essence of the church but with the complex inter-play of faith, culture and existential realities[3] represented through particular social constructions such as the metaphorical term "model." This discussion defines and discusses the integrative model of the Caribbean Diasporan church, which is one ecclesial pattern among many.

This is an understanding of the church that grows out of a relationship among diverse groups of people premised on faith in Jesus Christ within the context of the historic and contemporary church traditions predicated on ecclesial beliefs. For instance, most Caribbean Diasporan Christians were previously members of various churches – the historic or mainline denominational churches[4] – and the newer ones[5] prior to migrating to their resident homeland.[6] Because of this pre-existing relationship, when people migrate, denominational loyalty and polity form the basis of their membership in these Euro-American churches.

Concurring with this perspective, Black British theologian Anthony Reddie provides an invaluable insight into the nature of the integrative model of the Caribbean Diasporan church. He acknowledges that these are churches with African and Caribbean origin and function as "black enclaves within the overall white majority structure and membership of the ecclesiastical body as a whole."[7] The church, however, does not necessarily regard these non-Caucasian people as constitutive members.[8]

Reddie makes the important observation that not all the non-Caucasian churches can be considered in the Black theological tradition. He, however, identifies Black Methodism in Britain as representative of this tradition because of its commitment to, and practice of, liberation and understanding of Biblical faith through the prism of the Black experience and culture.[9] In this regard, the Caribbean Diasporan church can be considered as an agent of reconciliation and simultaneously as a prophetic presence in the society (2 Cor. 5:18-20; NIV). As such, attention is given to the factors that facilitate reconciliation and how it is understood and practiced by the Caribbean Diasporan church.

The Cords that Bind

As indicated above, the integrative model refers to the practice of Caribbean Diasporan Christians who have chosen to have membership in Euro-American churches. What are the factors that facilitate this kind of relationship? Among other factors, the ecclesial beliefs of denominational loyalty and polity[10] are the two primary factors that give rise to and facilitate reconciliation between the Caribbean Diasporan church and the Euro-American church. These two factors are now considered in turn.

Loyalty

Loyalty to the denominational church connects Caribbean Diasporan and Euro- American Christians. Writing of the Caribbean Diasporan church in the British society, Anita Jackson discusses the principle of loyalty in her book, *Catching Both Sides of the Wind: Conversations with Five Black Pastors.* She discovers that parental affinity, sense of belonging, means of their early education and support in a new country are some of the primary reasons Caribbean Diasporan Christians become members of the established churches in the adoptive homeland. Expressing this understanding, Jackson gives the account of an Anglican pastor. She reports: "My history is in the

Anglican tradition. I had an African past, but I do not know it ... I was always a High Anglican and will be that here as I was in the West Indies."[11]

Although Jackson's work records the experience of five pastors representing five different denominational churches, each pastor shared a common experience of being Black in a predominantly white denominational church.[12] The testimonies are also a record of the diasporan experience. Expressing this understanding, Jackson reports one pastor as saying:

> Each place had its own particular standard. But the fundamental thing is, and this is what I would underline, I had to say to myself: 'My church is the Methodist Church, and I'm not going to go because of you.' I told them loud and clear. I told them my grandfather was a Methodist. I told them I have a place here.[13]

The maintaining of relationship with the respective denominational church was central to their being Christians in a new society and no form of adversity could have changed it. Commitment to the church, therefore, precedes racial heritage. Underscoring this assertion, Anthony Reddie writes: "Black people stayed in [*the white church*] due to identity... conviction and temperament... theology, history and oral tradition... and the determination not to be forced out of 'their church.'"[14] Reddie's observation aptly summaries the important role loyalty plays in forging ecclesial relationships, but loyalty is not the only factor.

Polity

In addition to loyalty, denominational polity is a second factor of the integrative model of the Caribbean Diasporan church. The Reverend Alfred Johnson, a Jamaican Baptist pastor, who is now working as a Presbyterian pastor in the United States, demonstrates this factor. He expresses the reason for changing his denominational relationship. For Johnson, the similarity between the Jamaica Baptist Union and the mainline church in North America, in this case, the Presbyterian Church, U.S.A., facilitates such a relationship. He writes: "There are three aspects of the Presbyterian Church which made me begin to seek guidance from the Holy Spirit as to whether this is where the Lord wanted me to exercise ministry."[15] The reasons Johnson gives are the criteria for ordination, the connectional system and homiletical training.[16]

Johnson's statement may be representative of not only pastors but the members of these churches as well. These people came out of an established church culture and migrated with knowledge of the Christian faith. They were experienced in church life and had a clear understanding of the importance of the church in their life and society. Explaining their reasons for becoming members of a church, it is reported that they were instructed by their leaders or fellow parishioners to make it a priority on arrival in the new land or host country to locate and become members of a church, particularly a denominational one.[17] Baptist theology, for example, teaches that as soon as a member migrates to another community this person should actively seek membership in another church, particularly a denominational one. The advice to become affiliated with another whenever one migrates is stated in the Baptist church covenant. The covenant states:

> We moreover engage that, when we remove from this
> place, we will as soon as possible unite with some other
> church where we can carry out the spirit of this covenant
> and the principles of God's Word.[18]

Implicit in this practice are the issues of convenience and innocence. Many times, Caribbean people who migrate to countries such as the United States and the United Kingdom are not aware of the deeply ingrained racist and classist ideology that defines the world-view of the ecclesiastical system of which they become members. While these structures are incongruous with the reconciling purpose of Jesus Christ, for the church to be an agent of reconciliation it must move beyond the practice of integration and create new faith communities for people. But the church must acknowledge the difficulty involved in pursuing this kind of life in a society that makes it possible to reap the benefits of an unjust social system and at the same time, professes to be an agent of reconciliation. Fully cognizant of this reality, the factors that I have identified, denominational loyalty and denominational polity, as formulating the integrative model of the Caribbean Diasporan church, are based on a pre-existing relationship with a church in their homeland. This indicates that the integrative model assumes membership and acceptance in an affiliated church in the host country.

An Example of this Practice

A common practice of the integrative model, however, is that Caribbean Diasporan pastors are offered opportunity to serve struggling congregations.[19] These churches are usually located in communities with a declining white population. Since most African Americans neither belong nor or drawn to white churches, the denominational white church resorts to appointing Caribbean Diasporan pastors to their congregations. Social Scientist Omar M. McRoberts, writing of this practice, notes:

> The United Methodist Church therefore assigns a series of Caribbean pastors... in the hope of attracting immigrants from former British colonies in the West Indies and Africa, where British Methodism had laid deep roots.[20]

The Ascension Peace Presbyterian Church, in Florida, further illustrates this practice of assigning Caribbean Diasporan pastors to struggling congregations. Although located in an affluent community, the Ascension Peace Presbyterian Church is the product of the merging of two dying congregations. Prior to the merger, their individual names were Ascension and Peace Presbyterian Church. The Reverend Raymond Anglin, former pastor and General Secretary of the Jamaica Baptist Union, is now the pastor.[21]

The Ascension church was founded in 1959 and declined in the late 1980s when it was without a pastor for two years (1988-1990), prior to calling Raymond Anglin to be their pastor. The Peace church, on the other hand, was organized March 1, 1964. The church had one full time pastor, the Reverend Davis Haw, from 1964-1976. Therefore, for a seventeen year period from 1976-1993, the church did not have a full-time pastor. Similar to the Ascension church, the Peace church experienced decline in membership and was faced with the possibility of closure. This closure was averted when the Peace church and the Ascension church merged, thus becoming capable of affording a full-time pastor.[22] This merger seemed to be an act of good stewardship of the missionary task of the gospel since without the merger, both churches eventually would have died. The need for merger further indicates that the churches were either stagnant or in decline. The new church is currently flourishing under the leadership of the current pastor with much evidence of growth.[23] But more importantly, this serves to exemplify the formulating factors of the integrative model of the Caribbean Diasporan church and to identify an inherent weakness in the practice.

Practicing Reconciliation: A Way of Life

In describing the Caribbean Diasporan church as an agent of reconciliation, the discussion now turns to an examination of the manner in which the church practices reconciliation. An essential element of the integrative model of the Caribbean Diasporan church is reconciliation (Gal. 3:28; NIV). This element is not limited to the integrative model but it is a dominant theme that emerges from the theological works concerning the Caribbean Diasporan experience in the pre-dominantly Caucasian churches.

The work of Samuel Hines and Curtis Deyoung, *Beyond Rhetoric: Reconciliation as a Way of Life,* is a primary text that deals with this subject. The authors contend that reconciliation is a way of life and God's highest priority in the relationship between God and humanity and among persons.[24] Reconciliation, Hines asserts, precedes the creation of human beings. "God conceived of reconciliation before the formation of the world. Before the foundation of the world was in place, God provided a Lamb, slain ahead of time, for our AT-ONE-MENT."[25] This makes reconciliation normative for all persons because it is the way Jesus, the model of the faith, lived his life.[26] Those who are not reconciled with God, according to Hines, will consistently experience difficulties unless these persons accept reconciliation as God's primary purpose for humanity. Hines states:

> We must learn how to comprehend God's thoughts, because the concept of reconciliation does not originate in our minds. Reconciliation is God's idea. Therefore, our thoughts must conform to the mind of God. Until we can think God's thoughts we will struggle uselessly in our attempts to act as God would in a given situation.[27]

Caribbean Diasporan ecclesiology affirms that Jesus Christ is the basis and means of reconciliation between God and humanity and among persons. In Hines' version of reconciliation, the church is the agent of reconciliation. The church is given the task to carry out into the world the mission to work for unity, do God's will and to be a fellowship of the reconciled. "The church must insist on reconciliation," Hines writes, "and not settle for lesser goals like integration, accommodation, and toleration."[28] He continues to say:

> The church, the body of Christ is uniquely significant in carrying out God's one–item agenda. It is primarily in the church that the union between God and human beings is most regularly proclaimed, confessed, and realized and it is through the church that godly precepts and principles can be most readily taught and modeled.[29]

The question Hines' perspective leaves unanswered, however, is the role of humans in the realization of reconciliation. By omitting human involvement in the work of reconciliation, Hines makes it a one-dimensional affair. As a corrective to this limitation in Hines' perspective of reconciliation, African American theologian J. Deotis Roberts addresses this issue in his classic text, *Liberation and Reconciliation: A Black Theology*. Roberts concurs with Hines that reconciliation is God's purpose for humanity but goes further by arguing that reconciliation is both vertical and horizontal. Hence, Roberts contends:

> Christianity is rooted in the belief, 'God was in Christ reconciling the world to Godself' (2 Cor. 5:19; NIV), and that reconciliation between God and humans can be effected only through reconciliation between persons.[30]

Roberts continues his departure from Hines by demonstrating the scope and means of reconciliation. The church is not the only agent of liberation but institutions such as political movements that are working for the same purpose as the church. Thus, according to Roberts:

> Churches' involvement in empowerment and development programs among blacks must use their example, their influence, and their political strength

to activate an entire nation to heal the wounds of an oppressive race.[31]

Further reflection on Hines' version of reconciliation makes no mention of liberation. By defining God's purpose to be solely reconciliation, Hines runs the risk of limiting God's purpose to one issue. God's purpose also involves liberation. In his definitive work in Black theology, *A Black Theology of Liberation,* James Cone declares, "The Christian theology is a theology of liberation."[32] Cone defends this thesis by arguing that the life and resurrection of Jesus was to liberate the oppressed. Black people are an oppressed people and their oppression is God's way of identifying with them in Jesus Christ. For Cone, reconciliation is objective and subjective. God took the initiative for reconciliation and human beings respond. This response to God's reconciliation is the realization of liberation.[33]

Reconciliation takes place within the context of human existential conditions. Jesus Christ came into this existence as the Incarnation of God to reconcile all beings and creation to God and to each other but in order for this to take place, he also had to liberate. The Christ who reconciles is also the one who liberates. These are two dialectical dimensions of the Christian gospel that must be held in complementary relationship so that all persons can fully participate in God's purpose. Liberation and reconciliation, J. Deotis Roberts affirms "are the two main poles of Black theology. They are not antithetical – one moves naturally from one to the other in the light of the Christian understanding of God and humanity."[34]

Reconciliation relates directly to liberation. Christ liberates before he reconciles. The only reason, according to the biblical witness, he can reconcile, is because he liberates:

> For God was pleased to have all his fullness dwell in him, and through him to reconcile to himself all things… by making peace through his blood on the cross. Once you were alienated from God and were enemies … but now he has reconciled you by Christ's physical body through death … (Col. 1:19-22; NIV).

Therefore, an ecclesiology that is based on Jesus Christ affirms that liberation and reconciliation are essential dimensions of the purpose and identity of the church.

Taking these two perspectives of reconciliation into account, Anthony Reddie argues for a contextualized understanding of reconciliation where the life and death of Jesus is the norm[35] and no distinction should be made between the secular and sacred which correlate between the notions of the Christ of faith and Jesus of history. Reddie indicts Euro-American theology as a participant in the crime of murdering the historical Jesus by undervaluing his life and work on earth. He urges that "by downplaying the concrete reality of Jesus' life, Christian theology could focus upon the spirit and the abstract notion of the atoning work of God's Son, which reconciles us to all people."[36] Joining the communion of Black Liberation theologians in arguing for this contextualized approach to reconciliation, Reddie is adamant in locating reconciliation in both the life and death of Jesus Christ.[37] Reddie insists that:

> A Black theological perspective that takes the radical Black Jesus as its norm offers new hope for a more contextualized approach to reconciliation, which justice, reparations and equity are central to any formulation. This radical Black Jesus is one who sides with the poor and oppressed, and asks rich exploiters to repent, for the Kingdom of God is close at hand. This Jesus becomes the model for an alternative form of reconciliation.[38]

In Reddie's opinion, reconciliation as it is defined within Euro-American theology is spiritualized and consequently bears no relationship to the concrete existential reality of Black life. The importance of this notion of reconciliation resides in recognizing the continued presence of white supremacy, economic exploitation, political oppression and cultural degradation. Describing this nadir of human existence, Reddie notes that "in a world where white privilege and advantage is the norm and Blacks continue to die from starvation and economic exploitation, God has sided with these marginalized people through Jesus, who lived his life on earth as a colonized and oppressed Jew."[39]

Gayraud Wilmore attempts to address the issue of how people of African descent and Euro-Americans can live as members of the same church and society with the understanding that it is God's will and with full awareness of the history of racism in society and church.[40]

Wilmore acknowledges the continued existence of racism and other forms of oppressive and unjust practices in the church but he contends that the Black experience advances God's purpose by teaching the unity of the faith and being an example of God's new humanity.[41]

It would appear from the account of such initiatives that it is generally Black people who are the ones to seek whites' acceptance and the question is, why is it not a mutual endeavor? In the Euro-American churches, Blacks are always the ones to assimilate while whites usually do not become integrated into Black churches.[42] In this regard, it is a misnomer to argue that by virtue of having membership in the same church community Blacks and whites are one. How can this be true? As Anthony Reddie observes: "The church has learned to ignore the material needs and the embodied nature of human subjectivity, particularly if those human subjects are Black or people of color."

What this suggests is that the emphasis on reconciliation has not adequately addressed some fundamental questions. How is reconciliation an expression of God's purpose without a commitment to dismantle the system and structures that divide, alienate but confer unearned rights and privileges especially on those people of light pigmentation? How do we express and affirm our collective identity without denying the particularity of personal and cultural identity?

Certainly, reconciliation does not mean we should all be the same as symbolized by the Pauline metaphor of the Church as the body of Christ. While this metaphor characterizes the church as one body, it is constituted of many and diverse members (1 Cor. 12:12:31; Rom. 14:4-5). All the members are not alike but they all belong to the same body. In fact, it is the various members that make the body what it is. Similarly, the Caribbean Diasporan church as an agent of reconciliation represents this ideal of God's purpose for humanity. Reconciliation, however, is only one aspect of the integrative model of the Caribbean Diasporan church.

What then should be the ultimate aim of the Caribbean Diasporan church as an agent of reconciliation? Should it be to advance God's cause of reconciliation or to obtain the acceptance of white people? While the integrative model raises these questions, I assert that this model of the church symbolizes the tensions between the African and Euro-American heritage in Caribbean Diasporan Christianity as well as the dialectical relationship between these two traditions of faith that is discussed elsewhere.[43]

The integrative model, nevertheless, is not an autonomous representative of the Caribbean Diasporan community. It does not represent a Caribbean Diasporan constituency nor is it a distinct Caribbean community except through congregational presence in these churches. As such, the integrative model serves the interest of the institutional church, is marginalized and devoid of any self-determined communal representation.

The insight of the integrative model is that it is institutionally based and takes relationships seriously. Dismissing this insight and significance of this model of the church would be eliminating the communal character of faith but at the same time, the model does not take into account the particularity of faith. Notwithstanding this limitation, the prophetic posture and the holistic nature of salvation[44] are reasons that church should move beyond integration to active participation in the praxis of Divine reconciliation.

NOTES

[1] I am conscious of the ideological and political understandings of the terms Caribbean Diaspora, Caribbean Diasporan theology, Black Church and Black theology. Caribbean Diaspora (Commonwealth Caribbean) and Caribbean theology are species of Black Church and Black theology. The terms are used interchangeably respectively.

[2] Delroy A. Reid-Salmon, *Home Away From Home: The Caribbean Diaporan Church in the Black Atlantic Tradition* (London: Equinox Publishing Ltd., 2008); See also Elaine Bauer and Paul Thompson, *Jamaica Hands Across the Atlantic* (Kingston: Ian Randle Publishers, 2006), 160-179. I acknowledge the growing numbers of Caribbean Diasporan religions. This study, however, is distinct and different in its Christian identity and perspectives. It has similarities, nevertheless, with these other non-Christian Caribbean Diasporan religions. See for example, Bettina Schmidt, *Caribbean Diaspora in the US: Diversity of Religions in New York City* (Surrey: Ashgate Publishing Ltd., 2008); Paul Christopher Johnson, *Diasporan Conversions: Black Carib Religion and the Recovery of Africa* (Berkeley: University of California Press, 2007).

[3] Delroy A. Reid-Salmon, "Out of Every Tribe and Nation," in *Post Colonial Black British Theology; New Texture and Themes*, eds., Michael N. Jagessar & Anthony G. Reddie (Peterborough: Epworth, 2007), 73-100.

[4] See Arthur Charles Dayfoot, *The Shaping of the West Indian Church. 1492-1962* (Kingston: University of the West Indies Press, 1999). This work gives a general overview of the European influence on Caribbean Christianity.

Sylvia Frey and Betty Wood, *Come Shouting to Zion: African Protestantism in the American South and the British Caribbean* (Chapel Hill: The University of North Carolina Press, 1998), 118-213.

[5] Diane J. Austin-Broos, *Jamaica Genesis: Religion and the Politics of Moral Orders* (Kingston: Ian Randle Publishers, 1997), 93-116. While Austin-Broos study concerns the Pentecostal church tradition in Jamaica, she acknowledges its American influence. Concerning the Caribbean Diasporan Church in the British context , see Roswith I. H. Gerloff, *A Plea For British Black Theologies* Vols. 1 & 2 (Oregon; Wipf and Stock). See also, Anthony Reddie, *Working Against the Grain: Re-imaging Black Theology in the 21st Century* (London: Equinox Publishing Ltd., 2008), 111-136; Nicole Rodriguez, *Believing Identity Pentecostalism and the Mediation of Jamaican Ethnicity and Gender in England* (New York: Berg, 997), 1-120.

[6] See Diane J. Austin-Broos, *Jamaica Genesis: Religion and The Politics of Moral Order,* (Kingston: Ian Randle Publishers, 1997). Although the work focuses on the Pentecostal Church tradition in Jamaica, it can be regarded as representative of the Caribbean church. It gives an account of the American influence on the rise and development of Pentecostalism particularly in Jamaica and the Caribbean in general. Historically, Europe was the primary source of influence in the Caribbean but the influence has shifted to North America.

[7] Anthony G. Reddie, *Black Theology in Transatlantic Dialogue* (New York: Palgrave Macmillion, 2006), 50.

[8] Reddie, 78.

[9] Reddie, 17, 80.

[10] This idea stands in the American integrationist tradition. For an excellent study, see James H. Cone, *Martin & Malcolm & America: A Dream or a Nightmare* (New York: Orbis Books, 1991). Cone describes two traditions of racial justice in America but there is a third, the contemplative model represented by Howard Thurman. He was one of the founders of the *Fellowship Church* in San Francisco. This can be regarded as an integrative model of the church. See Howard Thurman, *With Head and Heart: The Autobiography of Howard Thurman* (New York: A Harvest /HBJ Book, 1979); Barbara A. Holmes, *Joy Unspeakable: Contemplative Practices of the Black Church* (Minneapolis: Fortress Press, 2004).

[11] Jackson, 67.

[12] Anita Jackson, *Catching Both Sides of the Wind: Conversations with Five Black Pastors* (London: British Council of Churches, 1985), ix.

[13] Jackson, 37.

[14] Anthony Reddie, *Black Theology in Transatlantic Dialogue* (New York: Palgrave Macmillion, 2006), 78.

[15] Alfred Johnson, Letter to the Author, Dated 12th November, 2003.

[16] Alfred Johnson, Letter to the Author, Dated 12th November, 2003.

[17] Elaine Reid-Salmon, Personal Communication. 1982.

[18] Wayne C. Clark, *The Meaning of Church Membership* (Valley Forge: Judson Press, 1992), 52.

[19] Omar M. McRoberts, *Streets of Glory: Church and Community in a Black Neighborhood* (Chicago: University of Chicago Press, 2003), 51.

[20] McRoberts, 51.

[21] *Ascension Peace Presbyterian Church Tenth Anniversary*, (Fla.: July, 2003).

[22] *Ascension Peace.*

[23] *Ascension Peace.*

[24] Samuel George Hines and Curtis Paul Deyoung, *Beyond Rhetoric: Reconciliation as a Way of Life* (Valley Forge: Judson Press, 2000), xxii. The issue of reconciliation is central to American Christianity. See Joseph Barndt, *Dismantling Racism: The Continuing Challenge to White America* (Minneapolis: Augsburg Press, 1991); Tony Campolo and Michael Battle, *The Church Enslaved: A Spirituality of Racial Reconciliation* (Minneapolis: Fortress Press, 2005); Curtiss Paul DeYoung, Michael O. Emerson, et al., "All Churches Should be Multiracial: The biblical case," in *Christianity Today* (April 2005): 32-43.

[25] Hines, xxii. This represents an other-worldly view of reconciliation. Reconciliation is only relevant when it applies to the reality of contemporary life. The Atonement is not only for personal or inter-personal relationships but for structural and systemic evil and oppression. This emphasis on the Atonement ignores its social and contextual implications.

[26] Hines, 3.

[27] Hines, 3.

[28] Hines, 51.

[29] Hines, 51.

[30] J. Deotis Roberts, *Liberation and Reconciliation: A Black Theology* (New York: Orbis Books, 1994), 9. For a study on the relationship between liberation and reconciliation in Roberts' thought, see Michael Battle, ed., *The Quest for Liberation and Reconciliation: Essays in Honor of J. Deotis Roberts* (Louisville: Westminster John Knox Press, 2005).

[31] Roberts, 13.

[32] James Cone, *Black Theology of Liberation* (New York: J. B. Lippicott Co., 1970), 17.

[33] James Cone, *God of the Oppressed* (New York: Seabury Press, 1975), 226-246. See also his *Black Theology and Black Power* (New York: Seabury Press, 1969).

[34] Roberts, 8. Liberation and reconciliation are major issues in Black Theology but a variety of perspectives exist. For Roberts, the starting point for liberation is reconciliation and for Cone, it is liberation. It is not a question of one or the other but which comes first. This debate will continue. The importance of the issue is to consider the source because it is not a matter of order but the source of both reconciliation and liberator. The Christ is both

Liberator and Reconciler. See Samuel K. Roberts, *African American Christian Ethics* (Cleveland: The Pilgrim Press, 2001). Some theologians consider Christ to be a Mediator rather than Reconciler. James Evans, *An African American Systematic Theology: We Been Believers* (Minnesota: Fortress Press, 1992). It is unfortunate that this important work as a Systematic Theology omits the issue of reconciliation when it is such a major issue in Black Theology.

[35] Reddie, "A Black Theological Approach to Reconciliation," in *Black Theology: An International Journal* 5.2 (2007): 184-202.

[36] Reddie, "A Black Theological Approach to Reconciliation,"193

[37] Reddie, "A Black Theological Approach to Reconciliation," 201.

[38] Reddie, "A Black Theological Approach to Reconciliation," 199.

[39] Reddie, "A Black Theological Approach to Reconciliation,"197.

[40] Gayraud Wilmore, *Black and Presbyterian: The Heritage and the Hope* (Phil: Geneva Press, 1983), 14.

[41] Wilmore, 73-87.

[42] Reddie, "A Black Theological Approach to Reconciliation," in *Black Theology: An International Journal* 5.2 (2007): 190.

[43] Delroy A. Reid-Salmon, *Home Away from Home: The Caribbean Diasporan Church in the Black Atlantic Tradition* (London: Equinox Publishing Ltd., 2008), 60-75.

[44] Reddie, *Black Theology in Transatlantic Dialogue*, 17; 79- 80.

Appendix
Contributing Authors

Lina Andronoviene, from Lithuania, is Course Leader in Applied Theology at the International Baptist Theological Seminary of the European Baptist Federation, Prague, Czech Republic, and Interim Director of the Non-residential Bible School of the Baptist Union of Lithuania.

Cawley Bolt is a church historian from Jamaica. He is a pastor in the Jamaica Baptist Union who has taught for many years at the United Theological College of the West Indies, Kingston, Jamaica.

Karen O'Dell Bullock is Fellow and Professor of Christian Heritage and Director of Ph.D. Program, B. H. Carroll Theological Institute, Arlington, Texas, USA.

Brian C. Brewer is an Assistant Professor of Christian Theology at the George W. Truett Theological Seminary at Baylor University, Waco, Texas, USA.

Neville Callam is the General Secretary of the Baptist World Alliance.

Regina Claas is General Secretary of the Union of Evangelical Free Churches (Baptists) in Germany.

Ross Clifford is Principal of Morling College, Sydney, Australia.

David Coffey served as President of the Baptist World Alliance (2005-2010) and is currently Global Ambassador for BMS World Mission.

Kenneth Edmonds is a member of the Ashburton Baptist Church in Melbourne, Australia. He is a practicing architect with extensive experience in the design of Baptist places of worship.

Christopher J. Ellis, from the UK, is pastor of West Bridgford Baptist Church, Nottingham, UK, and former principal of Bristol Baptist College, Bristol, UK.

Paul Fiddes is Professor of Systematic Theology, University of Oxford, and Director of Research, Regent's Park College, Oxford, UK.

Curtis Freeman is Research Professor of Theology and Director of the Baptist House of Studies at Duke University Divinity School in Durham, North Carolina, USA.

David P. Gushee is Distinguished University Professor of Christian Ethics, Mercer University, Atlanta, Georgia, USA.

Solomon A. Ishola is the General Secretary of the Nigerian Baptist Convention.

Dinorah B. Méndez is a Mexican Baptist who serves as Professor of Theology and Christian History at Mexican Baptist Theological Seminary, Mexico City, Mexico.

Teodor Oprenov is the General Secretary of the Baptist Union of Bulgaria and Senior Pastor of First Baptist Church in Sofia, Bulgaria.

Michael J. Quicke, a former Principal of Spurgeon's College, London, is the C. W. Koller Professor of Preaching at Northern Seminary, Lombard, Illinois, USA.

Delroy A. Reid-Salmon is pastor of Grace Baptist Chapel in New York City, New York, USA. He is a visiting Fellow at the Centre for Christianity and Culture, Regent's Park College, Oxford University, UK.

Anna Robbins is Senior Lecturer in Theology and Contemporary Culture at the London School of Theology, UK.

Kenneth B. E. Roxburgh is the S. Louis and Ann W. Armstrong Professor and Chair of the Department of Religion, Samford University, Birmingham, Alabama, USA.

Dennis L. Sansom is the Chair of the Department of Philosophy at Samford University, Birmingham, Alabama, USA.

Joel Sierra is from Mexico. He is a hymn writer and pastor, and currently serves as Senior Pastor of the First Baptist Church, Managua, Nicaragua.

William M. Tillman, Jr. is the T. B. Maston Professor of Christian Ethics at Logsdon School of Theology, Hardin-Simmons University, Abilene, Texas, USA.

Kirsten T. Timmer is from the Netherlands. She is a religious education teacher (7th -12th grade), an occasional preacher in the Netherlands and a Ph.D. student (Christian History) at B.H. Carroll Theological Seminary, Arlington, Texas, USA.

Fausto A. Vasconcelos is Director of Mission, Evangelism and Theological Reflection in the Baptist World Alliance.

Brian Winslade is National Director of the Baptist Union of Australia.